Manliness in Britain, 1760–1900

Manchester University Press

also available in the series

Windows for the world
Nineteenth-century stained glass and the international exhibitions, 1851–1900
JASMINE ALLEN

The matter of art
Materials, practices, cultural logics, c.1250–1750
EDITED BY CHRISTY ANDERSON, ANNE DUNLOP AND PAMELA H. SMITH

European fashion
The creation of a global industry
EDITED BY REGINA LEE BLASZCZYK AND VÉRONIQUE POUILLARD

The culture of fashion
A new history of fashionable dress
CHRISTOPHER BREWARD

The factory in a garden
A history of corporate landscapes from the industrial to the digital age
HELENA CHANCE

'The autobiography of a nation'
The 1951 Festival of Britain
BECKY E. CONEKIN

The culture of craft
Status and future
EDITED BY PETER DORMER

Material relations
Domestic interiors and the middle-class family, 1850–1910
JANE HAMLETT

Arts and Crafts objects
IMOGEN HART

Comradely objects
Design and material culture in Soviet Russia, 1960s–80s
YULIA KARPOVA

Interior decorating in nineteenth-century France
The visual culture of a new profession
ANCA I. LASC

Building reputations
Architecture and the artisan, 1750–1830
CONOR LUCEY

The material Renaissance
MICHELLE O'MALLEY AND EVELYN WELCH

Bachelors of a different sort
Queer aesthetics, material culture and the modern interior in Britain
JOHN POTVIN

Crafting design in Italy
From post-war to postmodernism
CATHARINE ROSSI

Chinoiserie
Commerce and critical ornament in eighteenth-century Britain
STACEY SLOBODA

Material goods, moving hands
Perceiving production in England, 1700–1830
KATE SMITH

Hot metal
Material culture and tangible labour
JESSE ADAMS STEIN

Ideal homes, 1918–39
Domestic design and suburban modernism
DEBORAH SUGG RYAN

The study of dress history
LOU TAYLOR

general editors
Christopher Breward
and
James Ryan

founding editor
Paul Greenhalgh

Manliness in Britain, 1760–1900

Bodies, emotion, and material culture

Joanne Begiato

Manchester University Press

Copyright © Joanne Begiato 2020

The right of Joanne Begiato to be identified as the author of this work has been asserted by her in accordance with the Copyright, Designs and Patents Act 1988.

Published by Manchester University Press
Altrincham Street, Manchester M1 7JA
www.manchesteruniversitypress.co.uk

British Library Cataloguing-in-Publication Data
A catalogue record for this book is available from the British Library

ISBN   978 1 5261 2857 7   hardback

First published 2020

The publisher has no responsibility for the persistence or accuracy of URLs for any external or third-party internet websites referred to in this book and does not guarantee that any content on such websites is, or will remain, accurate or appropriate.

Typeset in 10/12.5 Compatil Text by
Servis Filmsetting Ltd, Stockport, Cheshire

For Mike, my destiny and my destination

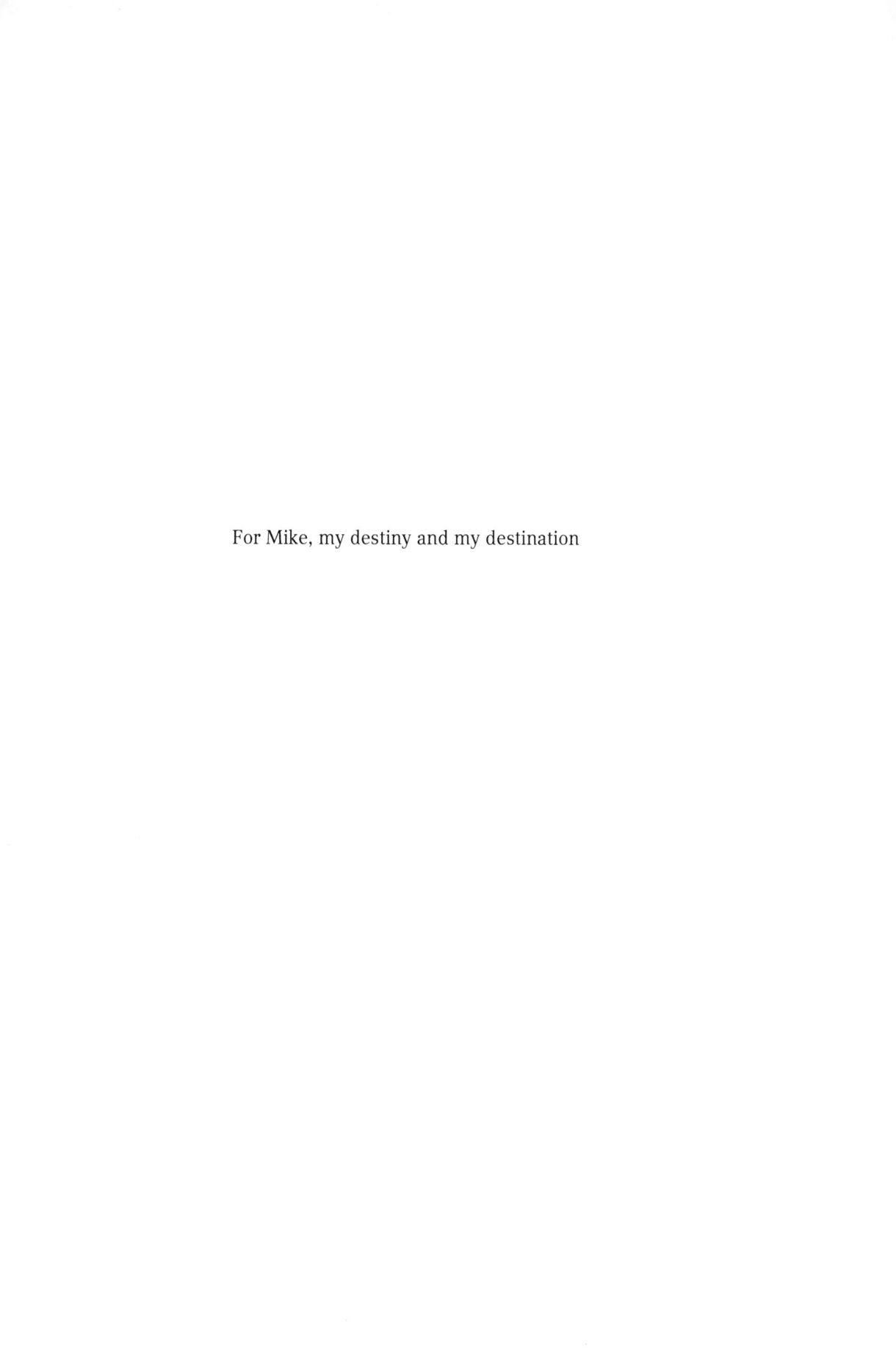

Contents

List of figures		viii
Acknowledgements		xi
	Making manliness manifest: an introduction	1
1	Figures, faces, and desire: male bodies and manliness	34
2	Appetites, passions, and disgust: the penalties and paradoxes of unmanliness	68
3	Hearts of oak: martial manliness and material culture	101
4	Homeward bound: manliness and the home	136
5	Brawn and bravery: glorifying the working body	168
	The measure of a man: an epilogue	203
	Select bibliography	215
	Index	222

Figures

0.1 Lord Byron's screen, after conservation by Britton & Storey Art Conservation and before hinging: pugilists' side shown. John Murray Collection. Reproduced courtesy of the John Murray Collection.   2

0.2 *A Father's Lessons on the Illustrated Wall-Papers*, British Workman (2 May 1870), p. 20. Reproduced courtesy of the Working-Class Movement Library, Salford.   18

1.1 'Orlando, the Outcast of Milan: A Heroic Story of the Olden Time', *Our Young Folks Weekly Budget of Tales, News, Sketches, Fun, Puzzles, Riddles &c* 208 (1874), p. 397. © The British Library Board.   39

1.2 *A View of the Fight between Gully and Gregson*, wood engraving by unknown artist (1807). Private collection © The British Sporting Art Trust, Reference: 2005.020. Reproduced courtesy of Bridgeman Images.   44

1.3 Staffordshire jug featuring Daniel Mendoza, Jewish Museum, Object Number: JM 686. Reproduced courtesy of Jewish Museum, London.   46

1.4 The first English touring team, pictured on board ship at Liverpool (1859). Public Domain by Wikimedia Commons.   48

2.1 'Moral and Physical Thermometer', in John Coakley Lettsom, *Hints Designed to Promote Beneficence, Temperance, and Medical Science*, vol. 1 (1797). Reproduced courtesy of the Wellcome Collection. CC BY.   75

2.2 *A Drunken Man Sits at Home with his Family who Must Sell Clothes to Pay for his Habit*, etching by G. Cruikshank (1847), after himself. Reproduced courtesy of Wellcome Collection. CC BY.   76

2.3	*Loss! Gain!*, British Workman 7 (1855), p. 28. Reproduced courtesy of BLT19, Nineteenth-Century Business, Labour, Temperance, & Trade Periodicals.	78
2.4	*The Brave Old Coxswain*, British Workman (1870). Reproduced courtesy of the Working-Class Movement Library, Salford.	93
3.1	HMS *Daring* figurehead. National Maritime Museum (1844), FHD0073. Reproduced courtesy of the Royal Museums Greenwich Picture Library.	102
3.2	White earthenware bowl decorated with pink lustreing, enamelling, and transfer-printed designs (c.1860–70), manufactured by Moore's Pottery, Sunderland. © Tyne & Wear Archives & Museums, TWCMS: D2037. Reproduced courtesy of Bridgeman Images.	114
3.3	Royal Patriotic Fund jug, Crimean War (1855), Samuel Alcock & Co. (maker). National Army Museum, NAM. 1961-03-24-1. Reproduced courtesy of National Army Museum.	115
3.4	*The Patchwork Quilt*, British Workman (Nov 1872), p. 138. Reproduced courtesy of the Working-Class Movement Library, Salford.	117
3.5	*Jack Crawford*, by Daniel Orme, line and stipple engraving, published 1797. National Portrait Gallery, Reference Collection, NPG D23301. Reproduced courtesy of © National Portrait Gallery, London.	123
4.1	*The Soldier's Dream of Home* (New York: Currier & Ives, 1861–65). Library of Congress Reproduction Number: LC-USZC2–3014.	143
4.2	*Please Father, Come Home Early*, British Workman 20 (1856), p. 76. Reproduced courtesy of BLT19, Nineteenth-Century Business, Labour, Temperance, & Trade Periodicals.	150
4.3	*The Beneficial Effects of Temperance on a Man and his Family*, lithograph by W. Gunthrop (c.1840), after himself. Reproduced courtesy of Wellcome Collection. CC BY.	152
4.4	'The Poor Man's House Repaired', British Workman (1858), p. 37. Reproduced courtesy of BLT19, Nineteenth-Century Business, Labour, Temperance, & Trade Periodicals.	156
4.5	*A Real Hard Case. (The Rough's Last Wrong.)*, by Charles Keene. Reproduced courtesy of Punch Cartoon Library, TopFoto.	159
5.1	*Getting in the Thin Edge of the Wedge; Or, Strike while the Iron's Hot*, British Workman (1868), p. 182. Copyright free: Archive.org.	170
5.2	*The Brave Fireman*, British Workman (Jan 1874). Reproduced courtesy of the Working-Class Movement Library, Salford.	182

5.3 Wooden hinged emblem, Stockport Branch of the Friendly United Mechanics (*c*.1830). People's History Museum, exhibition. Author's photograph. Reproduced courtesy of the People's History Museum. 187

5.4 Steam Engine Makers' Society certificate (1854). Working-Class Movement Library, Salford, certificates from 'Framed/241 Box 3'. Author's photograph. Reproduced courtesy of the Working-Class Movement Library, Salford. 189

5.5 Brass Founders, Turners, Fitters, Finishers & Coppersmiths Association certificate (*c*.1890s). Working-Class Movement Library, Salford, certificates from 'Framed/241 Box 3'. Author's photograph. Reproduced courtesy of the Working-Class Movement Library, Salford. 190

Acknowledgements

This book began in 2012 when I designed and taught a third-year module at Oxford Brookes, called Making Men: Masculinities in England 1700–1918. As I taught it, I realised that there was more to be said on the matter of manliness and the role that bodies, emotions, and material culture played in its construction. This study is the result of my curiosity in these matters. It has antecedents in numerous seminar and conference papers and parts of Chapters 1, 2, and 5 are developed from my publications 'Between poise and power: embodied manliness in eighteenth- and nineteenth-century British culture', *Transactions of the Royal Historical Society* 26:2 (29 December 2016), 125–47, and 'Punishing the unregulated manly body and emotions in early Victorian England', in Ruth Heholt and Joanne Parsons (eds), *The Victorian Male Body* (Edinburgh: Edinburgh University Press, 2018), pp. 46–64.

Of course, this book also owes much to the generosity and help of other people. First, I owe thanks to Oxford Brookes University for supporting my research with funding and a sabbatical to write it in 2018. My fellow members of the Faculty Executive have been accommodating and supportive. I am also grateful to the Oxford Centre for Methodism and Church History for a semester of teaching relief, which enabled me to do additional research. I owe much to Melanie Reynolds, who acted as a research assistant in the early stages of the project, collecting valuable sources relating to the concepts of manly and manliness. I am also grateful to the various universities and academic colleagues that have invited me to talk about this research in the years since it began. Numerous friends have discussed aspects of it with me, including Katie Barclay, Gary Browning, Matthew Craske, Bill Gibson, Sally Holloway, Simon Kövesi, David Nash, Christiana Payne, and Jane Stevens Crawshaw. This is not a complete list and I have a bad memory, so I hope those who are not listed here will forgive me; I am still grateful! I would also like to thank my parents-in-law, Monika and Steve Brown, for their enormous help over the last few years, which has enabled me to go on research trips and attend conferences.

The book has been a companion in times of enormous personal change. My mother died in 2016, her illness worsening as the project matured. I wish she had seen the book realised. She was central to its formation and development. We had countless entertaining conversations about masculine identity, and it is thanks to her memories of Jack Crawford and his importance in Sunderland, where she grew up, that I include him in this book. She reassured me through my constant anxieties, laboured endlessly to provide me with household and childcare so that I could work, and consoled me in difficult times. In the end our roles reversed, and I became her carer. During this dreadful time, there were two people who ensured I endured. First, my son Gabriel who was twelve when this book first entered my mind. He is a man now, emotionally mature, hard-working, funny, and my joy. I don't know where the time has gone, but every minute watching him grow and develop has been precious. The other person who saved me is my husband Mike. He came into my life and remade everything. He is my manly ideal: handsome, charming, funny, caring, and kind. He is the best stepfather and the best husband. He is also the best historian: I have benefited enormously from talking over my ideas with him and I doubt I could have written this without his enthusiasm and support.

Making manliness manifest: an introduction

Among 'Lord Byron's Relics', a collection of 'treasures' owned by the Murray family, there is a beautiful six-foot-high decoupage dressing screen that Robert Murray purchased from Byron in 1816. One side is covered with theatrical actors and productions, the other is 'crowded with his heroes in the boxing ring'.[1] The four panels of famous prize fighters, cut out and glued to the screen in chronological order, are a decorative paean to British manliness (Figure 0.1).[2] Posed in fighting stance, stripped to the waist and wearing boxing breeches and silk stockings, the pugilists' images are reproductions of well-known engravings and paintings.[3] Individual boxers grace the lower third of each panel, reproduced in black and white, unaccompanied by text, and framed by a painted border; the top two thirds teem with large colour portraits of pugilists, surrounded by head and shoulder portraits, pictures of notable matches in the ring, and newspaper cuttings describing fights and fighters, interspersed with handwritten titles and descriptions.[4] The cuttings celebrate the depicted boxers' bodies. Those placed next to 'Gentleman' Jackson, for example, admire his strength, initiative, and 'bottom'. One text box praises his 'anatomical beauty, and ... athletic and muscular appearance'. The paragraph selected for Bob Gregson, known as 'Dutch Sam', similarly commends his physique:

> To Nature he is indebted for a fine figure, and his appearance is manly and imposing; and who has been considered so good an anatomical subject to descant upon that Mr. CARLISLE, the celebrated Professor of Anatomy at the Royal Academy, has selected BOB to stand several times for that purpose; and who has likewise been the subject of the pencils of LAWRENCE, DAW.

Strikingly, these corporeal accounts also attach emotions to bodies. The text chosen for Tom Johnson describes him as 'extremely active, cheerful,

0.1 Lord Byron's screen, after conservation by Britton & Storey Art Conservation, and before hinging, pugilists' side shown.

and good-tempered', winning in 1789 although his opponent Isaac Perrins was three stone heavier. That for Richard Humphries ascribes to him 'gaiety' and 'impetuosity'. Two black American boxers are placed alongside each other: Tom Molineaux and Bill Richmond, both born in slavery. Richmond, who lived in England for most of his life, trained Molineaux when he visited to fight Tom Crib. Posed like the white fighters, the cuttings acknowledge their race, applauding Richmond's ability as 'a Man of Colour' to remain 'good tempered and placid' in the face of the racial 'taunts and insults' he received.

It is not clear who crafted the screen. In the 1820s, Pierce Egan claimed that it was compiled from the first volume of his *Boxiana*. Calling it 'Angelo's Screen', he stated that Henry Angelo made it for his pupil, Byron, who, he also said, bought it for the astounding price of £250, before selling it to his publisher John Murray for £16 5s 6d, in 1816, when he left England.[5] By the twentieth century, the screen, now designated a 'relic', was understood to have been made by Byron's own hands.[6] Describing the artefacts displayed in the Murray's London home, *The Globe* professed in 1906 that 'the erratic genius' had designed the screen.[7] By the time the *Worthing Herald* reviewed Bohun Lynch's book *The Prize Ring* – which included an illustration of Byron's screen – in 1937, Byron had 'made' the screen, between 1812 and 1816, 'when he was a close friend of John Jackson, the fighter'.[8] Byron's interaction with the collaged screen certainly may have extended beyond purchasing it, since it was further embellished with painted 'blood' splatters.[9]

Whatever its origin, Byron's screen does more than showcase his love of boxing and membership of the Fancy, a fraternal community devoted to pugilism.[10] It is the physical manifestation of a homosocial culture of masculinity predicated on 'social promiscuity' and the mixing of patrician and plebeian men brought into close proximity by their love of prize-fighting.[11] On these four panels we also witness elite men's admiration for white and black working-class men's sporting skill, strength, and fortitude. More than this, they thrum with erotic potential in their celebration of men's physicality and beauty. As Gary Dyer remarks, the 'boxing subculture was one of the rare arenas where one could celebrate the male body ... and depictions that foster aesthetic responses have been known to foster erotic ones as well, whether deliberately or inadvertently'.[12] As such, Byron's screen is a three-dimensional object that materialised working-class manliness and the desire and emotions that it stimulated.[13]

Desire dominates the decoupage. For Byron, who enjoyed sex with men and women, the boxers' bodies were homoerotically charged.[14] As Dyer shows, the Fancy's slang of 'flash' facilitated Byron's coded communication of his same-sex desires with his friends; secrecy was essential when anal sex was a felony.[15] The allure of the pugilists' bodies extended further than sexual desire, however. In their muscularity, athleticism, and agility, they perhaps reminded Byron of his own bodily aspirations and shortcomings. He was obsessed by his body throughout life; born with a club foot, which caused pain and lameness, he also persistently fought a tendency to corpulence.[16] Moreover, once Byron attained celebrity status, reactions to his body were ambiguous and complex. Though commentators were beguiled by his beauty, they also noticed his foot and gait, intrigued that for all his handsomeness, his body did not conform to notions of health, vigour, and shapeliness.[17] As such, this screen was an emotional object onto which he may have projected anxieties about his own body, his desire for the perfect, anatomically 'correct', male figure, and the values associated with it: in other words, his desire for manliness itself.

Although Byron cannot be assumed to be representative of all men, he was a model of masculinity that some men admired, including those of lower social status, as labouring-class poetic responses to him reveal.[18] Furthermore, other men shared his admiration and desire for men's idealised and emotionalised bodies and the capacity to use them in material form as a prompt for manly virtue and to evaluate their own manly performances.[19] This book focuses on these features of gender construction to argue that manliness in Britain was produced, maintained, and disseminated in the long nineteenth century through men's bodies, very often working-class ones, and the emotions and material culture with which they were associated. In so doing, it disrupts the received picture of nineteenth-century masculinity. Its account of manliness is more corporeal and material, more emotional, more cross-class, and less heteronormative than many other studies.[20] It therefore contributes to recent advances in scholarship which seek to disrupt heteronormative accounts of gender and sex and to flesh out masculine identities by attending to emotions and material culture.[21] It offers several innovations.

First, it seeks to queer the history of masculinity, to 'view it sceptically, to pull apart its constitutive pieces and analyse them from a variety of perspectives, taking nothing for granted'.[22] This book is not a history of same-sex activities and makes no assumptions about sexual identities, though it sees men's sexuality as intrinsic to ideas about manliness and their transmission.[23] In so doing, it challenges the heteronormativity of older histories of masculinity wherein desire, sex, intimacy, and kinship are assumed to be heterosexual, itself a self-explanatory, ubiquitous category, by recognising that male and female desire for idealised male bodies was integral to the success of manliness.[24] Such idealised bodies aroused erotic feelings in some who encountered them, which rendered the associated gender qualities they possessed appealing beyond any immediate sexual gratification. For others, the enchantment of a manly body might be non-sexual or not genitally based but still charged with desire for the gender attributes it embodied; their yearning was to become him, to possess him, to display him, to be admired or saved by him.[25] Correspondingly, those whose behaviour did not conform to these ideals were depicted in ways that prompted disgust, deploying aversion to steer men away from unmanliness.

Secondly, in challenging conventional accounts of masculine identity, *Manliness in Britain* breaks with conventional chronologies, stretching from the ages of feeling, revolution, and reform to those of militarism, imperialism, representative democracy, and mass media.[26] It deliberately spans periods often dealt with discretely by historians of masculinity, to focus on what contemporaries saw as the most important measure of masculinity: manliness.

Thirdly, the book reveals the centrality of the imagined working-class man and his materiality to ideas of manliness and unmanliness. For the middle classes, the working classes were 'good to think with' in terms of class, national, racial, and gender identities.[27] Their representations of idealised working men – fair of face, strong, and brave – offered didactic lessons for the working classes, blending instruction, guidance, and discipline.[28] In a time of change, upheaval, and crisis, this endeavour also rendered the labouring ranks 'safer' for both the middle and working classes, by modelling a patriotic, well-behaved, hard-working, trustworthy citizen. Literature and court records show that the idealised, eroticised young working man was desired by some elite men as a lover; for others, it will be argued, he was desirable because his physical and emotional allure displayed ideal manliness.[29] As such, depictions of working-class men offer insights into the production of middle-class men's identities, since the former served both as a 'brute' form of manliness to avoid when visualised as degenerate, violent, or malformed, or to aspire to when imagined as a 'natural', purer, physically perfect version.[30]

The book's fourth innovative feature is that it moves beyond families, education, employment, recreation, and print culture as sites of gender formation, to argue that manliness was made manifest through emotionalised bodies and material culture, where materiality and emotions combined to fix qualities of manliness in people from childhood through adulthood. One of the deliberate intentions of this book, therefore, is to put emotions' history into practice, offering a way to move beyond theorising to show how historicised emotions help us understand praxis.[31]

As this indicates, *Manliness in Britain* lies at the intersection of several key historiographical areas: masculinities, emotions, bodies, and material culture. All of these are relatively recent, are growing exponentially, and have been extensively summarised elsewhere. Thus, this introduction explores only the aspects of historiography most relevant to the book's overarching thesis of emotionalised bodies and material culture. It offers an overview of histories relating to 'being' a man in the long nineteenth century, focusing on the embodied qualities of manliness and on self-control, the primary means by which men were supposed to achieve idealised manly behaviour. It then assesses the scholarship relating to three domains in which manliness was understood to be performed and tested: war, home, and work.[32] Next, it describes the primary sources used to develop claims about manliness and their cultural forms, which deployed emotions as their modus operandi. This leads into an explanation of the concept of emotionalised bodies and material culture, followed by the chapter findings.

Being manly

The history of British masculinities has settled into a periodisation of successive masculine 'typologies', from the urban refined gentleman, via the man of feeling, to the muscular Christian. Change over time is presented by proposed shifts from the inner to the outer man – or soft to hard, and back again – as cultural trends such as politeness and sensibility gave way to cosy domestic quietude, till overturned by adventurous muscularity and stiff upper lips. However, these 'types' of masculinity, which are often associated with white, literate, middle-class and genteel men, and are derived largely from literary terms, only go part of the way to capture masculinities as perceived and experienced by a broad range of men.

Their capacity to encompass masculine identity in all its forms and over time becomes especially inadequate when different social classes, races, ethnicities and their intersections are explored over a longer period, along with more extensive domains for the performance of masculinity. One way to tackle this afresh is to explore masculine identities through another term that was widely used throughout the long nineteenth century: manliness, a primary evaluator of masculine identity and behaviour. Manly values did not map onto existing typologies, although they shared qualities, since the broader cultural and social trends of sensibility, romanticism, domesticity, realism, imperialism, and athleticism underpinned and informed them. Where manliness differs is that it was a set of attributes that combined both corporeality and emotionality.

There is no shortage of research on men's bodies from the eighteenth to the twentieth centuries, since human bodies are vessels for abstract cultural values and can be read as sites for cultural meaning and social practice.[33] Cultural histories of war explore how states shaped men's bodies in recruiting and fighting wars, bodies that themselves were deployed to represent abstract notions such as nation, empire, and modernity. They also delineate the ways in which military shortcomings were interpreted as signs of national, physical, and gender decline.[34] Historians of race, colonialism, and empire deconstruct whiteness to expose how it was constructed against racialised 'others', with bodies as one of the means by which this was achieved.[35] Analysis of the damaged male body also confirms the significance of physicality to masculine identity, since maimed or incapacitated men were unmanned in their own, and society's, eyes.[36]

Histories of sex and the print culture of erotica provide insights into changing medical understandings of bodies and the cultural force of the eroticised male body.[37] Studies charting the relationship between science and gender expose the changing notions underpinning scientific knowledge of masculine minds and bodies, and analyses of eighteenth- and nineteenth-century physiognomy – the scientific study of faces – show how appearances were read for character and identity.[38] Work on new photographic technologies and later nineteenth-century scientific disciplines investigate how anthropometric methodologies measured men's bodies to construct and naturalise racial typologies and hierarchies, with white middle-class men's bodies at the apex and men of colour's at the base.[39]

Research into nineteenth-century judicial, health, and medical initiatives to control and reform unruly poor bodies also reveals the centrality of male bodily reform to these endeavours, carried out through discipline, physical training, and education.[40] Scholars of consumption and fashion identify men's bodies as sites of anxieties about luxury and effeminacy and external markers of race, sex, virility, maturity, civility, and cosmopolitanism.[41] Finally, historians of entertainment, recreation, and sport map the changing aesthetics of the male body and the market for 'bodily spectacle'.[42]

For all its range and, increasingly, attention to imperial and racial imperatives and ideologies, this scholarship does not easily illuminate gender constructions, since it is attuned to different research questions and focuses on specific eras of interest. Indeed, the belief that the later Victorian and Edwardian periods were distinctively embodied persists.[43] In this view, several factors collided in the last decade of the nineteenth century to create a new emphasis on men's bodies, located in the notion of muscular Christianity (c.1850s–1914). These included fears of emasculation through the rise of sedentary jobs and racial degeneracy due to the strains of modern urban lifestyles and industrialisation, and society's responses in the form of 'new athleticism' and race science.[44] Elspeth Brown, for example, who convincingly demonstrates how race defined 'an emerging model for a new embodied masculinity', still positions this as part of a shift from 'older notions of "manhood", characterised by inner virtues and adult responsibilities to emerging ideas of modern "masculinity", where self-control became legible through the muscled body'.[45]

The evidence assembled here shows that there was no increase over time in the significance the male body lent to masculine identity.[46] The evaluation of men's classed and raced bodies in performing and representing manliness was just as critical in the eighteenth century.[47] Thus, this book shows that Georgian and Victorian British manliness was not a composite of cerebral and bloodless values and behaviours, but was conveyed through men's classed, racialised, and sexualised bodies. It thus shares the concerns of Katie Barclay's work on Irish masculinity in the first half of the nineteenth century, which uses emotions and embodiment to explore masculinity in the performative space of the Irish courtroom.[48] Like her study, this book addresses class and reflects on the recent emotional and material-culture 'turns', though it focuses instead on Britain and considers a broader range of social and institutional domains in which manliness was constructed and deployed.

Although scholarship on masculinities tends to survey ideals, with the features that threatened it left implicit, it also offers glimpses into what undermined masculine identities across time. Since the early modern period, the inability to achieve occupational, economic, and marital markers that denoted full manhood undermined men's gender identities. Men who were thus excluded might adopt anti-patriarchal masculinities such as drinking, womanising, and fighting, qualities that by the nineteenth century came to be associated with working-class men as a whole.[49] Scholarship on social practices and reforming initiatives in the long nineteenth century shows that this constellation of vices was understood to render men brutalised, desensitised, and bestial.[50] Similarly, failure to conform to abstract ideal manly characteristics, like bravery and strength, led to men being deemed cowards, weak, or effeminate.[51] This was both classed and raced, as research on imperial and colonial masculinities reveals, with British (white) manliness constructed in contrast to the imagined qualities of the racialised 'other', a phenomenon that helped justify colonial rule.[52] As Mrinalini Sinha observes, late nineteenth-century 'middle-class Bengali Hindus, became the quintessential referents for a category designated as odious, the "effeminate *babus*"', whose unmanliness was rooted in their supposed weak bodies, sexual deviancy, and lack of self-control.[53] Studies of emotions also reveal that men needed to control and channel specific feelings because the excessive display of tears, rage, fear, or love, betokened, amongst other things, irrationality, mental inadequacy, and ill-health.[54]

The connecting strand throughout this scholarship is that masculinity was compromised by men's inability to resist temptation and excess. Self-control was thus held up as the only answer to deterring unmanliness. Scholarship on religion and emotion demonstrates that religion had long been formulated around the governance of passions, imagined as a force which encompassed selfishness and unregulated feelings and bodily actions that led to vice.[55] Passions were thus the enemy of virtue, a positive force, which for men indicated strength and power; indeed, this force was so intimately bound up with masculine identity that its Latin root, *virtus*, meant manliness. Early nineteenth-century evangelicals redefined manliness to be less about outer reputation and more about inner character, requiring a more severe form of self-repression expressed through moderation and self-denial.[56] Self-control took on even greater significance in the 'disciplinary individualism' of Victorian Britain, wherein the conventions of governmentality sought 'a universal and voluntary surrender of self to the larger whole'.[57]

From the 1860s, the 'self-help' movement, under the umbrella of Victorian liberalism, raised self-control to a cult, harnessing piety, morals, character, and bodies in a mythology of self-improvement.[58] The male Victorian character was thus forged in independence and self-discipline: a panacea held out to working- as well as middle-class men for advancement, to be cultivated through abstinence, hard work, and a pious mind and heart.[59] By the 1880s, in the aftermath of the campaigns to repeal the Contagious Diseases Acts and to pass the Criminal Law Amendment Bill, it was harnessed to a rhetoric of cleanliness and purity, which equated physical hygiene with moral purity and sought to reform male sexuality.[60] This model of purity was disseminated to youths through the romantic fashion for chivalric ideals and within social purity movements, especially via the virtuous and appealing forms of St George and Sir Galahad.[61] It was also demanded by feminist-led moral reform movements, which attacked male vice and the sexual double standard.[62] A mainstream version was commercialised to sell products, and by the turn of the nineteenth century, possessing a strong, clean, regulated, chaste body and mind was conceived as the primary means by which men could withstand passions.

Embodied manliness thus became ever more important in the context of modernity, which was seen to cause mental dysfunction and physical degeneracy in men.[63] Indeed, the era saw the responsibility for gender failure devolve upon the individual. In some ways, therefore, deviation from conformity to the ideal male body was less tolerated and more disciplined.[64] In the early eighteenth century, for example, obese bodies indicated health and comfort and some degree of prosperity. A century later they denoted lack of virility, self-control, and will power, although, simultaneously, puny men were considered weak; both fell short of 'more physically heroic and martial forms of masculinity'.[65] This had implications for masculine privileges. As Ellen Bayuk Rosenman comments in her account of the Victorian spermatorrhea (excessive discharge of semen) panic, 'man and body are not perfectly aligned in an attitude of domination; in fact, what needed to be dominated was the body itself'.[66]

Men were instructed how to dominate their bodies and selves directly and by implication. The most explicit and intimate mechanism for inculcating self-control was religion. Men who attended church were warned that their spiritual well-being in the present and afterlife was predicated upon learning to master their desires to avoid sin. Shame and guilt were the emotions deployed to persuade them of the need to exert enough will to avoid sinful acts.[67] In addition to the church, home, school, workplace, and print culture were all spaces in which men were informed of the necessity to exercise self-control and disciplined when unsuccessful, while also demonstrating that failure of will denied individuals the privileges of masculinity.[68] Increasingly, Victorian men operated within broader disciplinary processes at the level of state and institutions, which sought to cultivate the 'mastered self'.[69] Much of the scholarly attention paid to the role of training, discipline, and punishment in constructing and reinforcing manliness, however, focuses on boys and youths, rather than men. What remains to be investigated is the role of emotions, bodies, and material culture in sustaining and inculcating self-control in adult men. Moreover, there is more to be said on the ambivalences of unmanly behaviours for men, since male bodies were understood to differ due to factors like age, illness, and disability.

Martial manliness, for example, could be ambiguous.[70] It combined the physique, valour, and self-control of the manly ideal; at the same time, it was linked with behaviours deemed problematic in other men, such as fighting, drinking, and sexual liberty. Such behaviour might be excused or tolerated, as with Jack Tar (a popular name for a sailor), who combined carousing with comradeship and sexual prowess with bravery.[71] Soldiers were also considered to turn women's heads and resort to drink when bored, yet they were not always castigated in the same way as other working men in popular culture for succumbing to temptation. Ironically, men may well have found martial manliness appealing because it united these components of masculine identity. Military men were therefore useful role models because they battled with and overcame the challenges of self-mastery, often in extreme situations. In 1863, an author in the *Boy's Own Magazine* told his youthful readers about a sergeant of the Guards at the Battle of Alma, who had been able to 'vanquish' swearing and other evil habits, and 'for many years had been looked up to by his comrades as a man of exemplary character'. Yet when he failed to rally his company after suffering losses and being forced to retreat, he was overpowered with shame and rage, succumbing 'to a sort of madness'. His fearful oaths shocked his company and he spent the night of the battle in prayer and sobbing like a child. There was a lesson in his outburst, his manliness was tested in battle, and, if he temporarily lost self-control, he mastered it once more, to emerge as the middle classes' ideal respectable working-class man: 'more humble, kind and considerate in his bearing towards' his men than before.[72]

Performing and testing manliness

The three key spaces in which manliness was performed and tested in this period were war, home, and work. All have been subjected to considerable research and thus this introduction offers the briefest of overviews for each in so far as they align with the book's focus on manly bodies, emotions, and material culture.

War is profoundly associated with masculinity and in this period martial manliness shaped civilian masculinities in numerous ways. The aftermath of Waterloo ushered in what Graham Dawson has termed the 'pleasure culture of war', wherein war became normalised and romanticised, and those who fought in it glamorised and lionised.[73] It escalated from the mid-century with the development of mass entertainment, mass media, and popular militarism.[74] Scientific racism and new imperialism in the final quarter of the century instilled the idea that war was the way for the fittest, warlike races to succeed, generating a hyper-aggressive competitive masculinity.[75] By the turn of the century, a more brutal, jingoistic, less romantic version of the warrior emerged.[76] Throughout the long nineteenth century, war could be perceived either as causing a crisis in national masculinity or reinvigorating it.[77] In the post-Waterloo era, men who experienced combat were increasingly considered to be different from civilians;[78] some used this to fashion distinctive self-identities in published narratives of serving and fighting, a new genre that in turn helped reconfigure the ordinary soldier into a hero.[79] Similarly, Jack Tar held enormous cultural appeal, imagined as stalwart defender of sweethearts, comrades, and nation; member of a 'cosmopolitan cohort' who moved goods around the globe and enforced imperial policies.[80] Crucially, military language and metaphors, practices, and models not only shaped soldiers' and sailors' experiences of the army and the navy, but shaped civilian men's identities and self-representations too.[81]

One of the concerns of this scholarship is to show the variety of ways in which martial values were disseminated into civilian life. War as entertainment saturated print culture aimed at youths.[82] People were persuaded to purchase consumables by advertising featuring soldiers and sailors.[83] They also encountered martial themes through the performance of military battles in theatres, circuses, and pageants.[84] The army and navy offered spectacle in the form of reviews, parades, and drills, processions, music, and the military accoutrements of flags and trophies.[85] People also took trips to see new warships, dubbed 'naval gazing'.[86] Yet the ways in which valorised martial values entered the popular psyche have still not been fully enumerated. This is worth pursuing, since war even shaped male psychoses, as Thomas West's admission to Middlesex County Lunatic Asylum, Colney Hatch, on 23 May 1854, indicates. Ill during the Crimean War, this twenty-one-year-old single man, dissenter, and railway engine cleaner, suffered delusions that manifested in the belief that he was driving a locomotive to fight the Russians.[87]

Recently, scholars have turned to the role of emotions in representations of military men. Sensibility saturated accounts of soldiers and sailors in the Romantic era and depictions of their suffering encouraged sympathy in viewers.[88] The notion of 'military men of feeling', who could combine gentleness and caring with combat, was still powerful in the Crimean era. This was not inimical to bellicosity: the gentle soldier ameliorated the shame of the spectator by allowing him to empathise with the combatant and legitimated war as a humanitarian effort.[89] Racially inflected imperial ideas of military men changed the nature of warrior feelings by the end of the century. A short story in *Hearth and Home*, 1894, describes its protagonist thus: 'Captain Murchison was a man of pluck and backbone, possessing great self-control and endurance, a man of iron will and fortitude.'[90] Even though, by now, hard physicality was not merged with ready tears of sensibility, the military man could still shed a tear when in extremity. For Murchison it was when facing total blindness. The impact on civilian manliness of the range of emotions associated with military men – not just courage and fortitude, but the mutually constitutive mix of self-sacrifice, longing and loss, nostalgia, and patriotism – needs the further investigation explored in *Manliness in Britain*.

The significance of these feelings is clear from their depiction in print, visual, and material cultures, consumed both on battle and home fronts. Indeed, the scholarship on the close relationship between these two domains has grown rapidly since the start of the twenty-first century. The *Boy's Own Magazine* author mentioned was a reverend, and he told his young audience that when he attended wounded and dying soldiers in the Crimea, they feared they had 'led a bad life' and asked him: 'can there be any hope for us now?' In his view, they 'may have been bad men, but they are always truthful: they never try to make themselves out to be better than they really are. Their last thought is generally of home.'[91] This book therefore traces the significance of the domestic sphere and its material culture in projecting martial values and manliness into the civilian sphere.[92]

Home, family relationships, and the concept of domesticity have been identified as central to masculine identity from early modern through to modern periods for most social classes.[93] Collectively, these studies show that men gained authority and advertised their manhood through their mastery over dependents and the sexual control of female members in their households; moreover, their status was threatened when this was not achieved. The home was fetishised in Victorian Britain as a symbol of morality within which masculine identity was increasingly monitored.[94] John Tosh shows that from the 1830s to 1880s, domesticity, as an emotional and psychological category, added a further dimension to these markers of status for middle-class men, who derived from it a profound sense of self.[95] Furthermore, historians reveal that masculine identity was evaluated in the long nineteenth century through men's care, nurture, and affection for their children.[96] This applied beyond the middle classes. Recent studies of working-class men as fathers rescue them from the contempt of posterity and nineteenth-century social investigators, who regularly cast them as neglectfully absent from the home and, when present, a disruptive force.[97]

The place of 'home' remained significant for manliness even in the period that John Tosh has identified as the 'flight from domesticity' – from the 1880s onwards.[98] In recent years this 'flight' has been revised and it is now considered to be an era when domesticity was projected beyond the home and family; merely displaced or postponed while men endeavoured to make their living, rather than rejected outright. As the shifts in tone of fictional representations of manliness to more adventurous, harder styles indicate, the 'flight' was primarily a feature of men's imaginative lives, rather than a social practice. Nevertheless, there was a tension between work and home, as this book demonstrates. This was not new. As Karen Downing's neat concept of 'restlessness' demonstrates, it can be traced in print to the plot of Daniel Defoe's *Robinson Crusoe* (1719) and retained its popularity for over a century afterwards.[99] Nonetheless, it became more acute during the long nineteenth century as attachment to home came to be seen as a marker of inadequacy and individuals were praised for launching themselves into the unknown of an imperial world where migration was normalised and sought after.[100] Even so, this was still a world in which tender feelings about and by men were encouraged, so long as those men also conformed to dominant notions of rugged, hardy manliness.[101]

Thus the home, and the emotions it generated, were significant to manliness throughout the century, since men were no more alienated from the home at its end than they had been before, although their reason for being absent might be imagined differently.

Collectively, this scholarship challenges any supposition that men were peripheral to the home, demonstrating that public and domestic spheres were neither separate nor rigidly gendered. While acknowledging difference and complexity, it shows that many men were frequently absent from the home because they were working to provide for the domestic economy and were considered by their families to perform affection, nurture, and devotion through this labour.[102] Similarly, when present, such fathers were tactile, playful, and caring, all factors which boosted their masculine identity.[103] This body of work is valuable and important, and its findings are not questioned here. However, this book takes a different tack, which is to explore why cultural representations of men frequently imagined them as physically absent from home, though never peripheral to it; and how this sense of them as a centripetal or centrifugal force within the home and family unit shaped their manliness.[104]

The workplace was one of the acceptable locations where men were expected to be when away from home. Employment, after all, enabled men to provide for their dependents and kept them busy and out of trouble. As such, work was a primary marker of masculine identity, whether in terms of middle-class professional identity or working-class skilled and unskilled labour. The relationship between work and men's bodies was a matter of contemporary concern. The increasingly sedentary nature of middle-class men's work was understood to undermine their bodies and minds, making the former flaccid and weak, the latter subject to neurasthenia, a psychological condition of modern life and its stresses.[105] Working men's bodies were subjected to greater scrutiny than elite men's, since state and society utilised them for industrial and economical success and national and imperial defence.[106] At any one time they were, thus, objects of both concern and emulation. As such, a variety of scholarly works address Victorian working-class men's corporeality. Social historians explore mid-century 'condition of England' fears that industrialisation stunted industrial workers, while economic and demographic historians reconstruct the working population's diets and stature.[107] Social Darwinism and urban industrialisation raised the spectre of a generation of physically deficient working-class men, and, thus, historical scholarship alludes to the working-man's body when exploring institutionalised attempts in the later nineteenth century to salvage the 'degenerate' physicality of the British working man.[108]

Art historical scholarship shows the ways in which working-class men's bodies were also celebrated and appropriated by elite audiences. Artists used representations of labourers, particularly navvies, harvesters, blacksmiths, and colonial craftsmen, to construct gender, class, national, and imperial identities.[109] Urban labouring men in art emphasised that Britain was a modern, technologically advanced industrial and imperial nation.[110] Agricultural labourers' depiction in art served many cultural functions over the eighteenth and nineteenth centuries.[111] By the Victorian period, such men were often represented as downtrodden or working in teams. This contrasted with portrayals, both in paint and photography, of seafaring men who were deemed independent and resilient and, therefore, less intimidating than the urban worker.[112] Indeed, one way to render the urban working classes more reassuring in an era of expanding democracy and working-class political demands was to ascribe heroism to them. Working-class men's physicality is, therefore, also considered in scholarship on the democratisation of heroism in the nineteenth century, when civilians of lower social status were honoured for saving lives and other acts of bravery.

Descriptions of this new hero's strength and character in a print culture intended for a popular readership served several purposes.[113] As exemplars and aspirational models of behaviour for the lower classes they were intended to secure social compliance.[114] The ways in which depictions of working men shaped middle-class men's masculine identities has been less fully considered. There are useful insights to build on. Middle-class artists, for example, explored their own labour through such art.[115] Radical socialists also saw working men's bodies as exemplars for their own visions of a socialist utopia: in some cases homoerotic desire was envisioned to bridge class divisions.[116] This book examines more broadly the middle-class fascination and desire for working-class men's labouring bodies to scrutinise the latter's relationship with ideals of manliness. It also addresses working-class accounts and representations of men at work to show how far they shared and contrasted with elite versions.

Sources, methodology, and concepts

In order to identify the meanings of manliness, a wide range of diverse sources that are not conventionally analysed together are surveyed in *Manliness in Britain*. These include print culture, such as advice literature, popular health guides, works of history and literature, sermons, friendly society regulations, periodicals and magazines, especially the popular *British Workman* temperance publication, as well as commercial advertisements. It also encompasses fiction, poetry, and songs, along with life writings. Visual images of idealised men in engravings and genre paintings are considered, together with photographs and lithographs. Insane asylum case notes are deployed to trace the relationship between men's bodies and the language of manliness.[117] Material culture is also assessed through a variety of objects, including trade union, friendly societies, and temperance ephemera, such as certificates, banners, quilts, and aprons, as well as pottery figures. Martial material culture like toys, textiles, and colours are assessed, as well as domestic objects such as plates, jugs, mugs, and hand-sewn furnishings.

The intention to elicit emotions unites much of the visual, material, and print culture that is examined here. This is partly because the decades studied were shaped by sensibility and the sentimental, two phases of the same urge to shape the world and encourage people's actions by stimulating feelings.[118] Its influence was deepened by its moral content.[119] Nicola Bown observes that sentimentality did not just 'sweeten ideological messages', it had aesthetic qualities that invited tears and feelings that were predicated on a shared humanity.[120] In this way, as Rebecca Bedell shows, the cultures of feeling that animated the long nineteenth century sought to forge human connectedness and thus achieve social transformation. She points out that sentiment was 'politically multivalent'. In some hands it aimed at reform, in others it sought to control, and even those people typically excluded from power might deploy its rhetoric to effect more radical change.[121] This worked because people shared the tools to interpret its meanings. Readers and viewers responded similarly to sentimental works, shaped by their familiarity with social codes, signs, and symbols; sentiment was thus 'predicated on a mutual understanding of the cogs of homogenised emotion'.[122] Such motifs had affective power throughout the long nineteenth century, which they carried with them wherever they were encountered, whether in art, material culture, poetry, or advertising.[123]

This study therefore argues that feeling is central to the formation of gender identities. As it demonstrates, many of the positive representations of idealised manliness were deployed through sensibility and sentiment, cultivating feelings of admiration, love, pride, and patriotism in those who encountered them. Powerful in themselves, these emotions were the more potent because they were repeatedly linked to exemplary manly bodies. The attractive male forms, figures, and faces which embodied manly values and elicited these emotional responses, it is proposed, also stimulated desire in their male and female spectators.[124] This desire could have many facets, whether erotic and sexual, or simply gratifying and pleasurable. The homo- and heteroerotic gaze was thus evoked in the service of gender and class constructions, since the male bodies objectified were frequently working class.[125] Negative accounts of men deemed unmanly also intentionally provoked feelings to strengthen their message, though these were not the tender emotions of the sentimental, but raw visceral feelings like disgust, revulsion, fear, and hate – the very antitheses of pleasurable desire. These representations of unmanliness, intended to warn men against excess in all its forms, deployed sensationalism and melodrama. When men were shown as disrupting homes, especially through marital violence, for instance, the motifs of melodrama are easily detected.[126] This cultural movement typically attached emotions to bodies too. Good and evil characters were written onto bodies, respectively beautiful or ugly, externalising what might otherwise be hidden.[127] Given the class and racial structures in which these systems of feeling operated in the nineteenth century, it was often working-class men and those defined as racial and ethnic 'others' whose bodies were thus imagined.

It was the nexus of bodies, emotions, and objects that embedded ideas about manliness in people's minds and influenced corporeal behaviour and actions: a phenomenon that is, to date, little recognised.[128] There are numerous conceptual frameworks for analysing bodies in the past. Roger Cooter's survey of the 'somatic turn' in history arranges these into four broad categories. First, the Foucauldian concept of biopower, which exposes the regulatory techniques that use the body to control populations and the systems that encourage self-actualisation through the personal shaping of the corporeal.[129] Next is the new cultural history's 'body': a culturally constructed entity that is historicised in its 'representational regime'.[130] The 'lived-experience' body is a reaction to this discursive emphasis, whose proponents argue that a representational approach risks de-essentialising the reality of flesh. Instead they seek to understand embodiment.[131] Karen Harvey's attempt to 'study the lived, embodied experience of gender' is driven by this agenda.[132] She advocates drawing on one's 'own material experiences', combined with documentary evidence, to investigate the physical experience of labour skills in the past.[133] Cooter goes on to critique what he sees as the return of 'biological essentialism' in other disciplines in the first decade of the twenty-first century. Some of these scholars adopt neuroscience to understand bodies, others implement 'presentationalism'; that is, the ontological quest for presence and authenticity in history.[134] Cooter completes his survey with Nikolas Rose's 'politics of life', in which the 'entanglements of power constituted in and through body/knowledge' are foregrounded.[135]

As its starting point, this book is perhaps most influenced by the 'representational regime' outlined, in that it focuses on textual, visual, and material culture representations of gendered male bodies to historicise their meaning.[136] Its source base is not, therefore, equipped to evoke men's embodied experience, which in any case would appear to be illusory: how, after all, can historians divest themselves of their own somatic sense, their own social and cultural context, their own sex and gender, to imagine themselves into a historical actor's very different body and mentality? By recognising the emotional moods created by these accounts of the manly body, nonetheless, this analysis seeks to do more than identify the meanings of manliness that were projected onto the body, through their association with feelings. It proposes that these emotions were forms of communication and that emotional expressions provide information about gender. In doing so, it adapts social-psychologist Gerben van Cleef's 'Emotion as Social Information' model, which contends that 'emotional expressions provide information to observers, which may influence their behaviour' through inferential processes and eliciting affective reactions.[137] It is proposed that this melding of approved manly bodies with particular emotions created 'emotionalised bodies', akin to emotional objects, which created and communicated what was deemed to be acceptable or unacceptable manliness (through inferences related to other knowledge about masculine identity) and elicited feelings in people that helped them find these qualities appealing and respond positively or be repulsed by and reject them.

The central tenet of this book's argument is that it was the intermateriality of text, image, object and their conjunction with bodies and emotions that facilitated the conveying, reproducing, and fixing of manly values.[138] An expansive definition of material culture is adopted for this reason, since text and images from print culture were frequently reproduced upon an object or repurposed into an object – their form and location extending the reach of their messages.[139] The theoretical concept that is deployed throughout to underpin this argument is cultural theorist Sara Ahmed's notion of 'stickiness'. She shows that objects, signs, and bodies become sticky with meaning. This meaning – in her application disgust – is transferred through a process of substitution from one object to another. The objects are not inherently disgusting but become sticky with such affect. For her, this process is an 'effect of the histories of contact between bodies, objects, and signs'. Repetition makes the meanings intrinsic and has a binding effect.[140] This book proposes that positive as well as negative emotions are projected onto and transferred between bodies and objects, which carry and transmit messages about gender to those who encounter them and their signs.

Contemporaries were aware of the potential of such material culture. The *British Workman*, for instance, sold packs of illustrated 'wall-paper', posters of the beautiful illustrations that it published each month intended to inculcate temperance through moral lessons. Their purpose was itself depicted in a 1870 wall-paper entitled 'A Father's Lessons on the Illustrated Wall-Papers'. It shows a working father sitting in front of a wall displaying several wall-papers (Figure 0.2), simultaneously labouring and using the illustrations to teach his daughter, who has brought him his lunch. Like this image, the wall-paper not only offered moral instruction and good behaviour, but modelled the performance of manliness. Such intermateriality meant that meanings travelled, often transcending or complicating their original intentions. When different audiences met these meanings, they had the potential to break free from the wealth, class, or gender constraints imposed by more conventional print culture. This is very apparent in objects that brought political, national, and imperial values into the home (such as textiles, ceramics, and figurines). Indeed, location and use could directly impact upon meaning and need to be taken

0.2 *A Father's Lessons on the Illustrated Wall-Papers*, British Workman (2 May 1870), p. 20.

into consideration when investigating cultural import and trends. Thus, considering the intersection of emotions and gender reshapes our understandings of power and its exercise by moving away from more simplistic, often heteronormative, binary models such as domination and subordination, or ideals and reality.[141]

Intermateriality also deepened the role of objects as emotional artefacts, a concept that takes us beyond text to addresses the intersections of bodies, emotions, and material culture.[142] As Ahmed argues, contact with imagined and material objects generates feeling.[143] This burgeoning area of research demonstrates that objects stimulate feelings and maintain and spread values and ideas. There is evidence that contemporaries recognised this capacity of material culture and deployed it to shape and monitor their own behaviours and beliefs.[144] The abolitionist iconography of the kneeling slave, for example, was a powerful tool in the campaign to abolish the slave trade. In 1834, William Lloyd Garrison introduced his 'Sonnet', inspired by Wedgwood's medallion of the kneeling slave, explaining:

> In order to keep my sympathies from flagging ... and to nourish my detestation of slavery by a tangible though imperfect representation of it, I have placed on my mantel-piece the figure of a slave (made of plaster) kneeling in a supplicant position and chained by the ankles and wrists.[145]

As this neatly demonstrates, emotions are more likely to be stimulated through sensorial encounters with three-dimensional objects. The juxtaposition of multiple forms in one object that could be handled, viewed, possessed, gifted, bequeathed, and treasured made emotional artefacts so powerful that they acted as agents in influencing people's actions, behaviours, and views.[146]

Manliness in Britain unfolds its arguments through these conjunctions of emotions and materiality. Chapter 1, 'Figures, faces, and desire: male bodies and manliness', queers our received knowledge of the transmission of gender by asking different questions about the part played by men's idealised figures, forms, and faces in the process. Setting out the general trends in manly ideal bodies over time, it contextualises them in the factors triggering discussions of manhood, which were frequently expressed through concerns over men's bodies, appearance, and function, and driven by fears about modernity. It follows in the footsteps of George Mosse's work on manliness in Germany and other parts of Europe, which places the beautiful male body at its heart.[147] What makes this approach novel, however, is that the chapter charts the various feelings and states of mind promoted by these attractive bodies and their consequences, including romantic and parental love, grief, cheerfulness, resolve, and security. All promoted characteristics of manliness, making this concept appealing and easy to recognise, feel, and to share. It contends that desire was the most fundamental factor in this process, since idealised male bodies had erotic potential for women and men, and were objects of the gaze in ways similar to feminine, sexualised bodies.[148] An explicit example of this is the furore over Richard Westmacott's eighteen-foot-high statue, Achilles, intended to commemorate the nation's gratitude to the Duke of Wellington, cast from French cannon captured during the Napoleonic Wars and erected in 1822.[149] Its nudity caused consternation, especially since it was funded by public female subscription; thus a fig leaf was added.[150] Originally intended to be titled 'The Ladies' Trophy', it was humorously titled 'the ladies' fancy'. George Cruikshank satirised it in *Making Decent!!* and *Backside and Front View of the Ladies Fancy-Man, Paddy Carey* (both 1822).[151] Replete with phallic innuendo, the latter centres on female viewers' fascination with the larger-than-life naked muscular male form. As the drapery banner declares: 'His Brawny Shoulders 4 ft Square/His Cheeks like thumping Kidney tatees/His legs would make a Chairman Stare/And Pat was loved by all the Ladies "The Ladies Joy &c &c" Paddy Carey.'[152] Such male bodies appealed to men as well as women, it is argued, rendering the gender qualities associated with them desirable too.[153]

Their antitheses: revulsion and ugliness constructed notions of unmanliness too, as Chapter 2, 'Appetites, passions, and disgust: the penalties and paradoxes of unmanliness', demonstrates. It builds on Stephanie Olsen's work on the emotional education of juveniles from 1880 to 1914, which deployed both positive and negative feelings.[154] It shows that adult men were instructed on how to avoid unmanliness through emotionalised bodies: failing, uncontrolled, unattractive bodies created by unchecked appetites and bad habits, prompted disgust, fear, and shame. Men were thus taught that the inability to master one's self caused literal physical, mental, and moral disintegration, and attracted society's contempt. The chapter shows that lack of self-restraint became more dangerous in the nineteenth century as excessive passions, bodily appetites, and feelings were increasingly pathologised as causes of disease.[155] To borrow Ellen Bayuk Rosenman's account of spermatorrhea, diseases were 'imagined into existence to embody historically specific anxieties'.[156] The same unregulated bodies and emotions were also increasingly seen to lead to insanity. Throughout the nineteenth century insanity was attributed to and located in disordered nervous systems. Nonetheless, it retained moral associations, with its hereditary explanations and causal factors of poverty, stress, bodily appetites, and emotional problems often moralised. In these understandings, responsibility was placed upon the male individual for failing to exert sufficient moral control to avoid his illness. Not all unregulated, non-normative male bodies were read as disgusting, however. Youths, old men, disabled and ill men, for example, were partially exempted from conforming to the rigid rules set by the beautiful emotionalised bodies of Chapter 1. Even so, all these men were deemed compromised and less manly as a result.

In Chapter 3, 'Hearts of oak: martial manliness and material culture', bodies and emotions are brought together with objects through the most desirable idealised man of all: the military man. Fictional and real martial men were imagined through emotionalised bodies, with material culture often acting as the point of entry for the cultural work they performed in producing and disseminating manliness. This included the romanticised 'stuff' of martial glory or, later in the century, the new technology of annihilation, or, across the period, the everyday domestic artefacts decorated with martial themes.[157] This martial material culture was emotionally dense and played a vital part in constructing manliness for civilians as much as soldiers and sailors. Uniforms, weaponry, battlefield objects, medals, and regimental colours functioned in print culture as entry points into wider imaginings of military men's admirable characters and qualities.[158] In their domestic lives, people frequently interacted with objects which resonated with martial manliness, those decorated with, or in the form of, sailors, soldiers, and military events, including military-themed toys, ceramic ornaments, and textiles, some of which were made by military men. Domestic in nature and scale, these objects also strengthen recent findings that there was no hard separation between the spheres of battlefront and home, military and civilian life.[159] What makes them even more significant for the book's argument, is that when objects imbued with martial masculinities were encountered in other spaces and times they continued to carry and convey these associations to a broader audience. This is evident in the impact of 'celebrity' military men in material culture, and this chapter therefore analyses two men from lower social origins who were feted in material culture, in performance, and later through funded memorials. The objects analysed acted as vessels for emotions, helping to 'fix' manly ideals in people's minds and sense of selves. Indeed, some, in the form of remains of military men's bodies and military colours, were treated as 'relics' and devotional artefacts. In the end, this chapter shows that objects are not merely symbolic but material agents in constructing gender.

Chapter 4, 'Homeward bound: manliness and the home', develops the analysis of materiality further by considering the relationship between the space of home and manliness. At marriage, men announced their sexual maturity and achieved their masculine privileges. As this chapter shows, however, there was a tension between a masculine identity that was conceptualised as rooted in the emotional sphere and physical space of the domestic, but only achieved by men being outside it, toiling to earn a living. As such, it addresses men's absence from home through the popular motifs of men leaving and returning home, dreaming of home, and their absent presence; that is, material reminders of men obliged to be away from home for long periods.[160] It then analyses the parallel consequences of men's presence in the home. Men could create 'happy' homes through their economic provision, frugality, kindness, and, crucially, displays of love and affection. Or their disruptive unmanly behaviours could result in 'unhappy' homes. The chapter focuses on working-class men, though, of course, cultural representations of absent middle-class men were not at all unusual. Some were positive, including men who were away from home carrying out duties in empire or war, or industrious businessmen striving at work before returning to their home refuges, so central to the concept of domesticity and the formation of middle-class identity.[161] Other absences from home, however, were marked as unmanly. A story in the 1883 *Illustrated London News*, for example, established that John Adair was a bad husband and father through his failure to return home after work to support his wife when his child was ill.[162] Nonetheless, the chapter addresses representations of working-class men because middle-class imaginations so often situated them in relation to home, scrutinising their emotional and sexual performances in that sphere since the home was deemed central to a successful society and nation. It also functioned to remind middle-class men what they should aspire to and avoid being. As such, it further disrupts the notion of a flight from domesticity from the 1870s.[163]

'Brawn and bravery: glorifying the working body' draws together emotionalised bodies, spaces, and objects in the final chapter by examining the performance of manliness in work. The representations of working men analysed in this chapter were especially amendable to a middle-class gaze and agenda. Their glorified emotionalised bodies conveyed respectability and reliability, constructing a safe type of manliness that drew on traditional motifs to counter anxieties about working-class men as a politically or socially disruptive force. These were 'heroic' forms of working-class masculine employees, either because their labour was deemed aesthetically and morally 'heroic', symbolised by their muscular forms, or because they risked their lives to save others as part of their profession. Some wore uniform, such as the firemen and railway guards; others had a distinctive and recognisable working dress that could be romanticised, such as miners, mariners, and blacksmiths. Several bore the symbol of the archetypical unskilled and skilled labourer: sleeves rolled up to show muscular forearms. A further common feature was that kindness was attributed to both brawn and brave stereotypes. This emotional 'cluster' of goodwill, moral responsibility, and benevolence tamed the muscular and reckless body.[164] This was not the only function of these manly workers for a middle-class audience, since the same combination of alluring physical and emotional qualities embodied in the male working-class body also rendered it desirable as a manly ideal.[165] Yet working bodies should not be read solely in terms of condescension, passivity, and subordination, nor through erotic desire and projection.

The final section of the chapter therefore explores working men's agency in constructing gendered identities through emotionalised bodies and material culture, evident in working-class artists' depiction of labouring men on images and objects intended for a working-class audience and consumer.[166] As Simon Newman's work on 'seafaring bodies' demonstrates, the agency of early Philadelphia sailors can be traced in their bodies: their distinctive gait, their injuries, and their tattoos, which were 'emblems of trade, experience, and proficiency'.[167] The banners and ephemera used in processions by workers in nineteenth-century Britain, often decorated with proud images of idealised working men, did similar work. Of course, given the dependence of the working classes on their labouring bodies, this also emphasises the precarity and vulnerability of a working man's sense of self and his classed position in the world, his body undermined by poverty, dangerous working conditions, and ill-health. Thus, while the cultural alignment of emotionalised bodies and objects strengthened the power of manliness for society, it simultaneously underwrote its vulnerabilities and instabilities.

The book's epilogue brings emotionalised bodies and material culture up to date to show how men's bodies and their associated emotions continue to be exploited for a variety of ends, some of which, in a world that appears to be rejecting progressive liberal values, are remarkably dangerous. In this way, it foregrounds the importance of bodies, emotions, and material culture for our understanding of masculinity and all of its social, cultural, and political implications.

Notes

1. *Manchester Courier and Lancashire General Advertiser* (Fri, 8 February 1907).
2. The other side of the panel has a theatrical theme of actors and productions.
3. John Jackson is the only one of the large figures of boxers to be depicted fully clothed.
4. The main boxers on the top two thirds of the panels are: Jack Broughton; George Stevenson; Tom Cribb and Tom Molineaux; John Jackson. Pugilists depicted or described around the main figures include James Figg, Ben Brian, Thomas Johnson, Jack Slack, Isaac Perrins, Tom Johnson, Jem Belcher, Caleb Stephen, George Moore, Bill Richmond, and Bob Gregson.
5. Henry Angelo was Bryon's fencing instructor. Pierce Egan, *Boxiana, or Sketches of Modern Pugilism from the Championship of Cribb to the Present Time*, 2 vols (London, vol. 2), p. 502. The screen is listed in Byron's Sale Catalogue of 1816, lot 382, 'A Screen six feet high, covered with NUMEROUS PORTRAITS OF ACTORS, Scene Prints, Portraits of Pugilists, and Representations of Boxing Matches'. From Peter Cochran's transcription of the three catalogues: https://petercochran.files.wordpress.com/2009/03/byrons_library.pdf (accessed 2 February 2019). In 1885, it was claimed it had been bought for £15, two years before, at 'Angelo's School of Arms', but was worth far more. *Edinburgh Evening News* (Fri, 6 February 1885).
6. *Manchester Courier and Lancashire General Advertiser* (Fri, 8 February 1907).
7. *The Globe* (Wed, 17 October 1906), p. 10.
8. *Worthing Herald* (Sat, 12 June 1937); for an illustration of Murray's drawing room, which housed the screen, see *Pall Mall Gazette* (6 March 1913), p. 9.
9. For example, panel 3.
10. Egan, *Boxiana*, pp. 26–8.
11. Kasia Boddy, *Boxing: A Cultural History* (London: Reaktion Books, 2008), pp. 52–3. Gary Dyer, 'Thieves, boxers, sodomites, poets: being flash to Byron's Don Juan', *Proceedings of the Modern Language Association* 116:3 (2001), 564.
12. Dyer, 'Thieves, boxers, sodomites, poets', 570.
13. For an overview of boxing in this period see Boddy, *Boxing*, chs 2 and 3.
14. Byron preferred youths over mature men, Fiona McCarthy, *Byron: Life and Legend* (London: Faber & Faber, 2003), passim.
15. Dyer, 'Thieves, boxers, sodomites, poets', 563, 567–70.
16. McCarthy, *Byron*, pp. 3–4, 25–6, 30–1, 479.
17. Deigo Saglia, 'Touching Byron: masculinity and the celebrity body in the Romantic

period', in Rainer Emig and Antony Rowland (eds), *Performing Masculinity* (Basingstoke: Palgrave, 2010), pp. 14, 15.

18 Examples from the Database of British and Irish Labouring-Class Poets and Poetry 1700–1900 (March 2019) include: Alexander Anderson, James Bird, Jem Blackaby, John Clare, Richard Herd, and Robert Millhouse. The poor also knew Byron was a radical, sympathetic to their plight.

19 Desire for the male body, and its relationship with race, class, and power is discussed in Anthea Callen, *Looking at Men: Anatomy, Masculinity and the Modern Male Body* (New Haven and London: Yale University Press, 2018), pp. 19–21.

20 For the roles of elite urban men and lower-ranking Highland men in the formation of Highland martial masculinity see Rosalind Carr, 'The gentleman and the soldier: patriotic masculinities in eighteenth-century Scotland', *Journal of Scottish Historical Studies* 28:2 (2008), 102–21.

21 Katie Barclay, *Men on Trial: Performing Emotion, Embodiment and Identity in Ireland, 1800–1845* (Manchester: Manchester University Press, 2018); Katie Barclay, 'Performing emotion and reading the male body in the Irish court, c. 1800–1845', *Journal of Social History* 51:2 (2017), 293–312; Ana de Freitas Boe and Abby Coyendall (eds), *Heteronormativity in Eighteenth-Century Literature and Culture* (Farnham: Ashgate, 2014); Simon Goldhill, *A Very Queer Family Indeed: Sex, Religion and the Bensons in Victorian Britain* (Chicago: University of Chicago Press, 2016); Karen Harvey, 'Craftsmen in common: objects, skills and masculinity in the eighteenth and nineteenth centuries', in Hannah Grieg, Jane Hamlett, and Leonie Hannan (eds), *Gender and Material Culture in Britain since 1600* (London: Palgrave Macmillan, 2016), 68–89 ; Karen Harvey, 'Men of parts: masculine embodiment and the male leg in eighteenth-century England', *Journal of British Studies* 54:4 (2015), 797–821; Dominic Janes, *Oscar Wilde Prefigured: Queer Fashioning and British Caricature, 1750–1900* (Chicago and London: University of Chicago Press, 2016); Declan Kavanagh, *Effeminate Years: Literature, Politics, and Aesthetics in Mid-Eighteenth-Century Britain* (Lewisburg, PA: Bucknell University Press, 2017); Matthew McCormack, *Embodying the Militia in Georgian England* (Oxford: Oxford University Press, 2015); Simon Newman, *Embodied History: The Lives of the Poor in Early Philadelphia* (Philadelphia: University of Pennsylvania Press, 2003).

22 Jennifer Evans, 'Introduction: Why queer German history?', *German History* 34:3 (2016), 371. For examples in eighteenth-century studies see the contributions to de Freitas Boe and Coyendall, *Heteronormativity in Eighteenth-Century Literature and Culture*.

23 There are some important works on same-sex desire that establish the lack of fixed binaries of categories of heterosexuality and homosexuality, including: Harry Cocks, *Nameless Offences: Homosexual Desire in the 19th Century* (London: I.B. Tauris, 2003); Matt Cook, *London and the Culture of Homosexuality, 1885–1914* (Cambridge: Cambridge University Press, 2003); Matt Houlbrook, *Queer London: Perils and Pleasures in the Sexual Metropolis, 1918–1957* (Chicago: University of Chicago Press, 2005); Helen Smith, *Masculinity, Class and Same-Sex Desire in Industrial England, 1895–1957* (Basingstoke: Palgrave Macmillan, 2015).

24 George Mosse recognises the centrality of idealised male beauty to notions of manliness in Germany and other parts of Europe, though he is less concerned with exploring desire beyond same-sex activities. George L. Mosse, *The Image of Man: The Creation of Modern Masculinity* (Oxford: Oxford University Press, 1996). For desire, see de Freitas Boe and Coyendall, *Heteronormativity in Eighteenth-Century Literature and Culture*, pp. 3, 6–15. For the homoerotic appeal of the male body see Janes, *Oscar Wilde Prefigured*.

25 For the different meanings of desire over time, see Anna Clark, *Desire: A History of European Sexuality* (New York and Abingdon: Routledge, 2008). For legitimate spaces for the homo-erotic gaze, see Anthea Callen, *Looking at Men: Anatomy,*

Masculinity and the Modern Male Body (New Haven and London: Yale University Press, 2018), pp. 22–3.
26 Again, it follows the lead of George Mosse's work, which extended from the eighteenth to the twentieth centuries. Mosse, *The Image of Man*.
27 'Good to think with' is French structural anthropologist Claude Lévi-Strauss's phrase. For its origin and problems see Marjorie Garber, *Loaded Words* (New York: Fordham University Press, 2012), pp. 96–7. The middle classes scrutinised working-class marital violence when constructing their views on marriage and violence: Lisa Surridge, *Bleak Houses: Marital Violence in Victorian Fiction* (Athens: Ohio University Press, c.2005); men constructed masculinities through classed and racialised bodies: Louis Moore, *I Fight for a Living: Boxing and the Battle for Black Manhood. 1880–1915* (Urbana and Chicago: University of Illinois Press, 2017).
28 The middle classes positioned the working-class home as a politicised construct, which carried with it moralizing and regulative dimensions: Mary Poovey, 'Domesticity and class formation: Chadwick's 1842 *Sanitary Report*', in Mary Poovey, *Making a Social Body: British Cultural Formation, 1830–1864* (Chicago: University of Chicago Press, 1995), pp. 116–18.
29 Smith, *Masculinity, Class and Same-Sex Desire*, pp. 18–19.
30 Poovey, *Making a Social Body*, pp. 124–5.
31 An excellent example of this is Barclay, *Men on Trial*.
32 For the performance of manliness in the Irish justice system see *ibid*.
33 For overviews of this literature, see Joanne Begiato, 'Between poise and power: embodied manliness in eighteenth- and nineteenth-century British culture', *Transactions of the Royal Historical Society* 26:2 (2016), 125–47; Roberta Park, 'Muscles, symmetry and action: "Do you measure up". Defining masculinity in Britain and America from the 1860s to the early 1900s', *International Journal of the History of Sport* 22:3 (2007), 366–7. For the classic account of the changing role of men's bodies in relation to shifting economic, political, cultural, industrial, and martial conditions, see Michael Anton Budd, *The Sculpture Machine: Physical Culture and Body Politics in the Age of Empire* (Basingstoke and London: Palgrave Macmillan, 1997). For the historiography of the body more broadly see Roger Cooter, 'The turn of the body: history and the politics of the corporeal', *Arbor, Clencia, Pensamiento y Cultura* 186:743 (2010), 393–405.
34 Budd sees Britain's participation in war as one of the key factors determining idealisations and fears about men's physical state, Budd, *Sculpture Machine*, passim. See also Michael Brown, 'Cold steel, weak flesh: mechanism, masculinity and the anxieties of late Victorian empire', *Cultural and Social History* 14:2 (2017), 155–81; Michael Brown and Chris Lawrence, 'Quintessentially modern heroes: surgeons, explorers, and empire, c. 1840–1914', *Journal of Social History* 50:1 (2016), 148–78; McCormack, *Embodying the Militia*, ch. 4; George L. Mosse, *Fallen Soldiers: Reshaping the Memory of the World Wars* (Oxford: Oxford University Press, 1990); R. A. Nye, 'Review essay: Western masculinities in war and peace', *American Historical Review* 112:2 (2007), 417–38.
35 Elspeth H. Brown, 'Racialising the virile body: Eadweard Muybridge's locomotion studies 1883–1887', *Gender & History* 17:3 (2005), 627–56; Cynthia S. Hamilton, 'Hercules subdued: the visual rhetoric of the kneeling slave', *Slavery & Abolition* 34:4 (2013), 631–52; Moore, *I Fight for a Living*; Jonathan Saha, 'Whiteness, masculinity and the ambivalent embodiment of "British justice" in colonial Burma', *Cultural and Social History* 14:4 (2017), 527–42.
36 Joanna Bourke, *Dismembering the Male: Men's Bodies, Britain and the Great War* (Chicago: University of Chicago Press, 1996); Arthur McIvor and R. Johnston, 'Dangerous work, hard men and broken bodies: masculinity in the Clydeside heavy industries', *Labour History Review* 69 (2004), 135–52; David M. Turner, *Disability in*

Eighteenth-Century England: Imagining Physical Impairment (New York: Routledge, 2012).

37 Karen Harvey, *Reading Sex in the Eighteenth Century: Bodies and Gender in English Erotic Culture* (Cambridge: Cambridge University Press, 2004); for an overview of work on bodies and sex see Sarah Toulalan and Kate Fisher, *The Routledge History of Sex and the Body: 1500 to the Present* (Abingdon: Routledge, 2013) and in an imperial context see Richard C. Sha, 'Othering sexual perversity: England, empire, race, and sexual science', in Michael Sappol and Stephen P. Rice (eds), *A Cultural History of the Human Body in the Age of Empire* (Oxford: Berg, 2010), pp. 87–105; Ellen Bayuk Rosenman, *Unauthorized Pleasures: Accounts of Victorian Erotic Experience* (Ithaca, NY: Cornell University Press, 2003).

38 Rob Boddice, 'The manly mind? Revisiting the Victorian "sex in brain" debate', *Gender & History* 23:2 (2011), 321–3, 325; Brown, 'Racialising the virile body', 627–56; Sharrona Pearl, *About Faces: Physiognomy in Nineteenth-Century Britain* (Cambridge, MA: Harvard University Press, 2010); Allan Sekula, 'The body and the archive', in Richard Bolton (ed.), *The Context of Meaning: Critical Histories of Photography* (Cambridge, MA: MIT Press, 1989), pp. 347–9; Kathryn Woods, '"Facing" identity in a "faceless" society: physiognomy, facial appearance and identity perception in eighteenth-century London', *Cultural and Social History* 14:2 (2017), 137–53.

39 Brown, 'Racialising the virile body', 632 and passim; Peter Hamilton and Roger Hargreaves, *The Beautiful and the Damned: The Creation of Identity in Nineteenth-Century Photography* (London: National Portrait Gallery, 2001), passim; Stephen P. Rice, 'Picturing bodies in the nineteenth century', in Sappol and Rice (eds), *A Cultural History of the Human Body*, passim; Sekula, 'The body and the archive', pp. 349, 371.

40 Budd, *Sculpture Machine*, ch. 1; Michael Hau, 'The normal, the ideal, and the beautiful: perfect bodies during the age of empire', in Sappol and Rice (eds), *A Cultural History of the Human Body*, p. 158; Newman, *Embodied History*, passim.

41 Matt Houlbrook, 'Queer things: men and make-up between the wars', in Grieg, Hamlett, and Hannan (eds), *Gender and Material Culture in Britain*, pp. 120–37; D. Kuchta, *The Three-Piece Suit and Modern Masculinity: England, 1550–1850* (Berkeley: University of California Press, 2002); Christopher Oldstone-Moore, *Of Beards and Men: The Revealing History of Facial Hair* (Chicago: University of Chicago Press, 2016); Beverly Lemire, 'A question of trousers: seafarers, masculinity and empire in the shaping of British male dress, c. 1600–1800', *Cultural and Social History* 13:1 (2016), 1–22.

42 This phrase is Budd's, *Sculpture Machine*, p. 56, also pp. 1, 7; Park, 'Muscles, symmetry and action', 365–95; Roberta Park, 'Biological thought, athletics and the formation of a "man of character": 1830–1900', *International Journal of the History of Sport* 24 (2007), 154–69.

43 James Mangan and James Walvin, 'Introduction', in J. Mangan and J. Walvin (eds), *Manliness and Morality: Middle-Class Masculinity in Britain and America 1800–1940* (Manchester: Manchester University Press, 1987), p. 3; Ava Baron, 'Masculinity, the embodied male worker, and the historian's gaze', *International Labor and Working-Class History* 69 (2006), 146–7.

44 Joane Nagel, 'Masculinity and nationalism: gender and sexuality in the making of nations', *Ethnic and Racial Studies* 21:2 (1998), 242–69; Park, 'Biological thought', passim.

45 Brown, 'Racialising the virile body', 637. For a similar focus see Pamela Gilbert, 'Popular beliefs and the body: "a nation of good animals"', in Sappol and Rice (eds), *A Cultural History of the Human Body*, pp. 144–5.

46 Scholars have come to delineate the differences between the Christian socialist version of muscular Christianity and the hyper-masculine muscular masculinity of

the imperial age, see John J. MacAloon, 'Introduction: muscular Christianity after 150 years', *International Journal of the History of Sport* 23:5 (2006), 687–700.
47 Rice, 'Picturing bodies in the nineteenth century', p. 230. Budd shows that the impulse to improve, regulate, and male control bodies was long-standing, *Sculpture Machine*, intro. and passim.
48 Barclay, *Men on Trial*, passim.
49 Alexandra Shepard, *Meanings of Manhood in Early Modern England* (Oxford: Oxford University Press, 2003).
50 Joanne Bailey, *Unquiet Lives: Marriage and Marriage Breakdown in England 1660–1800* (Cambridge: Cambridge University Press, 2003); Bernard Capp, 'The double standard revisited: plebeian women and male sexual reputation in early modern England', *Past & Present* 162:1 (1999), 70–100; Elizabeth Foyster, *Marital Violence: An English Family History, 1660–1857* (Cambridge: Cambridge University Press, 2005); Mark Rothery and Henry French (eds), *Making Men: The Formation of Elite Male Identities in England c. 1660–1900: Sourcebook* (Basingstoke: Palgrave Macmillan, 2012); David Turner, *Fashioning Adultery: Gender, Sex and Civility in England, 1660–1740* (Cambridge: Cambridge University Press, 2002).
51 For consideration of various periods see articles in Karen Harvey and Alex Shepard (eds), 'Special Feature on Masculinities', *Journal of British Studies* 44:2 (2005).
52 Saha, 'Whiteness, masculinity', passim.
53 Mrinalini Sinha, *Colonial Masculinity: The 'Manly Englishman' and the 'Effeminate Bengali' in the Late Nineteenth Century* (Manchester: Manchester University Press, 1995), p. 2.
54 Thomas Dixon, *Weeping Britannia: Portrait of a Nation in Tears* (Oxford: Oxford University Press, 2015); Elizabeth Foyster, 'Boys will be boys? Manhood and aggression, 1660–1800', in Tim Hitchcock and Michèle Cohen (eds), *English Masculinities, 1660–1800* (Harlow: Addison Wesley, 1999), pp. 151–77; Michael Roper, 'Between manliness and masculinity: the "war generation" and the psychology of fear in Britain, 1914–1950', *Journal of British Studies* 44:2 (2005), 343–62; Peter N. Stearns, 'Men, boys and anger in American society, 1860–1940', in Mangan and Walvin (eds), *Manliness and Morality*, pp. 74–88.
55 Thomas Dixon, '"Emotion": the history of a keyword in crisis', *Emotion Review* 4:4 (2012), 341; David Thorley, 'Towards a history of emotion 1562–1660', *The Seventeenth Century* 28:1 (2013), 5.
56 Christopher E. Forth, '"Manhood incorporated": diet and the embodiment of "civilised" masculinity', *Men and Masculinities* 11:5 (2009), 588, 590; John Tosh, 'The old Adam and the new man: emerging themes in the history of English masculinities, 1750–1850', in John Tosh, *Manliness and Masculinities in Nineteenth-Century Britain: Essays on Gender, Family and Empire* (Harlow: Pearson Education, 2004), pp. 73–5.
57 Poovey, *Making a Social Body*, p. 106; Lauren Goodlad, *Victorian Literature and the Victorian State: Character and Governance in a Liberal Society* (Baltimore, MD: John Hopkins University Press, 2003).
58 Goodlad, *Victorian Literature and the Victorian State*, passim.
59 Tosh, 'The old Adam and the new man', p. 75.
60 Frank Mort, *Dangerous Sexualities: Medico-Moral Politics in England since 1830* (London: Routledge, 2nd edn, 2000), pp. 67–77, 81–117.
61 Lesley Hall, 'Forbidden by God, despised by men: masturbation, medical warnings, moral panic, and manhood in Great Britain, 1850–1950', *Journal of the History of Sexuality in Modern Europe* 2:3 (1992), 371–2; Diane Mason, *Secret Vice: Masturbation in Victorian Fiction and Medical Culture* (Manchester: Manchester University Press, 2008), pp. 17–18.
62 Lucy Bland, *Banishing the Beast: English Feminism and Sexual Morality, 1885–1914* (London: Penguin, 1st pb edn, 1995), p. 245; Mort, *Dangerous Sexualities*,

pp. 81–117; Susan Kingsley-Kent, *Sex and Suffrage in Britain 1860–1914* (London: Routledge, 1990), pp. 5, 9, 177.
63 Hau, 'The normal, the ideal, and the beautiful', p. 158.
64 For the manipulation of men's bodies in war, see Emma Newlands, *Civilians into Soldiers: War, the Body and British Army Recruits 1939–45* (Manchester: Manchester University Press, 2014).
65 Hau, 'The normal, the ideal, and the beautiful', p. 158.
66 Ellen Bayuk Rosenman, 'Body doubles: the spermatorrhea panic', *Journal of the History of Sexuality* 12:3 (2003), 371.
67 David Nash and Anne-Marie Kilday, *Cultures of Shame: Exploring Crime and Morality in Britain 1600–1900* (London: Palgrave Macmillan, 2010); David Nash and Anne-Marie Kilday, *Shame and Modernity in Britain, 1890 to the Present* (London: Palgrave Macmillan, 2017).
68 Stephanie Olsen, *Juvenile Nation: Youth, Emotions and the Making of the Modern British Citizen, 1880–1914* (London: Bloomsbury, 2014), p. 3 and passim; Rothery and French, *Making Men*, p. 17.
69 Goodlad, *Victorian Literature and the Victorian State*, p. 43. For a Foucauldian reading of Victorian masculinity as the regulation of the self, especially for the bourgeois man, see Herbert Sussman, *Victorian Masculinities: Manhood and Masculine Poetics in Early Victorian Literature and Art* (Cambridge: Cambridge University Press, 1995), pp. 10–11.
70 There were criticisms of the armed forces and their personnel, but cultural representations were generally positive. For the ambivalences, see Catriona Kennedy, *Narratives of the Revolutionary and Napoleonic Wars: Military and Civilian Experience in Britain and Ireland* (Basingstoke: Palgrave Macmillan, 2013), pp. 37–8; Michael Paris, *Warrior Nation: Images of War in British Popular Culture, 1850–2000* (London: Reaktion, 2000), pp. 30–1.
71 Joanne Begiato, 'Tears and the manly sailor in England, c.1760–1860', *Journal for Maritime Research* 17:2 (2015), 117–33.
72 *Boy's Own Magazine: An Illustrated Journal of Fact, Fiction, History, and Adventure* 2 (1863), p. 311.
73 Graham Dawson, *Soldier Heroes: British Adventure, Empire, and the Imagining of Masculinities* (London and New York: Routledge, 1994); Kennedy, *Narratives of the Revolutionary and Napoleonic Wars*, pp. 9, 171–8 and passim; Paris, *Warrior Nation*, pp. 11–12.
74 Paris, *Warrior Nation*, p. 8.
75 Bradley Deane, *Masculinity and the New Imperialism: Rewriting Manhood in British Popular Literature, 1870–1914* (Cambridge, Cambridge University Press, 2014), pp. 1–19.
76 Paris, *Warrior Nation*, pp. 28, 54, 58, 69; Heather Streets-Salter, *Martial Races: The Military, Race and Masculinity in British Imperial Culture* (Manchester: Manchester University Press, 2004).
77 For example: McCormack, *Embodying the Militia*, ch. 1; Holly Furneaux, *Military Men of Feeling: Emotion, Touch, and Masculinity in the Crimean War* (Oxford: Oxford University Press, 2016), pp. 4–5.
78 Yuval Noah Harari, *Ultimate Experience: Battlefield Revelations and the Making of Modern War Culture, 1450–2000* (New York: Palgrave, 2008).
79 Kennedy, *Narratives of the Revolutionary and Napoleonic Wars*, pp. 19, 194–6 and ch. 2; Neil Ramsay, '"A real English soldier": suffering, manliness and class in the mid-nineteenth century soldiers' tale', in Catriona Kennedy and Matthew McCormack (eds), *Soldiering in Britain, and Ireland, 1750–1850: Men of Arms* (New York: Palgrave Macmillan, 2013), pp. 136–55.
80 Begiato, 'Tears and the manly sailor'; Mary Conley, *From Jack Tar to Union Jack: Representing Naval Manhood in the British Empire, 1870–1918* (Manchester:

Manchester University Press, 2009); Paul Gilje, *To Swear Like a Sailor: Maritime Culture in America 1750–1850* (Cambridge: Cambridge University Press, 2016), pp. 3–4, 7; Isaac Land, *War, Nationalism and the British Sailor, 1750–1850* (New York: Palgrave Macmillan, 2009); Lemire, 'Question of trousers', 6–8, 13.

81 Michael Brown, '"Like a devoted army": medicine, heroic masculinity, and the military paradigm in Victorian Britain', *Journal of British Studies* 49:3 (2010), 592–622; McCormack, *Embodying the Militia*, pp. 13–32, 99–102.
82 Paris, *Warrior Nation*, pp. 8, 9, 42.
83 Ibid., pp. 46–7.
84 Ibid., p. 19. Scott Hughes Myerly, *British Military Spectacle from the Napoleonic Wars through the Crimea* (Cambridge, MA: Harvard University Press, 1996), pp. 144–50.
85 Myerly, *British Military Spectacle*, passim.
86 Kennedy, *Narratives of the Revolutionary and Napoleonic Wars*, pp. 172–3.
87 Thomas West, London Metropolitan Archives (LMA), Middlesex County Lunatic Asylum Colney Hatch, Case Book for Male Patients: H12/CH/B13/004 (1854).
88 Philip Shaw, 'Wars of seeing: suffering and sentiments in Joseph Wright's "The Dead Soldier"', in Kennedy and McCormack (eds), *Soldiering in Britain and Ireland*, pp. 76–95.
89 Furneaux, *Military Men of Feeling*, pp. 16–24.
90 'Only two months more!', *Hearth and Home* (15 February 1894), p. 52.
91 *Boy's Own Magazine* 2 (1863), p. 316.
92 Holly Furneaux has explored the 'stuff of war' from the soldiers' perspective, considering the parcels they received from home, trench art, and the sketches and objects that they sent home. *Military Men of Feeling*, ch. 5.
93 Joanne Bailey, *Parenting in England, 1760–1830: Emotion, Identity, and Generation* (Oxford: Oxford University Press, 2012); Karen Harvey, *The Little Republic: Masculinity and Domestic Authority in Eighteenth-Century Britain* (Oxford: Oxford University Press, 2012); John Tosh, *A Man's Place: Masculinity and the Middle-Class Home in Victorian England* (New Haven, CT and London: Yale University Press, 1999).
94 For an examination of this in literary culture, see Karen Chase and Michael Levenson, *The Spectacle of Intimacy: A Public Life for the Victorian Family* (Princeton, NJ: Princeton University Press, 2000).
95 Tosh, *A Man's Place*. For an example in colonial Australia see Stephen Garton, 'The scales of suffering: love, death and Victorian masculinity', *Social History* 27:1 (2002), 40–58.
96 Bailey, *Parenting in England*; Trev Lynn Broughton and Helen Rogers, *Gender and Fatherhood in the Nineteenth Century* (Basingstoke: Palgrave Macmillan, 2007); Julie-Marie Strange, *Fatherhood and the British Working Class* (Cambridge: Cambridge University Press, 2015).
97 Broughton and Rogers, *Gender and Fatherhood*, intro.; Julie-Marie Strange, 'Fathers at home: life writing and late-Victorian and Edwardian plebeian domestic masculinities', *Gender & History* 27:3 (2015), 703–5.
98 John Tosh, 'Home and away: the flight from domesticity in late-nineteenth-century England re-visited', *Gender and History* 3 (2015), 561–75.
99 Karen Downing, *Restless Men: Masculinity and Robinson Crusoe 1788–1840* (Basingstoke: Palgrave Macmillan, 2014), pp. 3, 5 and passim.
100 Joanne Begiato, 'Selfhood and "nostalgia": sensory and material memories of the childhood home in late Georgian Britain', *Journal for Eighteenth-Century Studies* 42:2 (2019), 229–46.
101 Melissa Bellanta, '"Poor Gordon": what the Australian cult of Adam Lindsay Gordon tells us about turn-of-the-twentieth-century masculine sentimentality', *Gender & History* 28:2 (2016), 401–21.

102 Strange, *Fatherhood and the British Working Class*, passim.
103 Strange, 'Fathers at home', 703; Tosh, *A Man's Place*, ch. 4.
104 This develops Broughton and Rogers' reading of Frederick Harvey's *The Volunteer, 1860*: 'Introduction: the empire of the father', in Broughton and Rogers, *Gender and Fatherhood*, pp. 2–5. For this phenomenon in its broader and global perspective see K. H. Adler and Carrie Hamilton (eds), *Homes and Homecomings: Gendered Histories of Domesticity and Return* (Chichester: Wiley-Blackwell, 2010).
105 Janet Oppenheim, *Shattered Nerves: Doctors, Patients, and Depression in Victorian England* (New York: Oxford University Press, 1991), ch. 5.
106 For the role of the worker in conceptualisations of national character and the differences between the mid-nineteenth century and last quarter of that century, see Peter Mandler, *The English National Character: The History of an Idea from Edmund Burke to Tony Blair* (New Haven, CT, and London: Yale University Press, 2006), pp. 103–4, 107.
107 Michael Brown, 'Making sense of modernity's maladies: health and disease in the Industrial Revolution', *Endeavour* 30:3 (2006), 108–12; Chris Hamlin, *Public Health and Social Justice in the Age of Chadwick: Britain, 1800–1854* (Cambridge: Cambridge University Press, 1998), p. 116 n55; Sara Horrell, David Meredith, and Deborah Oxley, 'Measuring misery: body mass among Victorian London's poor', *Explorations in Economic History* 46 (2009), 93–119; Sara Horrell and Deborah Oxley, 'Bringing home the bacon? Regional nutrition, stature and gender in the industrial revolution', *Economic History Review* 65:4 (2012), 1354–79.
108 Budd, *Sculpture Machine*, pp. 18, 25. For similar fears of degeneration in France, Germany, and the USA see Hau, 'The normal, the ideal, and the beautiful', pp. 15–19.
109 Michael Barringer, *Men at Work: Art and Labour in Victorian Britain* (New Haven, CT, London: Yale University Press, 2005), pp. 1–2, 14–16.
110 Robert Dare, 'History, progress and industry: William Bell Scott's *Iron and Coal*', *Word & Image* 12:3 (1996), 275–6.
111 John Barrell, *The Dark Side of the Landscape: The Rural Poor in English Painting 1730 – 1840* (Cambridge: Cambridge University Press, 1983); Christiana Payne, *Toil and Plenty: Images of the Agricultural Landscape in England 1780–1890* (New Haven, CT, and London: Yale University Press, 1993).
112 For contemporary photographs of seafaring communities, see Colin Ford, *An Early Victorian Album: The Photographic Masterpieces (1843–1847) of David Octavius Hill and Robert Adamson* (New York: Alfred A. Knopf, 1976), pp. 155–91. Also, Christiana Payne, *Where the Sea Meets the Land: Artists on the Coast in Nineteenth-Century Britain* (Bristol: Sansom & Co. Ltd, 2007), pp. 157–63.
113 Simon Wendt (ed.), *Extraordinary Ordinariness: Everyday Heroism in the United States, Germany, and Britain, 1800–2015* (Frankfurt am Main: Campus Verlag, 2016).
114 Craig Barclay, '"Our heroes of to-day": the Royal Humane Society and the creation of heroes in Victorian Britain', in Wendt (ed.), *Extraordinary Ordinariness*, pp. 25–52; Christiane Hadamitzky and Barbara Korte, 'Everyday heroism for the Victorian industrial classes: the British workman and the British workwoman, 1855–1880', in Wendt (ed.), *Extraordinary Ordinariness*, pp. 53–78.
115 Barringer, *Men at Work*, pp. 76–81.
116 Michael Hatt, 'Near and far: Hamo Thornycroft's mower and the homoerotics of labour', *Art History* 26:1 (2003), 26–55.
117 Men's case notes were sampled from Colney Hatch Lunatic Asylum. LMA, Middlesex County Lunatic Asylum, Colney Hatch, Case Books for Male Patients: H12/CH/B13/001–004 (1851–54), H12/CH/B13/020 (1872), and H12/CH/B13/035 (1886).
118 The similarities between the two movements are increasingly recognised. Rebecca

Bedell, *Moved to Tears: Rethinking the Art of the Sentimental in the United States* (Princeton, NJ, and Oxford: Princeton University Press, 2018), p. 66.

119 For an introduction to sentimental genre painting's focus on family relationships see James Kilroy, *The Nineteenth-Century English Novel: Family Ideology and Narrative Form* (Basingstoke: Palgrave Macmillan, 2007), pp. 2–5.

120 Nicola Bown, 'Tender beauty: Victorian painting and the problem of sentimentality', *Journal of Victorian Culture* 16:2 (2011), 215.

121 Bedell, *Moved to Tears*, pp. 4, 7, 8, 11.

122 S. Solicari, 'Selling sentiment: the commodification of emotion in Victorian visual culture', *19: Interdisciplinary Studies in the Long Nineteenth Century* 4 (2007).

123 Carolyn Burdett, 'New agenda sentimentalities: introduction', *Journal of Victorian Culture* 16:2 (2011), 187–94. For an excellent commentary on sentimentality and its continued cultural valence into the twentieth century see Bellanta, '"Poor Gordon"', 402–3, 405.

124 The male body was positioned as an object of erotic desire for the female and male gaze in pornography. Sarah Toulalan, *Imagining Sex: Pornography and Bodies in Seventeenth-Century England* (Oxford: Oxford University Press, 2007), pp. 66, 68, 70–1, 173–4.

125 For different gazes and their relationship with the male body see Anthea Callen, *Looking at Men: Anatomy, Masculinity and the Modern Male Body* (New Haven and London: Yale University Press, 2018), pp. 15–16, 22–3.

126 Juliet John, 'Melodrama and its criticism: an essay in memory of Sally Ledger', *19: Interdisciplinary Studies in the Long Nineteenth Century*, 8 (2008).

127 Bridget Walsh, *Domestic Murder in Nineteenth-Century England: Literary and Cultural Representations* (Farnham: Ashgate Publishing, 2014), pp. 8, 24; Surridge, *Bleak Houses*, ch. 1; John, 'Melodrama and its criticism', 3.

128 George Mosse's ground-breaking work on men's idealised bodies and male beauty in Germany was in the vanguard, and this study is inspired by its focus on the male body as a public symbol. Mosse, *The Image of Man*, passim. Katie Barclay is unusual in identifying how reading emotions were understood as performed through bodies and manifesting character. For example, see Katie Barclay, 'Performing emotions and reading the male body in the Irish court, c. 1800–1845', *Journal of Social History* 51:2 (2017) 293–312.

129 Cooter, 'The turn of the body', 395–6. An example is Newman, *Embodied History*, passim.

130 Cooter, 'The turn of the body', 396–7.

131 *Ibid.*, 397–8.

132 Harvey, 'Men of parts'.

133 Harvey, 'Craftsmen in common', p. 83.

134 Cooter, 'The turn of the body', 399–401.

135 *Ibid.*, 401–2.

136 For an insightful example of this approach see Matthew McCormack, 'Boots, material culture and Georgian masculinities', *Social History* 42:4 (2017), 461–79.

137 Gerben Van Kleef, 'How emotions regulate social life: the emotions as social information (EASI) model', *Current Directions in Psychological Science* 18:3 (2009), 184, 186.

138 Many Staffordshire portrait figures were inspired by paintings and prints. P. D. Gordon Pugh, *Staffordshire Portrait Figures and Allied Subjects of the Victorian Era* (London: Barrie & Jenkins, 1970), pp. 24–84.

139 Material culture history is another expanding field and this introduction therefore can only touch on the diverse ways to practise it and the innumerable objects and spaces that can be investigated. For two introductions to the field see: Karen Harvey (ed.), *History and Material Culture: A Student's Guide to Approaching Alternative Sources* (London: Routledge, 2009) and Leonie Hannan and Sarah Longair, *History*

140 Sara Ahmed, *The Cultural Politics of Emotion* (New York and London: Routledge Taylor & Francis Group, 2004), pp. 89–92.
141 For the impact of emotions on binary models see Susan Broomhall (ed.), *Emotions in the Household, 1200–1900* (Basingstoke: Palgrave Macmillan, 2008); for the decentring of heteronormativity as a way to rethink expectations and experiences of gender, sexuality, and their consequent impact on social structures, see de Freitas Boe and Coyendall, *Heteronormativity in Eighteenth-Century Literature and Culture*, pp. 6–9 and passim.
142 For an introduction to the concept and examples of its use, see Stephanie Downes, Sally Holloway, and Sarah Randles (eds), *Feeling Things: Objects and Emotions through History* (Oxford: Oxford University Press, 2018).
143 Ahmed, *The Cultural Politics of Emotion*.
144 Downes, Holloway, and Randles (eds), *Feeling Things*, pp. 11–13.
145 Cited in Hamilton, 'Hercules subdued', 646.
146 Stephanie Downes, Sally Holloway, and Sarah Randles, 'A feeling for things, past and present', in Downes, Holloway, and Randles (eds), *Feeling Things*, pp. 8–23.
147 Mosse, *The Image of Man*, passim.
148 For the male body as a potentially erotic object, see Janes, *Oscar Wilde Prefigured*. On the tensions between naked human bodies as subjects of scientific knowledge and objects of desire see, Rice, 'Picturing bodies in the nineteenth century', pp. 232–3.
149 Janes, *Oscar Wilde Prefigured*, pp. 18–19. For a rich analysis of this statue see Henk de Smaele, 'Achilles or Adonis: controversies surrounding the male body as national symbol in Georgian England', *Gender & History* 28:1 (2016), 77–101.
150 Linda Colley, *Britons: Forging the Nation 1707–1837* (New Haven, CT, and London: Yale University Press, 1992), p. 258.
151 British Museum, no. 1868,0808.8555, George Cruikshank, 'Making decent – !! –' (1822), www.britishmuseum.org/research/collection_online/collection_object_details.aspx?objectId=1599943&partId=1&images=true; British Museum, no. 1865,1111.2120, George Cruikshank, 'Backside & front view of the ladies fancy-man, Paddy Carey' (1822), www.britishmuseum.org/research/collection_online/collection_object_details.aspx?objectId=1650556&partId=1&people=125596&peoA=125596-2-70&page=1 (accessed 30 March 2019).
152 Paddy Carey was the protagonist of a song about a good-looking Irish man who was appealing to women, and the phrasing echoes the song's lyrics. Other attractive men were compared to Paddy Carey, see Barclay, 'Performing emotions and reading the male body', 301–2.
153 Budd, *Sculpture Machine*, p. 44.
154 Olsen, *Juvenile Nation*, passim.
155 Dixon, '"Emotion": the history of a keyword', 341.
156 Rosenman, 'Body doubles', 366.
157 Brown, 'Cold steel, weak flesh', 155–81; Myerly, *British Military Spectacle*, passim.
158 Myerly was one of the first to consider the role of military material culture in this way, *British Military Spectacle*, p. 8, passim.
159 Holly Furneaux and Sue Prichard, 'Contested objects: curating soldier art', *Museum & Society* 13:4 (2015), 453. For another examination of the lack of hard distinctions between home and war see Kennedy, *Narratives of the Revolutionary and Napoleonic Wars*, pp. 14–16.
160 For a longer history of returning artisans, see Brian Maidment, 'Coming through the cottage door: work, leisure, family, and gender in artisan interiors', in Brian

Maidment, *Reading Popular Prints 1790–1870* (Manchester: Manchester University Press, 2001), pp. 101–37.
161 Leonore Davidoff and Catherine Hall, *Family Fortunes: Men and Women of the English Middle Class, 1780–1850* (Chicago: Chicago University Press, 1987); Tosh, *A Man's Place*, passim.
162 *Illustrated London News* (27 October 1863), p. 19. Also see 'A Safe Cure', *Funny Folks* (1 October 1892), p. 317; see also 'Look Before you Leap-Year', *Funny Folks* (31 December 1887), pp. 436–7 in which a 'Lady Special gets her Husband home early for once'.
163 Tosh, 'Home and away', 561.
164 Linda A. Pollock, 'The practice of kindness in early modern elite society', *Past & Present* 211:1 (2011), 121–58.
165 Begiato, 'Between poise and power', 125–47.
166 The place of the body in forming working men's subjectivity is explored by Stuart James Hogarth, 'Reluctant patients: health, sickness and the embodiment of plebeian masculinity in nineteenth-century Britain. Evidence from working men's autobiographies' (PhD dissertation, Metropolitan University of London, 2010); Ying Lee, *Masculinity and the English Working Class: Studies in Victorian Autobiography and Fiction* (London: Routledge, 2016), pp. 15, 19, 20.
167 Newman, *Embodied History*, p. 122.

1

Figures, faces, and desire: male bodies and manliness

Introduction

Manliness was conveyed through beautiful, virile, male bodies; men's muscles, hair, stance, movement, and facial features delineated, even rhapsodised, in print, visual, and material culture.[1] Such appealing male figures and faces were associated with positive emotions that were coded as both manly and moral.[2] This chapter explores their changing forms over time, but also addresses the question raised by such bodies. Intended to promulgate and disseminate exemplary masculinity, what purpose did their beauty serve? Scholarship that explores attractive, eroticised male bodies often considers them as unusual or transgressive, either because they are found in erotic or pornographic works, or because they are considered to primarily appeal to a homoerotic viewer.[3] Depictions of a 'normative' male body are also deemed problematic within the framework of the gendered gaze, which positions the male viewer as active and dominant and the object of his gaze as female and subordinate.[4] Henk de Smaele, for instance, argues that Richard Westmacott's monument to the Duke of Wellington (unveiled in 1822) failed in its attempt to deploy the naked idealised male body to contribute to hegemonic ideals of masculine citizenship. This was because 'turning the male body into an object of the gaze evokes the possibility of female and homosexual desire', resulting in 'disorder and confusion' rather than the virtuous order the spectacular body was meant to achieve. While contemporary satire mocked women's sexual interest in the statue, and it was later used in anti-government criticism, de Smaele's reading of the image is selective and certainly does not bear the weight of his conclusion that 'masculine power rests on the absence of a fixed embodied standard against which one can be measured'.[5]

In contrast, and to answer the question of the role of male beauty in disseminating ideals of manliness, this chapter takes a queer approach which deliberately makes strange the conjunction between physical beauty and masculine values. It adopts the techniques of scholarship that queers sexual constructions and rejects assumptions about normative masculinities and how they were created and circulated.[6] Thus, it recognises the desirability of idealised male bodies and makes this the foremost object of scrutiny.[7] Overall, it proposes that beautiful male forms and appearances were intended to arouse desire for the *gender* that these bodies bore, whilst also, no doubt, stimulating erotic feelings in some of their male and female viewers. This nuances our understanding of the gaze. It shows that the idealised manly body was active, since it was an agent of prized gender values. Yet it was also passive, as the object of a female and male desirous gaze, and subordinate, for although some of the descriptions of idealised male bodies in this chapter were elite, as it and later chapters show, many manly and unmanly bodies were those of white working-class men.[8] Due to the sources used, it is white bodies that are the focus here, but it is acknowledged throughout that in the imperial context of the long nineteenth century, the idealised manly body was also racialised, with whiteness constructed through accounts of ethnic and racial 'others'.[9] Throughout, manliness was measured through bodies and the emotions they symbolised and aroused.[10]

Viewing the manly form: poise, power, and pose

In art, and, later in film, idealised men's bodies were often described in dynamic motion: fighting, wrestling, throwing, lifting, and working.[11] Other bodies were caught at rest, between labours, or adopting a pugilistic, athletic, or muscular pose, all of which still gestured to a more active state. Attention to this movement exposes the plethora of ways in which the male body was viewed and evaluated by spectators, often to discipline and categorise it. Motion was a marker and privilege of mature manhood, for example, and a long-standing moralistic trope insisted that male youths work or exercise to distract them from sin. In 1750, for example, the Ordinary of Newgate explained that Anthony Byrne, who was convicted for breaking and entering, was put to apprentice once he had arrived 'at a proper Age to undergo Fatigue, and to keep his robust and manly Faculties in Agitation, in order to shield him against the Sallies of Idleness, the Root of all Evil'.[12] Anthony failed because he rejected active work. A century later, Samuel Smiles advised readers of his chapter on 'Self-Culture' that the only remedy for youths prone to 'discontent, unhappiness, inaction' was 'abundant physical exercise, – action, work, and bodily occupation of any sort'.[13] Under the shadow of race science in the later nineteenth century, as Elspeth Brown observes, 'movement emerged as a key indicator of racial evolution'. Anthropometric photography in the 1880s was aligned with developments in physical anthropology to use human locomotion as an identifier of racial difference, with bodies of colour placed lowest on the hierarchical scale.[14]

Men's moving bodies were also viewed for pleasure and entertainment. Pamela Gilbert shows that men participated in popular rural sports, including wrestling, fighting games, hurling stones, and bare-knuckle boxing, to make money, win prizes, and resolve disputes, but also 'to affirm masculinity through the demonstration of strength, competitiveness, and the ability to endure pain stoically'.[15] Pleasure in men's moving bodies was clearly understood to be the draw for a paying audience and marketed thus in the press. Frank E. McNish, an American acrobat performing in London, was described in 'Heroes of the Hour' (1889), as possessing a 'fine athletic frame – a remarkable combination of grace, agility, and strength'.[16] The representation of men as bodies in motion, therefore, offers insights into the ways in which embodied manliness was consistently scrutinised although its form changed over time.[17]

The variation in men's bodies, bodily styles, and form can be captured by three convenient, if somewhat simplified, terms: 'poise', 'power', and 'pose'. These conform to a rough chronology, wherein the idealised manly form shifted from slender, graceful strength to more bulky, solid heft, to sculpted muscularity from the 1760s to 1900.[18] Two very different definitions of exercise at 1755 and 1897 capture the changing nature of the goals of male exercise regimes, from moulding elite bodies to a more democratic commercialised physical culture. In his 1755 *Dictionary of the English Language*, Samuel Johnson defined exercise as 'Habitual action by which the body is formed to gracefulness, air, and agility.'[19] One hundred and fifty years later, Eugen Sandow's regime of physical exercise targeted specific muscles to bulk them up, accompanied by a table enabling the user to record 'before' and 'after' measurements.[20] Sandow headed a physical culture iconography in which the male pose was a signifier of fitness to which men from a variety of social classes could aspire.[21] The following section offers a broad-brush chronological model of these bodily types to demonstrate how they stimulated desire for the manliness they embodied.

First, though, it must be noted that poise, power, and pose were not successive, distinct bodily categories since they shared several qualities.[22] Most obvious is that the classical body influenced by Greek antique sculptures was at the core of all formulations of male physical beauty and health.[23] Two classical male body types were especially potent: the young, slim athleticism of the Ephebes and the mature, hefty, heroic Herculean form; the first clean-shaven, the other bearded.[24] In 'The Marquis and the Maiden' (1857), for example, the stalwart heroic groom was described as 'faultless in his form and build, a young Apollo, with that careless ease of manner, and with a certain bold frankness of air'.[25] Martin Myrone's study of masculinities in British art suggests that Georgian ideals of manly beauty focused upon the less brawny Greek model, while the mature Herculean body type came to symbolise the muscular Christianity dominating the second half of the nineteenth century.[26] Roberta Park's assertion that until 1850 idealised men were represented either as 'lithe and slim' or 'ponderous' pugilists is, however, somewhat simplistic.[27] After all, the art that resulted from using boxers as life models in the early nineteenth century depicted muscular bodies that would have satisfied Sandow. Furthermore, the symbolism of Hercules conveyed dignity and agency to many kinds of men's bodies in the eighteenth century, though somewhat ambiguously when applied to well-developed black bodies. The kneeling African slave, designed in 1787 to symbolise and help effect the abolition of the slave trade, for example, was muscular and posed like images of the kneeling Hercules. His emotionalised body conveyed nobility and endurance, as well as supplication and victimhood. However, as the image was more widely disseminated the representative slave was 'reconfigured as an object of pity and gratification'.[28]

Moreover, the two classical body types were equally valid forms of attractive manliness. The tale 'Holroyd of St. Anselm's Meets an Old Acquaintance' in the 1900 *Big Budget*, for instance, described two Oxford undergraduates at St Anselm's, 'a college famous for its scholarship as well as its athleticism'. They were popular, sporty Tippy Guthrie, runner, rugby player, and footballer, and rower Jack Lucas:

> both splendid specimens of young British manhood – Guthrie, lightly but beautifully built, erect and supple as a poplar, with sparkling, devil-may-care eyes, and features, if irregular, made attractive by their strong vitality; and Jack Lucas, captain of the college boat, a young Hercules of six feet and fourteen stone, with a face open as the day, and a great cheery laugh that was as good as a tonic to it hearers.[29]

Here, classical bodies are aligned with hearty values of humour, risk, and openness to evoke pride in British manliness. And, of course, as the inspirational classical male body indicates, the muscular male pose was as much a feature of early nineteenth-century art as late nineteenth-century photography, whether signifying poise or power.

In fact, strength did not reside only in the mighty muscular manliness of the later nineteenth century. Men's bodies had always been required to be well proportioned and strong. The Ordinary of Newgate's description of the a forty-six-year-old highwayman, William Gordon, in 1733, conceded that 'He was a Man strong in his Person, and well limbed.' This bodily conformity signalled other manly characteristics: 'and as to inward Accomplishments, he was bold to a prodigious Degree, had a large Share of personal Courage, and would fight resolutely on any Occasion'.[30] Gordon had the basic stuff to have been manly, though he had made the wrong decisions. So too did William Smith, the thirty-year-old son of the Rector of Killmare, Ireland, who was indicted for forgery, depicted in 1750 in *The Ordinary of Newgate's Account* as around five feet eight inches tall, with a 'good manly Countenance, and … well proportioned in his Limbs'.[31] Although physical symmetry was one of the corporeal measures of anthropometry, it had long existed as an ideal of manly beauty, as this shows. An 1807 account of Cambridge-educated Charles Mordant described him thus: 'Nature had in every respect been bountiful to Charles Mordant; for to a person moulded in the most exact form of symmetry, was added not only a beautiful, but a manly face.'[32] Indeed, the emphasis in the later nineteenth century on a muscular development that forged harmonious, symmetrical bodies was simply a historically specific form of poise.[33]

It is also worth pointing out that the precise delineations of the athletic, muscular body were open to the viewers' interpretation. An excellent example is 'Orlando, the Outcast of Milan: A Heroic Story of the Olden Time' (1874) who is described as being around twenty years of age,

> though his frame had reached the proportions and developments of athletic vigour. He was not taller than the average height of men, but when he stood erect, so straight and comely was he, and such a breadth of bosom did he present, that the eye, taking its cue from his evident strength of nerve and muscle, gave him proportions of frame beyond his real measure. His face was somewhat bronzed by exposure, but his features were regular and handsome.[34]

At first read, one imagines Orlando as strapping, broad-chested, and muscular. Yet, in the accompanying illustration (Figure 1.1), he is pretty, slight, and graceful, rather than bulky and muscular. And in fact, the text gestures to this; not yet mature and of average height, Orlando assumed a larger frame thanks to the manly signifiers of nerve, upright pose, facial hair, and beauty.

These qualifications aside, it is still possible to historicise the ideals to which male corporeality was meant to conform and to which manly values were attached. The eighteenth- and early nineteenth-century ideal possessed a dexterous carriage and poise and clean-shaven face; a bodily shape influenced by factors as diverse as polite sociability and the culture of sensibility, Georgian military techniques, and ideas about physical exercise and health and diet regimes.[35] Politeness had established a distinctive set of poses for men that presented their sociability and civility to onlookers.[36] Sensibility added inner dimensions to these external bodily manners. In 'The Story of Selina' in *The Lady's Magazine* of 1804, the sixteen-year-old eponymous heroine was wooed by Edward. No wonder: 'his form wore every manly grace; his manners were soft, persuasive, elegant; his mind well stored with useful and accomplished learning; [and] his fortune competently independent'. His physical grace was thus profoundly entwined with the emotions praised in the culture of sensibility: sympathy, compassion, and benevolence. He was so appealing that even her parents encouraged him as a suitor.[37]

ORLANDO,
THE OUTCAST OF MILAN.
A HEROIC STORY OF THE OLDEN TIME.
By the Author of "Theseus, the Young Hero of Attica."

CHAPTER I.
THE ROBBER KNIGHTS—THE OUTCAST'S STORY.

THE tenth century was drawing to a close, and the monarchs of Europe were taking a respite from the labours of war and conquest. Petty princes were lifting their heads into notice, and the knights of Christendom who sought only honourable combat were resting upon their arms. But all knights were not thus quiet. Many there were who, with no other use for their weapons, betook themselves to the darker passes of the highway, and turned robbers.

Towards the close of a pleasant day in midsummer, a young man sat alone upon the greensward, beneath an olive tree, not many miles north of Milan. It was a lovely spot—a vast garden of tree and shrub, with fruit and flowers, with there an open space and there a dense, shadowy thicket of dark leaved trees. Close at hand was the highway, but for more than an hour no traveller had stirred the dust of the beaten track. The man to whom we have alluded could not have been more than twenty years of age, though his frame had reached the proportions and developments of athletic vigour. He was not taller than the average height of men, but when he stood erect, so straight and comely was he, and such a breadth of shoulders and such a swell of bosom did he present, that the eye, taking its cue from his evident strength of nerve and muscle, gave him proportions of frame beyond his real measure. His face was somewhat bronzed by exposure, but his features were regular and handsome, and his eye, large and full, looked out with a soft, liquid light, seeming almost tearful when resting from the call of passion. His hair was very dark—almost black—and hung in wavy masses over his shoulders, while upon his lip curled a graceful moustache. His dress was soiled and much worn. The hose, which had once been a fawn-coloured silk, had grown to a dingy brown; the shirt, once white and fair, was stained and crumpled; and the doublet of blue velvet, slashed with white and crimson, edged with gold, had lost its newness, and in more than one place some of its fabric was missing. His hat was looped up upon one side by a silver brooch, which held the remains of a much-abused ostrich plume. A faded red sash confined his shirt about the loins, also holding his sword-scarf in its place.

The youth arose from his recumbent posture, and gazed about him.

"Where to-night?" he muttered, in a half mournful tone.

He took out his purse—a network of silk and gold—and held it up between his eye and the horizon.

"Empty—the last denier gone. For my bed the warm earth will answer, but this body of mine will not thrive upon fruits and herbs. I must have bread and meat. And my poor garments—they will not stand me much longer. This is my only possession which moth doth not corrupt."

As he thus spoke, he drew his sword from its scabbard, and gazed upon it with a fond look. The blade was long and stout, as bright as when first it came from the hands of its maker, and evidently of the finest metal. The hilt was of silver, inlaid with flowers of gold, and in the pommel was set a carbuncle of rare brilliancy and large size.

"As yet," he said, still gazing upon his weapon, "thou hast never been drawn in a dishonourable cause, but how long it shall be so, God only knows. I must either turn my heart away from Milan, and bid farewell to the home of my birth, or I must find some means of sustenance where honour stands not in the way. If I join the robber knights I may find more than bread and meat—I may find some means of revenge upon my enemy. Oh, Saint Ambrose, help me in this strait! My father's son must not come to dishonour."

As he ceased speaking, he cast his eyes to the northward, and saw what appeared a party of horsemen coming from the direction of Monza. They were upon the brow of a hill, and as they came down the slope he saw that they were six in number, and that they were clad in glistening armour.

"Who can this be, in such knightly array, I wonder?" he said to himself, as he watched the party descend the hill. "They are not robbers, for those gentry never appear in bright armour. They are rather those who come armed against the robbers."

In a little while the party had descended the hill, and were lost to view behind intervening trees, and as the youth was upon the point of sitting down again upon the grass, he saw another party of horsemen issuing from a wood to the left. They were twelve in number, and were clad in black armour.

"Now, by my soul," cried the observer, "we are to have a clash. This smells of conflict. These black rascals are of the robber band, and yonder bright-armed travellers are marked."

By-and-bye the first party came into sight again, and as they approached, the black knights drew back into the wood. The watcher could see both parties, and he knew that they must soon come together. The travellers were now so near that he could distinguish their bearing, and he knew them to be gentlemen. Four of them were stout knights, one seemed to be a servant, while the sixth was without armour, and apparently but a mere boy. They rode on at an easy canter, laughing and chatting, thinking, probably, that all danger had been left behind them. But they were soon to be undeceived. As they emerged from behind a grove of olives, and entered upon the open plain, the robber knights came sweeping from their cover, and with a wild battle-cry, dashed forward to the onset.

"God and Saint Stephen defend us!" cried the leader of the travelling party; and as he spoke, he and his armed companions brought their lances to a rest, with their youthful companion behind them.

"This will never do," said the watcher. "Those gentlemen will be quickly swept down if they have not help. It must not be said that a Vendorme refused his help to a suffering fellow. Come now, my faithful blade, live or die, I'll have a hand in this!"

By a short cut he reached the place of meeting just as the onset took place.

"What, ho!" he shouted at the top of his voice; "are ye not rather near to the city of Milan for such dastard work? Give way. Twelve against six is cowardly."

"Ho, ho!" returned the robber chieftain, "here we have the duke's outcast! If you would save your head, Master Vendorme, get thee gone quickly."

"Not if thou meanest harm to these honest travellers."

"What meanest thou?"

"I mean to fight if ye do not leave these gentlemen to pursue their way in peace."

Upon this the robber chieftain laughed outright, and in a moment more he poked his lance derisively at the intruder. But he did not advance his lance a second time; for with one sweep of his sword the adventurer cleft it in twain, and on the next instant the chief lay dead upon the ground. As soon as the robbers saw that their leader was dead, three of them set upon Vendorme, as though they would have made quick work with their vengeance.

"How now, outcast!" one of them cried. "We would have given you a station of power with us, but now you turn against us. But your doom is sealed. Take that!"

The robber's lance was turned from the youth's body as though it had struck a surface of solid rock, and before he could recover himself he was thrown from his saddle, and his neck pierced through and through.

Vendorme now sprang to where the fight was gathering thick and hot around the travellers; and sounding the war-cry of God and Saint Ambrose, he

ORLANDO PERFORMS MIGHTY DEEDS OF VALOUR.

1.1 'Orlando, the Outcast of Milan: A Heroic Story of the Olden Time', *Our Young Folks Weekly Budget of Tales, News, Sketches, Fun, Puzzles, Riddles &c* 208 (1874), p. 397.

Elegance and soft manners did not suggest effeminacy. Dexterity and fluidity were military fighting techniques as well as dance movements, where manly strength was conveyed through deft movement, rather than bulk.[38] The author of *An Essay on the Art of War* (1761) advised readers:

> Let an officer also accustom himself to a laborious, simple, and frugal Way of Life; let him as much as possible acquire Agility and Nimbleness, by dancing, fencing, riding, playing at Tennis, walking, hunting, in short, by every Exercise fit to form and strengthen his constitution; let him never avoid exposing himself to the Air, or ever attach himself to any Commodity. Exercise of the body Content of Mind, and Regularity of Manners, are the sure Means to preserve that manly Vigour, which ought ever to distinguish a military man.[39]

Physical exercise like fencing was thus promoted for its own sake in the second half of the eighteenth century, rather than for self-defence alone. A 1763 publication, translated into English in 1787 – Domenico Angelo's *School of Fencing* – emphasised that it gave persons of rank 'additional strength of body, proper confidence, grace, activity, and address'.[40]

Although strength did not have to map onto a stout body, it was marked out by ethnicity. On 14 October 1759, Thomas Robinson (1738–1786), a Yorkshire gentleman on his Grand Tour, wrote to his brother Frederick, deploying national stereotypes about continental effeminate men:

> I am sure to meet several very pretty young Counts and Marquis, with bags & swords, but I always think when I see them how easily you would lick them, & that tho' they should draw their swords, that a knock on the mark would lay these tough Fellows flat. Any but you would think that tough meant hardy & stout, but tell them to look tough out in the Westminster Dictionary, & they will find the meaning of it to be Proud ... & conceited of themselves.[41]

For Thomas, strength was not only corporeal, but betokened British self-confidence and authenticity over 'foreign' artificiality and conceit.[42]

This type of plain manliness was in the ascendant by the early nineteenth century, along with the more grounded body that it matched. Ideal bodies were defined by adjectives that conveyed size: 'hearty', 'mighty', 'rugged'.[43] Cruikshank's breakdown of body parts that the ladies desired most in the 1822 statue of Achilles celebrating Wellington's victories would certainly suggest that size mattered: 'Brawny Shoulders 4 ft Square', large pronounced buttocks, and legs that 'would make a Chairman Stare' (the men who carried sedan chairs were notable for their powerful thighs and calves).[44] In 1847, *Bell's Life in London and Sporting Chronicle* described a cricketer as fighting 'to win every inch of ground with mighty manliness'.[45] Stolidity and robustness, therefore, made corporeally manifest the manly values of fortitude and endurance. By the mid-Victorian period, the idealised manly body was brisker in motion, erect rather than graceful in posture. The eponymous hero of 'Stonio, the Stone-Cutter: A Story of Lisbon and the Great Earthquake' in the *Young Folks Paper* of 1889 was described thus: 'He is scarcely twenty-five years old, erect as the mast of a ship, athletic, and full-bearded.'[46] As well as denoting a phallic sexuality, which is discussed in the section 'Desiring manly vigour: virile and erect forms', uprightness was both embodied and a set of moral behaviours. Signifying its virtuous connotations, in 1822 the periodical *John Bull* praised a London Lord Mayor and Member of Parliament, commenting on his 'manly and UPRIGHT conduct'.[47] Uprightness was also emotionalised, associated especially with pride. In an 1851 example of the former, one youthful sailor was described as being physically straighter as the result of becoming manly: 'In about fifteen or twenty minutes he came down, and straightened himself up with the conscious pride of having performed a manly act, he walked aft with a smile on his countenance.'[48]

Several cultural, political, and social factors converged to make this sturdier, rugged male body so aspirational. Artifice was rejected by the political revolutions of the late eighteenth century. The 'natural' was increasingly fashionable in hair, with wigs abandoned and whiskers grown.[49] Neoclassicism offered new clothing fashions, which hinted at the classical, nude, muscular form.[50] But perhaps most influential was a period of national crisis and war that demanded hardy, fighting-fit male bodies. Military men's faces signified this, with elite cavalry units adopting the hussar moustache from 1806 and most regular army officers sporting a military upper lip by mid-century.[51] Essentially, the feeling, graceful, and refined body appeared less useful in an age of revolution and war; certainly, the more robust fighting working-class bodies of sailors, soldiers, and boxers were depicted as particularly appealing and reassuring.[52]

The hardy Jack Tar's bodily endurance, strength, and agility, for example, were ubiquitous in popular representations of his fighting and cosmopolitan activities in the service of his nation.[53] His body bore and made visible his professional identity through his metaphorical arms and heart of oak and his literally distinctive skin and clothing. Sun-burned seamen took up tattooing in large numbers from the later eighteenth century, with 90 per cent sporting a tattoo by the early nineteenth century. For them it displayed the trademarks of their job: ship-based skills, the capacity to fight, and extensive travel; it also indicated fraternal fellowship and romantic love, and, no doubt, their capacity to withstand pain.[54] When combined with their specialised clothing – trousers whose fabric and shape marked the sailor out as a man of cosmopolitan, global significance – it is not surprising that men and women desired and consumed the erotic frisson of the general image of the sailor with numerous youths aspiring to possess this brand of manliness.[55]

The idealised male form of the late Victorian era can be similarly historicised as it bore the hallmarks of modernity: urbanisation, industrialisation, imperialism, and militarism. It was hearty and plucky, as befitted the adventurous man of empire, and had a military carriage that was determined by new weaponry that required skirmish and light infantry battle techniques.[56] Middle-class men clearly desired and attempted to acquire the physical markers of this rugged daring manliness. As beards were divested of their association with Romantic radicals and working-class revolutionaries, they were taken up with enthusiasm: grown from the 1860s to represent a modern manliness that combined authenticity with patriarchal authority.[57] This was a profoundly racialised manliness. New imperialism ushered in what Bradley Deane calls 'competitive manliness' where, paradoxically, encounters with non-European men did not simply consolidate scientific racism; instead, they offered examples of 'primitive', 'pure' manliness that were considered admirable and aspirational. Adventure stories, for example, delineated the magnificent physiques of races deemed inherently warrior-like, such as Zulus and Sikhs. The exotic 'other' formulated conceptions of white British manliness, therefore, due to the 'ability of British heroes to hold their own on the frontier'.[58] Often, the male subject of the desirous white gaze was black, as Richard Smith shows in his analysis of West Indian soldiers in the white imagination during the First World War.[59] White men admiring the masculine beauty of indigenous men not only served to display the former's own sense of superiority. In some cases, as Anne O'Brien observes, the homoerotic gaze occasionally strengthened opposition to injustice against the latter.[60]

Modernity triggered fears about manly bodies too. Although the urban labourer was celebrated in mid-century visual and textual representations, as will be discussed in detail in Chapter 5, this was partly to remind middle-class men of their potential bodily enfeeblement due to new forms of sedentary work.[61] Alongside the idea of heroic workers, according to a social Darwinist discourse working-class men's bodies were identified as degenerating and unsuitable to play their role in building and maintaining a strong nation and empire. Numerous commentators from different professional and disciplinary backgrounds proffered solutions to the bodily weaknesses of all these men, ranging from advocating physical exercise, to organising athletic clubs, to integrating exercise in education at all levels.[62] Sport was essential to this effort to remake manly bodies, catalysed in the 'new athleticism' of the last quarter of the nineteenth century, which advocated organised sports and games to produce physical prowess, skills, and team spirit.[63] Indeed, the role of desire for the manly body and its qualities was most explicit and visible in the commercialised sportsman's body, as the following case studies of boxer, cricketer, and strongman display.[64]

From the second half of the eighteenth century, the boxer represented a type of manliness cultivated through the body, since the sport was predicated upon a physical stance and technique, and body appearance and shape developed through diet and training regimes.[65] Thus, the pugilist's body challenges any suggestion that masculinity became more embodied in the later Victorian era. The biographical accounts published in the late nineteenth century of famous, long-deceased prize fighters offer considerable continuity in visual depiction. Consider, for instance, the *Licensed Victuallers' Mirror*'s 1888 biography of John Broughton's last fight, accompanied by a line drawing of him in fighting pose.[66] Broughton is described in his final fight as looking like 'a fine specimen of a gladiator – big, burly, powerful – the well-developed muscles showing prominently on his huge arms and vast chest; but to critical eyes he was much too fleshy, especially about the face'. The qualifying statement was about his age rather than any preference for one kind of muscularity. Nor does the illustration define his muscularity differently to meet new corporeal standards; it was based on contemporary depictions of him. Facially it is similar to John Ellys' mezzotint, possibly 1787, while the torso, breeches, and shoes are influenced by John Hamilton Mortimer's 1767 painting of the match.[67]

As Broughton's illustration indicates, demand for reproductions of the boxer's idealised corporeal form was high.[68] Artists such as William Hogarth, Thomas Lawrence, and John Rossi sought out boxers as artists' models in preference to, or as living evocations of, classical statuary.[69] Surgeons also admired boxers as perfect anatomical specimens. In a letter dated 26 July 1808, Charles Bell complained that he had missed recent 'comparisons of the modern athletes and the antique', such as 'exhibitions of Jackson, the boxer'. He noted, however, that on Saturday Lord Elgin had invited him to see 'an exhibition of the principal sparrers naked in his museum. I went, and was much pleased. The intention was that we might compare them with the remains of antiquity. There were Flaxman, Fuseli, and several other Academicians.'[70] Aristocratic patrons in the late eighteenth and nineteenth centuries commissioned boxers' portraits for their collections and enjoyment. Benjamin Marshall's *Mr John Jackson* (1810) posed the boxer alongside a classical statue, and while, unusually, Jackson is not in fighting pose or clothing, his attractive muscled form and his legs are displayed as equivalent to the statue's.

Lower-ranking artists also painted boxers' portraits to satisfy demand, and depictions of humble pubs and homes indicate that people displayed cheaper engravings of such portraits on their walls.[71] Charles Hunt's aquatint portrait of Bendigo William Thompson (1811–1880) has him in typical fighting pose: planted feet with muscular torso and arms.[72] Illustrations of fights were marketed too. Thomas Rowlandson's etching of the *Boxing Match for 200 Guineas between Dutch Sam and Medley* presents the two boxers in an aesthetically appealing form. A less illustrious example can be found in the *View of the Fight between Gully and Gregson* (1807) (Figure 1.2), which uses the same lexicon: naked torsos, solid legs planted apart in form-fitting breeches, arms raised, fists clenched.[73] With the improvement in photographic techniques, photographs of boxers were sold on postcards and cigarette cards to an even wider audience. A representative example is

1.2 *A View of the Fight between Gully and Gregson*, wood engraving by unknown artist (1807).

the 1890 collotype of Lieutenant-Colonel Sir Walter Edgeworth-Johnstone (1863–1936), Irish heavyweight boxer, posing in shorts and vest, long socks, and boxing gloves.[74] Billy Edwards's *Portrait Gallery of Pugilists of England, America, Australia* (1894) is a large-form version collected into one volume with a short description of each boxer followed by a full plate photograph (and in one or two cases an illustration from a photograph).[75] In these, the boxers were similarly posed, mostly bare-chested, wearing pale close-fitting tights that ended below the knee with socks and a belt or elaborate scarf tied around the middle, and several sported fashionable moustaches. They differed only in that some were in fighting poses while others faced the camera with arms crossed.

People also paid to see these boxers' bodies outside of the ring in entertainment venues such as the stage or music hall.[76] Peter Jackson, a man of West Indian origin, champion of Australia, arrived in the USA in 1888 and beat numerous contenders, then toured in 1894, appearing as Uncle Tom in Harriet Beecher Stowe's *Uncle Tom's Cabin*.[77] Daniel Mendoza took part in pantomimes and fought as spectacle on stage in Manchester and London.[78] People desired and consumed the boxer's neat, muscular pose, balance, nimbleness, mobility, and sturdy grace through material culture too.[79] A Staffordshire jug, dated around 1800 (Figure 1.3), depicted the famous fight between Daniel Mendoza and Richard Humphreys in 1788.[80] Mendoza's victories in the late 1780s and 1790s also saw his face emblazoned on coins and beer mugs.[81] Staffordshire portrait figures of pugilists created the fighting stance in three-dimensional form. Some were posed as a fighting pair on one base, such as the figurine depicting the American boxer John Heenan and the English boxer Tom Sayers, circa 1860.[82] Others were separate, like the pair depicting Tom Cribb and his opponent Tom Molineaux (c.1810–15), an American-born former slave, who fought in 1810 and 1811.[83] Objects like this were collected and displayed in the home, disseminating the partially stripped body of the boxer, black-skinned as well as white, still further, appealingly displayed in their pastel-coloured breeches and on pale bases.[84] These widely collectable 'pin-ups', memorabilia, and ornaments displayed skin, power, and form that evoked manly values of endurance, courage, fortitude, and self-mastery and stimulated desire, pride, admiration, and excitement.[85] As argued throughout this book, the possession of such objects and the feelings attributed to them, and inspired by them, communicated and fixed notions of manliness in owners and handlers.

As these examples denote, the popular and public figure of the 'prize fighter' embodied national and racial characteristics in his manly form.[86] In his 1823 work *Boxiana*, Pierce Egan drew distinctions between national fighting styles: 'In Holland the long knife decides too frequently; scarcely any person in Italy is without the stiletto; and France and Germany are not particular in using stones, sticks, etc. to gratify revenge; but, in England, the FIST only is used.' Thus, Egan could claim that sincerity, honesty, generosity, and fairness were 'inherent' in Englishmen.[87] Similarly, the white boxer was used in the popular press as possessing the ideal qualities of ideal British manliness, 'mild and sociable in demeanour, conducting himself with discretion and civility'.[88] Representations of minority boxers contributed to these constructions in complex ways.[89] The fine bodies of Jewish pugilists, like Daniel Mendoza, helped challenge anti-Semitic stereotypes about Jewish weakness and effeminacy, as the term 'Hefty Hebrews' indicates.[90] Similarly, images of African Americans like Molineaux celebrated their physical beauty and equal prowess to white British boxers. However, in both cases, as Ruti Ungar shows, even this praise marked them out as different, signalling the supposed superiority of white British manliness in the process. Nevertheless, the appeal of minority boxers showed that neither national identity nor manliness was a unitary ideal.[91]

Cricketing was another example of a sport that celebrated manly pose and behaviour, though one that offered a rather different type of bodily appeal to its viewer.[92] This 'manly sport', according to Samuel Smiles, developed a youth's 'arms and legs'. Indeed, it was, he declared, thanks to 'the boating and cricketing sports, still cultivated at our best public schools

1.3 Staffordshire jug featuring Daniel Mendoza.

and universities, that they produce so many specimens of healthy, manly, and vigorous men, of the true Hodson stamp'.[93] As this suggests, cricket was England's national sport and appealed to a range of social groups, producing along the way cricketer heroes whose batting skills displayed courage and whose bowling demonstrated strength and ferocity.[94] The

Lillywhite family of cricketers offer an example of their allure. William Lillywhite (1792–1854), eventually known as 'Old Lilly', the renowned Sussex bowler, headed a notable family of cricketers and cricketing entrepreneurs. They included John (1826–1874), a batsman and umpire, who was a member of the first national All-England Eleven touring team that visited America and Canada in 1859 and was chronicled by Frederick Lillywhite in 1860.[95] Depictions of the men were used in publications from specialised sports titles to boys' magazines and marketed through visual and material culture as well as recorded in photography – all conveying standards of manliness to viewers.[96] The Staffordshire pitcher of 'Old Lillywhite at Lord's', for example, based on a lithograph by John Corbett Anderson, shows the rather portly figure of Old Lilly grasping his cricket ball. The leaner-bodied image of John Lillywhite, from around 1874, is somewhat different to his father's familiar image, though both suggest the rural nature of the sport.[97] The sport was perhaps most embodied in the person of William Gilbert Grace, who played in the final three decades of the century: heavy-set and sporting a majestic beard he exemplified a 'natural' sporting manliness.[98]

Perhaps this was a feature of the sport's amateur status in the period, which mythologised the 'natural' in terms of skill and, it seems, bodies.[99] Indeed, Richard Holt observes that the early cricketing heroes of the mid-nineteenth century fell into two types: 'countrymen, tall, broad, decent … or the skilled, wily supremely determined players'.[100] Both offered a different kind of manly body to the boxer, though still one to be admired and consumed and one that was perhaps attainable for more men. Their posture in photographs also differed. Like boxers, cricketers dressed in their distinctive clothing and had fashionable facial hair, but their manliness centred on homosocial and same-sex affection rather than competitive aggression.[101] In portrait photos cricketers held the bat or ball that marked out their skill; batsmen largely posed at rest rather than ready to hit the ball, leaning on the bat as if it were a cane. In team portraits, they were grouped standing and sitting: men of action, but pictured at ease (see Figure 1.4). The text accompanying a team lithograph published in *Harpers Weekly*, 1863, describes cricket as 'a constant exercise of muscle in batting and running, and skill in bowling and catching the ball'.[102] Yet, rather than overt muscularity, it is casual grace, confidence, and, notably, affectionate camaraderie that mark out their manly bodies, as they lean together, their arms around each other. David Deitcher has written of the 'mildly erotic pleasures of looking at affectionate men' in his work on same-sex intimacy in portraits of American men posed together. These team photographs were produced to record sporting events and achievements and advertise the cricketers' skills, and, in choosing attractive affectionate poses, they surely capitalised on the desirous gaze to market their game and sporting manliness.[103]

1.4 The first English touring team, pictured on board ship at Liverpool (1859).

By the turn of the nineteenth century, physical culture was commercialised, facilitated by the growth of mass society, democracy, and the belief that bodies could be constantly reshaped and improved for national and personal benefit.[104] As such, the posed male body was ever more familiar to viewers and, in the case of the strongman, marketed for popular enjoyment. The most notable strongman example was Eugen Sandow, born Ernst Muller in East Prussia, who came to London in 1889, aged twenty-three, to embark on a music hall career, performing feats of strength and displaying his muscular body in classical poses. He epitomised a new manly look based on the muscular athlete who eschewed the heavy beard of W. G. Grace in favour of a moustache that emphasised youth and vigour.[105] Sandow reached celebrity status and further monetised his shaven sculpted body and Prussian-moustached face through objects like cigarette cards and postcards with his image on them, as well as various publishing endeavours, including *Sandow's Magazine of Physical Culture* in 1898, which disseminated the ideals of muscular manliness to a socially diverse readership.[106] Strongmen were objects of desire, for both female and male gazes and appreciation. They epitomised muscular manliness in image and person, selling their bodies on stage, in *cartes de visite* and postcard form, in photography book collections, in periodicals and magazines, and in guides for other men to improve their bodies, using the measurements of their own muscled limbs and torsos as exemplary models.[107]

Measuring humankind, especially men, was normalised and popularised in the late nineteenth century.[108] The measurement of human bodies was at its least benign, however, under the guise of scientific anthropology, particularly anthropometry, which used new technologies to record, document, and measure human bodies and thus categorise them according to race, class, gender, and degrees of 'deviance', insanity, criminality, and intelligence.[109] Archibald MacLaren's *A System of Physical Education Theoretical and Practical*, published in 1869, for example, deployed bodily data from his measurements of men enrolled in gymnastic training at the Royal Military Academy, non-commissioned officers training as military gymnastic instructors, and youths. The geneticist Francis Galton (1822–1911) set up an Anthropometric Laboratory at the International Health Exhibition, held in South Kensington, in 1884, which offered visitors the opportunity to have their senses of hearing, sight, and smell tested, their strength calculated, their weight and height taken, and the results entered on a card to take away with them, for the sum of 3d. He gathered data from over two thousand individuals and used them for his quantitative analysis of human populations.[110] One of the aims in assessing men's bodies was to prevent racial regression in white working-class men, and preserve and secure professional men from the risks of illnesses of modernity and civilisation, such as neurasthenia.[111] Thus, not only did anthropometry make manifest the assumed hierarchies between groups of people based on race and social class, it marked out gender, quantifying ideal and 'deviant' forms of masculinity and femininity.[112]

As part of this anthropometric impulse, the moving body was captured using the new forms of still and moving photography, returning us to the manly motion with which this section began.[113] The British photographer Eadweard Muybridge's sequential photography, which captured the naked human body in motion in a research project undertaken at the University of Pennsylvania between 1884 and 1887, is the best-known example.[114] The white male models who were selected for his project included university students who were prominent in athletics and sports such as cricket, rowing, and cycling, as well as professional athletes, mechanics, and labourers. Their physical form was intended to display the 'perfect' movement of an athletic or work-related activity.[115] As Stephen Rice notes, even Muybridge's contemporaries were concerned about the tensions in his photography between presenting the bodies 'as objects of scientific knowledge' and 'of looking at bodies as objects of desire'. One of the reasons the images were marketed in expensive formats was to prevent their consumption for reasons of pleasure only. As Rice observes, however, the erotic element never fully recedes.[116] At the turn of the nineteenth century, cinema captured the moving bodies of boxers and strongmen.[117] In the 1890s, Eugen Sandow's nearly naked sculpted body was displayed to paying audiences in a fifty-foot filmstrip shown in projection theatres.[118] By this period, men's bodies were not only categorised in more elaborate ways, their emotionalised, gendered forms were communicated in new ways for audiences to consume. Desire played no small part in this process.

Desiring manly vigour: virile and erect forms

In his chapter 'Sculpting the Heroic and the Homoerotic', Michael Budd argues that the dissemination of photographic images made possible the 'pleasures of possession and the fetishization of [male] body parts'.[119] This is powerfully demonstrated by the photographic portraits of ordinary men who entered Eugen Sandow's 'Great Competitions', seeking to win prizes and have photographs of their own bodies published in his magazine, wearing singlets or bare-chested, arms crossed. As Budd notes, they all shared the desire 'to express a solidity of strength and potent force'.[120] Indeed, it was perhaps the erect male pose, adopted by men whose bodies were proffered for admiration, and used to describe idealised men, which conveyed manliness most. Recall Stonio the stone-cutter (1889), discussed in the section 'Viewing the manly form: poise, power, and pose', who stood 'erect as the mast of a ship'.[121] As Budd explains, 'the body is exhibited as totally taut; both literally statuesque and yet always capable of exercising force and power'.[122] The phallic language of the erect pose was especially common in later nineteenth-century descriptions of ideal manliness, yet the manly form was always understood to betoken sexual appeal and virility, often through the coded terms of vigour and vitality. The 1761 *Essay on the Art of War*, for example, commended dance for producing manly vigour.[123] In 1764, a physician outlined the general features of a man: 'superior courage, Manliness of deportment, hirsute, robust Habit of Body, base Tone of Voice, and other signs of Virility, which men perfect in their kind'.[124] In the 1900 *Big Budget*, undergraduate and all-round athlete Tippy Guthrie was commended for his supple, erect body and his 'strong vitality'.[125] Vigour, virility, and vitality all signify the extent to which manliness was generally associated with potent male sexuality throughout the long nineteenth century.

Sailors and soldiers were often held up as having the manly bodies upon which ideas of sexual vigour and potency were projected. Bawdy songs are a useful source indicating the association of sailors with priapic sexuality. 'Jack Junk on Board of Molly Brown' is typical, published in the 1830s and 1840s and sung in late-night supper rooms. Jack courts Molly until he leaves on a voyage. A squire and a captain woo her during his absence. On Jack's return, to help her select which of the three men to marry, Molly's father recommends the squire because he owns land and her mother supports the captain because he has ships at sea. Molly chooses Jack, however, because of his 'long bowsprit'.[126] A case of libel from 1872 reveals particularly well the extent to which military men's bodies were associated with male sexual vigour.[127] In January 1873, Lieutenant-Colonel Gordon Maynard Ives, Colonel of the 36th Middlesex Rifles, and previously an officer in the Coldstream Guards, prosecuted the proprietors of the *Paddington Times* at Marylebone Police Court for publishing a libellous letter. The letter, signed 'Decency' (and printed in several newspapers when reporting the trial), declared that Colonel Ives' speech at the prize-giving ceremony to the 36th Rifles (Paddington) Volunteer Regiment in December 1872 was 'improper' and a 'gross insult' to the volunteers' attending female relatives. The letter did not specify the nature of the prurient remarks, but the report of the cross-examination in the police court offers insights. Denying he was drunk, the colonel confirmed that he had:

> suggested the propriety of young women to marry volunteers. He said that men were better after joining the volunteers than they were before. He did not advise the young women to look at the volunteers' feet, their legs, their everything. He did not say, 'Do not believe these fellows, they will give you this thing, that thing, or the other thing. The volunteers can give you everything.'[128]

Ives refused to accept an apology, and the case eventually went before the Old Bailey on 3 February. When cross-examined, Ives reiterated that his speech had 'not a single word or thought of indecency' and that no one complained about it at the time. He agreed that he had remarked that the volunteer life improved 'their figures and their limbs', but 'did not recommend to the ladies the manly and vigorous form of the volunteers'. He conceded that he wished ladies to marry men of manly character; nevertheless, 'I never alluded to any visible part of man'. Various captains and their wives, a colonel, a surgeon, and a private all offered testimony as to the inoffensiveness of Ives' speech. Even so, for Ives and his witnesses, it was men's parts that formed the manly, vigorous whole. Captain Clark, the regiment adjutant, recalled Colonel Ives as saying: 'Look at the man, look at his head, look at his shoulders, look at him all over, he is everything a man would wish to be.' Similarly, in reporting Ives' speech it is clear that motion and training were key to this appeal: 'If you notice a man drilled he looks a man and he looks a soldier, and it is to the credit of the country that he should look so.'

For these officers, perhaps still drawing on earlier connections between drill and dance, it was volunteers' manly legs that signalled their fitness for service, and for satisfying marital unions, along with their coyly worded 'everything'. Clark was, after all, adamant that Ives was correct, observing: 'I believe the ladies do love men of manly character, for I have got a very good one; I am sure you will be very glad to see her.' His wife did indeed testify next.[129] Even though the proprietor of the *Paddington Times* was found guilty and fined five pounds, this case shows that there was a humorous and, in some situations, bawdy association of manly, healthy, trained men's bodies with virility and sexual appeal. As Budd so accurately observes, the 'male body was beautiful, good and heroic. Each of these were qualities that could also be erotized.'[130] Through that eroticisation, the manly body acted as a vessel for desirable gender qualities.

Reading the manly face: beauty, character, and emotions

The final section of this chapter explores the relationship between handsome faces, moral worth, and manliness. There are numerous descriptions of men and youths as handsome, good-looking, even beautiful. Captain James C. Dailey, an American boxer of Irish parentage, was described in Edwards's *The Portrait Gallery of Pugilists* as 'the *beau ideal* of manly beauty' with handsome face and clean-cut limbs.[131] Attractive, manly faces varied over time, especially as fashions for facial hair altered. Regardless of decade however, a beautiful face conveyed specific manly qualities. Thus, the character of the male protagonist of the 1897 story 'Platonic Friends' by Russell Grey was embodied in his description as a 'tall lithe fellow, with grave deep eyes and a manly eager strength in his handsome, earnest face'.[132] Such visual depictions of character were evident in all types of periodical, whether their intended readerships were adults or youths, female or male. It signalled good or bad character without having to delineate specific manly (or unmanly) qualities. For instance, the author of 'Geraniums and Roses' in *Young Folks*, 1880, asked the reader:

> Would you like to know anything of Jack Brenton's appearance? He has a good figure – that essential point in a man – a sunburnt face, and a pair of honest, merry blue eyes; his hair is curly, and like his slight moustache, dark brown in colour. He has a manly face, and a manly nature. You could not help liking Jack Brenton.[133]

These physical attributes were simply a shorthand for what was widely known as manly: sincerity, honesty, frankness, openness, integrity, and dignity.

The point was often made through contrast. In the 1882 tale, 'The Haunted Wreck, or The Dismal School by the Sea', two handsome fourteen-year-old twins, Harry and Frank, reminded each other of the story of their father and Uncle Bobadil. Much younger than his brother, their 'dear father' 'was very handsome too, whereas uncle was very plain, and not only that, but his temper had always a twist in it as well'. As Harry explained, Uncle Bobadil had a 'surly, morose disposition'. Their father's 'handsome face, manly form, and hearty, genial ways', however, won over their mother, the woman both brothers loved.[134] It should be noted that manly qualities could be subtle and did not map exactly onto only one type of face and form. In *Chums*, an 1895 tale of imperial daring, 'Old "Fire and Sword's Nephew": The "Plucking" of Cuthbert Delancey', introduced two cousins: 'Cuthbert, tall, well set up, soldierly in the fullest sense of the term, with a frank manly face and a firm chin; Arthur, slight, a little inclined to stoop from close application to his studies, also open-faced, but not of that type that takes the initiative and leads the world in its wake by the magnetism of its personality'.[135]

Attractiveness of face was an increasingly prevalent way to evaluate a man in print and visual culture over the period examined. As noted, boxers were always judged on their corporeal qualities and alignment with anatomical and aesthetic notions of idealised male bodies. Yet their handsomeness was also noted in later nineteenth-century descriptions. This is clear from comparing two descriptions of William Hooper, the 'Tinman', a pugilist who fought in the late 1780s. The first volume of Pierce Egan's *Boxiana* (1830), describes Hooper's fighting career. Egan mentions his short stature and weight, but focuses on fights and patronage, and their impact on Tinman's character. Thus, he was valiant and determined, but led astray by fame and the fancy.[136] In 1888, the *Licensed Victuallers' Mirror* published an account of Hooper's fights in which his appearance was much more intimately traced than in Egan's account:

> He was splendidly made – with those compact, well-knit shoulders which are always indicative of tremendous hitting power. His face too, was really handsome. His well-shaped head was surrounded with a crop of crisp auburn curls, and his brown eyes were as keen and bright as a falcon's. He looked what he was – a dare-devil fighter.

His opponent, a carpenter named Wright, was appealingly described as 'a fine strapping fellow of the type that George Eliot has portrayed in *Adam Bede*: 'tall, broad shoulders, muscular arms, and a resolute face'. Following the fight, the Tinman attended a masquerade and supper where the Prince of Wales presided. The author noted that although 'The Tinman still bore on his manly face the marks of his opponent's fists', he remained 'good-looking'.[137]

As these examples illustrate, it is important to analyse the ways in which attractiveness was a shorthand for manly values that served aspirational and didactic ends. Of course, to some extent, handsomeness could be self-defeating as a moralising tool, since those not considered thus blessed might feel unable to attain its associated qualities. Who, after all, could match the male beauty which was specified by feature, often in historical fiction, and shared much with descriptions of female beauty, centring on youth, luxurious hair, large, liquid, long-lashed eyes, and expansive bosoms? Take the lustrous Orlando (1874), for example: 'his eye, large and full, looked out with a soft, liquid light, seeming almost tearful when resting from the call of passion. His hair was very dark – almost black – and hung in wavy masses over his shoulders, while upon his lip curled a graceful moustache.'[138] It is perhaps unsurprising, therefore, that manly features deemed beautiful in text were not often detailed.[139] In the novel *Belinda*, published 1789, Edmond was described as possessing a 'face in the most perfect stile of manly beauty'.[140] Writing in 1836, Elizabeth Johnson described her son, Andrew, who died at twenty-five years of age, as possessed of 'vigorous health, manly beauty (he was, as I have said, tall, well-proportioned, and with a face such as is seldom seen)'.[141] Thus, health was also used as an indicator of, or synonym for, attractiveness, marked out by signs such as the strong and hardy form, well-proportioned limbs, or brown, ruddy, or bronzed face. The latter signified fitness, as a quote from James Thomson's poem 'A Youth' suggests: 'brown with meridian toil/Healthful and strong'.[142] Such 'healthy' signs were potentially more easily achieved, particularly when exercise and useful recreation were understood to facilitate them.

Accordingly, handsome manly faces could adorn many kinds of men, from humble to noble, from unremarkable professionals to active heroes, since they functioned simply to demonstrate manly attributes. In David Ker's 'The White Fawn and its Mother', for instance, 'one of the greatest generals and bravest warriors in all Southern Asia' was noticeable in his isolated, lost state only because of 'a quiet dignity in his look and bearing, and an air of power and command in his firm, manly face (which though somewhat haggard from long fatigue and want of food, was still strikingly handsome)'.[143] More rarely, a morally compromised man might be described as possessing a beautiful face, primarily to show why those who encountered him might be duped. In an 1839 *Ladies' Cabinet* story, Juliet became progressively suspicious of her Venetian husband, Leone Leoni, whose beauty excused her initial gullibility. Her description is telling: 'Truly was he the son of those men with black beards and alabaster hands, the type of whom has been immortalized by Vandyke. Leoni had their eagle profile, their fine and delicate features, their majestic figure.' As Juliet says,

> 'how could I resist my passion for that matchless being, supreme alike in good or evil. How amiable, how beautiful was he in those moments. How well the sallow tints became his manly face, while they spared his high pale fore-head, relieved by his jet black eyebrows. How he could feel and give expression to his feelings.'

It is likely that his eagle profile, sallow skin, and delicate features signalled foreignness to readers, and, therefore, an untrustworthy beauty intended to contrast with British manly 'open' features. Indeed, Juliet articulated her growing suspicion that Leoni worked upon her romantic disposition by using his appearance and emotions.[144]

As historians of physiognomy explain, the link between external appearance and internal morals and character was readily and frequently made by artists, medical practitioners, scientists, and philosophers; beauty indicated virtue and moral worth, ugliness was the manifestation of vice and moral failure.[145] The long-standing art of physiognomy became a science with Johann Caspar Lavater's empirical techniques, which contributed to its revival in the 1790s and widespread popularity in the nineteenth century.[146] As Lavater pronounced: 'If you would know Men's Hearts, Look in their Faces.'[147] Samuel Smiles espoused this in its mid-Victorian form: 'It is in the physical man that the moral as well as the intellectual man lies hid.'[148] The desire to accurately assess others became more acute over the period, since modernity in all its forms, as industrialisation, urbanisation, and migration, increased the anonymity of encounters.[149] Physiognomy was thus a technology of reassurance that enabled personal encounters to be less threatening.[150] It moved from a way to read individuals' characters to characterise groups, such as Jews, the Irish, criminals, the insane, and the poor, and was eventually used in building data about racial, ethnic types (in some cases through composite photography).[151] Physiognomy also facilitated readings of gender. Kathryn Woods' exposition of physiognomy's changing nature across the eighteenth century notes that from mid-century 'facial beauty began to operate as a measure of a person's femininity or masculinity'. Though in her work she considers this only where femininity is concerned, this concept was also central to assessing masculine identities.[152]

As such, physiognomy informed the depictions of handsome faces as indicators of a man's moral core.[153] In 1874, *Bell's Life in London and Sporting Chronicle* announced the death, aged forty-eight, of the cricketer John Lillywhite, explaining that 'his very presence to persons of ordinary perception must have struck them as being the personification of all that was manly and true; no man's character was ever more faithfully depicted in his countenance'.[154] *John Bull* (1847) reviewed Mr Warren's new publication *Now and Then*, summarising the story of Adam Ayliffe, an 'upright yeoman' wrongly accused of murder a century earlier, whose appearance signified his innocence to those looking on in the court. This 'tall marvellously well-proportioned man's countenance said instantly to all present – that it could never be that of a MURDERER ... It was a frank manly face, of a dauntless English cast.' His blue eyes were 'full of intelligence and spirit, and indicative of goodness'.[155] The 1879 story 'Guy's Fortunes: A Stirring Tale of the Sea', described Guy Kendrick's 'physical condition' as 'literally perfect'. In it, the captain and chief mate agree that Guy was 'the handsomest man' they had seen, thanks to his 'form and face, the manly strength and vigour, and the intellectual grace and beauty'. He was contrasted with Loren Beauchamp whom the casual observer might think 'extremely good-looking and even handsome'. But a 'close observer and one versed in physiognomy, in judging the man's characteristics from his face', would have identified the signs of Beauchamp's poor character written in his forehead, nose, and eyes, which indicated his lack of steadiness and strength.[156]

Popular physiognomic readings of men's faces also helped commentators to navigate and evaluate the changing styles of manly bodies described in the 'Introduction' of this chapter. The word portraits and short biographies of famous eighteenth-century male writers in *Young Folks*, 1889, offer excellent case studies.[157] The author's intention was to use portraits to gauge the mind within, enabling readers to understand these past authors and enjoy their literary products more effectively. The writer acknowledged the difficulties of reading mind from face, through the example of an imagined visualisation of George Augustus Sala, a journalist for *Household Words*. This was informed by his writing style: dashing, stalwart, boasting whiskers and a 'bold front'. The author was disappointed on seeing Sala's portrait, however, because his features were awkwardly conformed, with lopsided eyebrows and a snub nose. After reflection, the author concluded, however, that Sala's irregularity of face 'only sets out the more strongly the brave heart and tender spirit enshrined therein'. Robert Louis Stevenson was another author whose face did not match his writing style, since his 'portrait shows a long, dreamy, oval face, thick lips, an apology of a moustache … that gives no hint of the fire and energy within'.[158]

To some extent, then, the author struggled to deploy physiognomy effectively.[159] For example, Oliver Goldsmith was 'a collection of bumps; and yet he was a kindly man'. Indeed, what is detectable is a suspicion of earlier definitions of male beauty when they did not match with what was, in the nineteenth century, deemed a manly character. Byron's curly hair and piercing gaze, for example, 'show forth every beauty except that of humility'. Similarly, a comparison of Walter Scott, whose face was 'full of manly power', with Percy Shelley was coded through manliness: 'Whilst Scott is robust and manly, Shelley is delicate and feminine; whilst Scott, for the time, is popular, Shelley, for the time is unpopular.' Shelley's face, the author contended, was witness to his 'tameless and proud' flawed character:

> His face is almost romantically beautiful, and the effect is enhanced by the thick masses of wavy hair with which his head is adorned. His eyes are large and expressive, and his glance piercing, as suits the poet of 'The Beautiful', while his mouth is small and exquisite, as suits the uttering of the beauties which he saw. Poor, sensitive Shelley! placed amidst 'the thorns of life' without the skill to avoid or the strength to bear them. His great need was self-control.[160]

Here Shelley was deemed inferior to Scott, due to his lack of robustness, which at the time of writing in 1889 was clear marker of manliness. Similarly, his face indicated excessive sensitivity, which by this point meant he conformed less closely with notions of embodied manliness. Even so, the author deployed feelings to help divine mind and manly behaviour from men's faces. The author William Thackeray, for example, resembled a benevolent country minister who had an easy smooth life, when in fact he had experienced a difficult life with hard duties. These sufferings had neither soured his disposition nor 'quench[ed] the cheerfulness of his spirit'. Still, the author decided, Thackeray's face was not entirely dissimulating, since his writings made him a minister of the parish of the world.[161]

It was common for textual accounts of manly faces to intimately link appearances with emotions. A manly face was often a cheerful one. In 'The Unpleasant Passenger' by Horace Lashbroke, the captain of a merchantman was introduced as 'warm-hearted, weather-beaten, jovial Uncle Tom' who wore a 'manly cheerful face'.[162] Scholars have argued that cheerfulness was deployed in representations of the lower orders to make them less threatening, apparently satisfied with their lot in life.[163] This is true, but it was also indicative of a 'natural' manliness and a man's ease with his masculine identity, betokening lack of dissimulation. An 1893 defence of cycling declared that 'Cyclists in their ordinary calling are invariably men well put together, firm, strong, healthy, cheerful, temperate and manly.'[164] Clearly, the manly whole was important, a 'well put together' man merged physical beauty with good spirits and moderate behaviour.

This was integral to another quality that was repeatedly read from the manly countenance: openness. At one level, an open face was simply a physiognomic marker, gesturing that an individual's gendered values, morals, and intellect were exposed to the viewer. Yet openness was a profoundly masculine quality, meaning 'absence of dissimulation; frankness, candour, and sincerity'.[165] It was a metonym for a man untroubled by and comfortable with his gender identity, master of his masculine privileges. *John Bull*, in 1844, offered 'The Philosophy of Good Clothes', which pointed out that 'genteel apparel' produced in men energy, independence, and delicacy of sentiment, shaping their very bodies so they walk with confidence, and making their face 'manly, bold, and free; the brow open, and the eye clear'.[166] Though this might imply that manliness was put on like a suit, physiognomic readings were extended to clothing and hair. Pearl's analysis of the photographs of asylum patients, for example, reveals that the condition and orderliness of apparel and hair signalled state of mind and selfhood, with ordered clothing and hair indicating patients' recovery.[167] Thus, good clothes released or made visible the inner, 'essentialised' man rather than the insincere, inauthentic one.

The manly face was emotionally expressive in other ways too. In 1890, *Chatterbox* informed its young readers in a poem that manliness encompassed several kinds of feeling. Its protagonist was a youth who had a 'manly look', which 'told of a stedfast purpose,/Of a brave and daring will'. This did not preclude other emotions. When he met his mother at the gate on returning home, the youth kissed her loving face and the poem concluded: 'From lads in love with their mothers/Our bravest heroes grew;/Earth's grandest hearts have been loving hearts/Since time and earth began;/And the boy who kisses his mother/Is every inch a man!'[168] A story in the *Ladies' Cabinet of Fashion* characterised Mary's fisherman father in terms that could stand for every ideal man of this period: 'fine-looking ... with his erect figure and open, manly face'. Fathers were particularly associated with feeling.[169] As Mary declares, 'I never met him in my life, no matter how short had been our parting, but he embraced me.'[170] In the 1870 poem 'The Village School', a small girl's life hangs in the balance while her parents fret over her fate. As her apparent demise loomed, her father, a miller, combines frank manliness with tears: 'His manly face the Miller hid/In those strong hands that earn her bread,/Tears through the big brown fingers slid,/And dropp'd upon his Rosy's bed.'[171] As this touchingly reminds us, manliness in the later nineteenth century did not adhere to a stereotypically stiff upper lip. Indeed, manly faces ameliorated any potential discomfort with men's tears in the last quarter of the nineteenth century. Thus, in 'Phantom Lives' (1886), the author deployed the male character's tears to convey his emotional crisis without undermining his masculinity. Maurice's 'handsome manly face was almost convulsed – great tears were blinding him'. His tears also indicated to his sister – and the reader – the shocking enormity of the information he was about to reveal.[172]

Overall, therefore, the descriptions of manly faces were frequently associated with moments of high feeling, whether thwarted or threatened romantic love, paternal or filial affection, kindness to children (frequently located in the rescue of a child), grief, or despair, or, between male friends and enemies, anger or resolution. Typically, the manly man's role was to resolve or ameliorate these emotional crises. Thus, he also signalled security and safety. In the 1900 tale 'Jack's Luck', a girl is saved primarily because she can read the hero's face. Ned, a sailor, needs to escort her to safety, which requires taking an isolated forest path. She accompanies him, because a glance at his 'manly face' is enough to reassure her, 'for it showed her that she was absolutely safe with him, no matter where she might choose to go'.[173] Similarly, in an 1864 tale, Margaret Gordon, a desperate young woman trying to work to keep her orphaned half-brother's children from falling into penury, was addressed by a man in his thirties 'with a manly face – a face to be trusted, to be believed in anywhere; a resolute mouth'.[174]

In effect, characters with manly faces were evoked at moments of heightened emotion to enact approved forms of masculine behaviour. The didactic power of such faces was thus strengthened through an existing knowledge of the qualities of manliness and the affective reactions they elicited in their viewer or reader. While the link was often made implicitly through context, more explicit fictional evocations can be found. In the 1899 story 'A Felon's Gold: or, The Search for the Hidden Millions', Evandra is in peril and thought of 'someone who would fight for her, protect her. A picture of Hubert Mayrick's handsome, manly face ... the grey eyes so full of strength and determination, and yet so tender, had risen up before her. And the picture, painted by her imagining, sent a throp of joy and hope through her whole being.'[175] Similarly, the sympathetic football master in a 'New Leaf', a tale of schoolboys tackling bullies, explained that one could see why he was popular: 'there was strength written in every movement of his athletic frame, while in his manly face there was the unmistakable sign of that glorious accompaniment to physical power – a kind and generous heart'.[176]

These handsome manly faces return us to where this chapter began, with desire, for they were understood to possess allure. Their sexual attraction was identified in accounts of marital selection. A review of *Eberhard; or, The Mystery of Rathsbeck* in *John Bull* (1883) describes the heroine becoming beguiled by the medical student Eberhard Evers, for example, because 'she is struck with his handsome face, manly bearing, and romantic disposition'.[177] In the story of the Errols, a socially mismatched Scottish married couple, Ronald Errol, a nobleman, falls in love with Mary, a dowerless clergyman's daughter and choses disinheritance in order to marry for love. Mary and her father resist his decision, fearing his eventual disappointment on giving up honours and wealth. However, his protestations, 'coupled with his handsome face and manly form, overcame the modest girl's scruples, and ere long they were married'.[178] More generally, men's attractive faces, when associated with a range of positive emotions, were considered desirable, ensuring that the manly qualities they represented were alluring for the men and women who encountered them.

Conclusion

Men's bodies and emotions made manliness desirable and appealing. This might be through the fictional cheerful athletic undergraduate or reports about the real boxer who possessed 'bottom', or romantic tales of muscular youths with heaving bosoms and tearful eyes. Their attractiveness might be transmitted via hardy men with honest, open-faced countenances, or bawdy songs conjuring the vital desirability of soldiers or sailors. Such men's bodies were collected, consumed, and gazed at in paintings, engravings, photographs, and eventually, film. In all cases, their emotionalised bodies influenced people's ideas about manliness. As Chapter 2 shows, men's bodies and faces were likewise used to inculcate negative emotions that worked to fix ideas about unmanliness.

Notes

1 George L. Mosse, *The Image of Man: The Creation of Modern Masculinity* (Oxford: Oxford University Press, 1996). Anthea Callen, *Looking at Men: Anatomy, Masculinity and the Modern Male Body* (New Haven and London: Yale University Press, 2018), p. 12 and passim.
2 Bodies were read for information about morals and guided justice in the court room, Katie Barclay, 'Performing emotion and reading the male body in the Irish court, c. 1800–1845', *Journal of Social History* 51:2 (2017), 293–312.
3 For example, Dominic Janes, *Oscar Wilde Prefigured: Queer Fashioning and British Caricature, 1750–1900* (Chicago and London: University of Chicago Press, 2016); Sarah Toulalan, *Imagining Sex: Pornography and Bodies in Seventeenth-Century England* (Oxford: Oxford University Press, 2007).
4 The seminal article on the gaze is Laura Mulvey, 'Visual pleasure and narrative cinema', *Screen* 16:3 (1975), 6–18. It has been the subject of much debate since.
5 Henk de Smaele, 'Achilles or Adonis: controversies surrounding the male body as national symbol in Georgian England', *Gender & History* 28:1 (2016), 56.
6 Ana De Freitas Boe and Abby Coyendall (eds), *Heteronormativity in Eighteenth-Century Literature and Culture* (Farnham: Ashgate, 2014); Jennifer Evans, 'Introduction: Why queer German history?', *German History* 34:3 (2016), 371–84; Janes, *Oscar Wilde Prefigured*.
7 This is where it hopes to build on George Mosse's classic work in this area, by exploring aspects of the idealised male body beyond its relationship with nation-building and nationalism. Mosse, *The Image of Man*.
8 The same is true of the objectification of black men's bodies, where desire enforced control, although admiring representations of their bodies in the fields of military, sport, and entertainment could offer one means to contest racial inferiority. Richard Smith, *Jamaican Volunteers in the First World War: Race, Masculinity and the Development of National Consciousness* (Manchester: Manchester University Press, 2004), pp. 104 and ch. 5.
9 For considerations of white desire for bodies of colour see Anne O'Brien, 'Missionary masculinities, the homoerotic gaze and the politics of race: Gilbert White in northern Australia, 1885–1915', *Gender & History* 20:1 (2008), 68–85; Elspeth H. Brown, 'Racialising the virile body: Eadweard Muybridge's locomotion studies 1883–1887', *Gender & History* 17:3 (2005), 638; Smith, *Jamaican Volunteers in the First World War*.
10 This is true also of men with the least independence. Thus, the bodies of enslaved men embodied black manhood, and they used their physique, comportment, clothing, and hair to portray masculine identity. This had risks as well as limits. Kathleen M. Brown, '"Strength of the lion … arms like polished iron": embodying black masculinity in an age of slavery and propertied manhood', in Thomas A. Foster (ed.), *New Men: Manliness in Early America* (New York and London: New York University Press, 2011), pp. 172–92.
11 This has long roots: Rosemary Barrow, *Gender, Identity and the Body in Greek and Roman Sculpture* (Cambridge: Cambridge University Press, 2018), p. 3.
12 Old Bailey Proceedings Online (hereafter OBPO), www.oldbaileyonline.org (accessed 20 November 2018), *Ordinary of Newgate's Account*, December 1750 (OA17501231).
13 Samuel Smiles, *Self-Help: With Illustrations of Character and Conduct* (Boston, 1st edn, 1859), p. 241.
14 Brown, 'Racialising the virile body', 642.
15 Pamela Gilbert, 'Popular beliefs and the body: "a nation of good animals"', in Michael Sappol and Stephen P. Rice (eds), *A Cultural History of the Human Body in the Age of Empire* (Oxford: Berg, 2010), p. 142.

16 *Licensed Victuallers' Mirror* 68 (14 May 1889), p. 181.
17 This contrasts with Mosse, who proposes that the idealised male body differed little from the mid-eighteenth century. Mosse, *The Image of Man*, p. 12.
18 For an account of varying body types in the Christian era see Roberta Park, 'Muscles, symmetry and action: "Do you measure up". Defining masculinity in Britain and America from the 1860s to the early 1900s', *International Journal of the History of Sport* 22:3 (2007), 368.
19 Cited in Julia Allen, *Swimming with Dr Johnson and Mrs Thrale: Sport, Health and Exercise in Eighteenth-Century England* (Cambridge: Lutterworth Press, 2012), p. 5.
20 Eugen Sandow, *Strength and How to Obtain it: With Anatomical Chart Illustrating the Exercises for Physical Development* (London: Gale & Polden, 1897).
21 For the role of physical culture in working-class self-actualisation see Michael Budd, *The Sculpture Machine: Physical Culture and Body Politics in the Age of Empire* (Basingstoke and London: Palgrave Macmillan, 1997).
22 Park, 'Muscles, symmetry and action', 367–8.
23 Michael Hau, 'The normal, the ideal, and the beautiful: perfect bodies during the age of empire', in Sappol and Rice (eds), *A Cultural History of the Human Body*, pp. 149–52; Mosse, *The Image of Man*, ch. 2; Park, 'Muscles, symmetry and action', 367–8, 370, 373, 376–7. Callen, *Looking at Men*, 14-15, 21–2.
24 For an examination of the European-wide appeal of these bodily types see Hau, 'The normal, the ideal, and the beautiful', passim; Joseph A. Kestner, *Masculinities in Victorian Painting* (Aldershot: Scolar, c.1995), p. 54. For its classical antecedents, see Barrow, *Gender, Identity, and the Body*, p. 76.
25 *Englishwoman's Domestic Magazine* 6 (October 1857), p. 168.
26 Martin Myrone, *Body-Building: Reforming Masculinities in British Art, 1750–1810* (New Haven, CT: Yale University Press, 2006), pp. 48, 70.
27 Park, 'Muscles, symmetry and action', 378.
28 Cynthia S. Hamilton, 'Hercules subdued: the visual rhetoric of the kneeling slave', *Slavery & Abolition* 34:4 (2013), 646. Also, see a similar use when applied to a Jamaican volunteer in 1917, Smith, *Jamaican Volunteers in the First World War*, pp. 107–8.
29 'Holroyd of St. Anselm's meets an old acquaintance', *Big Budget* 182 (8 December 1900), p. 410.
30 OBPO, *Ordinary of Newgate's Account*, 25 April 1733 (OA17330425).
31 OBPO, *Ordinary of Newgate's Account*, 3 October 1750 (OA17501003).
32 *Lady's Monthly Museum* (1807), p. 175.
33 Park, 'Muscles, symmetry and action', 363, 380–1; Christopher Oldstone-Moore, *Of Beards and Men: The Revealing History of Facial Hair* (Chicago: University of Chicago Press, 2016), p. 204.
34 *Our Young Folk's Weekly Budget of Tales, News, Sketches, Fun, Puzzles, Riddles &c* 208 (1874), p. 397.
35 Gentility had a smooth face. Oldstone-Moore, *Of Beards and Men*, pp. 144–50.
36 Philip Carter, *Men and the Emergence of Polite Society, Britain 1660–1800* (London: Longman, 2001).
37 *Lady's Magazine* 35 (1804), p. 146.
38 Matthew McCormack, 'Dance and drill: polite accomplishments and military masculinities in Georgian Britain', *Cultural and Social History* 8:3 (2011), 315–30.
39 Anon., *Essay on the Art of War: In Which the General Principles of All the Operations of War in the Field are Fully Explained. The Whole Collected from the Opinions of the Best Authors* (London: A. Millar, 1761), p. 603.
40 R. B. Shoemaker, 'The taming of the duel: masculinity, honour and ritual violence in London, 1600–1800', *The Historical Journal* 45:3 (2002), 525–45.
41 Cited in Myrone, *Bodybuilding*, p. 50.

42 Michele Cohen, *Fashioning Masculinities: National Identity and Language in the Eighteenth Century* (London and New York: Routledge, 1996).
43 *Young Folks Paper* 996 (28 December 1889), p. 401.
44 The British Museum, no. 1865,1111.2120, George Cruikshank, 'Backside & front view of the ladies fancy-man, Paddy Carey' (1822), www.britishmuseum.org/research/collection_online/collection_object_details.aspx?objectId=1650556&partId=1&people=125596&peoA=125596-2-70&page=1 (accessed 30 March 2019).
45 'Cricketer's Register', *Bell's Life in London and Sporting Chronicle* (Sunday, 12 September 1847), p. 6.
46 *Young Folks Paper* (1889).
47 'To John Bull', *John Bull* 85 (29 July 1822), p. 677.
48 'The praying sailor-boy', *Children's Friend* 332 (1 August 1851), p. 182. Gale document no. DX1902089021.
49 Oldstone-Moore, *Of Beards and Men*, pp. 155–6.
50 Karen Harvey, 'Men of parts: masculine embodiment and the male leg in eighteenth-century England', *Journal of British Studies* 54:4 (2015), 812.
51 Oldstone-Moore, *Of Beards and Men*, pp. 166–70.
52 Karen Downing, 'The gentleman boxer: boxing, manners, and masculinity in eighteenth-century England', *Men and Masculinities* 12:3 (2010), 328–52.
53 Joanne Begiato, 'Tears and the manly sailor in England, c.1760–1860', *Journal for Maritime Research* 17:2 (2015), 117–33.
54 Tessa Dunlop, 'Tattoos: the legacy of a seafaring heritage', *History Today* 62:6 (2012), 36-7; Louise Moore, 'Tattoos, tars and sailortown culture', http://porttowns.port.ac.uk/tattoos-tars-sailortown-culture/ (accessed 2 January 2019); Simon Newman, *Embodied History: The Lives of the Poor in Early Philadelphia* (Philadelphia: University of Pennsylvania Press, 2003), ch. 5.
55 Beverly Lemire, 'A question of trousers: seafarers, masculinity and empire in the shaping of British male dress, c. 1600–1800', *Cultural and Social History* 13:1 (2016), 1–22.
56 Michael Brown, 'Cold steel, weak flesh: mechanism, masculinity and the anxieties of late Victorian empire', *Cultural and Social History* 14:2 (2017), 155–81.
57 Oldstone-Moore, *Of Beards and Men*, pp. 181–91.
58 Bradley Deane, *Masculinity and the New Imperialism: Rewriting Manhood in British Popular Literature, 1870–1914* (Cambridge: Cambridge University Press, 2014), pp. 3–4, 12, 15, 164, ch. 5.
59 Smith, *Jamaican Volunteers in the First World War*, pp. 101–2, 104, 108.
60 O'Brien, 'Missionary masculinities', 73, 74, 76, 82.
61 Ava Baron, 'Masculinity, the embodied male worker, and the historian's gaze', *International Labor and Working-Class History* 69 (2006), 143–60.
62 Park, 'Muscles, symmetry and action', 373–8.
63 J. A. Mangan, 'Athleticism: a case study of the evolution of an educational ideology', *International Journal of the History of Sport* 27:1–2 (2010), 60–77. For several examples of the links made between sports and athletics and muscular masculinity from the 1860s in Britain and the USA see Park, 'Muscles, symmetry and action', 371–8.
64 Budd, *Sculpture Machine*, ch. 2, pp. 35, 36.
65 Kasia Boddy, *Boxing: A Cultural History* (London: Reaktion Books, 2008), p. 33; Downing, 'The gentleman boxer', 341–2; Dave Day, '"Science", "wind" and "bottom": eighteenth-century boxing manuals', *International Journal of the History of Sport* 29:10 (2012), 1446–65. For the relationship of representations of boxers and wrestlers with anatomy, art, and masculinity, see Anthea Callen, *Looking at Men: Anatomy, Masculinity and the Modern Male Body* (New Haven and London: Yale University Press, 2018), pp. 66–109.
66 *Licensed Victuallers' Mirror* (24 April 1888), p. 3.

67 British Sporting Trust, John Ellys, *Mr John Broughton*, mezzotint (possibly 1787), www.bsat.co.uk/image_collections/photo_more?id=28 (accessed 15 February 2019); Yale Center for British Art, Paul Mellon Collection, John Hamilton Mortimer, *Jack Broughton, the Boxer* (c.1767), Accession Number B1981.25.462, http://collections.britishart.yale.edu/vufind/Record/1669193 (accessed 15 February 2019).

68 For example, the depiction of John Jackson in Sir Thomas Lawrence, *Satan Summoning his Legions*, 1796–7, Royal Academy of Arts, Object Number: 03/1094. The general value of using sporting images is explored in Mike Huggins and Mike O'Mahony, 'Prologue: extending study of the visual in the history of sport', *International Journal of the History of Sport* 28:8–9 (2011), 1089–104.

69 Boddy, *Boxing*, pp. 66–73.

70 C. Bell, *Letters of Sir Charles Bell, Selected [Chiefly] from his Correspondence with G. J. Bell* (London: John Murray, 1870), pp. 125–6. For the boxer as the anatomists' ideal model, see Anthea Callen, *Looking at Men: Anatomy, Masculinity and the Modern Male Body* (New Haven and London: Yale University Press, 2018), pp. 78–85.

71 Boddy, *Boxing*, pp. 81, 84.

72 British Sporting Art Trust, Charles Hunt, *Bendigo*, aquatint, Reference: 2005.015, https://bsat.co.uk/image_collections/photo_more?id=56 (accessed 15 February 2019).

73 British Sporting Art Trust, Thomas Rowlandson, *Boxing Match for 200 Guineas between Dutch Sam and Medley*, etching with later hand-colouring, Reference: 2005.036, https://bsat.co.uk/image_collections/photo_more?id=39 (accessed 15 February 2019); Unknown artist, *A View of the Fight between Gully and Gregson*, wood engraving, Reference: 2005.020.

74 National Portrait Gallery, *Sir Walter Edgeworth-Johnstone*, by Ernest Clarence Elliott, for Elliott & Fry, collotype, 1904; Edgeworth-Johnstone's photograph was included in a collection of sporting celebrities, Peter Hamilton and Roger Hargreaves, *The Beautiful and the Damned: The Creation of Identity in Nineteenth-Century Photography* (London: National Portrait Gallery, 2001), p. 40.

75 Billy Edwards, *The Portrait Gallery of Pugilists of England, America, Australia from James J. Corbett Running Back to Tom Sayers* (London and Philadelphia: Pugilistic Publishing Co., 1894).

76 Budd, *Sculpture Machine*, pp. 35–7, 42.

77 Edwards, *The Portrait Gallery of Pugilists*.

78 Cited in Day, 'Boxing manuals', 1460; Boddy, *Boxing*, p. 40.

79 Boddy, *Boxing*, passim.

80 Jewish Museum, London, Object Number: JM 686, https://jewishmuseum.org.uk/50-objects/jm-686/ (accessed 12 September 2019). For examples of portrait figurines see P. D. Gordon Pugh, *Staffordshire Portrait Figures and Allied Subjects of the Victorian Era* (London: Barrie & Jenkins, 1970), pp. 533–4.

81 Boddy, *Boxing*, p. 39.

82 An example can be seen at www.mearsandboyer.com/antique/217/staffordshire-boxers- (accessed 2 January 2019).

83 Boddy, *Boxing*, p. 45.

84 For a range of boxer figures, see '81. Boxing: Staffordshire figures, 1780–1840: supplementary archive', www.earlystaffordshirefigures.com/81-boxing.html (accessed 2 January 2019).

85 For the spread of literary flash, or the widespread use of boxing metaphors from the 1820s see Boddy, *Boxing*, pp. 56–66.

86 For the ways in which black men in America used boxing to assert their manhood, challenging white America's ideas about race, class, and manhood, see Louis Moore, *I Fight for a Living: Boxing and the Battle for Black Manhood. 1880–1915* (Urbana and Chicago: University of Illinois, 2017); Ronald Schechter and Liz

Clarke, *Mendoza the Jew: Boxing, Manliness, and Nationalism, a Graphic History* (New York: Oxford University Press, 2014).
87 Pierce Egan, *Boxiana; or, Sketches of Ancient and Modern Pugilism, by One of the Fancy* (London, 1823), pp. 14–15.
88 Downing, 'The gentleman boxer', 334; Boddy, *Boxing*, pp. 43, 46–7, 106–9.
89 In America, black boxers demonstrated the myth of black inferiority as well as contributing to constructions of black working-class manliness. Moore, *I Fight for a Living*; Louis Moore, 'Fine specimens of manhood: the black boxer's body and the avenue to equality, racial advancement, and manhood in the nineteenth century', *MELUS* 35:4 (2010), 59–84.
90 David Dee, '"The hefty Hebrew": boxing and British-Jewish identity, 1890–1960', *Sport in History* 32:3 (2012), 361–81.
91 Ruti Ungar, 'The boxing discourse in late Georgian Britain, 1780–1820: a study in civic humanism, class and race' (PhD dissertation, Humboldt University of Berlin, 2010), pp. 132, 133, 149–50, 153–5.
92 Boddy, *Boxing*, p. 109.
93 Smiles, *Self-Help*, p. 242.
94 Richard Holt, 'Cricket and Englishness: the batsman as hero', in Richard Holt, J. A. Mangan, and Pierre Lanfranchi (eds), *European Heroes: Myth, Identity, Sport* (London and New York: Routledge, 2013), pp. 48–50.
95 For various biographies and objects, see the Lillywhite Family Museum, www.thelillywhitefamilymuseum.com/The_Lillywhite_Family_Museum/Welcome.html (accessed 17 January 2019); Frederick Lillywhite, *The English Cricketers' Trip to Canada and the United States* (London, 1860).
96 Holt, 'Cricket and Englishness', pp. 50–3. For the visual and material culture produced in their lifetimes, see Pugh, *Staffordshire Portrait Figures*, pp. 530–1; Lillywhite Family Museum, Cricket Collection, www.thelillywhitefamilymuseum.com/The_Lillywhite_Family_Museum/The_Cricket_Collection.html (accessed 17 January 2019).
97 Lillywhite Family Museum, Cricket Collection, Staffordshire pitcher of 'Old Lillywhite at Lord's' taken from a lithograph by John Corbett Anderson for Fred. Lillywhite & Wisden, 2 Coventry St, Leicester Square. John Lillywhite, Getty Images *c*.1874, www.gettyimages.co.uk/detail/news-photo/vintage-illustration-featuring-english-cricketer-and-umpire-news-photo/458900902 (accessed 17 January 2019).
98 Oldstone-Moore, *Of Beards and Men*, pp. 198–203. For Grace as a national sporting hero, see Derek Birley, *A Social History of English Cricket* (London: Aurum Press, 2000), ch. 8.
99 Holt, 'Cricket and Englishness', p. 52.
100 *Ibid*.
101 For illustrations and photographs of cricketers of the 1830s to 1850s and of later Victorian and Edwardian periods see Birley, *Social History of English Cricket*.
102 Lillywhite Family Museum, Cricket Collection, All-England Team of 1863, including James Lillywhite, Jr., from their tour of the United States, in *Harpers Weekly*, www.thelillywhitefamilymuseum.com/The_Lillywhite_Family_Museum/The_Cricket_Collection.html (accessed 17 January 2019).
103 David Deitcher, *Dear Friends: American Photographs of Men Together, 1840–1918* (New York: Harry N. Abrams, Inc., 2001), p. 19 and passim.
104 This section is based on Budd, *Sculpture Machine*, pp. x, xii.
105 Oldstone-Moore, *Of Beards and Men*, pp. 203–4.
106 Budd, *Sculpture Machine*, pp. 38–40. For Sandow's cultivation of a smooth body, see Oldstone-Moore, *Of Beards and Men*, pp. 204–8.
107 Budd, *Sculpture Machine*, pp. 26–7, 42–3. For the popularity of athletes pictured on *cartes de visite*, a form of reproduction on mass scale, see Hamilton and Hargreaves, *The Beautiful and the Damned*, pp. 31, 43–54.

108 Elise Smith, '"Why do we measure mankind?" Marketing anthropometry in late-Victorian Britain', *History of Science* (2019), 1–24.
109 Park, 'Muscles, symmetry and action', 378–87.
110 Both examples cited in *ibid.*, 379. For Galton's endeavours to get popular buy-in to build his anthropometric data, see Smith, '"Why do we measure mankind?"' 18–22. Also see Allan Sekula, 'The body and the archive', in Richard Bolton (ed.), *The Context of Meaning: Critical Histories of Photography* (Cambridge, MA: MIT Press, 1989), p. 372, and 'International Health Exhibition, 1884', http://blogs.lshtm.ac.uk/library/2016/07/07/international-health-exhibition-1884/ (accessed 5 January 2018).
111 Brown, 'Racialising the virile body', 646–7.
112 Smith, '"Why do we measure mankind?"' 17. For an overview see Stephen P. Rice, 'Picturing bodies in the nineteenth century', in Sappol and Rice (eds), *A Cultural History of the Human Body*, p. 214.
113 This was a widespread European and American phenomenon, see Hau, 'The normal, the ideal, and the beautiful', pp. 161–7; Sekula, 'The body and the archive', pp. 353–73.
114 For an account of the project and its racialising imperatives see Brown, 'Racialising the virile body', 627–56.
115 *Ibid.*, 642–3.
116 Rice, 'Picturing bodies in the nineteenth century', pp. 232–4.
117 Dan Streible, 'On the canvas: boxing, art, and cinema', in Nancy Mowll Mathews, Charles Musser, and Marta Braun, *Moving Pictures: American Art and Early Film 1880–1910* (Manchester, VT: Hudson Hills Press LLC, 2005), p. 111.
118 Budd, *Sculpture Machine*, p. 56 and ch. 3.
119 *Ibid.*, p. 62.
120 *Ibid.*, pp. 59, 62.
121 *Young Folks Paper* (1889).
122 Budd, *Sculpture Machine*, pp. 62–3.
123 Anon., *Essay on the Art of War*, p. 603.
124 Physician of Bristol, *Table Dorsalis: or, The Cause of Consumption in Young Men and Women. With an Explication of its Symptoms, Precautions and the Method of Cure* (London, 1764).
125 'Holroyd of St. Anselm's meets an old acquaintance', *Big Budget* 182 (8 December 1900), p. 410.
126 Ed Cray (ed.), *Bawdy Songbooks of the Romantic Period*, vol. 1: *Items Published by William West (1834–6)* (London: Pickering & Chatto, 2011), pp. 112–13.
127 For the representation of French soldiers' virility, see David Hopkin, 'Sons and lovers: popular images of the conscript, 1798–1870', *Modern & Contemporary France* 9:1 (2001), 31–4.
128 Charge of libel', *Morning Post* (8 January 1873), p. 3; also see 'The police courts', *Daily News* (8 January 1873); and 'Summary of this morning's news', *Pall Mall Gazette* (8 January 1873).
129 OBPO, February 1873, trial of EDWARD AMBLER (51) (t18730203-193).
130 Budd, *Sculpture Machine*, p. 73.
131 Edwards, *The Portrait Gallery of Pugilists*, n.p.
132 *Hearth and Home* (7 January 1897), p. 343.
133 'Geraniums and roses', *Young Folks* 482 (28 February 1880), p. 180.
134 *Boys of England: A Journal of Sport, Travel, Fun and Instruction for the Youths of Nations* (8 December 1882) p. 2.
135 *Chums* 125 (30 January 1895), p. 356.
136 Egan, *Boxiana*, pp. 187–94.
137 *Licensed Victuallers' Mirror* (17 July 1888), p. 291.

138 *Our Young Folks Weekly Budget of Tales, News, Sketches, Fun, Puzzles, Riddles &c* 19(208) (December 1874), p. 397.
139 For changing physiognomic readings of beauty, see Kathryn Woods, '"Facing" identity in a "faceless" society: physiognomy, facial appearance and identity perception in eighteenth-century London', *Cultural and Social History* 14:2 (2017), 146.
140 *Belinda, or, the Fair Fugitive. A Novel. By Mrs. C---- Dedicated to her Grace the Duchess of Marlborough. A New Edition. In Two Volumes* (1789), vol. 1, p. 24.
141 Elizabeth Lichtenstein Johnston, *Recollections of a Georgia Loyalist* (New York and London, 1901), p. 99.
142 Cited in *Pawsey's Ladies' Fashionable Repository* (n.d.), p. 13.
143 *Little Folks* (n.d.), p. 422.
144 *Ladies' Cabinet of Fashion* (1839), p. 375.
145 For the longer history of physiognomy see Woods, '"Facing" identity in a "faceless" society', 137–53. Sharrona Pearl, *About Faces: Physiognomy in Nineteenth-Century Britain* (Cambridge, MA: Harvard University Press, 2010).
146 Its popularity fluctuated over its long history. Woods, '"Facing" identity in a "faceless" society', 141–3. Pearl, *About Faces*, pp. 11–13.
147 James Gillray's satire claiming to read politicians' hidden characters used this quote as a subtitle in 1798. Cited in Pearl, *About Faces*, p. 88
148 Smiles, *Self-Help*, p. 246.
149 Pearl, *About Faces*, ch. 1.
150 *Ibid.*, pp. 10–11.
151 *Ibid.*, p. 4 and ch. 4; Woods, '"Facing" identity in a "faceless" society', 140–3; Sekula, 'The body and the archive', pp. 353–73.
152 Woods, '"Facing" identity in a "faceless" society', 145–7.
153 Pearl, *About Faces*, p. 27.
154 *Bell's Life in London and Sporting Chronicle* (1874), p. 5.
155 *John Bull* 18:1 (1847), p. 809.
156 *Young Folks* 466 (1879), p. 329. Pearl, *About Faces*, pp. 43, 47–56; for the links between physiognomy and photography see Hamilton and Hargreaves, *The Beautiful and the Damned*, pp. 63–84.
157 *Young Folks* 954 (9 March 1889), p. 156.
158 For the way authors might be playful with physiognomy, see Pearl, *About Faces*, p. 13.
159 *Ibid.*, p. 6.
160 *Young Folks* 954 (9 March 1889), p. 156.
161 *Ibid.*
162 Routledge's *Every Boy's Annual* 31 (n.d.), p. 337.
163 Nicole Eustace, *Passion is the Gale: Emotion, Power, and the Coming of the American Revolution* (Chapel Hill: University of North Carolina Press, 2008), pp. 68–9; Joanne Bailey, *Parenting in England, 1760–1830: Emotion, Identity, and Generation* (Oxford: Oxford University Press, 2012), pp. 117–18.
164 'Degenerating the human race', *Cycling* (London, England), 146 (Sat, 4 November 1893), p. 253.
165 *Oxford English Dictionary*.
166 Extract from 'Traits and stories of the Irish peasantry', *John Bull* (26 August 1844), p. 537.
167 Pearl, *About Faces*, ch. 5.
168 *Chatterbox* 51 (1890), p. 403.
169 Joanne Bailey, 'A very sensible man: imagining fatherhood in England c.1750–1830', *History: The Journal of the Historical Association* 95:319 (2010), 267–92.
170 *Ladies' Cabinet of Fashion* 322 (n.d.), p. 1.
171 *Good Words for the Young* (1 September 1870), p. 596.

172 '"Phantom Lives" by Annette Lyster', *The Monthly Packet* 67 (1 July 1886), p. 8.
173 *Up-to-Date Boys Journal & Novelettes* 35 (23 February 1900), p. 289.
174 *Ladies' Treasury* (1 January 1864), p. 12.
175 *The Big Budget* 88 (18 February 1899), p. 157.
176 *Young England: An Illustrated Magazine for Recreation and Instruction* (n.d.), p. 552.
177 *John Bull* 3 (7 April 1883), p. 218.
178 *Atalanta: The Victorian Magazine* (n.d.), pp. 198–200.

2

Appetites, passions, and disgust: the penalties and paradoxes of unmanliness

Introduction

Unmanliness was emblazoned on emotionalised bodies, written onto ill-formed, unappealing forms and faces, and deployed through disgust, the very antitheses of desire. This too had physiognomic roots and moral associations. Johann Caspar Lavater, for example, explained: 'the morally best, the most beautiful. The morally worst, the most deformed.'[1] Eighteenth-century British moral philosophers similarly drew analogies between the corporeal and the moral, applying a 'moralization of aesthetics' in which morality was rooted in the 'natural' capacities of the body: its senses, affections, and passions.[2] Already associated with vice and immorality, 'ugliness' was increasingly physiognomically read in the nineteenth century to embody class, race, and ethnic inferiority.[3] People encountered this philosophical and scientific premise in popular culture, perhaps most obviously in children's stories, which frequently contrasted good and bad characters through heroes' and villains' bodies. In *Young Folks Paper*, 1888, Noel Claythorpe is hauled into the baronet's court to stand trial for beating the baronet's cruel son. Noel's virtue is signalled by his appearance: 'a flood of sunlight, softened by the dingy panes of a tall and narrow, closely lozenged window, poured upon him, lighting up his handsome face and manly form, and producing an effect that was heroic'. Norman Anwick's duplicity and corruptness, on the other hand, is flagged by his obese body and blood corrupted by alcohol.[4]

The description of Anwick is especially telling, for his failure to measure up to an idealised physique was caused by his excessive appetites. This chapter explores the ways in which unmanliness was imagined through such unrestrained appetites and feelings, and their impact upon bodies, minds, morals, and, therefore, gender. These are critical factors to explore in the long nineteenth century, when the penalties for unmanliness became less abstract and collective and more visceral and personalised. In the early modern period, failure to control bodily appetites and emotions had been recognised as the road to crime, sin, punishment, and, eventually, redemption.[5] With modernity, which Mary Poovey defines, in part, as 'the repetition at the level of subjectivity and the body of the disciplinary dynamics played out more ostentatiously in various domains', the failure of self-control was pathologised.[6] The connection between succumbing to temptation and escalating vice remained, but additionally was considered to fuel a descent into degeneracy and madness. As such, unmanliness was increasingly conceptualised as a failure of the self, a form of self-destruction. The discussion of the relationship between unmanliness, bodies, and emotions that follows reveals the inherent paradox of masculine identity, since many unmanly behaviours were also those which, in a managed form, were central to the performance of normative masculinity. Thus, men had to navigate considerable ambiguities in performing their gender. These challenges are further exposed by the ways in which men from different social classes deployed different emotions in their calls for self-control. Finally, the chapter shows how unmanliness was especially complicated for those men whose bodies were lacking, regardless of their volition, due to disability, age, or infirmity.

Unrestrained appetites and passions

In *An Account of the Marine Society* (1759), Jonas Hanway declared: 'Reason and experience urge; Heaven itself importunes us to convert our luxury and vanity, our puerility and effeminacy, into pious, manly, and martial labours.'[7] This conversion necessitated the restraint of certain appetites, which were ascribed moral qualities and positioned as the enemies of manliness.[8] Culturally and socially constructed, such appetites encompassed sensual and carnal desires and behaviours, including food and sex, substances like alcohol and tobacco, activities like gambling and consumption, and a raft of behaviours deemed to distract men from productivity, such as idleness.[9] This section focuses in particular upon eating and drinking, and their associated vices, such as masturbation, to show the ways in which they were condemned through their projection onto unmanly bodies that stirred aversion.

The regulation of these appetites was adjusted to prevailing cultural trends, a shift illustrated by three examples of advice for boys, youths, and men. James Fordyce's *Addresses to Young Men*, published in 1777, aimed at the middle and professional ranks, positioned the failure of manliness in what he called 'effeminacy', that is, the pursuit of 'pleasure' and 'luxury', which included gaming, excess in fashion, and worldly habits. All led to the loss of affection, sympathy, sense of worth, and understanding of moral beauty, truth, and virtue. The consequences of such indulgence were bodily disassembly: 'the tone of your minds is broken; you are frittered by vanity; you are dissolved in vice'.[10] Its physical results were 'distorted beings' with 'lax nerves' who decorated their bodies and simpered.[11] To some extent, these men were the victims of their times: 'when a masculine virtue and deportment are become so unfashionable' thanks to the worldly temptations of civilised society.[12] Modernity corrupted, with its 'new orders of pleasure, ruinous by their expense, inflammatory to the passions, productive of softness, idleness, sensuality, debauchery'.[13] Britain itself was under 'imminent danger from the prodigality, profligacy, and unfeeling luxury of her inhabitants', who had exchanged 'the strictness, the hardiness, and the noble spirit of our ancestors' for 'a selfish and vicious effeminacy'.[14] Nevertheless, bodily control in the form of frugality, sobriety, simplicity, plainness, and hardness would restore the nation to its rightful historical eminence. Fordyce not only blamed urban luxury: poor child-rearing and education similarly misled male youths. Indeed, he cited Samuel Richardson who blamed society for prioritising pleasure, which led 'the man of body' to take 'the greatest care to set out and adorn the part for which he thinks himself most valuable. Better the man of mind, who would bestow most pains in improving that mind.'[15]

Nearly one hundred years later, Samuel Smiles' *Self-Help*, aimed this time at working-class men, likewise located unmanliness in modernity and physical excesses, for which the only response was self-control.[16] Smiles informed his male readers that the highest object of life was 'to form a manly character, and to work out the best development possible, of body and spirit, – of mind, conscience, heart, and soul'.[17] Manly character was sustained by not giving in to physical desire, whether for sexual gratification or food and alcohol, by controlling inappropriate passions and feelings such as anger and fear, and by physical hard work. His recommendation was to 'be a temperate man, and exercise the virtue of self-denial … nothing is so much calculated to give strength to the character'.[18] Lack of self-control produced discontented poor men, who manifested 'weakness, self-indulgence, and perverseness'.[19] He also disparaged middle-class 'ambition to bring up boys as gentlemen, or rather "genteel" men', through which they 'acquire a taste for dress, style, luxuries, and amusements, which can never form any solid foundation for manly or gentlemanly character'.[20] Yet, unlike Fordyce, writing a century earlier, he did not situate the causes of unmanly appetites in upbringing and institutions; in fact, 'It may be of comparatively little consequence how a man is governed from without, whilst everything depends upon how he governs himself from within.'[21] In effect, he placed the blame upon the character flaws of the individual man. His examples of successful men were intended to show his readers that 'their happiness and well-being as individuals in afterlife, must necessarily depend mainly upon themselves, – upon their own diligent self-culture, self-discipline, and self-control, – and, above all, on that honest and upright performance of individual duty, which is the glory of manly character'.[22] In the 1866 edition of *Self-Help*, he was even more explicit, asserting that such individualism was responsible for the state of the nation, since 'progress is the sum of individual industry, energy, and uprightness, as national decay is of individual idleness, selfishness, and vice'.[23]

Robert Baden-Powell took individualism to its extreme in his goal of creating entirely self-sufficient, individualistic men, who nevertheless gave up everything for 'King, fellow countrymen or employers'. In 1908, he published his handbook for scouts, which contained guidance for instructors, as well as 'yarns' intended to inspire boys in learning scouts' work. *Scouting for Boys* aimed to inculcate the skills of 'peace scouts', those 'frontiersmen of all parts of our Empire', such as pioneers, explorers, missionaries: 'real men in every sense of the word'. Such men knew how to look after themselves when far from help or support: 'they are accustomed to take their lives in their hands, and to fling them down without hesitation if they can help their country by doing so'. If Smiles' generation replaced moderation with abstinence, then Baden-Powell's demanded that 'real' men 'give up everything, their personal comforts, and desires, in order to get their work done'.[24] What is similar to all these campaigns for self-control, as we shall see, is that men's bodies, along with a range of associated emotions, were deployed as the main weapons in the drive to persuade men to exercise self-control.

First, self-mastery of food. Food consumption offers valuable insights into unmanliness since, as Christopher Forth argues, commentators envisaged food as impacting on nervous, digestive, and reproductive systems to thereby craft the materiality of manhood.[25] Dietary moderation had long been commended, with religion a motivating force for such restrictions. Fasting was part of Christian observance and a simple diet was seen as producing not only faith and morals, but a harder male body, resistant to sexual temptations.[26] In the Christian tradition, after all, meat excited the body and temperament and stimulated a further urge for alcohol or carnal desires.[27] In the later seventeenth century, for instance, Thomas Tyron saw excessive eating and drinking as leading to corruption, with meat inciting men to violence.[28] Evangelicalism influenced the vegetarian movement, which adhered to the idea that dietary indulgence led to moral corruption.[29] In 1903 it was still proposed that flesh food 'tends to irritate the nerves and to excite the passions, thus giving the balance of power to the lower propensities'.[30] Although excessive abstinence was disparaged in the seventeenth and eighteenth centuries, due to its associations with popery, something more than moderation became necessary as the nineteenth century unfolded.

All this had extensive implications for masculine identity, particularly when combined with the other motivating factor for restraint: modernity, imagined to soften the body, causing obesity, laziness, and a propensity for masturbation and sodomy.[31] Strikingly, the bodies produced were described in terms intended to elicit distaste. As Samuel Smiles pronounced in 1859: 'in this age of progress, we find so many stomachs weak as blotting-paper, – hearts indicating "fatty degeneration", – unused, pithless hands, calveless legs and limp bodies, without any elastic spring in them'.[32] By the nineteenth century there was a new stress on cultivating a healthy constitution, designed to produce a hard male body, which implied virility and manliness. A 'hardening' regime of exercise and restricted diet in turn regulated men's passions.[33] For W. Wadd, for instance, the only way to prevent obesity was 'rigid abstemiousness, and a strict and constant attention to diet and exercise'.[34] This had different meanings for different classes. Stuart Hogarth states that middle-class men practised it to protect against overindulgence and rich living, while working-class men used it to toughen the body to bear the burden of excessive hard work.[35]

These invocations about healthy manly bodies worked. In the 1820s, Thomas Bewick (1753–1828) explained that a doctor advised him to take up 'temperance and exercise' after he became unwell from intensive application to books and his indoor work as an apprentice engraver.[36] Acting upon this advice, he read '"Lewis Cornaro", and other books, which treated of temperance'.[37] He walked for exercise, ate only a small amount of 'animal food' to avoid his constitution being overstimulated, and had frugal amounts of bread and milk. He also habituated himself 'to temperance and exercise, which hardened the constitution to such a pitch that neither wet nor cold had any bad effect' upon him. As a result, he reported, his 'health, strength, and agility' improved.[38] He was motivated by medical advice, although the experience of a failing body and fear of permanent illness played no small part; ultimately, Bewick located his masculine identity in his bodily moderation. Dietary restriction continued to be understood to dampen the passions, thereby facilitating self-improvement. A Manchester man wrote in the *Vegetarian Advocate* in 1848 that his 'self-denial' in eating meat increased his health and wealth, improving him morally, intellectually, and physically.[39] All were features that demonstrated ideal masculinity, as well as creating a hard, self-mastered body.

Roy Porter observes that if the 'Christian distrust of the flesh was undermined' by the end of the eighteenth century, it was 'reborn in the guise of fashion's horror at excessive ponderousness, especially when associated with aging and decline'.[40] Porter's use of 'horror' captures the emotional freight of descriptions of bodies deemed unacceptable and thus unmanly. An account of Jack Broughton's last fight in 1750, in *The Licensed Victuallers' Mirror* (1888), is an excellent example. Describing the crowd, the author notes that present in the highest-priced seats 'was Broughton's old patron, the Duke of Cumberland – no longer the stalwart, handsome, athletic youth, whose portrait adorned our last chapter, but grown gross and corpulent, coarse in features and in manners – the most inveterate gambler, and the most reckless roué of his day'. Frederick, Prince of Wales, his brother, accompanied him: 'a far bigger blackguard in every respect, and now rapidly nearing his end, gouty, dropsical, obese'.[41] These visceral descriptions of the damage done to young athletic bodies by excess were intended to stir revulsion and disgust for unattractive male bodies marked as physically and morally diseased. Moreover, they were rendered more loathsome by contrast with those of Broughton and his opponent John Slack, both ideals of burly, muscular manliness.

As the nineteenth century wore on, appetite became a useful means to differentiate supposedly stoical, self-denying, middle-class masculinity from that of both self-indulgent aristocrats and undiscriminating, impulsive working men.[42] Aristocrats were portrayed in fiction, for example, as corpulent gourmands who overindulged in foreign foodstuffs, signalling lack of will.[43] As Joanne Parsons comments of Count Fosco, in Wilkie Collins' *Woman in White* (1860), his fat 'exists as a visible symbol of lack of gastronomic control and therefore tends to act as an indicator of other undesirable traits': in his case effeminacy and villainy.[44] Ignoring the reality of poverty and restricted access to food, the middle classes conceptualised the working classes as possessing animalistic and brutish cravings and appetites.[45] In middle-class reforming logic, the working classes only needed to curb their hunger for sensual gratification in order to satisfy their dietary needs. Men's emotionalised bodies were key in such instances of class 'othering', with both aristocratic and poor men demonstrating voracious hunger that was deemed either revolting or bestial.

The rhetoric directed at working-class men, which demanded their self-control over other habits, also deployed emotionalised bodies. Thus, in 'The Smoker', in the *Children's Treasury and Advocate of the Homeless and Destitute* of 1879, a young brisk, cheerful middle-class man confronts 'Bob Speaker, as he sits idly smoking on the doorstep', asking him if he has nothing to do. Bob confirms that he has potatoes to plant and digging to do, but needs a rest. His interlocutor replies 'A great strong fellow like you, I'm ashamed of you! I see you've an enemy very near you taking away all your energy.' He then explains to Bob,

> if you had never begun smoking you would have had a good bit more money, a good bit more manliness, a good bit more health, and you would have given a good bit less suffering to other people. Throw away your pipe and be a man, and seek to live a clean, pure life.[46]

For Baden-Powell, smoking damaged men's senses and faculties. He warned boy scouts that it weakened men's eye-sight, rendered them shaky and nervous, spoiled their ability to smell, and through the light and odour of tobacco, gave them away to the (imagined) enemy.[47] The manipulation of fear to effect restraint could be taken to ludicrous lengths. In the 1855 *British Workman's* tale, 'Fire! Fire! Or a Costly Pipe', a cautionary account of a man employed in a printing works unfolds. 'Like too many working men', he would not give up his smoke after his meal. Lighting his tobacco, he threw the burning match into what he thought was a pot of water. It turned out to be camphor, and though he escaped with his life, his lack of self-control meant that the works and surrounding buildings were burnt down, and 2,000 people lost their jobs.[48]

The temperance movement similarly harnessed emotionalised male bodies to their ends. There had been concerns about the dangerous effects of certain alcoholic beverages, especially spirits, throughout the eighteenth century, accompanied by calls for moderation. From the 1830s, the non-denominational temperance movement advocated complete abstinence, or teetotalism.[49] John Coakley Lettsom's 'Moral and Physical Thermometer', 1797 (Figure 2.1), illustrates the shift in emphasis. He includes small beer in the category 'Temperance', along with milk and water, all of which produced good health, wealth, and morals. In the same category are wine, cider, porter, and strong beer; less wholesome, but, if taken moderately at meals, still associated with cheerfulness, strength, and nourishment. The category of 'Intemperance' links spirits to various vices, diseases, and punishments, which illustrate how the consumption of spirits caused progressive deterioration and eventually death. These dire eventualities were not associated with specific types of people. Increasingly, however, warnings of the risks of drunkenness were represented through the bodily and material decline of the respectable working-class family man.[50] In 1855, the *British Workman* published 'The Loaf Lecture', which contrasts the differences wrought by intoxicating drink on two working men who earned the same wages. The abstainer possesses a neat and comfortable house, is respectably dressed, and has wholesome food. The drinker 'occupies one miserable room, a two-pair back; not twenty shillings' worth of furniture in the place; 'a shabby, dirty-looking fellow, who keeps his wife and little ones in rags, and doesn't perhaps see a decent joint of meat on his table once a month'. The accompanying illustration depicts the drunkard's badly kempt hair, worn-out clothing, bare ankles, and badly shod feet. He sits, slumped, while the teetotal stands erect, in decent jacket and trousers, good boots, waistcoat, and necktie.[51] These tropes were practically ubiquitous, decorating ceramics and processions. In 1862, for instance, the Preston Temperance Society marched through the streets at the Preston Guild Jubilee with the same visual devices on their banners.[52] While prompting admiration for the temperate and revulsion for the intemperate, the emotionalised bodies deployed also conveyed lessons about manliness and unmanliness.

One of the most popular examples was George Cruikshank's 1847 series *The Bottle*, which sold 100,000 copies and was seen by many since

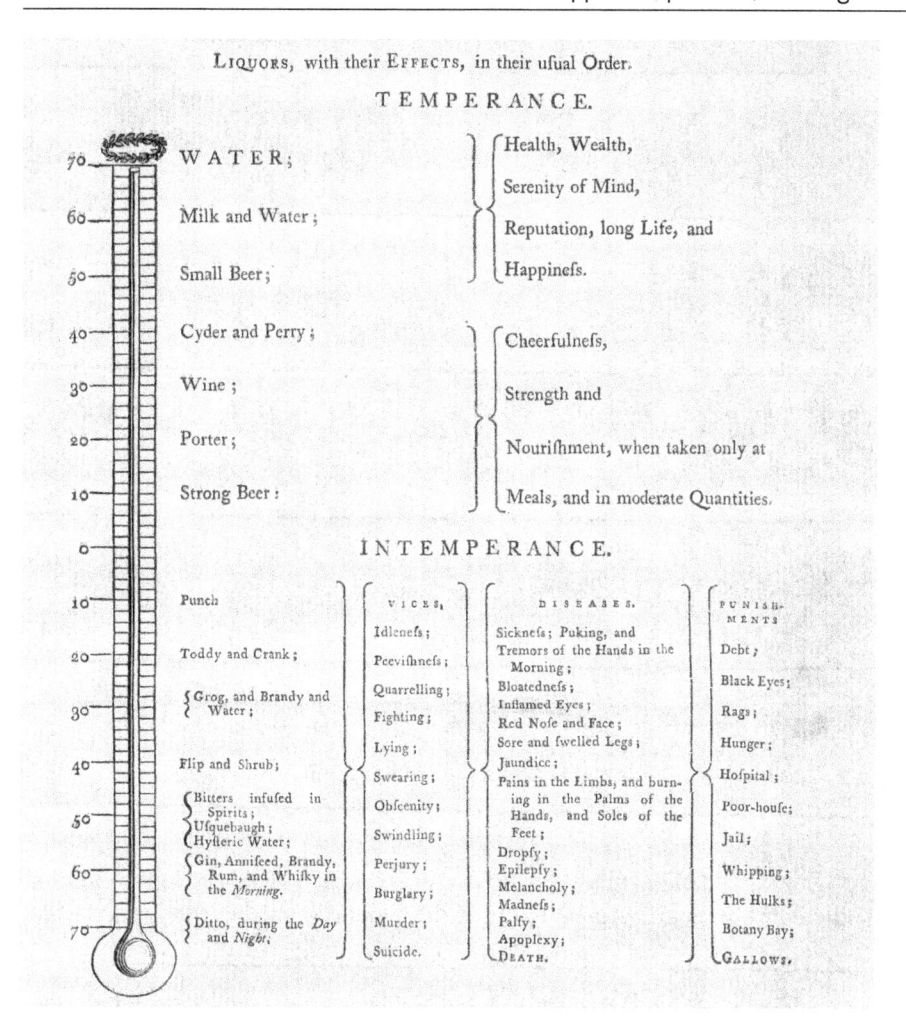

```
       Liquors, with their Effects, in their usual Order.
                        TEMPERANCE.

70  WATER;                        ⎫  ⎧ Health, Wealth,
                                  ⎪  ⎪
60  Milk and Water;               ⎪  ⎨ Serenity of Mind,
                                  ⎬  ⎪ Reputation, long Life, and
50  Small Beer;                   ⎪  ⎩ Happiness.
                                  ⎭
40  Cyder and Perry;              ⎫  ⎧ Cheerfulness,
                                  ⎪  ⎪
30  Wine;                         ⎪  ⎨ Strength and
                                  ⎬  ⎪
20  Porter;                       ⎪  ⎪ Nourishment, when taken only at
                                  ⎭  ⎩
10  Strong Beer:                     Meals, and in moderate Quantities.

0                      INTEMPERANCE.

10  Punch              ⎫ VICES,      DISEASES.              PUNISH-
                       ⎪                                    MENTS
                       ⎪ Idleness;   Sickness; Puking, and
20  Toddy and Crank;   ⎪ Peevishness; Tremors of the Hands in the   Debt;
                       ⎪             Morning;
   ⎰ Grog, and Brandy  ⎪ Quarrelling;  Bloatedness;                 Black Eyes;
30 ⎱   and Water;      ⎪              Inflamed Eyes;
                       ⎪ Fighting;   Red Nose and Face;             Rags;
40  Flip and Shrub;    ⎬              Sore and swelled Legs;        Hunger;
                       ⎪ Lying;      Jaundice;
   ⎧ Bitters infused in⎪ Swearing;   Pains in the Limbs, and burn-  Hospital;
50 ⎨   Spirits;        ⎪ Obscenity;  ing in the Palms of the
   ⎩ Usquebaugh;       ⎪              Hands, and Soles of the       Poor-house;
     Hysteric Water;   ⎪ Swindling;  Feet;                          Jail;
   ⎧ Gin, Anniseed, Bran-⎪            Dropsy;
60 ⎨   dy, Rum, and Whisky⎪ Perjury;   Epilepsy;                     Whipping;
   ⎩   in the Morning. ⎪ Burglary;   Melancholy;
                       ⎪              Madness;                      The Hulks;
   ⎰ Ditto, during the ⎪ Murder;     Palsy;
70 ⎱   Day and Night;  ⎪              Apoplexy;                     Botany Bay;
                       ⎭ Suicide.    DEATH.                         GALLOWS.
```

2.1 'Moral and Physical Thermometer', in John Coakley Lettsom, *Hints Designed to Promote Beneficence, Temperance, and Medical Science*, vol. 1 (1797).

it was marched in the streets on temperance banners, displayed in shop windows, projected in magic lantern 'dissolving view' performances, and transferred onto decorative ceramics, such as wall plaques, plates, and teapots.[53] Unappealing uncontrolled bodies that evoke revulsion and terrors are palpable throughout the series. In the first plate a man introduces alcohol to his comfortable home and family. It is perhaps Christmas, since a garland decorates the door of a well-stocked pantry. The room is replete with further signs of a manly ability to provide: food on the table, a grandfather clock, a hearth with a mantelpiece above displaying portraits, figurines, and a miniature cottage. The family are well dressed, the two smallest children play at their own stool, a book beside them; even the

2.2 *A Drunken Man Sits at Home with his Family who Must Sell Clothes to Pay for his Habit*, etching by G. Cruikshank (1847), after himself.

cat is well fed. The man is upright and healthy, if worryingly ebullient, indicated by his arm gesticulating wildly, hand grasping the bottle. In the plates that follow, he is discharged from his job for drunkenness and the family pawn their clothing to buy alcohol. Next, he slumps in his chair, body slouching, hands in pocket, hat tilting on his head, half asleep with his pipe gripped in his teeth; further signs of the associated vices of indolence and smoking. The room is cold, the ornaments broken, there is no food, the cat is emaciated, and the children lack playthings (Figure 2.2). Thereafter, the bailiffs remove the remaining furniture, and the furniture of death replaces domestic comforts since the youngest child has died and is laid out in a tiny coffin. By plate six, the husband is transformed into a wife-beating brute: wild-eyed, grimacing, hair disarrayed. Next, we see that he has murdered his wife with the alcohol bottle: the police and neighbours enter the bare room, now a crime scene. *The Bottle*'s final series of plates graphically depict the consequences of excessive alcohol consumption for men's bodies and minds, with the once upright husband and father now a 'hopeless maniac' in a cell, hair torn from his shrivelled face and body, arms grasping his sides. The children do not escape this as they mature, reduced to vice via the gin palace and beer shop; the prostitute daughter dead by her own hand, the criminal son transported for robbery.⁵⁴

Stories for children ran on similar lines. In 'The Unpleasant Passenger' by Horace Lashbroke in *Every Boy's Annual*, Uncle Tom, captain of a merchantman, tells his nephew the story of an 'adventure' on his ship as it sailed home from Melbourne. Its 'hero', Silas Wording, 'was a dark, strong-built man' in his late thirties. Uncle Tom thought him handsome, although 'the charm his face would otherwise have possessed' was marred by 'the wildness visible in the expression of his eyes'. Tom speculates, 'Had I seen him indulging largely in wine or spirits, I should naturally have concluded that the origin of his behavior was an over-indulgence in these potent luxuries.' He is correct, for Silas eventually admits that he has 'been going the whole hog lately – half-killing' himself. Silas is thus presented as weakened and subordinated by his lack of self-control. He eventually throws himself into the sea and drowns. Tom tells his nephews that he discovered, some months later, that the 'unpleasant passenger' had murdered his partner at 'Owen's Diggings' and absconded with their joint fortune.⁵⁵ The lesson was clear for boys: the failure to master oneself led to greed and intemperance, then murder and suicide.

Adult men were instructed using the same rhetoric of fear rooted in bodies. In 'Death on the Rail', a didactic *British Workman* tale (1855), a drunk twenty-four-year-old farm servant headed home from the tavern by walking along the railway line. '[T]oo stupefied with drink to keep on the right side of the rails', he is struck by a train. A graphic account of the state of his body follows; the engine driver finds to his horror that 'a portion of a man's body [was] stuck to one of the carriage wheels', while those who collect the 'mangled remains of the poor inebriate' found his 'head was cut off as if by a knife – his heart was laid in another direction – while other portions of his body were strewed on both sides of the rail'.⁵⁶ This 'victim to the sin of intemperance' was dismembered for his lack of self-control. In an 1890 article aimed at sailors to persuade them to give up alcohol, Agnes Weston similarly deployed corporeality and the feelings it stirred, expostulating that 'the fine, manly, stalwart form of a man-o'-war's man reeling up the street, all his manliness gone, and the kindly, pleasant-spoken fellow turned either into a drivelling idiot or a rough swearing bully, is a spectacle sad enough to make men and angels weep'.⁵⁷

The physical characteristics of the drunken male body often evoked the corporeal inadequacies of men who manifested other failures of will. In 'Penny Puffs; or the £90', in the *British Workman*, 1856, a labouring man is informed to his amazement that he has spent £90 in a lifetime on tobacco. The illustration of his face demonstrates a crudeness of feature similar to the drunkard in the 1855 *Loss! Gain!* (Figure 2.3) in the same periodical.⁵⁸ Both depict what Sharrona Pearl describes as 'caricature physiognomy', their simian features indicating that intemperate bodies

2.3 *Loss! Gain!*, British Workman 7 (1855), p. 28.

were subject to racial degeneration.[59] This was about the construction of difference, usually deployed against Irish, Jewish, and black people, but which also included a bodily othering of white working-class men to differentiate manliness from unmanliness.[60] In 'Our Gin-Shops', published in the *British Workman* in 1855, the reader is asked to look at the men standing at the counter, to witness the:

> pale-faced, pallid-looking gin-drinker; see the eyes large and sunk deep in the sockets, as with his fingers, like the claws of an unclean bird .... It is horrible to look at him. And yet that is a man! See that other standing; the dull waters of disease stagnant in his eye – sensuality seated upon his cracked, swollen, parched lip; see him gibbering in all the idiocy of drunkenness. That is a man![61]

The repeated incredulous refrain 'that is a man!' takes its power from the disjuncture between the drunkard's dirty, ill, avian body and the ideal manly body described in Chapter 1.

The descriptions of the gin-drinkers' bodies are almost identical to those of masturbators, whose self-indulgence was seen as a consequence and cause of other forms of sensuality and wayward appetites.[62] Generally, those who succumbed to the 'secret vice' were considered to be pale, weak, and nervous.[63] In 1767 John Wesley published *Thoughts on the Sin of Onan, Chiefly Extracted from a Late Writer*, observing that masturbators:

> frequently contract the infirmities of old age. They become pale, effeminate, dull, inactive; they lose their Appetite, weaken their sight, their memory, their understanding, and contract all the disorders attending weak nerves. Many bring on thereby a general weakness, and paralytic disorders of all kinds: Yea, lethargies, epilepsies, madness, blindness, convulsions, dropsies, and the most painful of all gouts.[64]

Just over a century later, Robert Ritchie stated that the asylum patient whose insanity was caused by masturbation was marked out by his pale colouring, emaciated slouching frame, and flaccid muscles.[65] In 1876, R. V. Pierce detailed the degeneration that ensued from 'abuse of the sexual organs': sunken eyes, bloated and pale face, rank body odour, then, increasingly, weakness in legs, trembling hands, melancholy, and suicidal thoughts.[66] All these bodily incapacities and inadequacies stirred fear and deployed disgust to strengthen their didactic power.

The same fears can be read in the condition of spermatorrhea, which was of particular concern from the 1830s to the 1870s.[67] As Ellen Bayuk Rosenman remarks, spermatorrhea literature 'provides an encyclopedic rendering of non-normative masculinity', since all its traits were associated with lack of male control over bodies and emotions.[68] Sellers of patent medicine for the condition, for example, advertised in the press using an emotive language of physical decline. In 1843, *The Age* contained a review of the book *Manly Vigour: A Popular Inquiry into the Concealed Causes of Premature Decline*. Offered more as an advert than a critical review, it stated that the book showed that 'fond parents' mistakenly ascribe their youthful offspring's 'attenuation of the frame, palpitation of the heart, derangement of the nervous system, cough, indigestion, and a train of symptoms' to 'consumption or general decay'. Instead, they should be alert to the consequences of the 'alluring and pernicious practice, destruction of mind and body'.⁶⁹ Bodily disgust and the manipulation of emotions were critical in this process. In R. and L. Perry's *The Silent Friend* (1847), a head-and-shoulder portrait of the progress of the masturbator contrasts his handsome face 'before' his habit took hold with his drooling counterpart 'after', whose tongue protrudes from his mouth.⁷⁰ Dr Henery's *Vital Hints on Health and Strength, and their Dependence on the State of the Generative Organization*, in the 1860s, explained the emotions consequent upon masturbation: 'secret misery, disgust and despair'.⁷¹ The solution to avoiding masturbation was the same as building manliness: restricted diet, bodily exercise, outdoor living, cold baths, healthy eating, and prayer.⁷²

As these examples indicate, the unmanly man's ultimate fate was disease and insanity. Medical texts, temperance advocates, and popular culture linked excessive appetites with several diseases by the nineteenth century. A pathological condition categorised as 'abulia', seen as a diminishment of motivation and disorder of the will, was identified in the mid-nineteenth century, for example. Obese men were considered to suffer from it; deemed unable to overcome their desire to consume excessively.⁷³ Intemperance, as we have seen, along with spermatorrhea, was popularly understood to send men mad.⁷⁴ Alienists also saw men's strength and constitution as broken down by intemperance, their muscles rendered flaccid, and their bodies subject to impotency, trembling, and mental derangement.⁷⁵ William Acton declared in the fourth edition (1867) of his *The Functions and Disorders of the Reproductive Organs*: 'That insanity is a consequence of this habit [masturbation], is now beyond doubt.'⁷⁶ All excesses of appetites and emotions were included in the causes that medical writers identified as leading to insanity.⁷⁷ In 1813, Samuel Tuke, for instance, noted that 'Intemperance is another very prevalent, and less ambiguous cause of insanity.'⁷⁸ It was still considered one of the 'physical' causes of insanity in the second half of the nineteenth century, along with emotional causes – such as mental worry, domestic trouble (including bereavement), religious excitement, and fright and nervous shock – and adverse circumstances like disappointment in business and love affairs.⁷⁹

Restoring the capacity to master one's appetites and passions was seen as an aid to recovery.⁸⁰ One aspect of moral therapy, initially a lay treatment influenced by continental models, for example, was inculcating self-control to enable recovery. As Samuel Tuke remarked: 'most insane persons, have a considerable degree of self command; and ... the employment and cultivation of this remaining power, is found to be attended with the most salutary effects'.⁸¹ Louis Charland describes this treatment as 'ultimately a therapy of the passions. It worked on the passions, through the passions.'⁸² Moral treatment of the insane was adopted by the medical superintendents of new county pauper asylums from the mid-century, though, by the latter part of the century, 'moral management' was in the ascendant in large institutions.⁸³ Even so, emphasis was still placed on patients' own responsibility to regulate their behaviour and to conform to the routines and bureaucratic rules that replaced more individualised treatment.[84]

Men's asylum case notes illustrate the importance that men and their families placed on intemperance and lack of self-control as a cause of insanity. Several examples follow, based on a sample of case notes (from the 1850s, 1870s, and 1880s) of male patients admitted to Colney Hatch, the second pauper lunatic asylum for the County of Middlesex, which opened at Friern Barnet in July 1851.[85] Some patients, for instance, used this vocabulary of intemperate lifestyle to explain their condition. Dwigne Leopold self-reported in 1851:

> that when on his way from Ireland to visit France, passing through London he was mixed up with very bad company – and became intemperate – his brain was attacked and he became maniacal – after passing through many deprivations and much sorrow he found himself in the Insane Ward of the Workhouse.[86]

Similarly, in 1854 Thomas West 'states that he is a native of Warwick and has been 17 months in London and that he has succumbed to the vices and temptations of the metropolis'.[87]

Patients' families similarly identified failure to control passions as a significant factor in the men's downfall. When Lewis Aaron was admitted 22 August 1851, aged thirty-five, a married clothes salesman, he was recorded as:

> A Jew with very marked features of that persuasion. He has been married about two years previous to which time he had a very Debauched life which evidently has caused the maniacal attack that he at present labours under. He has had two or three Epileptic Fits. His health is good and he affirms there only to have been fits of passion over which he had no control. His wife says that his passion and tempers are so ungovernable that it is impossible to live with him. His conversation is rational, though excessive and he complains bitterly of the confinement.[88]

Bernard Fitzpatrick, aged fifty, married, formerly a soldier and more recently a hawker, was admitted for a third time to Colney Hatch in June 1854, having been discharged as recovered in February that year. He had served in the army from 1827 until he was pensioned out in 1839, having succumbed to yellow fever in the West Indies. Although this disease was identified as causing his insanity, his questionable lifestyle and problematic self-restraint were recorded as exacerbating the problems. Since the attack of fever he had been prone to insanity, 'which has been excited by drinking beer'. The information about his service and drinking was added in 1855 and further details were reported by his wife and recorded in the case notes.[89] The failure in both Aaron and Fitzpatrick to restrain passions was related to their previously debauched or intemperate lives, and as the institution's comments indicate, this was linked to their respective Jewish and Irish ethnicities. When the cause of insanity was not completely obvious, the medical officer would gesture to intemperance. James Fidler was recorded in 1854 as suffering from: 'Recurrent attack, of about 6 weeks duration – cause unknown – (probably intemperance)'; while of Charles Langley it was said: 'There is a vagueness and difficulty about him which is suggestive of a fear of his having led a very irregular life.'[90]

Mastering one's appetites and vices was viewed as the key to recovery. The notes recording the admission, recovery, and discharge of John Black were framed thus. A married, thirty-seven-year-old tailor, he was admitted on 8 May 1886. The 'supposed cause' was recorded 'Not Known', and the facts indicating insanity were that he was suicidal and melancholic, due to his delusion that he was full of devils. According to the observations that day, he was a well-nourished middle-aged man with brown hair and beard. Next, however, the medical officer noted, 'his appearance is suggestive of intemperance, and he acknowledges that he drinks too much'. This was the cause of insanity that was taken forward, with 'Drink' added in red ink as a cause to the column 'Not Known'. The next observation dates from 12 May, where John is recorded as admitting that he had drunk too much whisky for some time. His bodily appearance was now read through the lens of his intemperance: 'a bearded and hairy faced … with somewhat muddy complexion and frowzy eye'. On 20 May, his wife's statement that he had taken 'too much whiskey and beer for weeks before his admission' was added. Black's trajectory to recovery was signified by his return to domestic attachments. His bodily and emotional restoration, presumably by being denied alcohol, was indicated by a sequence of entries, where he was sleeping and eating well, laughing at the notion of devils, and writing affectionate letters home to his wife. He was discharged recovered on 18 June.[91]

The references to patients' masturbation in Colney Hatch used the same language of bodies damaged by men succumbing to bad habits. The account of James Fitzgerald, for example, in 1851, states:

> His friends say that until seven years since he was a sharp active lad of regular habits – intelligent and very respectable – about that time it was noticed that he absented himself shutting himself in his room and gave way to the habits of masturbator under which evil practices his mind seemed entirely to break down.[92]

This clearly presaged Ritchie's 'premonitory symptoms' of the typical masturbatory inmate in the insane asylum, in which the youth gradually altered from being 'quiet and studious', of good behaviour and abilities, to an isolated, slovenly, apathetic, unmanageable character.[93] Robert Brealey, admitted 5 December 1872, was twenty-three years old, single, a compositor, and recorded as never before having been in an asylum. The

'Observations as to state of patient' noted: 'A pale young man with sandy hair, and a countenance of dazed and bewildered expression. He has spots of acne on the face, and has the heavy leaden look of a masturbator.' This was linked to Brealey's other failures. The notes also recorded that his 'Father says that he was discharged from the artillery for some breach of discipline (probably striking an officer) and sentenced to nine months imprisonment … He says that his son was always well behaved, as a lad, and was considered fairly intelligent at school.'[94]

Non-conforming bodies, frequently those of white working-class men, as well as those ethnically and racially marginalised, were marked out as uncontrolled, ugly, and, consequently, disgusting. This was culturally useful in making unmanliness frightening, unappealing, and to be avoided. For most men, therefore, the risks to manliness caused by excessive eating, drinking, smoking, and sexual activity, or simply indulging in pleasurable bodily habits instead of rigorous self-mastery, were very visible and visceral. This was compounded by the understanding that ill-health and insanity were caused by unrestrained appetites and emotions. As such, the penalties for unmanliness were shockingly real, endangering a man's place in his family and community, and the root of the dissolution of self.

The paradoxes of unmanliness and vulnerable bodies

This picture of unmanliness, rooted in abject bodies, must, however, be complicated in several ways. First, negative emotions were not always deployed in directives to be temperate. Working-class men's own invocations to their peers to avoid alcohol used a very different emotional register. An excellent example is found in the Manchester Oddfellows lectures, dated 1834.[95] Skilled working men joined such friendly societies to protect themselves and their families against illness, accidents, and death. The Oddfellows motto was 'Friendship, Love and Truth', symbolised by the emblem of a heart on an open hand.[96] In 1834, the Independent Order of Oddfellows Manchester Unity rewrote their ritual practices to avoid being categorised as an illegal society, rather than a benefit society.[97] One of the 'Duties of Odd Fellowship' was to 'Be honest, loving and temperate'. Members were advised to work diligently at an occupation to provide 'decent' things and help relieve the distress of others, fellow brethren in particular; to be honest to neighbours; and to act candidly. Although they shared a broader conviction that temperance was beneficial and achieved through self-will, they often deployed positive rather than negative emotions to make their case. The lectures advised:

> be temperate in the enjoyment of all those good things Providence may have favoured you with in this life. Be temperate in the exercise of all the powers and passions of the body and mind, that you hurt not the circumstances, or the feelings of any man, but more especially of a brother.[98]

Here the benefits of temperance were delivered with words like 'enjoyment' and through feelings of care and kindness. Personal dignity and agency were identified as the outcome:

> Be temperate in the exercise of any power, right, prerogative, or influence you may possess, either in common life, civil society, or more especially in the affairs of our honourable Order. Be also temperate in forming your opinion, in expressing your thoughts, and in attempting to obtain your wishes.[99]

Bodies were still critical in these recommendations for self-control, but they were not used to elicit disgust. The regulations listed the duties of 'The First Degree or White', which newly initiated brothers received on the first lecture night. Taking the form of questions and answers, a brother was informed that his duties were: 'a strict adherence to temperance, sobriety, and chastity'. Temperance was defined as a 'well-regulated employment of our faculties, which prevents our ever exceeding in our pleasures the end of nature'. Critically, the response to 'Why do our laws enjoin temperance?' is:

> Because it has a powerful ascendancy over us; it produces peace of mind and health of body, and teaches us to delight in combatting our passions, and glory in conquering our evil habits; thus, we grow old, free from sickness, and enjoy, with good humour, the comforts which fortune or industry has procured for us.[100]

Here is a thoroughly benign mirror image of the frightening, repulsive emotionalised bodies employed elsewhere. Working men define the positive aspects of controlling their appetites: good health, long life, savings; all imagined through delight, glory, good humour, and comforts.

When describing the physical decline of the drunkard, these authors still returned to the body to make their moral lesson more powerful. They denounced drunkenness as:

> the vilest and most pernicious of vices. The drunkard, deprived of the sense and reason given him by God, profanes the gift of Divinity, and lowers himself to the condition of a brute: incapable of directing his steps, he totters and falls, as in a fit; he wounds himself and endangers his own life; his weakness, in this state, renders him the plaything and scorn of all around him; he contracts ruinous engagements; neglects the management of his affairs; fills his house with trouble; and concludes by a premature death; or, when old age comes on, he is comfortless, diseased and deserted.[101]

This drunkard, like the middle-class reformers' version, is subjected to moral judgement, since in being reduced by alcohol to a 'brute' he also turns his face against God. Arguably, though, his body is not so revolting. Instead, it is diminished by being vulnerable and pathetic. The words selected for his fall, such as wounds, weakness, plaything, comfortless, and deserted, and his 'tottering' gait, prompt a degree of pity, a sentiment which is singularly absent in the cultural accounts in the section

'Unrestrained appetites and passions'. Instead, the joys and dignity of temperance are most prominent. Thus, the book states that the charitable man is blessed 'with that peace of mind which the profligate and abandoned can never enjoy .... Matured in his manners he is respected by all ranks: the rich esteem him for his manly actions, and the poor bless him for his charities.'[102] It is surely no coincidence that the unrestrained, unmanly working-class body was less a prompt for disgust when it was deployed by the working classes themselves. Instead they used morals and fraternity to achieve their ends.

Furthermore, the manly, unmanly dichotomy does not entirely fit within a typical binary formulation of identity, wherein, as Chris Mounsey puts it, 'the dominant "we" of a culture defines itself negatively as "not you"'; 'so white against non-white; upper classes against working classes; men against women; heterosexual against homosexual; and able-bodied against disabled'.[103] For, even as one type of imagined man was pitted against another, the distinctions between them were not that clear-cut. Richard Stott's study of 'jolly fellowship' in America argues that men's fighting, drinking, gaming, and joking were seen as a natural part of manhood at the outset of the nineteenth century but increasingly marginalised from the mid-century, due to evangelicalism, temperance, and ideas of respectability. Jolly fellowship was resilient, but marginalised.[104] In Britain, in contrast, such a successive chronology of behaviour is less apparent. Unmanliness, in the form of carnal and sensual appetites, was considered man's base level, with debauchery and intemperance understood as natural behaviours of the male body and temperament rather than a lack or deficiency. As such, many of these appetites could also be associated with qualities deemed masculine in certain situations, locations, and social classes, rooted, as they were, in male conviviality and notions of virility.[105]

Eighteenth-century middling and genteel men, for example, could enjoy bawdy and lewd behaviour in the company of close male friends. Kate Davison identifies this as legitimised incivility, not anti-civilised behaviour, because it occurred in private homosocial spaces and places.[106] Regular alcohol drinking was part of everyday life for many and was bound up with ideas of nutrition and male strength: a culture of drinking that the temperance movement recognised and sought to counter. For example, the first issue of the *British Workman* had a teetotal working man explain to his drunkard counterpart the fallacy of the notion that 'strong ale made men strong' because it had 'more nourishment and strength'.[107] Tobacco is a particularly paradoxical case in point. It was powerfully associated with male companionableness and with masculinity in general. While women smoked pipes in the eighteenth century, it was increasingly seen as a male habit that evoked contemplation and, in the nineteenth century, a certain kind of mature virility.[108] It was associated favourably with soldiers' fortitude, for example. In 1863, in '"Lucknow" Kavanagh and the Victoria Cross' in the *Boy's Own Magazine*, the author states, 'We have heard many a soldier say that he would rather go without his dinner than his pipe' to advertise the men's fortitude during the siege of the garrison.[109] Given that some examples of masculine identities were predicated upon the very appetites that manliness shunned, it is no wonder that those who sought to inculcate manly behaviour more widely did so through profoundly emotionalised bodies.

Male sexuality had similar ambivalences.[110] There is evidence that masturbation might have been encouraged in youths as a stage of sexual development and preparation for virile manhood. Some male youths, for example, learned to masturbate from their peers as a precursor to learning to have sex with women.[111] Lesley Hall found evidence of men explaining in the early twentieth century that they had been told that it 'will make a man of you', not that it was harmful.[112] The proprietary medicines that were advertised to restore manly vigour in men, and the literature offering advice on tackling spermatorrhea, were similarly contradictory. The middle-class victims who were targeted in this medical and moral pathologisation of sexuality were aware of the sexual double standard in their favour. They were immersed in a language of manhood that alluded constantly to sexual virility (hardness, firmness, erectness). Yet they were required to exert enormous self-control over any erotic pleasures. Indeed, Rosenman describes spermatorrhea literature as reflecting this 'impasse of opportunity and punishment'.[113] Perhaps most confusing for those men who sought to tackle their sexual 'problems' was that the literature and patent medicines deployed case studies claiming to restore men to sexual potency.[114] For example, press adverts for the 'Cordial Balm of Rakasiri' in the 1820s claimed to cure disorders brought on 'by dissipation in Youth, and a gross violation of those rules which prudence dictates for health'.[115] An 1861 advert for Perry's 'Cordial Balm of Syriacumf', in *Bell's Life* announced that it was 'Established nearly a century, and known throughout the world as the greatest regenerator: a never-failing remedy for the loss of manly power, produced by early indiscretions of any other causes'.[116] Furthermore, the review of a patent medicine in 1842, explained that while 'MANLY VIGOUR temporarily impaired, and mental and physical emasculation', were produced 'by uncontrolled indulgence of the passions', reassured sufferers that they would be restored to 'the vigour of health and moral courage'.[117]

Even the intemperate or uncontrolled man who became insane was not simply the antithesis of ideal manliness. This is demonstrated in the ambivalent views of men who displayed the symptoms of General Paralysis of the Insane (GPI) in the second half of the nineteenth century. Jennifer Wallis remarks that its features of bodily atrophy and flaccidness denoted men as the antithesis of idealised masculinity, since these implied lives of apathy, laziness, and cowardice, in contrast to the ideals of bodily hardness and self-control.[118] Juliet Hurn, nonetheless, reveals the variety of alienists' views as to the type of masculinity which they associated with male sufferers. Some doctors discerned 'admirable aspects' within GPI sufferers, because they understood it as a disease of middle-class men who had been struck down when successful, having previously 'lived hard'. Thus it betokened former virility, as well as energy, ambition, and strength; indeed a few alienists argued that sexual excess was a symptom rather than a cause.[119] As this indicates, GPI was suspected to be linked to sexual behaviour, particularly too active a sexual life and alcoholic excess.[120] By the turn of the century, however, it was increasingly associated with syphilis and defined as a 'disease of civilisation', given its prevalence in cities.[121] British degenerationists increasingly saw GPI as moral deterioration leading to physical collapse, rather than due to ambition and business anxieties, with sufferers de-evolving to man's baser nature.[122]

A further way in which the account of unmanliness must be complicated is by considering those men who were unable to fully implement the bodily, mental, and emotional self-control necessary for manliness because their bodies were vulnerable through no fault their own: through youth, old age, disability, and ill-health. Stuart Hogarth's term 'vulnerable' can be adapted to describe such bodies. In his analysis of plebeian men's bodies, he explains that the 'vulnerable plebeian body ... was not entirely powerless or lacking in agency, but ... its progress through life was slowed by the physical accretion of multiple assaults on its physical integrity'.[123] Bodies in these life phases were less amenable to being attached to moral values. There is evidence, for example, that some of these traits were partially tolerated in youths, where they were seen as part of a passing phase before maturity was reached.[124] The remainder of this chapter suggests that expectations for such men could be adjusted, since their future potential and past acts were taken into consideration as context. In some cases, due to bodily vulnerabilities, more leeway was given in terms of the moral evaluation of behaviour. Critically, their bodies were not so likely to be labelled as disgusting.

In the eighteenth century, physical impairment was understood as part of life, a feature of human frailty to which all would eventually succumb.[125] Disabled and deformed bodies were, moreover, not always aligned with the 'moralization of aesthetics', since not all eighteenth-century writers followed the model that the physically deformed must be morally deficient. Paul Kelleher argues that the moral philosopher Lord Shaftesbury, for example, used bodily deformity to 'think with', since beauty, truth, and virtue were considered so intertwined; nonetheless, he did not see what we describe as disability as synonymous with moral deformity.[126] Stuart Hogarth shows that in the early nineteenth century, some plebeian men who encountered a period of ill-health used it to conform to existing ideas of manliness, where their sickness provided an opportunity for self-improvement, typically through education. Others constructed an alternative form of manliness. Joseph Gutteridge (1816–1899) and James Powell (born 1830), for example, who both suffered from lifelong chronic conditions, positioned themselves in opposition to 'the rougher elements of plebeian culture (drinking and fighting), signalling their sense of superiority in terms of a more refined sensibility'.[127] These men celebrated the qualities that made them different, namely their nerves and weaker bodies, to define something almost akin to a Romantic manliness.[128]

Bodies that were not whole did not necessarily map onto unmanliness either, despite an idealisation of physical harmony and perfection, the growing discomfort with visible signs of physical impairment, and the urge to 'normalise' bodily 'defects'.[129] Veteran sailors and soldiers who wore crude prosthetic stumps on arms or legs, for example, could be accorded manly status. In popular culture, as work on the representations of veterans indicates, stumps, crutches, and peg legs resulting from battle injuries indicated personal valour and national glory.[130] In *Bell's Life*, 1830, in a light-hearted account of the Chelsea Pensioners in 'Sketches of a Professional Character', the author noted that 'a round half-dozen of crippled heroes of the same order as himself joined us in the devout blessing, their stumps and crutches beating a round of approbation, not unlike an ill-fired "feu de joie" on a commemoration day'.[131] Here the prosthetics themselves were associated with military fire. In 'Old Soldiers, and Old Sailors' in the *Ladies' Cabinet*, 1843, the author contrasts the stories veterans tell of the excitement, turmoil, terror, and passions of battle with their fragmented bodies, exclaiming,

> as you look at the crippled narrator of all this, – old, infirm, mutilated, 'curtailed of man's fair proportions', a mere piece of patch-work made up for the great part of cork, or common timber, – it requires some exercise of the imaginative faculty to bring it home to you, that this is the creature who has been an actor in these things.[132]

Nevertheless, this is exactly what injured veterans' 'patchwork' bodies did. Numbers of male amputees increased from the mid-nineteenth century, due to industrial accidents, improvements in surgical techniques, and developments in prosthetic technology.[133] As Erin O'Connor reveals, these 'fractions' of men, whose stumps were 'othered' and assigned female qualities, were re-masculinised by the artificial limbs that made them 'whole', mobile, and able to undertake productive labour.[134]

Life course was also important in assessing the capacity to attain manliness. Youth has long been recognised as a period of lack of control, when the juvenile male has not yet fully learned to master temptations and control or channel emotions. This was a feature of the rhetoric of spiritual conversion and criminality. In 1730, the Ordinary of Newgate described a typical tale of youthful bodily excesses, which, unresisted, were 'the first Step to destruction'. In it, the apprentice soon 'wearied of close Imployment, joyn'd himself to bad Company and stopt at no Extravagancies'. This bad company drank and caroused, fell 'a dancing, Singing, Squeaking and Crying out like so many Pigs and Geese; and often as drink comes in, with going out, they fall a fighting, beating and tearing one another'.[135] Such youthful indiscretions were associated with all social ranks. The Ordinary of Newgate in 1759 addressed: 'Ye giddy, headstrong youth of every rank, chiefly young mariners, in the vigour of vanity, or vice; who scarce ever think seriously, think on this!'[136] Without action, such young men would be 'cut down like flowers, by the scythe of an unmanly and shameful death!'[137]

As these warnings indicate, youths and young men were expected to make a physical and emotional journey to maturity. This was a trope of popular literature. 'The Divorce: A Tale, in Three Parts' in *The Ladies' Treasury*, 1861, tells of Richard Wilson and his wife Isabel, who had separated soon after marrying. It centres on their progress to self-knowledge. Richard's growth consists of mastering his emotions. When he glimpses his wife after not seeing her for a decade, a neighbour, not knowing his identity, recounts her history: 'I've heard said that her husband was a hot-headed, self-willed, young fellow, and no more fit to be married than to fly.' Five years later, a friend who has recently met Richard, tells Isabel that he seemed, 'as a man who had passed through years of discipline, and gained the mastery of himself'. Isabel reflects that when they were married they were both self-willed and hasty and their 'selfishness and passion' drove them asunder. Similarly, Richard explains to a friend that his marriage had failed because of 'pride, passion, and self-will'. Twenty years after they divorced they are reunited, having both, he says, been 'purified from the fire'.[138]

Emotional excess was thus more readily tolerated in youths, even young adults. For example, impulsiveness, which was to be avoided in adulthood, might be excused in the immature. 'Our Hero: A Tale of the Franco-English War Ninety Years Ago' by Agnes Giberne, in the *Girl's Own Paper*, 1898, is hagiography of Lieutenant-General John Moore (1761–1809), who was fatally wounded at the Battle of Corunna. At the high point of popular militarism in the late nineteenth century, Giberne makes over Moore into a model of manliness. His attractive body announces his valour: he is handsome, brave, and adored by his men. Pretty and charming in his youth, she explains that he beguiled 'the high and mighty' while accompanying his father, a Scottish physician and guardian of the Duke of Hamilton, on the latter's Grand Tour. She excuses his youthful emotional excesses, which led him to receive an accidental injury from the Duke's sword when playing, fight a boxing match with two French boys at Tuileries, and even nearly kill a servant girl because he was meddling with loaded pistols. As Giberne acknowledges, 'Although he early learnt self-control, he was as a child very impulsive and hasty-tempered and addicted to fighting.' Nonetheless, his impulsiveness was offset by his youth, his devotion to duty, and his eventual adoption of self-control. This 1898 biography even uses Moore to represent the prevalent moral values of the day. Thus, he is described in adulthood as a disciplinarian who enforced obedience, in 'an age when hard drinking was the fashion, he set his face like a flint against habits of intemperance', so that his regiment 'became widely known for its exceptional sobriety and dependableness'.[139]

Youth stimulated compassion where failure of will was evident. When twenty-six-year-old William Smith was admitted to Colney Hatch Lunatic Asylum for a third time, in 1851, he was recorded in the case book as a 'young man of pleasing appearance and open expression of countenance'. In some ways, this ameliorated and contextualised his mental health problem, which was identified as an inability to

> resist the impulse whether for good or evil – In the present case he was desirous of breaking some windows and although he acknowledged that it was absurd and wrong, the desire must be and was carried out. These impulsions are as occasional as they are sudden – He is in very good health.[140]

Even in the early twentieth century, sympathy was expressed about the expectations placed upon boys' capacity to learn the restraint demanded of adult men. In *At the Works* (1907), Lady Bell bemoaned the fate of boys taken from school in Middlesbrough by their parents at the age of thirteen, 'for no reason at all'. With nothing to do until he was sixteen, such a boy would run a few errands but mostly loaf around the streets. Yet, still, she observed,

> we are going to demand from this boy and his fellows, arrived at manhood, many qualities – stern self-denial, consistent purpose, unceasing industry, self-sacrifice, temperance in its widest sense – not always, in spite of our well-meaning attempts both at home and at school to induce them, found either in boyhood or in manhood in the sons of the well-to-do.[141]

In effect, youths' bodies and emotions were conceived of as nascent and fluid. Thus, the causes of such excess were often differently conceived to their counterpart in mature men. An article in the *Spectator* in 1888 discussed the 'rough' and offered the reasons for working-class youths' roughness, which were based on

> mere health and strength and the tumult of the blood natural at that age, rough at other times from the craving for physical exertion which the rich expend upon a hundred games, rough always from want of the self-restraint which is the first, some philosophers say the only, gift of continuous civilisation.[142]

As such, youths were given time, admittedly a bounded period, to master their appetites and feelings. Schooling, organisations such as temperance societies and youth groups, and print culture, especially magazines for boys, joined forces to instil in male youths the capacity to resist temptation.[143] Boys were to be trained to achieve their appropriate masculine identity through emotional and bodily management and restraint, although this might vary with social class. The Boys Brigade, for instance, proclaimed its objective to be the advancement of Christ's kingdom among boys and the promotion of habits of 'Obedience, reverence, Discipline, Self-Respect and all that tend towards a true Christian Manliness'. Here the hierarchical values of obedience and discipline were the routes to self-mastery.[144]

If the period of youth was about attaining a manly body through self-restraint, then that of old age was about marshalling an increasingly infirm body. There were, perhaps, fewer positive representations of aged male bodies. This is because the aged man's body symbolised a reversion to dependence since it was less capable of working; nor did it conform readily to the active motion that defined the idealised manly body.[145] Old men's bodies were precarious. In the 1871 tale 'Health of the Aged' in the *British Workman*, an elderly man is compared to 'an old waggon: with light loading and careful usage it will last for years; but one heavy load or sudden strain will break it and ruin it for ever'. The author acknowledges that some make it through their later years, even to seventy, free from infirmities, with a cheery heart, good health, and wisdom, and reasonable prospects and opportunities for usefulness. Nevertheless, the author warns that they should be 'careful', for

> An old constitution is like an old bone; broken with ease, mended with difficulty. A young tree bends to the gale, an old one saps and falls before the blast. A single hard lift; an hour of heating work; an evening of exposure to rain or damp; a severe chill; an excess of food; the unusual indulgence of any appetite or passion; a sudden fit of anger; an improper dose of medicine; – any of these or other similar things may cut off a valuable life in an hour and leave the fair hopes of usefulness and employment but a shapeless wreck.

Notably, nature and work, but also appetite and emotions, were threats. Though the old man's body was not intended to stir revulsion, fear and faith were used to invoke its weakness and the means to avoid this: 'let your moderation be known unto all men' and 'whether ye eat or drink, or whatever ye do, do all to the glory of God'.[146]

In some ways, if a youth's body had potential, the old man's body was spent and, therefore, unmanly. After all, the reality of harsh industrial working conditions, such as in mining and heavy industries, meant that the elderly, the disabled, and those prematurely aged by ill-health felt emasculated by their physical weakness and inability to work and provide.[147] Yet in cultural representations, personal histories of manliness were used to mitigate the diminishing effects of age. This was perhaps most noticeable in the figure of aged veterans in the long nineteenth century. Although their bodies were injured and worn out, their needs catered for by state or charity, they could nonetheless be depicted positively because of their previous utility as fighting men. As such, they could retain some association of manliness despite their supposed physical inadequacy. An early example is the 1800 song 'Tom Tuff' by Charles Dibdin, which begins: 'My name it is Tom Tuff, I've seen a little service', with Howe, Jervis, Warren, and in Nelson's fleet. As with most refrains about Jack Tar, Tom is a combination of bluffness, bravery, and sentiment as he sighs and sheds tears for the wife and family he leaves behind. The song ends: 'I've only lost an eye and got a timber toe/Old ships in time must expect to be out of condition,/No longer to sail with a yo heave yo/ I'll smoke my pipe and sing old songs.' His present is thus secured by his valiant past, but also by his virility in fathering children. The song announces that his sons have grown up to be sailors who will revenge his foes and his 'girls will breed young sailors for to nobly face the foe'.[148]

Moreover, continued self-mastery and other favoured manly attributes such as virility and bravery offset encroaching infirmities. 'The Brave Old Coxswain' in the *British Workman*, 1870, recounts the most notable rescues of coxswain Joseph Cox, who saved over 200 lives during his career.[149] It emphasises his bodily fortitude; in rescuing an Austrian barque, for example, 'old Cox [was] much bruised, as he was jammed up against the counter, but his life-belt saved him'. The illustration beautifully depicts this (Figure 2.4), his sturdy body in action steadying the tiller in the face of huge waves, his forthright expression; the only concession to the 'old' of the title is in his grey whiskers. Joseph therefore retains his manliness, signified by his still attractive appearance, thanks to iron self-mastery and piety.[150] Joseph is also held up as a model of self-control, which control overcomes the potential feebleness of age. The narrator comments: 'The brave old coxswain's temperance principles are worthy of note.' In effect, his abstinence was the key to his continued manliness:

> Old Cox has seen so many Jack-tars ship-wrecked – both in body and soul – by drink, that he has a well-grounded antipathy against everything that can make a man drunk. We commend the worthy old coxswain's courage, firmness, and his testimony to the blessed truth of the Gospel, to all our readers.[151]

Even extreme longevity might not lead to the loss of manliness. *The Age* reported the death of a 'Chelsea Veteran' in 1827, noting 'He was a native of Wiltshire, and had been about ninety years in the army; he scarcely ever experienced a day's illness, and maintained his faculties perfect to the last, with the exception of his eyesight, which latterly became impaired.'[152] In a neat virtuous circle, self-control ensured longevity.

2.4 *The Brave Old Coxswain, British Workman* (1870).

Conclusion

If Chapter 1 focused on objectified bodies, then this chapter has considered bodies which were 'abjectified'. It has shown that just as manliness was encouraged by a combination of attractive bodies and positive emotions, unmanliness was condemned through ugly, degenerate bodies and negative emotions. However, unmanliness was not simply a counterpoint to a manliness easily achieved by exercising will over one's sensual appetites for food, alcohol, tobacco, and sex.

Alternative, if less respectable, forms of masculinity existed, which permitted and approved habits like heavy drinking and smoking and the display of sexual virility. When the behaviours proving masculinity were somewhat contentious, associating unrestrained appetites, emotions, and unappealing bodies with disgust, fear, and horror was especially useful. For middle-class commentators and reformers, it was also easier to map unmanly behaviours onto the emotionalised and moralised bodies of working-class men to serve as abject lessons to avoid. Some men were partially exempted from the relationship between 'ugly' bodies, unrestrained appetites, and negative emotions. The young, the elderly, the ill, and those whose bodies were disabled through war or workplace accidents were not described with disgust, though only a few of them were accorded full manliness. Generally, these few were men who had had military careers and whose bodily nonconformity was due to serving the nation. Indeed, as Chapter 3 shows, the emotionalised bodies and material culture of military men offered all classes an appealing and idealised manliness to be emulated and admired.

Notes

1. Cited in Sharrona Pearl, *About Faces: Physiognomy in Nineteenth-Century Britain* (Cambridge, MA: Harvard University Press, 2010), p. 27.
2. Paul Kelleher, 'Directions from nature: the rhetoric of deformity in Shaftesbury's *Characteristics*', in Chris Mounsey (ed.), *The Idea of Disability in the Eighteenth Century* (Lewisburg, PA: Bucknell University Press, 2014), pp. 72, 78.
3. Kathryn Woods, '"Facing" identity in a "faceless" society: physiognomy, facial appearance and identity perception in eighteenth-century London', *Cultural and Social History* 14:2 (2017), 147–9.
4. *Young Folks Paper: Literary Olympic and Tournament* 925 (4 August 1888), p. 106.
5. Joy Wiltenburg, 'True crime: the origins of modern sensationalism', *American Historical Review* 109:5 (2004), 1377–404.
6. Mary Poovey, *Making a Social Body: British Cultural Formation, 1830–1864* (Chicago: University of Chicago Press, 1995), p. 14.
7. Jonas Hanway, *An Account of the Marine Society Recommending the Piety and Policy of the Institution, and Pointing Out the Advantages Accruing to the Nation [Microform]: With the Motives for Establishing it: Also a Full Detail of their Rules and Forms of Business: With a List of the Subscribers, from the Commencement in July 1756, to September 30. 1759: Also a Proposal for Accommodating the Boys, Equipped by Them, in the Merchants Service, When the War is Finished* (London, 1759), p. 10.
8. Christopher E. Forth, '"Manhood incorporated": diet and the embodiment of "civilised" masculinity', *Men and Masculinities* 11:5 (2009), 578–601.
9. For the range of substances considered across Europe and North America to endanger bodies, see *ibid.*, 594–6.

10 James Fordyce, *Addresses to Young Men*, 2 vols (London, 1777), vol. 2, pp. 199–200.
11 *Ibid.*, p. 201.
12 *Ibid.*, p. 191.
13 *Ibid.*, p. 193.
14 *Ibid.*, pp. 192–3.
15 *Ibid.*, p. 204.
16 Samuel Smiles, *Self-Help; with Illustrations of Character and Conduct* (Boston, 1859).
17 *Ibid.*, p. 238.
18 *Ibid.*, p. 216.
19 *Ibid.*, p. 220.
20 *Ibid.*, p. 225.
21 Samuel Smiles *Self-Help, with Illustrations of Conduct and Perseverance* (London: IEA Health and Welfare Unit, 1996), 1866 edn, p. 2.
22 Smiles, *Self-Help*, 1859 edn, p. 6.
23 *Ibid.*, pp. 4, 42.
24 Robert Baden-Powell, *Scouting for Boys: A Handbook for Instruction in Good Citizenship* (1908; London: Dover, 2007), pp. 12–13.
25 Forth, '"Manhood incorporated"', 582.
26 Samantha Calvert, 'Eden's diet: Christianity and vegetarianism 1809–2009' (PhD dissertation, University of Birmingham, 2013). Anita Guerrini, 'A diet for a sensitive soul: vegetarianism in eighteenth-century Britain', *Eighteenth-Century Life* 23:2 (1999), 34–8. Joanne Begiato, 'Celibacy, "conjugal chastity", and "moral restraint"', in Joanne Begiato and William Gibson, *Sex and the Church in the Long Eighteenth Century: Religion, Enlightenment and the Sexual Revolution* (London and New York: I.B. Taurus, 2017), ch. 6.
27 Anita Guerrini, 'Health, national character and the English diet in 1700', *Studies in History and Philosophy of Biological and Biomedical Sciences* 43:2 (2012), 349–56. For diet and masculinity: Joanne Parsons, 'Fosco's fat: transgressive consumption and bodily control in Wilkie Collins' "The Woman in White"', in Joanne Parsons and Ruth Heholt (eds), *The Victorian Male Body* (Edinburgh: Edinburgh University Press, 2017), pp. 216–33.
28 Cited in Guerrini, 'Diet for a sensitive soul', 35–6.
29 Calvert, 'Eden's diet', 20, 56. Ian Miller, 'Evangelicalism and the early vegetarian movement in Britain c.1847–1860', *Journal of Religious History* 35:2 (2011), 199–210.
30 Calvert, 'Eden's diet', 39.
31 Forth, '"Manhood incorporated"', 580–1 and passim.
32 Smiles, *Self-Help*, 1859, p. 241.
33 Guerrini, 'Diet for a sensitive soul', 37.
34 *Cursory Remarks on Corpulence or Obesity Considered as a Disease* (1816), cited in Parsons, 'Fosco's fat', p. 222.
35 Stuart Hogarth, 'Reluctant patients: health, sickness and the embodiment of plebeian masculinity in nineteenth-century Britain. Evidence from working men's autobiographies' (PhD dissertation, Metropolitan University of London, 2010), p. 73.
36 Thomas Bewick, *A Memoir of Thomas Bewick* (Newcastle-on-Tyne and London, 1862), pp. 67–70.
37 This refers to Luigi Cornaro, *Discourses on a Sober and Temperate Life*, first published in Italian as *Discorsi della vita sobria* in 1558 and republished through the eighteenth and nineteenth centuries.
38 Bewick, *Memoir*, pp. 69, 112–13.
39 Cited in Miller, 'Evangelicalism and the early vegetarian movement', 209.
40 Roy Porter, *Flesh in the Age of Reason* (London: Penguin, 2004), p. 243.
41 *Licensed Victuallers' Mirror* (1888).

42 Charlotte Boyce, 'Suffering, asceticism, and the starving male body in Mary Barton', in Parsons and Heholt (eds), *The Victorian Male Body*, pp. 193–5, 198, 200.
43 For changing meanings of the obese male body over time, see Forth, '"Manhood incorporated"', 588–9.
44 Parsons, 'Fosco's fat', p. 216. For gastronomy, gourmandizing, masculinity, and class see Forth, '"Manhood incorporated"', 591–3.
45 For the use of the language of disease, filth, squalor, depravity, and threat in the medico-moral language of sexual reform, deployed from the 1830s against the working classes, see Frank Mort, *Dangerous Sexualities: Medico-Moral Politics in England since 1830* (London: Routledge, 2nd edn, 2000), pp. 17, 30–1.
46 *Children's Treasury and Advocate of the Homeless and Destitute* (24 May 1879), p. 250.
47 Baden-Powell, *Scouting for Boys*, p 28.
48 *British Workman* 1 (1855), p. 6.
49 Calvert, 'Eden's diet', 55, 99.
50 Frank Murray, "Picturing the "road to ruin": visual representations of a standard temperance narrative, 1830–1855', *Visual Resources: An International Journal of Documentation* 28:4 (2012), 291.
51 An economic argument is also deployed *British Workman* (1855), pp. 1–2.
52 'Teetotal-Bench' and 'Ale-Bench' by Obadiah Sherratt, c.1835, in Reginald G. Haggar, *Staffordshire Chimney Ornaments* (London: Phoenix House Ltd, 1955), p. 77; *Penny Illustrated Paper* (13 September 1862).
53 Joss Marsh, 'Dickensian "dissolving views": the magic lantern, visual story-telling, and the Victorian technological imagination', *Comparative Critical Studies* 6:3 (2009), 335–14. For the engraved images, see George Cruikshank, *The Bottle and the Drunkard's Children, in Sixteen Plates Designed and Etched by George Cruikshank* (London and Glasgow: Gowans & Gray Ltd, 1906). These were reproduced from first editions published in 1847 and 1848, www.archive.org/details/bottledrunkardsc00crui (accessed 4 May 2019). For examples of the ceramics, see examples in Tyne & Wear Archives & Museums, such as rectangular wall plaque, TWCMS: 2004.2567, and breakfast-sized plate, TWCMS: 2004.2566.6. For the images use on temperance banners see report of the Preston Guild Jubilee, *Penny Illustrated Paper* (13 September 1862).
54 There are similar depictions in Murray, 'Picturing the "road to ruin"', 296, 297, 301, 302.
55 *Every Boy's Annual* 41 (1878) p. 273.
56 *British Workman* 2 (1855) p. 10.
57 Quotation from Sophia Wintz, *Our Blue Jackets: Miss Weston's Life and Work among our Sailors* (London, 1890), cited in Mary Conley, '"You don't make a torpedo gunner out of a drunkard": Agnes Weston, temperance, and the British navy', *The Northern Mariner/Le Marin du nord* 9:1 (January 1999), 9.
58 *British Workman* 7 (1855) p. 28; *British Workman* 22 (1856), p. 87.
59 The notion that modern urban life could return poor people to a baser condition was in place by the 1840s. An example is found in the contributions of Thomas Southwood Smith to the *First Report of the Commissioners for Inquiring into the State of Large Towns and Populous Districts*, vol. 1 (1844), p. 32n73, cited and discussed in Michael Brown, 'From foetid air to filth: the cultural transformation of British epidemiological thought, ca. 1780–1848', *Bulletin of the History of Medicine* 82:3 (2008), 536.
60 Pearl, *About Faces*, ch. 4.
61 *British Workman* 2 (1855), p. 11.
62 For a discussion of masturbation, and celibacy more generally see Begiato, 'Celibacy, "conjugal chastity", and "moral restraint"'.

63 Diane Mason, *Secret Vice: Masturbation in Victorian Fiction and Medical Culture* (Manchester: Manchester University Press, 2008), p. 21.
64 J. Wesley, *Thoughts on the Sin of Onan: Chiefly Extracted from a Late Writer* (London, 1767), p. 4.
65 Cited by William Acton, *The Functions and Disorders of the Reproductive Organs in Youth, in Adult Age and in Advanced Life* (London, 6th edn, 1875), pp. 95–6, 97.
66 Ray Vaughn Pierce, *The People's Common Sense Medical Adviser in Plain English, or Medicine Simplified* (Buffalo, NY: World's Dispensary Printing Office and Bindery, 1876), pp. 801–2. There followed several editions published in London. For other examples see Mason, *Secret Vice*, ch. 1.
67 Ellen Bayuk Rosenman, 'Body doubles: the spermatorrhea panic', *Journal of the History of Sexuality* 12:3 (2003), 365.
68 *Ibid.*, 375.
69 C. J. Lucas, *Manly Vigour: A Popular Inquiry into the Concealed Causes of its Premature Decline: With Remarks on the Treatment of Gonorrhea, Gleet, Stricture and Syphilis* (London: C. J. Lucas, 1842). *Age* 87 (27 August 1843), p. 8.
70 Cited in Rosenman, 'Body doubles', 374.
71 Dr Alfred Field Henery, *Vital Hints on Health and Strength, and their Dependence on the State of the Generative Organization* (London: 53 Dorset Street, c.1860–64). Cited in Caroline Rance, 'Secret vices and silent friends: quackery in the treatment of spermatorrhoea, 1840–1870' (MA dissertation, Birkbeck, University of London, 2013), p. 21.
72 He was citing at length from Robert Ritchie, 'An inquiry into a frequent cause of insanity in young men', published in *The Lancet* in 1861. Wesley, *Thoughts on the Sin of Onan*, pp. 15–18. For later examples see Stephanie Olsen, *Juvenile Nation: Youth, Emotions and the Making of the Modern British Citizen, 1880–1914* (London: Bloomsbury, 2014), pp. 65–7.
73 Parsons, 'Fosco's fat', p. 227.
74 Rosenman, 'Body doubles', 365.
75 Kostas Makras, '"The poison that upsets my reason": men, madness and drunkenness in the Victorian period', in Thomas Knowles and Serena Trowbridge (eds), *Insanity and the Lunatic Asylum in the Nineteenth Century* (London: Pickering & Chatto, 2015), pp. 139–40; Lesley Hall, 'Forbidden by God, despised by men: masturbation, medical warnings, moral panic, and manhood in Great Britain, 1850–1950', *Journal of the History of Sexuality in Modern Europe* 2:3 (1992), 365–87; Mason, *Secret Vice*, ch. 1. For the treatment of the 'problem' in boys see Olsen, *Juvenile Nation*, pp. 65–6.
76 Acton, *Functions and Disorders*, p. 95.
77 Anna Shepherd, *Institutionalizing the Insane in Nineteenth-Century England* (London: Pickering & Chatto, 2014), pp. 124–5.
78 Samuel Tuke, *Description of the Retreat, an Institution near York for Insane Persons of the Society of Friends: Containing an Account of its Origins and Progress, the Modes of Treatment and a Statement of Cases* (York, 1813), p. 133.
79 Shepherd, *Institutionalizing the Insane*, pp. 124–5. See also Akihito Suzuki, 'Lunacy and labouring men: narratives of male vulnerability in mid-Victorian London', in R. Bivins and J. Pickstone (eds), *Medicine, Madness and Social History: Essays in Honour of Roy Porter* (Basingstoke: Palgrave Macmillan, 2007), pp. 118–28; Helen Goodman, 'Mad men: borderlines of insanity, masculinity and emotion in Victorian literature and culture' (PhD dissertation, Royal Holloway, University of London, 2015), p. 154.
80 Porter, *Flesh in the Age of Reason*, p. 314.
81 Shepherd, *Institutionalizing the Insane*, p. 116; Tuke, *Description of the Retreat*, p. 89.

82 Louis C. Charland, 'Benevolent theory: moral treatment at the York retreat', *History of Psychiatry* 18:1 (2007), 71, 72.
83 Charland, 'Benevolent theory', 66; Porter, *Flesh in the Age of Reason*, p. 318; Shepherd, *Institutionalizing the Insane*, pp. 116–17, 125; Louise Hide, *Gender and Class in English Asylums 1890–1914* (Basingstoke: Palgrave Macmillan, 2014), ch. 4.
84 Sarah Hayley York, 'Suicide, lunacy and the asylum in nineteenth-century England' (PhD dissertation, University of Birmingham, 2009), pp. 262–3.
85 The case notes typically record more than one cause of insanity. This is because a previous medical diagnosis or family opinion was first stated on the notes, and then added to by the Colney Hatch medical officer following observation. London Metropolitan Archives (LMA), Middlesex County Lunatic Asylum, Colney Hatch, Case Books for Male Patients: H12/CH/B13/001–004 (1851–54), H12/CH/B13/020 (1872), and H12/CH/B13/035 (1886).
86 Dwigne Leopold, LMA, Middlesex County Lunatic Asylum, Colney Hatch, Case Book for Male Patient H12/CH/B13/004 (1854).
87 Thomas West, LMA, Middlesex County Lunatic Asylum, Colney Hatch, Case Book for Male Patient H12/CH/B13/004 (1854).
88 Lewis Aaron, LMA, Middlesex County Lunatic Asylum, Colney Hatch, Case Book for Male Patient H12/CH/B13/001 (1851).
89 He had also spent time in other asylums, such as three months in the Kent County Asylum. In 1844 he had threatened to shoot the Duke of Wellington and Sir Robert Peel. Bernard Fitzpatrick, LMA, Middlesex County Lunatic Asylum, Colney Hatch, Case Book for Male Patient H12/CH/B13/004 (1854).
90 Charles Langley, Middlesex County Lunatic Asylum, Colney Hatch, Case Book for Male Patient H12/CH/B13/004 (1854).
91 John Black, LMA, Middlesex County Lunatic Asylum, Colney Hatch, Case Book for Male Patient H12/CH/B13/005 (1886).
92 James Fitzgerald, LMA, Middlesex County Lunatic Asylum, Colney Hatch, Case Book for Male Patient H12/CH/B13/001 (1851).
93 Acton, *Functions and Disorders*, pp. 95–6, 97.
94 Robert Brealey, LMA, Middlesex County Lunatic Asylum, Colney Hatch, Case Book for Male Patient H12/CH/B13/020 (1872).
95 *Lectures Used by the Manchester Unity of the Independent Order of Odd Fellows*, Manchester, 1834, People's History Museum, Manchester Unity Collection 5/10; 380 Book Lectures; 383 Book Lectures.
96 'A Library and Museum of Freemasonry information leaflet: the Oddfellows', https://docplayer.net/24489983-A-library-and-museum-of-freemasonry-informati on-leaflet-the-oddfellows.html (accessed 3 January 2019).
97 This was a response to the conviction of the Tolpuddle Martyrs for swearing an oath to their agricultural workers' friendly society in 1834. For a general history of the Oddfellows, see the Oddfellows website: www.oddfellows.co.uk/about/history/ (accessed 15 May 2019).
98 People's History Museum, Manchester Unity Collection 5/10; 380 Book Lectures; 383 Book Lectures, pp. 12–13.
99 *Ibid.*, pp. 12–13.
100 *Ibid.*, pp. 54–6.
101 *Ibid.*, pp. 54–6.
102 *Ibid.*, pp. 61–3.
103 Chris Mounsey, 'Variability: beyond sameness and difference', in Mounsey (ed.), *The Idea of Disability*, p. 2.
104 Richard Stott, *Jolly Fellows: Male Milieus in Nineteenth-Century America* (Baltimore, MD: John Hopkins University Press, 2009), pp. 2, 54, 283.
105 Forth, '"Manhood incorporated"', 594.

106 Kate Davis, 'Occasional politeness and gentlemen's laughter in eighteenth-century England', *The Historical Journal* 57: 4 (2014), 921–45.
107 *British Workman* 1 (1855), p. 2.
108 Forth, '"Manhood incorporated"', 595–6.
109 *Boy's Own Magazine: An Illustrated Journal of Fact, Fiction, History, and Adventure* 2 (1863), p. 415.
110 Herbert Sussman, *Victorian Masculinities: Manhood and Masculine Poetics in Early Victorian Literature and Art* (Cambridge: Cambridge University Press, 1995), pp. 3–7.
111 In his unpublished memoir, written in the 1730s and 1740s, John Cannon recalled such an incident from his youth in 1697. Cited in Thomas W. Laqueur, *Solitary Sex: A Cultural History of Masturbation* (New York: Zone Books, 2004), pp. 182–3.
112 Hall, 'Forbidden by God, despised by men', 375.
113 Rosenman, 'Body doubles', 367, 368, 371.
114 *Ibid.*, 392.
115 Cited in Rance, 'Secret vices and silent friends', pp. 17–18.
116 *Bell's Life in London and Sporting Chronicle* (Sun, 17 November 1861), p. 2. See also Dr Hammond's curative and restoration for manly vigour, *Bell's Life in London and Sporting Chronicle* 2 (Sat, 5 June 1869) p. 482.
117 *Age* 87 (Sun, 27 August 1843) p. 8.
118 Jennifer Wallis, '"Atrophied", "engorged", "debauched", muscle wastage, degenerative mass and moral worth in the general paralytic body', in Knowles and Trowbridge (eds), *Insanity and the Lunatic Asylum*, pp. 102, 110.
119 Juliet Hurn, 'The history of general paralysis of the insane in Britain 1830–1950' (PhD dissertation, University of London, 1998), pp. 75–86.
120 Jennifer Wallis, *Investigating the Body in the Victorian Asylum: Doctors, Patients, and Practices* (London: Palgrave Macmillan, 2017), p. 209.
121 *Ibid.*, p. 13.
122 *Ibid.*, p. 209; Hurn, 'The history of general paralysis', pp. 75, 85. Janet Oppenheim, *Shattered Nerves: Doctors, Patients, and Depression in Victorian England* (New York: Oxford University Press, 1991).
123 Hogarth, 'Reluctant patients', p. 119.
124 Henry French and Mark Rothery, *Man's Estate: Landed Gentry Masculinities 1660–1990* (Oxford: Oxford University Press, 2012), pp. 124–33.
125 David Turner, *Disability in Eighteenth-Century England: Imagining Physical Impairment* (New York: Routledge, 2012); Mounsey, *The Idea of Disability*, p. 3.
126 Kelleher, 'Directions from nature', pp. 73, 78, 86.
127 Hogarth, 'Reluctant patients', pp. 137, 156–68.
128 *Ibid.*, p. 160.
129 Claire L. Jones (ed.), *Rethinking Modern Prostheses in Anglo-American Commodity Cultures, 1820–1939* (Manchester: Manchester University Press, 2017), p. 4.
130 Joanne Begiato and Michael Brown, 'Visualising the aged veteran in nineteenth-century Britain: memory, masculinity and nation', in Michael Brown, Anna Maria Barry, and Joanne Begiato (eds), *Martial Masculinities: Experiencing and Imagining the Military in the Long Nineteenth Century* (Manchester: Manchester University Press, 2019), pp. 102–36.
131 *Bell's Life* (11 July 1830), p. 3.
132 'Old soldiers, and old sailors', *Ladies' Cabinet* (1 September 1843), p. 196.
133 For workplace accidents and their deleterious effect on masculine identity, see Jamie L. Bronstein, *Caught in the Machinery: Workplace Accidents and Injured Workers in Nineteenth-Century Britain* (Stanford, CA: Stanford University Press, 2008), pp. 85–91.
134 Erin O'Connor, *Raw Material: Producing Pathology in Victorian Culture* (Durham, NC, and London: Duke University Press, 2000), pp. 104, 108, 124, 126.

135 Old Bailey Proceedings Online (hereafter OBPO), *Ordinary of Newgate's Account*, November 1730 (OA17301116).
136 OBPO, *Ordinary of Newgate's Account*, 3 October 1759 (OA17591003).
137 OBPO, *Ordinary of Newgate's Account*, April 1761 (OA17610420).
138 *Ladies' Treasury* (1 August 1861), p. 238.
139 *Girl's Own Paper* (26 November 1898), p. 141.
140 William Smith, LMA, Middlesex County Lunatic Asylum, Colney Hatch, Case Book for Male Patient H12/CH/B13/001 (1851).
141 Lady Bell, *At the Works: A Study of a Manufacturing Town* (London, 1904).
142 *Spectator* (2 June 1888).
143 Olsen, *Juvenile Nation*, chs 1, 4, 5.
144 This remains the motto, see the Boys Brigade website: https://boys-brigade.org.uk/who-we-are/ (accessed 1 June 2019).
145 For premature ageing caused by employment, see Ben Curtis and Steven Thompson, '"This is the country of premature old men": ageing and aged miners in the South Wales coalfield c1880–1947', *Cultural and Social History* 12:4 (2015), 587–606.
146 *British Workman* 203 (1871), p. 91.
147 Curtis and Thompson, '"This is the country of premature old men"', 594–5.
148 Broadside Ballads Online, 1st Ballad – Roud Number: 13818 (Nottingham: Burbage and Stretton, 1800), http://ballads.bodleian.ox.ac.uk/view/edition/13068 (accessed 1 June 2019).
149 For heroic mariners and lifeboatmen, see Christiana Payne, *Where the Sea Meets the Land: Artists on the Coast in Nineteenth Century Britain* (Bristol: Sansom & Co. Ltd, 2007), pp. 35–5, 157–63.
150 Artists often depicted rescuers as saving their own souls when saving people from drowning due to their acts of mercy. Payne, *Where the Sea Meets the Land*, pp. 163–4.
151 The story was selected to accompany an article on the launch of a *British Workman* lifeboat, in connection with the National Lifeboat Institution. *British Workman* (1 November 1870), p. 42.
152 *Age* (7 October 1827), p. 149.

3

Hearts of oak:
martial manliness and material culture

Introduction

Of all the forms of manliness, without doubt the most appealing was that embodied by soldiers and sailors. They offered a potent example of the desirable emotionalised body surveyed in Chapter 1. Their glamorised appearance and feelings, deeds, and qualities were valorised in visual and print culture, commercialised in advertising, and celebrated in an expanding material culture. This chapter explores the ways in which the reach of their alluring form of manliness was extended through material culture. A magnificent example is the 1844 polychrome-painted figurehead of the twelve-gun brig HMS *Daring*: a bust of a seaman (Figure 3.1), arms folded in a manly pose, the name 'Daring' emblazoned on his cap ribbon and chest. He displays the sheer power of martial manliness for Victorian society, since figureheads had previously been mythological or royal subjects. Drawing on the concept of emotional objects, three types of material culture are examined in this chapter, which, it is argued, inspired feelings that reinforced ideas about idealised manliness. The first are the artefacts of war and the military, including uniforms, weapons, medals, ships, and regimental colours. The second are objects encountered at the domestic level, including toys, ceramics, and textiles, which depicted martial manliness or had intimate connections with soldiers and sailors. They appealed to all age groups, genders, and social classes, since many were priced for a modest pocket and had a domestic function or ornamental appeal. The third type considered consists of the material culture that celebrity military heroes generated, from consumable products that deployed their names and images, to the monuments that memorialised them, to the very stuff of their bodies. Such material culture conveyed martial values that were keenly associated with manliness. This irresistible nexus of emotionalised bodies and objects prompted affective

3.1 HMS *Daring* figurehead (1844).

responses, which disseminated, reinforced, and maintained civilian manly identities.

Manliness and martial material culture

Martial material culture was a catalyst for discussions of ideal military manliness and functioned as a metonym for its physical and emotional qualities, which were so appealing to civilians. An example is the account of Sir Charles Napier's deathbed in 1853, published in 1858 in *The Lady's Newspaper*.[1] Napier, the author declares, 'died amidst trophies of battle, and his camp-bed was his bier: the colours of the 22nd gently waved over him, and between them the grand picture of Meanee leaned forward above his pale heroic countenance'.[2] As Napier's 'last breath escaped', it reports, Major McMurdo snatched the old colours that had been borne at Meanee and Hyderabad, and swung them over him. Here, Napier's military past and superior manly qualities were symbolised by his martial accoutrements, including a painting of the Battle of Meanee, in which he fought in February 1843, and channelled through the grief of two veterans of his regiment who stood at the foot of his bed.[3]

These connections are not surprising. The martial man's appeal was frequently represented through his body, perfectly attired in regulation uniform, headgear, shoes, weapons, and equipment, and manifested in his size, gait, and posture.[4] Scott Myerly explains that uniform was designed to emphasise appearance over practicality: a psychological tactic intended to inculcate soldiers' obedience and loyalty and enforce discipline. Producing and symbolising the 'military machine', such display also intimidated, reassured, and delighted civilians. The latter is evident in a naval captain's recollection of transporting Napoleon to St Helena and seeing Napoleon's officers bidding him farewell. This was the passage selected in a review of his memoirs in 1849 in *John Bull*. It repeats Huntley's description of Napoleon's officers, particularly the 'tall, fine figure' of Savary, attired in the much-decorated 'light blue cavalry uniform of the Polish Lancers'.[5] This was not the only marker of Savary's manly status. Huntley says that when Savary met Napoleon, his tears 'burst through all restraint, to show the affection of the heart which glowed within the breast of this intrepid, able, and faithful soldier'. Napoleon, in contrast, 'was as cold as the bronze figure which so often represents him': an intriguing material culture analogy that evokes the importance of feelings to manliness.[6]

The Victoria Cross, first issued for gallantry in 1857, was one of the most popular objects that functioned as a point of entry for readers to imagine military manliness. The article for boys, 'Soldiers and the Victoria Cross by an Army Chaplain', published in 1863, opens with the disingenuous claim that English boys are less warlike than their French counterparts, for they neither worship 'la gloire' nor dress like soldiers: 'Swords and guns are not their only playthings, nor are feeble imitations of sanguinary contests their only pastimes.'[7] Of course, this distinction actually emphasises the centrality of martial material culture to boys' fascination with war.

It also highlights the significance of feelings in constructions of martial manliness. Rather than telling tales of soldiers' bravery, it focuses on the emotions of combat and the battlefield. The chaplain states: 'One early object of our curiosity was to ascertain what are the sensations or feelings of a soldier on entering battle.' He answers this through the sensory nature of fighting – 'as the bullet whizzed past the ear, and comrade after comrade dropped' – likening the experience to the disorientation of a bather plunging into water. The chaplain presents a powerful image of English soldiers as masters of self-restraint, noting that they were silent in hand-to-hand fighting, unlike the Russians who were noisy when advancing and fighting. His account does not pull its visceral punches; he describes a soldier going mad after his friend's brains splattered in his face.[8] For all its graphic nature, perhaps even because of it, this account of the materiality of combat conjures a striking picture of martial men who fight despite fear and comrades who support each other in battle, and may, though he suggests otherwise, shed furious tears in battle.

The article celebrates martial self-sacrifice through regimental colours, objects that personified manly bravery and selflessness for civilians as well as the military. The chaplain explains that one or two subalterns and several sergeants were nominated to guard the colours, while the bravest men in the regiment would rally round them when they were in danger. As he concludes, a 'Grateful country will not forget men who loved colours better than their lives'.[9] The article describes other objects that emphasise the poignancy and appeal of martial manliness, listing the 'Many small pledges of affection [that] were found on the persons of our soldiers who fell on the battle-fields of the Crimea.'[10] These included a lock of hair, a photograph, a last letter from home, a small Bible, and a father's gift of a watch: all explicitly understood to be repositories of emotions associated with the courage and endurance of military action and life.[11] Another account of men awarded the Victoria Cross, in the *Boy's Own Magazine*, 1863, similarly deployed material culture to emphasise military men's emotional intensity. At the siege of Bergen-op-Zoom (1814), Captain Fraser directed his servant, Donald, to remain in the garrison while he conducted his men to attack a battery. Engaged in this manoeuvre, the captain halted for a short time; on moving forward he found his path impeded. Putting his hand down he seized a plaid, and drew his dirk, thinking one of his men was deserting, only to discover his servant Donald. When asked why he was there, Donald answered: 'It was just my love for you.' He tells Fraser that he brought the plaid because

> How could I ever show my face to my mother (she was Fraser's foster-mother) had you been killed or wounded, and I not been there to carry you to the surgeon or to Christian burial? And how could I do either without a plaid to wrap you in?[12]

Same-sex affection clearly heightened the appeal of martial manliness for those who encountered it.

Though the narrative style was harder, more brutal, even vicious by the turn of the century, material culture and emotions nonetheless remained central to martial manliness. The demise of Harry Keston, in a tale set in the South African war in *The Marvel* (1899) deploys weaponry to horrific effect. When Harry is wounded in a rout, a scene of wild disorder, he throws aside his rifle and, holding a revolver in each hand, tries to secure higher ground. The Boers swarm the knoll; one of them, Paul Pieters, Harry's personal enemy, charges at him. Left only with an empty revolver, Harry fights like 'a wild animal … striking out heavily with his fists, kicking, snarling, butting savagely'. Taken prisoner and assured that Pieters will torture him the next day, Harry elects to end his own life. He is unable to fire a loaded gun he finds on the ground because his arms are bound. A chilling scene follows that unites innocent tropes of childhood pleasures with the aggressive, competitive version of manliness that dominated the imperial, militaristic culture of late nineteenth-century Britain.[13] First, the sight of his bare toes reminds him of a childhood visit to a circus in which an armless performer used his toes like fingers. Thus inspired,

> By the aid of his toes, and by lying on his side, Keston managed to get the barrel of the rifle between his knees. It was then an easy matter to work it up till the muzzle entered his mouth ... With his toes he felt for the trigger of the rifle, keeping the butt firmly against the ground, found it, and rested the big toe of his right foot upon it. A moment's hesitation. Bang![14]

These emotions were worlds away from earlier cheerfulness, sentimental fraternal comradeship, and tender feeling. Instead, they conveyed the individualistic and antagonistic model of martial manliness that underpinned Baden-Powell's scouting model of masculinity, with self-mastery enacted through self-annihilation, rather than laying down one's life for one's comrades. Nevertheless, for the youths reading this literature, the combination of excitement, admiration, and violence helped to make this version of aggressive manliness equally desirable.

The personal allure of martial manliness

Martial material culture embodied and spread the allure of sailors and soldiers. In the early nineteenth century, women were said to suffer 'scarlet fever', a wonderfully medical metaphor for the love of a man in uniform.[15] This was captured in a 'Military Catechism for Young Ladies', published in *Punch* in 1847, which, in the form of question and answer, satirised female adoration of soldiers. When asked 'Why should a woman prefer a soldier above all other male creatures?' the young lady answers: 'Because he wears such a very handsome dress; carries gold upon his shoulders; gold all over his coat; wears a sword at his side; and a love of a feather in his helmet or cap.' Her notion of 'military glory' is 'A review in Hyde Park' and 'laurels' are 'A ball, and supper afterwards.'[16]

Boys and youths were also drawn to the glamour of martial material culture, a fact that the army deployed in their recruiting tactics. It worked, since soldiers' life writings identify the desire to acquire the glamorous trappings of uniform and weapons motivating their enlistment.[17] William Cobbett (1763–1835) longed to join the navy for such reasons, although he was the son of a publican and farmer, bred, he claimed 'at the plough-tail'.[18] In autumn 1783, he visited a relation in Portsmouth and, 'for the first time, beheld the sea; and no sooner did I behold it, than I wished to be a sailor'. Cobbett saw this as a male universal: 'almost all English boys feel the same inclination: it would seem, that, like young ducks, instinct leads them to rush on the bosom of the water'.[19] The technology of warfare and the mythical status of Britain's naval glories and heroes were critical:

> But it was not the sea alone that I saw; the grand fleet was riding at anchor at Spithead. I had heard of the wooden walls of England; I had formed my ideas of a ship, and of a fleet: but, what I now beheld so far surpassed what I had ever been able to form a conception of, that I stood lost between astonishment and admiration. I had heard talk of the glorious deeds of our admirals and sailors, of the defeat of the Spanish Armada, and of all those memorable combats that good and true Englishmen never fail to relate to their children about a hundred times a year. The brave Rodney's victories had long been the theme of our praise and the burden of our songs. The sight of the fleet brought all these into my mind; in confused order, it is true, but with irresistible force.[20]

Cobbett failed to get a naval captain to take him on board ship, however, and returned home. The following year he ran away to London to work as a clerk. Nonetheless, the prospect of armed service beguiled him and a recruiting advertisement for 'His Majesty's marine service' announcing the potential for prizes caught his attention. Resolving to join this 'glorious corps', he mistakenly enlisted in a 'marching regiment', the 54th (West Norfolk) Regiment of Foot.[21] Stationed in North America between 1785 and 1791, he rose to sergeant major, before obtaining his discharge from the army in December 1791.

The glamour of the forces even appealed to those who did not go on to enlist. Henry Angelo (1780–1852), Master of Fencing, taught sword exercises to elite youths. His memoir, published in 1830, recounted his childhood martial ambitions, which centred on his adoration of martial material culture. At the age of six, an army officer had visited his family and 'pretended to be the bearer of a commission in Lord Pembroke's regiment, which being formally presented to me, my mother made a complete suit of regimentals'.[22] This, he says, rendered him spoiled and naughty; one of the reasons he was sent to school.[23] Soon after, another family friend, this time a naval captain, stirred his interest in the navy by playfully rating Angelo as a midshipman on his warship.[24] The captain visited after returning from his voyage, presenting Angelo's mother with twenty-five guineas, 'as my share of prize-money for that expedition'. The pampered Angelo was made yet another military outfit, and he 'strutted about in blue jacket and trowsers, and was intended for the sea', though this was never realised.[25]

In February 1828, a seventy-year-old clergyman, William Ettrick, of High Barnes in Sunderland, despairingly confided in his journal his efforts to persuade his eighteen-year-old son Anthony to train as a doctor. In response to his father's observation that the five years of medical training at St Bartholomew's Hospital, at the enormous cost of 300 guineas, was an excellent opportunity, Anthony insisted that he wanted to be a sailor.

William replied sarcastically that being a sailor was not all gold lace and showers of gold; Anthony would not, he cuttingly remarked, soon be a Nelson or a Codrington.[26] William stuck to his guns and Anthony undertook medical training. However, he never practised medicine, and in 1845, at age thirty-five, was still complaining to his now extremely elderly father about being forced to train for the medical profession despite his desire to go sea.[27]

For these men, martial materiality prompted visceral responses, evoking feelings such as desire for glory, riches, and honour, and wonder and awe at the military technology, spectacle, and pomp, and, especially, the uniforms.[28] For Ettrick it was gold lace, for Angelo it was dressing up in blue and red coats.[29] This was a literary trope. An 1807 account of Charles Mordant, in *The Lady's Monthly Museum*, explains that although 'His friends were desirous that he should embrace the clerical order ... he preferred a red coat to a black. A pair of colours were presented to him by his godfather, the celebrated Marquis of Granby.' The 'irresistible power' of these objects fired him with the love of glory.[30] For many boys, youths, and men, a uniform made them feel like a real man. The artist and illustrator George Cruikshank (1792–1878) recalled his youthful yearning to serve his country. At fourteen, an officer friend promised to get him appointed to his ship and George was thus supplied with a splendid outfit adorned with anchor buttons.[31] Making his appearance in public in this uniform was, he said, 'the only time in my life that I ever remember being vain and proud'.[32]

These accounts also testify to the sensory appeal of martial materiality. Military bands stirred pride and patriotism through the visual and auditory onslaught of elaborate uniforms and rousing music.[33] Other military songs had different effects. For example, Cobbett and Angelo referred to maritime songs, which evoked potent feelings of love and loss at military men's self-sacrifice.[34] Angelo even located his failure to join either armed service as the result of these moving ballads. He claimed that his intent to go to sea was blocked by his mother, for

> her singing the favourite air in Thomas and Sally, 'For my true love is gone to sea', operating on her too sensitive nerves, frequently set her weeping; and my infantine sympathy making me do the like, the blue jacket, as well as the red jacket, was laid aside, and my profession of arms was doomed to be a very harmless profession.[35]

Henry Angelo's mother accommodated her small son's childish longings until she sang a song from Isaac Bickerstaff's nautical opera 'Thomas and Sally or the Sailor's Return'. As it was designed to do, it prompted feelings of loss, reminding her of the risks to her son's safety. Nonetheless, military objects retained emotional power for Angelo. He kept his prize money of twenty-five guineas, 'in the shape of a piece of silver, as a memento of my public services as a son of Neptune'.[36]

Military emotional objects with familial connections could be especially powerful. The Birmingham bookseller and historian William Hutton (1723–1815) singled out his great-great-grandfather in his family history, published in 1816. This Yorkshire ancestor had served as a trooper on the parliamentary side in the English Civil War. Hutton listed his engagements at Marston Moor, Naseby, and Worcester, and explained that he had served in the regiment till 1658, after which he married, had ten children, and ran an alehouse. At the end of this narrative William recorded:

> Three pieces of antiquity belonging to this warrior fell into my possession, which I preserved as *relics*. A brass spoon of a singular construction, ill suited to the shape of the mouth, graced with the image of a Saint at the top. This he carried in his pocket for his own use during his military peregrinations. – His broad-sword, drawn for liberty, his companion and guard during sixteen years' service. These were both taken from me at the Riots. – The third was a fragment of a mug that had been daily used for fourscore years.[37]

These relics were repositories for William's pride in his 'warrior' ancestor and they preserved memories, aiding him and his family in constructing a familial identity of which they were proud. Given that he focused on this military forerunner for his autobiography, it is possible to propose that the dissenting radical thinker Hutton also formulated his own identity upon this manly, parliamentarian soldier.

In this small selection from men's life writings we see in action the desire that men felt for the manliness embodied in appealing military bodies and material culture. It informed their longings and aspirations, it shaped their actions, and it served as a reference point against which they measured their own masculine identity and performance.

The pleasure culture of war in material form

According to *Chums* (1894), 'Everyone has seen the toy soldiers, modelled of tin or lead, which are so beloved by boys.'[38] They included traditional wooden, peg-like dolls, mounted on a wooden lattice to keep them upright for play, paper soldiers, and tin and solid lead soldiers.[39] From 1893 they became more accessible, with the introduction of new hollow, cheaper versions that were manufactured in huge numbers.[40] They were very popular in periods of military enthusiasm; the account of tin soldiers in *Chums* explains that German manufacturing took off with Frederick the Great's exploits in the Seven Years' War, 'though, as would naturally be expected, the demand falls off in periods of prolonged peace, but revives again when a great international conflict takes place, like the war of 1870 between France and Germany'.[41] Historians who consider their role, along with related paraphernalia such as toy guns and uniforms, identify their importance in inculcating loyalism, popular militarism, and nationalism.[42] This had particular power for men, since the toy soldier craze exposed male children to images of war and imperial might, persuading them of their place in upholding both.[43]

The function of military toys in shaping gender construction, however, has been considered less thoroughly; yet this is an important line of enquiry, since playing with these toys was complex and not simply a means of turning civilian boys into war-hungry men. The privileged childhood of Liberal politician and landowner C. P. Trevelyan meant he had access to large numbers of toy soldiers, from which he derived great pleasure. However, when war broke out in 1914, he resigned from the cabinet because he hated war.[44] Military toys were thus repositories for masculine qualities, which, even if they did not inculcate bellicosity, disseminated ideas of manliness due to their association with the appeal of military men.

After all, toy soldiers were gendered as the archetypal little boy's toy in visual and print culture, even if girls also played with them and adults collected them. Thus, children's pretty 'scraps' often depicted boys playing with red-coated toy soldiers.[45] They were common in children's poems. 'The Plaything Sky' (1879), described the 'Hosts of tin soldier-men [who] wave their tin banners' in boys' dreams.[46] Inevitably, the toy soldier symbolised the masculine qualities of boyhood. In Fergus Hume's *Whom God Hath Joined*, 1891, the adoring mother looks at her son Sammy, who is surrounded by the ruins of his toys: a woolly if indeterminate quadruped with legs pulled off, 'an indecent-india-rubber doll', 'a drum (broken), a toy soldier (head missing)'.[47] Casual male destruction is thus dismissed and validated.

Toy soldiers were deployed to gendered didactic ends in stories. An early and long-lasting version was Hans Christian Anderson's 'The Brave Tin Soldier'; written in 1838, it was still being marketed in the late nineteenth century.[48] In 1875 *Funny Folks* praised it, using martial metaphors to good effect: 'In life's stern battle every raw recruit/May learn from his "Tin Soldier" useful love.'[49] The story is rather bleak for the boy 'recruit': a tin soldier falls in love with a paper ballerina, is thrown out of the nursery window by a goblin, damaged, washed away, eaten by a fish, and magically returned to the children. Momentarily reunited with his love, a child spitefully throws him onto the fire. Victim of the horrors of cruel fate, the tin soldier's problems are exacerbated by his refusal to call for help, convinced such an appeal would humiliate him and his uniform. The combination of almost wilful self-restraint, and consequent display of bravery, determination, fortitude, and steadfastness, certainly matched the idealisation of martial manliness.

Scholarship on the nationalistic qualities of military miniatures does not extend to toy boats. These toys were more ambivalent in terms of their martial qualities, as likely to arise from an interest in seagoing vessels, like fishing boats or pirate and merchant ships, as naval warships. Nor was there a comparative mass-produced version of the tin soldier, since they continued to be handmade well into the twentieth century, crafted from paper in their most ephemeral form, or carved from wood at home by father or child. Yet toy boats were also associated with broad martial values and patriotism. Like toy soldiers, they were closely associated with boys in paintings, watercolours, book illustrations, greeting cards, scraps, and photographs, which were consumed by adults for their pretty representations of childhood. Many show sailor-suited boys, often accompanied by girls, playing in attractive rural scenes beside a stream or pond, in a picturesquely poor cottage, or at the coast.[50] Thomas Webster's *Contrary Winds* is typical. Completed in 1843, and reproduced in the following decades, this oil painting of an interior cottage scene shows four children – three boys and a girl – gathered round their grandmother's washing tub in front of a large hearth, all blowing at the tiny boat on the water, while the old woman sits at one side looking on.[51]

These delightful depictions of childhood taught gendered lessons. In 'Good-Natured Jack', a Christmas tale published in *Our Young Folks* (1874), the toy boat functions as the signifier of manly aspirations. The story is set in the dirty, poverty-stricken 'Snag's Court' in the East End of London, near the docks and quays of the Thames. In it, Allan, a nine-year-old invalid son of a desperately poor widow, who has taken in the twelve-year-old orphan Jack of the title, has 'one great wish'. He wants 'to possess a boat – a wooden boat, with brightly painted sides, and masts and sails', like one that his neighbour, Ben Black, received from his uncle, a sailor. Unable to buy such a gift for his friend, Jack seeks help from his employer's wife on Christmas Eve. She enables him to purchase a small second-hand boat, which he lovingly improves with paint, and she also provides gifts of food and money for the poverty-stricken family. In this generic sentimental tale of middle-class seasonal charity, the working-class boy earns benevolence through his kindness and knowing his place. Yet it hints at the power of the martial ideal; in this court, says the author, everybody 'was in heart "a true-born sailor"'.[52]

Popular depictions of boys at play often had a military theme. Representations of aged Greenwich Pensioners, for example, frequently include a small boy sitting on the floor engrossed in his toy boat.[53] This was intended to invoke the generational transmission of military and patriotic values. A small boy plays with toy soldiers in the lithograph 'A Soldier's Wife; Or, Sunshine and Shadow' (c.1890), in which a priest stands alongside a seated, presumably grieving, wife, whose soldier husband is immortalised in a painting on the wall. Obliviously playing with five toy soldiers and a gun alongside his father's military helmet, the small boy embodies the stoicism recommended to withstand loss.[54] A rather different message is offered in the well-known poster *Daddy, what did YOU do in the Great War?* (1915), where the boy playing with his toy soldiers is an accusing figure, shaming men into volunteering for service.[55]

Increasingly, these archetypical boys' toys were bound up with nostalgia for lost childhood and family life. It was noted in the trade journal *Athletic Sports, Games and Toys*, in February 1896, that everyone remembers their toys, from the wooden horse, to 'the glittering hosts of French and Germans whom we disbanded ten years later on the threshold of youth'.[56] It is perhaps, therefore unsurprising that martial toys could become intensely emotional objects. This was obvious at the time. In the poem 'Treasures' in *Young Folks Paper* (1887), the treasures are relics of ages gone and childhood fled. When the author supposedly finds his 'treasures', they are stereotypical boys' playthings: 'Here we are! – a tin soldier whose limbs have been shattered,/And black is his coat, which was formerly red.' He then playfully skewers the trope of nostalgia, observing that although he should believe that 'these relics remind me/Of days when the sun shone as now 'tis not wont,/Of golden delight in the years far behind me', he is 'sorry to say that they don't!'[57] Despite the humorous cynicism of this poem, the convention that toy soldiers evoked childhood and the construction of self-identity was frequently deployed. Winston Churchill pronounced in *My Early Life*, for example, that his future career was set by his delight in playing with toy soldiers.[58]

The emotional resonance of toy soldiers and boats was such that they also signified the transience and risks of childhood and the vulnerability of masculinity. The lone toy boat or soldier could represent the boy in danger, missing, even dead: cultural associations prompted by harsh reality. In 1848, *John Bull*'s report of persons found dead in the Thames included a ten-year-old, 'amusing himself on the Surrey Side of Waterloo Bridge by playing with a toy-boat', who walked too far out in the water when it went beyond his grasp.[59] In print culture, the image of a vessel rendered vulnerable by nature made the boy's toy boat particularly poignant. Many depictions show a small boy leaning over a pond with a stick trying to hook his toy boat or being saved at the last moment from drowning.[60] The pathos inherent in abandoned military toys suggests mature masculinity unrealised. The poem 'Little Boy Blue', published in the 1890s, opens thus: 'the little toy soldier is red with rust, and the musket moulds in his hands', prompting the awful realisation that the soldier is left behind, waiting valiantly for his owner, because the boy has died in the night.[61] Again, these powerful feelings strengthened the appeal of martial manliness.

Like military toys, ceramic objects adorned with military subjects came in a variety of forms in the nineteenth century.[62] Popular during the French wars of the early nineteenth century and thereafter, they were reinvigorated during the Crimean War era. Staffordshire figurines, later called the 'poor man's porcelain', depicted naval and military heroic officers, as well as generic soldiers and Jack Tars.[63] New narrative figurines were introduced in the Crimean War, such as the 1854 'Wounded Soldier', which portrayed an injured French soldier leaning on an English sailor, reflecting and capitalising on the changing nature of Anglo-French relations.[64] Some objects depicted soldiers in less warlike scenes. Edward Moore & Co.'s earthenware pot lid (1870) has a soldier seated on a grassy bank watched by two flirtatious young women who have supplied him with water from their wooden pail.[65] Straightforwardly decorative, it alludes to soldiers' physical appeal for females. Lustre plaques, with a coloured border, also dubbed the 'poor man's picture', were often decorated with transfer verses and images with martial themes.[66] Potteries in the north-east and north-west produced lustreware in the form of bowls, mugs, jugs, and teapots, designed for display and decorative purposes rather than daily use. They combined verses, local landmarks, trade or society emblems, portraits of notable and celebrity figures and heroes, symbols of wars, and illustrations of soldiers and sailors.[67]

Some were explicitly commemorative and patriotic, intended to stir pride as well as pleasure. A pearlware jug from 1804 features large profile portraits of Admiral Nelson and Captain Berry on each side, separated by two rigged ships. With no accompanying text and somewhat generic portraits, their appeal assumed close knowledge of the two officers' acts in battle.[68] Others were more detailed, like a creamware mug, dated 1800, commemorating the Battle of the Nile in 1798, which depicts two warships engaging, and proudly states: 'The Young Alexander of France May boast of his prowess in vain, When Nelson appears tis confest That Britons are Lords of the Main.'[69] These did more than valorise officers' bravery. Although a Sunderland pink lustre jug boasts a portrait of Nelson beneath a figure of Fame, it extends admiration for martial valour beyond him to the ratings, in a verse that ends: 'All, all were Nelson's on that glorious DAY'.[70] Part of the 'general democratization of heroism' that developed in the nineteenth century, these objects cultivated and disseminated the charisma of martial manliness.[71]

Indeed, by the 1830s, in an era of apparent assured naval dominance, the verses on plaques and vessels regularly evoked martial manliness in the lower ranks, deploying songs celebrating Jack Tars, commissioned earlier in the French wars by the government to promote patriotism. For example, a plaque from the 1830s boasted a verse that deployed the bravery, physical strength, sacrifice, love, and kindness of idealised martial manliness:

> The walls of England are oak and they're strong
> And our tars have the heart of the oak they belong
> Oh! who is so brave and so kind and so free.
> As he who defendeth the Queen of the Sea.
> If a foe should advance he's then at your call
> If you crave his assistance he'll give you his all
> He loves you in peace and protects you in war
> Oh who is so kind as the brave British Tar.[72]

Such ceramics stirred feelings of pride, joy, even comfort. A plain plate, c.1860, with pink lustre border, contains the verse, 'The Sailor Boy', within a coloured rope; an appealing role model for youths immersed in the pleasure culture of war. In it the 'gallant sailor boy' is proud to carry his country's flag and name; he declares he will never shame his nation, but will 'fight her battles and share her fame./Sing: Hoy the gallant sailor boy.'[73]

One of the notable features of many of these ceramics throughout the century is the juxtaposition of illustrations and texts. Images and verses were recycled repeatedly in various combinations on jugs, mugs, bowls, and teapots, exploiting local and national identities and events and the close link between military and civilian spheres to appeal to buyers.[74] An earthenware bowl, c.1860–70, for example, depicts several broadly patriotic verses, praising England as the 'Empress of the elements' and diadem of the world, alongside maritime stanzas seeking the Lord's delivery from the dangers of the sea (Figure 3.2).[75] It also features a sailor's return, a sailor's farewell, a frigate in full sail, a view of the Wear Bridge – the biggest single-span bridge in the world when it opened in 1796 – as well as a Crimean War transfer with the word Crimea emblazoned on a central shield, a French eagle and British flag, and the phrases, 'May they ever be united; Vive L'Empreur God Save the Queen.'[76] Portraits of the Italian general Giuseppe Garibaldi were added to such ceramics in the 1850s and 1860s.[77] He became an icon of manliness in Britain following his visits to Tyneside and London.[78] Collectively, these motifs wove together Britain's imperial might and industrial progress and identified their defence and continued glory in sailors' and soldiers' manly deeds of courage and sacrifice.[79]

In conjunction with pride and patriotism, the prevailing emotions such items inspired were pity and pathos. Representations of the wounded soldier, like those modelled in Staffordshire figures from the Crimean War period, evoked sympathy for manly self-sacrifice. 'Miss Nightingale', c.1857, portrays Florence Nightingale standing next to a seated soldier with his arm in a sling.[80] The Royal Patriotic Fund made practical use of this. Established in 1854 to financially assist the widows and families of those who lost husbands or fathers in battle or on active service in the Crimean War, it raised funds through the sale of a Staffordshire Crimean War jug (Figure 3.3). It portrays a crying widow, her distressed children around her knees. On the other side is a battlefield scene with a Highlander being carried off the battlefield, and a wounded soldier supporting his bandaged head in his hand, a gesture indicating fatigue and grief and intended to stimulate pity and compassion in the beholder.[81] Many ceramics deployed military men's tears, a popular motif that evoked the sufferings of Christ, as well as the feeling, sentimental face of manliness that retained its strength in representations of military men.[82] The

3.2 White earthenware bowl decorated with pink lustreing, enamelling, and transfer-printed designs (c.1860–70), manufactured by Moore's Pottery, Sunderland.

'Sailor's Tear' (1835) was a typical verse on these earthenware objects.[83] Its stanzas took the soldier from his wife and infant to sea and fighting Britain's foes.[84] His tears formed the narrative device, each verse ending in him shedding a tear as he left his family behind until he was transformed into a magnificent fighting man. Verses from Lord Byron's 1806 poem 'The Tear' were transferred onto earthenware bowl which portrayed a sailor weeping when he realised he was to die and a soldier who in battle 'bathes every wound with a Tear'. These men shed tears of a Christian sensibility that symbolised resignation, lament, and pity rooted in manly duty.

These objects offered the body of the martial man in three-dimensional form to be touched, admired, and emoted over.[85] Their gender associations were made 'stickier' by the motif of tears and the emotions they provoked.[86] In the light of youths' responses to martial material culture, already discussed, it is not unreasonable to speculate that these objects generated similar aspirations and desire for military manliness and all it stood for. They also destabilised the distinctions between war and home and, in the case of men on armed service, as Chapter 4 will reveal, they acted as reminders of, and substitutes for the men within, homes and families.

Textiles were another form of material culture that showcased aspects of military masculinities, including men's capacity for domestic crafting. There are two types of 'wartime quilts' intended for use as bed or table

3.3 Royal Patriotic Fund jug, Crimean War (1855), Samuel Alcock & Co. (maker).

covers: those which incorporate pictorial military scenes and those made from martial uniform fabric such as woollen serge and worsted twill.[87] Both projected martial values into the domestic and civilian world.[88] Pictorial quilts had panels which depicted military individuals or events, often based on contemporary engravings. A very fine example by an unidentified woman is the 'George III coverlet' (c.1805), a Mariner's Compass design, made from plain and printed cottons.[89] Its centre is a pieced, embroidered circular panel showing George III reviewing volunteer troops in Hyde Park, copied from a 1799 print by John Singleton Copley. The forty vignette panels around its border were also influenced by prints of military themes, illustrating the extent to which these images penetrated domestic spaces and were consumed by women as well as men. The scenes include the ubiquitous sailor's and soldier's farewell and return, wounded military men, and, in various poses related to their service, carousing sailors, as well as celebrity heroes, such as Nelson and Major Peirson on his deathbed.[90] It is noteworthy that the female maker selected images that had emotional resonance, largely sailors' and soldiers' personal relationships with women, family, and comrades, as well as deathbed scenes.

One can only speculate as to the effect of sleeping under such coverings upon men. What is clear is that popular culture deployed such quilts to combine the domestic and martial to moral didactic ends, offering lessons of respectable civilian manliness. In 'The Patchwork Quilt' in the *British Workman* (1872), an army chaplain tells the story of a 'Scripture quilt' that a woman made and donated to a military hospital, to comfort soldiers' bodies and awaken their spirituality. The full-page illustration shows a sick, moustachioed soldier lying under a frilled patterned patchwork, closely scrutinising one of its scriptural patches (Figure 3.4). Desirably didactic, a tinted version of the engraving was available for one penny as an 'illustrated wall-paper'. The periodical hoped that 'many copies will find their way to Hospital Walls, Barrack Rooms, Cottage Walls'.[91] The sentimental motif of tears is again central. The chaplain explains that the woman had made the quilt with prayers, weeping for her own son who was in the army; soldiers who encountered it shed hundreds of tears in turn. Listing the wounded soldiers who were spiritually enlightened by the quilt, the story culminates with a young man who is observed to tearfully kiss one of the patterned pieces, as he recovers, because it reminds him of his mother's gown. Eventually they deduce that the quilt was made by the soldier's own mother and the chaplain triumphantly writes to 'tell her that her son who was dead is alive again – who was lost is found!' Redeemed, presumably, since this is a temperance magazine, by giving up alcohol, one of manliness's nemeses as Chapter 2 demonstrated.[92]

Although it is easy to assume that sewing quilts was a female, domestic craft, wartime quilts were made by sailors and soldiers who acquired needlework skills during service.[93] With geometric patterns, such quilts often had centrepieces that displayed their military origin, including motifs of ships, colonial locations, and regimental flags.[94] An exquisite patchwork in regimental colours made around 1855 from felted uniform wool, adorned with beadwork, has an embroidered middle panel consisting of regimental flags and the emblem of the 37th Regiment of Foot.[95] Some were made for family members.[96] While serving on HMS *Victory* in 1865, sailor James Cox made a bedspread from uniform fabric for his sister, Mary, who had brought him up after their mother died.[97] Mary bequeathed the bedspread to her granddaughter.[98] Others were sold or exchanged to settle a debt.[99] Many soldiers made exquisite quilts for public exhibition, generating income from viewing fees. The bed rug made by Sergeant Malcolm Macleod, sewn in India when he was serving with the 72nd Duke of Albany's Own Highlanders, blends the domestic with representations of

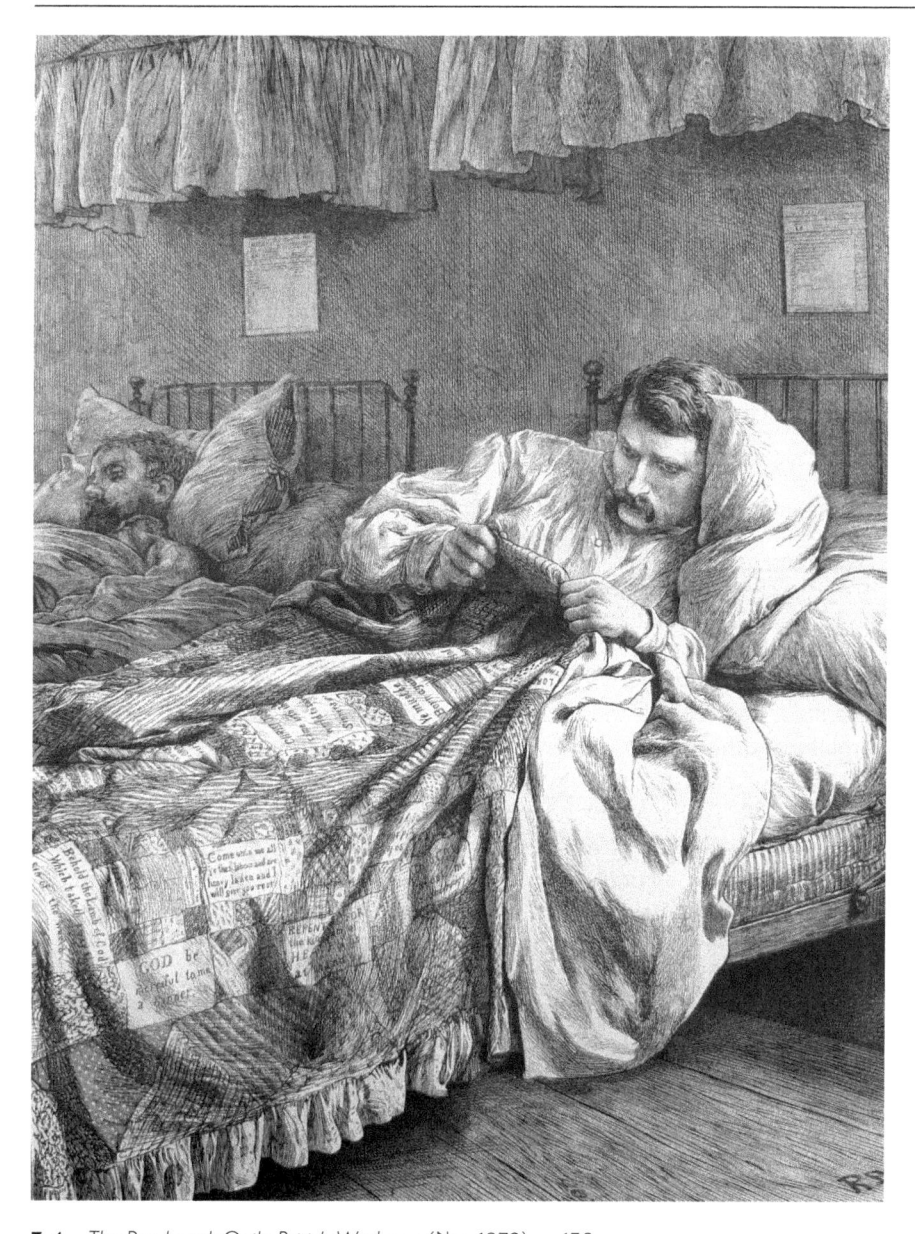

3.4 *The Patchwork Quilt, British Workman* (Nov 1872), p. 138.

both armed forces. Two embroidered panels, aligned to match on either side of a central panel, depict a Royal Navy sailor waving his hat and grasping a Union Jack and a Royal Navy ship. Macleod's regiment's two flags are worked in: the Queen's colour on the left, the regiment's colour on the right. He embroidered his name and rank across both, along with the names of places where the regiment served: Cape of Good Hope,

Sevastopol, Hindoostan, and Central India. He exhibited the bedspread at the Glasgow Industrial Exhibition 1865–66.[100]

In a society receptive to the pleasure culture of war, this juxtaposition of the martial and the domestic intrigued paying audiences which meant that large numbers of people from all social ranks encountered them. There were thirty woollen quilts made by military personnel displayed at the Great Exhibition of 1851, as well as at numerous industrial, charity, and military exhibitions thereafter.[101] They were one of the exhibits alongside the 'war material' in the Royal Military Exhibition in Chelsea, 1890, which was widely reported in London and provincial newspapers.[102] The *Daily News*, for example, enumerated them among the assembled 'treasures', which it predicted would be 'vastly' attractive for spectators. Its language is striking in domesticating the manly soldier:

> 'Tommy Atkins' in his leisure moments does not neglect the arts of peace … at fancy needlework some of them are accomplished experts. Patchwork rugs and quilts in great profusion bear testimony to labours on which the utmost patience and ingenuity must have been exercised; in the arrangement of colours much artistic taste is also displayed.[103]

This public fascination with the domesticated activities of military imperial men also undermines the concept of a 'flight from domesticity' at the cultural level, offering yet more evidence that domesticity could be masculine and was portable and not always fixed in the family home.[104]

The *Daily News* report concludes that these creations should reassure the public that soldiers of all ranks 'are more often profitably employed both abroad and at home'.[105] Indeed, these textiles were also agents in constructing the less threatening aspects of military manliness, playing their part in saving military men from temptation and depravity. As the report on the Royal Military Exhibition suggests, they were intended to occupy military men's spare time when not on the battlefield. Military authorities viewed needlecraft as an industrious activity that, if regularly practised, prevented soldiers resorting to alcohol when bored. In 1862, the British War Office promoted the setting up of workshops to train military personnel in various crafts and skills.[106]

In an interesting alliance, temperance periodicals similarly imagined patchwork as a guard against idle drinking. The *Band of Hope Review* published 'The Soldier-Boy's Patchwork Quilt' in 1871, in which the narrator, 'Uncle John', uses 'the well-known story of the soldier's patchwork quilt' to recommend that all soldiers take up 'useful employment' in the evenings to prevent them getting into trouble. His desire is 'that soldiers were as clever in the use of needles and thread as our "Jolly Jack Tars"'. The magazine was intended for poor, working-class children, so the story focuses on a 'little Band-boy' of the Royal Welsh Fusiliers, stationed at Chatham Barracks, who made a quilt for his grandfather. Here, the appeal of the military was deployed to inculcate a temperate, civilian manliness. Its message was intensified by an attractive illustration of three band-boys in uniform, two admiring the needlework of the third, while an adult soldier looks on approvingly through an open window. Presumably, the band-boys in their military uniforms were understood to appeal to boys seduced by the aesthetic allure of martial dress.[107] The *British Workman* commended soldiers' craftwork for its adult readership. In 1873 it published an article about Private Roberts who made patchwork quilts to raise an income when he gave up alcohol. He pointedly declares, 'I must be employed, or I shall get into mischief.'[108] The message was that working-class men could be as manly as military exemplars, without recourse to the pub. In the illustration Roberts holds up a beautiful quilt; the attractive combination of a uniformed soldier with a domestic textile intended to promote in its civilian readers the desire for self-controlled manliness.

Holly Furneaux and Sue Prichard have dismissed the traditions that military quilts were made to memorialise fallen comrades, or primarily sewn by recuperating wounded Crimean soldiers, although they recognise the cultural value such stories held.[109] Tales of their construction from the fragments of fallen soldiers' uniforms, for instance, inspired in viewers a patriotic intimacy and 'a desire for a rich narrative of the soldier maker's feeling'. Likewise, accounts of wounded soldiers creating them as occupational therapy provided a 'direct connection to the suffering body ... of the heroic survivor maker'.[110] They use both narratives to analyse Thomas Wood's well-known portrait of Private Thomas Walker making a quilt while convalescing in bed in Fort Pitt Military Hospital, Chatham, 1856, after a severe head injury in the Battle of Inkerman.[111] For them, the temperance framing of craftwork as an industrious and productive substitute for dangerous and immoral pastimes underpins the painting's celebration of Walker's dexterity and aesthetic taste.[112] In this way, the portrait domesticates the soldier into a more reassuring productive worker. The 'violence of war apparent in Walker's head wound' is transformed, 'as the trappings of militarism in the bold colours of the uniform are literally fragmented and remade into a form that gives comfort'.[113] They identify 'uneasiness', however, in Walker's 'inscrutable' facial expression, and in the scissors on his lap, 'directed to the centre of his crotch, uncomfortably suggest[ing] emasculation, even castration, by invalidism, and the craftwork of the sickbed'.[114]

The assertion that craft emasculates the soldier is overstated. Craftwork was an acceptable masculine activity, both in leisure and employment.[115] It was also a symbol of the ideal manly qualities of self-mastery in the face of dangerous appetites. As Chapter 2 has shown, this was a profound marker of approved masculinity. Contextualised in the other images of martial manliness, from bravery to suffering, therefore, the portrait of Walker conveys the glory and selflessness of idealised military manliness through wounds and craftwork, not its emasculation. His uniform, medal prominently displayed, and his expression of contented concentration remind the viewer of the glamour of martial life, men's self-sacrifice, and their role as physical protection for the nation. In sum, quilts served as emotional objects, stirring pride and patriotism and fashioning familial identity, all linked to the martial manliness at their heart.

Military celebrities and their material afterlife

This final section uses the changing representations in material culture of two military heroes to draw together the chapter's themes. Most accounts of celebrity military men focus upon officers, whose faces, forms, and feats appeared on commemorative objects and were used to market a variety of products. As we have seen, Admiral Nelson was regularly commemorated: a practice that continued where British military success permitted, as with an 1857 jug celebrating Sir Colin Campbell and Major General Sir Henry Havelock's relief of Lucknow.[116] Military celebrities were portrayed in figurines, such as the 1857 Staffordshire equestrian figure of Henry Havelock,[117] and General Charles George Gordon, dressed in fez and uniform, 1885.[118] More unusual is the wax and calico doll of Lord Frederick Roberts, c.1900, and, more common, the Gallaher 'Types of the British Army' cigarette cards issued in 1898.[119] The two military men discussed here, whose acts of courage were celebrated, commoditised, and memorialised in the years following their bravery, were of lower rank. Both were popular long after their deaths and thus their cultural meaning can be traced through the trajectory of the material culture that embodied them metaphorically – paintings, pottery, posters, toys, stone memorials, flagship colours, and regimental flags – and literally, in the form of corporeal relics.

Corporal John (Jack) Shaw was born in 1789 on a farm in Cossall, Nottinghamshire, and apprenticed as a boy to a wheelwright. Tall and large framed, at sixteen he began boxing, and at eighteen, in 1807, he joined the 2nd Life Guards.[120] Here he honed both his sporting prowess, trained by the champion boxers James Belcher and Gentleman John Jackson, and his sexual allure, as admired by the artist Benjamin Haydon who called him a 'satyr'. He put his physique to good use as a life model for artists, not only Haydon, but also William Hilton, Edwin Landseer, and William Etty.[121] Shaw went to war on the Iberian Peninsula in 1812, returned in 1814, and won a prize fight against Ned Painter in 1815. It was at Waterloo, however, that his posthumous reputation was forged, for it was here that he fought ferociously to the death against the French. The incident was lauded, if its details remain mired in myth.[122]

As his biographer Kasia Boddy reveals, Shaw was immediately 'turned into an object of vivid collective fantasy'.[123] He already possessed the raw materials for ideal manliness, combining a boxer's build, the swagger and glamour of the cavalry soldier, and the bravery and fortitude of the warrior. In the resulting 'Shawmania' that developed as Waterloo became a cultural artefact, Shaw was made over into a national emblem – a myth that served society's needs as well as the pleasure culture of war. Indeed, Boddy argues that the Duke of Wellington's calm modesty in the wake of victory was insufficient to satisfy the public's desire for an appropriate climax to the conflict. The spectacular charge of the heavy cavalry, personified in Shaw the Lifeguard, as he generally was described thereafter, was selected to serve this purpose.[124]

Boddy observes that Shaw's death came to act 'as a kind of synecdoche for the battle'. He was central to its commercialisation. The tours of Waterloo, which began almost immediately, included a visit to his grave. He featured as a symbol for martial heroism in novels, and as the virile poster boy of 'Old England' and its romanticised feudal relations for authors such as Sir Walter Scott and John Ruskin.[125] 'Shaw the Lifeguard' was the focus of military melodramas and tableaux across the country, like J. H. Amherst's 'The Battle of Waterloo', an equestrian, circus-style performance, popular for decades from 1824. The acts ended with a choreographed version of Shaw's sacrifice, often presented, however inaccurately, as the event on which the day turned.[126] A poster advertising Batty's Circus Royal on Wednesday, 5 February 1840, for example, promised a performance by Mr Wilkinson giving his 'celebrated impersonation of Shaw, The Life Guard's Man. Wherein he will depict the manly Prowess and Death of that individual at the Battle of Waterloo'.[127] These performances deployed a plethora of martial material culture, as an announcement in the *Chester Chronicle* of 1849 testifies. The 'Grand Military Piece' it advertises possesses 'every becoming necessary of dresses, flags, uniforms, combats, choruses' and culminated with the 'Terrific combat between Shaw, the Life Guardsman, and his opponents'. Deemed likely to entertain and, perhaps, educate, the event admitted the Charity Schools of Chester gratis.[128]

As the free showings to schools suggests, in this event and others Shaw was repackaged as an exemplar of martial manliness for boys. His legendary bravery was immortalised on objects marketed to children, including miniature Waterloo-themed theatrical sets, and he starred in boys' fiction published from the 1870s.[129] Somewhat belatedly, his natal village memorialised Shaw, along with two other men from Cossall who had served at Waterloo. In 1875, the *Ilkeston Pioneer* reported that a committee had been formed to raise funds for a tribute to these Cossall 'giants' and 'humble, noble heroes'; the white marble memorial adorned with two crossed swords and a plumed helmet was funded by local dignitaries and officers and unveiled on Waterloo Day in 1877.[130]

Next is Jack Crawford, who was born on 22 March 1775 in Sunderland. A keelman's son, at eleven he was apprenticed at South Shields, and in

1796 was either press-ganged or volunteered for the Royal Navy, serving on Admiral Duncan's HMS *Venerable*, the fleet's flagship. He became famous in 1797 at the Battle of Camperdown when the *Venerable*'s mast was hit, causing the Admiral's flag to fall – the customary sign of surrender. Crawford picked up the flag and, under heavy fire, which caused him facial injuries, climbed the broken mast and nailed the colours to it with a marlin spike. He was rewarded with an annual pension and a silver medal, given the honour of meeting George III, and, possibly, attended Nelson's state funeral.[131] Crawford returned to Sunderland to work on the keelboats and married, but became an alcoholic, purportedly a victim of his own celebrity, since he succumbed too readily to his admirers' offers of alcohol. As the *Manchester Times* reported, decades later, in 1890, Crawford had 'the improvident habits of the seamen of those days' and fell into 'hard straits', selling his medal to pay debts.[132] He was one of the first to die in the cholera outbreak in 1831 and, since he had drunk away his income, was buried in a pauper's grave.

His act of bravery was celebrated, romanticised, and immortalised almost immediately. He was portrayed on the mast, on the left of John Singleton Copley's 1799 painting, *The Surrender of the Dutch Admiral de Winter to Admiral Duncan at the Battle of Camperdown (The Victory of Lord Duncan)*.[133] Thereafter his image, in the act of nailing the colours, was commercialised, available both as engravings (see Figure 3.5) and transferred onto objects.[134] He appeared on Sunderland lustreware and commemorative pottery throughout the nineteenth century, typically bowls, jugs, teapots, and plates, which, like those discussed, included other motifs, such as the sailor's return and farewell.[135] By the 1860s, as this book's cover shows, Crawford was made over into a beautiful example of British manliness. Locks blowing in the wind, pretty face adorned by whiskers, his shirt provocatively revealing a muscular chest and shoulder, he practically pole-dances around the mast depicted in front of a Union Jack.[136] His fame was extensively exploited. In what appeared to be yet another retelling of his heroic actions, an 1890 article transformed halfway through into an advert for the patent medicine 'Prairie Flower and Sequah's Oil', which metaphorically nailed its colours to the mast to proclaim that the fight against illness was not lost: price 2s.[137]

There were performances at the Lyceum Sunderland in the 1870s: a play titled *Jack Crawford*, 'of a purely local interest' with 'many effective tableaux', and a 'Historical Picture Curtain; showing the nailing of the flag, seen by over 4000 people'.[138] Crawford was not just a local hero however: his name and actions cropped up across Britain in the second half of the nineteenth century. In 1841, the *Lancaster Gazette* included an elaborate imagined narrative of Crawford's actions as part of an account of Camperdown.[139] In 1887, the 'Hero of Camperdown' was the subject of Reverend Mr Hornby's 'popular lecture', delivered on this occasion at

3.5 *Jack Crawford*, by Daniel Orme, line and stipple engraving, published 1797.

the annual meeting of the Methodist New Connexion Missionary Society in Truro.[140] The emblematic, materialised form of Crawford was so powerful in conveying ideals of martial manliness that politicians and trade union leaders were depicted in his form. During polling for the general election in 1886, the arch-masculinist William Gladstone was depicted nailing colours to a mast, 'Jack-Crawford-like', on a screen hung in front of the Eleusis Club, Chelsea.[141] J. Havelock Wilson, who founded the sailors' and fireman's union in 1887, was portrayed as Crawford on the seamen's union banners.[142]

Once the legend of Crawford's bravery gained a powerful afterlife, Sunderland stepped up to honour his name and actions, and in doing so, stimulated local pride and identity. As noted, the memorabilia celebrating Crawford sometimes included images of Sunderland Bridge and performances of his actions were deemed to have a local audience. These links were made more material in a series of memorials. In 1866, Sunderland funded a memorial stone to be placed on Crawford's grave, along with constructing a public drinking fountain to his memory, perhaps more or less ironic given that his downfall was alcohol and temperance societies funded such fountains to encourage people not to drink beer. These actions were widely reported in provincial newspapers across Britain, in each instance announcing Crawford as 'the Sunderland tar who nailed Admiral Duncan's colours to the mast at the Battle of Camperdown'.[143] In the 1880s, however, in a time of escalating militarism, a local call was issued for a more substantial memorial to Crawford. The plans for a large obelisk, to be placed in the Sunderland Parish Churchyard, were widely reported in the British press from 1887, as was its unveiling in August 1888.[144] Reports noted the colours that were central to the obelisk, which had a sculpted mast with the flag nailed to it and draped down its front.[145] Indeed, at its unveiling, the flagship's colours were simultaneously present in two material forms. The *York Herald* commented that 'The identical flag which Jack nailed to the mast, and which is now the property of the Earl of Camperdown, draped the memorial.'[146]

Shortly after, another memorial was planned, this time in statue form. From 1889, local newspapers began reporting that a subscription was being raised by Sunderland Town Council to fund a statue on the knoll, Malakoff Hill, in Mowbray Park.[147] Depicted aloft nailing the colours to the mast, this version of Crawford is slightly different to previous ones. For one thing he nails the flag with the butt of a pistol, not a marlin spike. In earlier images such as Singleton Copley's painting, which influenced engravings, and in romanticised images that followed, like the bewhiskered version of 1866, he is a mature man. Yet, by 1890, he has acquired the proportions of a youth, with trousers rolled up to his knees. This indicates the extent to which martial manliness was co-opted to serve as an exemplar for boys.[148] Its elaborate unveiling in April 1890 by the Earl of Camperdown, Earl of Durham, and Mayor of Sunderland was a military spectacle that was widely reported in the metropolitan and provincial press. *Reynolds Newspaper* noted that 'A monster procession of trade societies, military and volunteer forces in the town, and a detachment of 300 bluejackets sent by the Admiral and Marines paraded the principal streets and then went to the park.'[149] Once again, the martial was linked to the domestic, as suggested by the advertisement announcing to parents the sale of 'Jack Crawford Sailor Suits' in May 1890.[150]

What makes the trajectories of both Shaw and Crawford so remarkable and similar is that both were associated with a corporeal relic. Shaw's body was recovered after the battle and buried near La Haye Sainte. In 1826, Sir Walter Scott wrote to Benjamin Haydon, mentioning that he possessed Shaw's skull, eventually displayed in his library at Abbotsford. It is still unclear how he acquired it, though what is evident is that Scott, like others, was fascinated by the Waterloo detritus that was sold as souvenirs and relics, obtaining cuirasses, bullets, and buttons, as well as Shaw's skull.[151] Scott's fascination allegedly stemmed from seeing Shaw when he was modelling his muscular physique for a sculpture.[152] Rather appropriately for a 'heart of oak', Jack Crawford's heart was donated to the Borough Museum of Sunderland in 1882 by a local councillor.[153] In 1887, the *Monthly Chronicle* mentioned 'a glass jar labelled as containing the heart of the hero of Camperdown' when it reported locals demanding a more appropriate memorial to Jack.[154] Only three years later, this had hardened into unease regarding the display of Jack's heart. The *Sunderland Daily Echo* reported in 1890 that the Museum and Library Committee had decided that the heart be removed from the shelves after hearing objections to its display. Arthur Laing said it gratified a 'morbid curiosity' and that there was no evidence it was Crawford's heart, while Mr Burns pointed out that since Crawford died from cholera it was unlikely that his heart would have been preserved.[155]

The physical remains of these military men's bodies had become devotional objects.[156] They resembled the preserved fragments of holy figures, which were not only vessels for emotions but were intended to incite emotional responses in those who encountered them.[157] The same occurred with other national heroes. In France, Leon Gambetta's heart was preserved following his death in 1882 and incorporated into a statue of Gambetta erected in 1891. As Charles Sowerwine comments, this shows the extent to which the body and emotions continued to be central in political and national rituals in the modern period.[158] In Shaw's and Crawford's cases, some of the emotions which resided in them had the potential to shape notions of gender. The nexus of body, material culture, and emotions still resounds today. Chris McHugh, a north-eastern artist, carried out a Community in Clay project using objects to engage the local community in Sunderland. As part of this he designed and executed a modern bravery medal (2011) embellished with Crawford's heart in a folk-art style, as well as a reconstruction of the heart is a glass jar which, rather aptly, resembles a reliquary.

Both the military heroes' 'charisma' was also intimately linked with that other military devotional object – the flag.[159] Crawford's fame centred on his physical act of nailing the colours and was central to his later persona as 'Champion of England', as this book's cover illustration shows to great effect. Shaw's combat was not originally linked with a flag, but it was introduced into the myth. By 1884, performances had Shaw 'retaining the English standard with his foot' while fighting off the French. He then 'faints from loss of blood, and falls across flag with a groan, kisses the standard, and crawls toward WELLINGTON, who gently takes the banner from his mouth. Shaw falls dead.'[160] Clearly, the cavalry equivalent of a regimental colour added to the dramatic spectacle. Regimental colours were, after all, understood to be imbued with military emotions. Each regiment possessed two flags: the royal colour (a union flag) and a flag that displayed the colours of the regiment, which were consecrated with a religious dedication. On them were embroidered the battles and campaigns in which the regiment had served. They were paraded when regiments were reviewed and taken into battle; when not in use they were housed in the officers' mess. When replaced by new colours, often in a public ceremony, the old ones were laid up, or put on permanent display in a location sacred to the regiment, such as the regimental chapel.[161]

As we have seen already, accounts of military bravery in the name of abstract regimental and patriotic values entered popular culture. It is important to note that it was their sacred quality that was revered. Thus, Agnes Giberne's 'Our Hero: A Tale of the Franco-English War Ninety Years Ago', published in the *Girl's Own Paper* in 1899, described Roy, who had the honour of bearing the King's Colour at the Battle of Corunna. She observed: 'The Royal and the Regimental Colours are, as we know, always consecrated with religious ceremony at the time of presentation, and they are looked upon with the most intense veneration and pride by every British soldier.'[162] Such objects promoted powerful feelings of pride in them and the men who cherished them. Not only recounted in stories, regimental colours were displayed in public and semi-public spaces and thus acted as emotional objects for civilians too. An 1886 account of 'Chelsea Pensioners at home' in the *Boy's Own Paper*, draws on their emotional resonance in its account of the hospital chapel:

> Against bright grey walls and roof the captured flags that form the chief decoration stand boldly out. Torn to tatters, most of them tender as tinder, they are now sewn on to silken nettings to support them in their decay; but often tiny pieces of the rotting silk come floating into the brown oak pews that line the walls.[163]

Every seven years when the chapel is cleaned, the article states, the 'precious trophies' are wrapped and laid in store: 'so delicate are they that slightest draught would blow them into dust'.[164] Here, their ephemerality rather than their glamour was forefront, since the intention was to capture the passage of time both through the artefacts of war and the bodies of the veterans, to imbue in boys a wonder at military men and their feats.[165]

Colours and the devotion they embodied were widely visible. They hung, at least in fiction, in ballrooms. In a tale of 'The Two Balls', 1863, set during the Crimean conflict, the ballroom's walls were adorned with regimental colours and military trophies, while French, Sardinian, and English flags, like 'three big bed-curtains', hung from the ceilings.[166] As we have seen, the colours were sometimes at the centre of soldiers' and sailors' quilts, thereby entering the domestic sphere. The *Birmingham Pictorial and Dart* described the art and needlework department of Jevons & Mellor in 1898; among the nightdress cases and bedspreads was a table-centre 'in white satin de luxe, embroidered in regimental colours, Indian style and design, edged with taped-headed fringe'.[167] In 1899, the *Country Gentleman: Sporting Gazette, Agricultural Journal* described Queen Victoria's fortieth birthday celebrations, when Colonel Inigo Jones, of the 2nd Battalion Scots Guards, presented her with an 'Empress' bouquet of forty crimson and white roses tied with a white satin sash sporting looped bows of regimental colours fixed with the silver star of the regiment.[168] By the late nineteenth century, bridesmaids attending the weddings of military grooms carried bouquets trimmed with streamers in regimental colours.[169]

The plethora of material culture surrounding celebrity martial heroes and the glamour that accrued to them, whether real or imagined, reveals the force of the conjunction of emotionalised bodies and material culture. The objects could evoke the feelings associated with idealised manliness and, thus, were not just storehouses of meaning, they acted upon those who encountered them, shaping notions of gender and self.[170]

Conclusion

This chapter unpicks the ways in which objects bearing martial connotations and representations of idealised military men conveyed manliness. Those who encountered the objects were familiar with the manly values they evoked, all associated with powerful feelings like love, duty, bravery, and stoicism, sacrifice, and grief. After all, the military men and associated material culture were often glamorous and charismatic, which stimulated desire for the manliness they embodied. Men recalled reacting in similar ways to military heroes and objects, demonstrating how emotional objects functioned as disseminators of values that people shared and interpreted within their pre-existing mutual knowledge of gender constructions. Collectively, the materiality of martial manliness also shows that the military and civilian spheres were not entirely distinct. Cultural imagination, as well as interactions between people and things, often spanned the geographical distance imposed by war and service. It also contributes to the nuancing of the thesis of the flight from domesticity, by offering more evidence of the place and role of the domestic within homosocial institutions, as well as the militarisation of the domestic environment, a location for objects that celebrated war and fighting men. Chapter 4 develops these themes by examining men's absence from home, whether serving the nation in the armed forces or in paid employment. In both cases, their manliness was bound up with their relationship with home and the feelings it wrought.

Notes

1 From the *Quarterly Review* originally, republished in the *Lady's Newspaper* (25 December 1858), p. 409.
2 *Ibid.*
3 The painting that is most likely referred to, and to which Napier is said to have offered information, is by George Jones: *The Battle of Meeanee, 17 February 1843*, Cheshire Military Museum, https://artuk.org/discover/artworks/the-battle-of-meeanee-17-february-1843-103077 (accessed 4 June 2019).
4 Scott Hughes Myerly, *British Military Spectacle: From the Napoleonic Wars through the Crimea* (Cambridge, MA, and London: Harvard University Press, 1996), chs 1 and 2.
5 Review of *Peregrine Scramble; or, Thirty Years' Adventure of a Blue Jacket* by Capt Sir H.V. Huntley, R.N., *John Bull* (10 March 1849), p. 151.
6 *Ibid.*
7 'Soldiers and the Victoria Cross by an army chaplain', *Boy's Own Magazine: An Illustrated Journal of Fact, Fiction, History, and Adventure* 2 (1863), p. 309. Also see 'The Victoria Cross and the Royal Welsh', *Boy's Own Magazine* 2 (1863), p. 476.
8 'Soldiers and the Victoria Cross by an army chaplain', p. 310–14.
9 *Ibid.*, p. 314.
10 *Ibid.*, p. 315.
11 *Ibid.*, p. 315. For the role of battlefield relics see James Marten, *Sing Not War: The Lives of Union and Confederate Veterans in Gilded Age America* (Chapel Hill: University of North Carolina Press, 2011), pp. 138–46.
12 *Boy's Own Magazine* 2 (1863), p. 483.
13 For an account of this form of manliness in literature see Bradley Deane, *Masculinity and the New Imperialism: Rewriting Manhood in British Popular Literature, 1870–1914* (Cambridge: Cambridge University Press, 2014).
14 *The Marvel* (9 December 1899), p. 13.
15 Louise Carter, 'Scarlet fever: female enthusiasm for men in uniform, 1780–1815', in Kevin Linch and Matthew McCormack (eds), *Britain's Soldiers: Rethinking War and Society, 1715–1815* (Liverpool: Liverpool University Press, 2014), pp. 155–80.
16 *Punch* (16 January 1847), p. 20.
17 Myerly, *British Military Spectacle*, ch. 3. For the wider motivation of men becoming soldiers and sailors in the Revolutionary and Napoleonic Wars see Catriona Kennedy, *Narratives of the Revolutionary and Napoleonic Wars: Military and Civilian Experience in Britain and Ireland* (Basingstoke: Palgrave Macmillan, 2013), ch. 3.
18 See Ian Dyck, 'William Cobbett', in *Dictionary of National Biography*, https://doi-org.oxfordbrookes.idm.oclc.org/10.1093/ref:odnb/5734 (accessed 30 March 2018).
19 *The Life of William Cobbett, Esq, Late MP for Oldham, Manchester* (1835), p. 8. For patriotism inspiring joining the navy, see Kennedy, *Narratives of the Revolutionary and Napoleonic Wars*, pp. 58–9.
20 *Life of William Cobbett*, p. 8. George Brydges Rodney, 1st Baron Rodney, KB (bap. 13 February 1718–24 May 1792), was a British naval officer who fought in the

American War of Independence. He was feted for his victory over the French at the Battle of the Saintes in 1782.
21 *Life of William Cobbett*, p. 12.
22 Henry Angelo, *Reminiscences of Henry Angelo* (London, 1904), p. 81.
23 *Ibid.*, p. 81.
24 *Ibid.*, p. 82.
25 *Ibid.*, p. 82.
26 Tyne & Wear Archives, Reverend William Ettrick's memorandum books, DF/ETT 2539/3 (1823–27). Admiral Sir Edward Codrington GCB RN (27 April 1770–28 April 1851) was a British admiral, hero of the Battle of Trafalgar and the Battle of Navarino.
27 E. E. Watts Moses, 'The Ettricks of High Barnes', *Antiquities of Sunderland* (The Sunderland Antiquarian Society), XX (1932–1943) (1951), p. 14. Dorset Record Office (DRO), Mrs Sherwood, 'Account of William Ettrick's life' (1980), D1854/3.
28 Kennedy, *Narratives of the Revolutionary and Napoleonic Wars*, pp. 38–9.
29 Myerly, *British Military Spectacle*, pp. 18–27.
30 *Lady's Monthly Museum* (1807), p. 174.
31 For the widespread popularity of children dressing as soldiers see Myerly, *British Military Spectacle*, p. 150.
32 Draft notes for his autobiographical *A Handbook for Posterity, or, Recollections of 'Twiddle Twaddle'*, published in 1896: *A Handbook for Posterity, or, Recollections of 'Twiddle Twaddle' / by George Cruikshank, about Himself and other People; a Series of Sixty-Two 'Etchings On Glass', with Descriptive Notes* (Houghton Library, Harvard University). Cited in Dominic Janes, *Oscar Wilde Prefigured: Queer Fashioning and British Caricature, 1750–1900* (Chicago and London: University of Chicago Press, 2016), p. 119.
33 Myerly, *British Military Spectacle*, pp. 63–4.
34 For an in-depth study of the power of such songs see Oskar Cox Jensen, David Kennerley, and Ian Newman (eds), *Charles Dibdin and Late Georgian Culture* (Oxford: Oxford University Press, 2018).
35 Henry Angelo, *Fencing Master: Reminiscences of Henry Angelo with Memoirs of his Late Father and Friends* (London, 1828), p. 82
36 *Ibid*.
37 *The Life of William Hutton, and the History of the Hutton Family. Edited from the Original MSS., with the Addition of Numerous Illustrative Notes, Original Matter, Examples of Hutton's Poetical Productions, and Notices of All his Works* (London, 1872), p. 9.
38 'Something about tin soldiers', *Chums* (17 January 1894), p. 334.
39 For example, Mary Evans Picture Library, 'Toy Soldiers at Attention', part of Box 134, Boswell Collection, Picture No. 11058848, *c*.1895 © The Boswell Collection, Bexley Heritage Trust/Mary Evans.
40 Kenneth Brown, 'Modelling for war? Toy soldiers in late Victorian and Edwardian Britain', *Journal of Social History* 24:2 (1990), 238, 243.
41 *Chums* (17 January 1894), p. 334.
42 For the first half of the nineteenth century see Kathryn Gleadle, 'Playing at soldiers: British loyalism and juvenile identities during the Napoleonic Wars', *Journal for Eighteenth-Century Studies* 38:3 (2015), 335–48; Bryan Ganaway, *Toys, Consumption, and Middle-Class Childhood in Imperial Germany, 1871–1918* (Bern: Peter Lang, 2009); David Hamlin, *Work and Play: The Production and Consumption of Toys in Germany 1870–1914* (Ann Arbor: University of Michigan Press, 2007); Myerly, *British Military Spectacle*, pp. 61–2, 143–4. Michael Paris, *Warrior Nation: Images of War in British Popular Culture, 1850–2000* (London: Reaktion, 2000), pp. 70–4.
43 Brown, 'Modelling for war?', passim.

44 *Ibid.*, 246.
45 For example, Mary Evans Picture Library, late nineteenth-century scrap, Picture No. 11075803.
46 *St Nicholas* (1 March 1879).
47 Fergus Hume, *Whom God Hath Joined, or A Question of Marriage* (London: F. V. White, 1891), p. 183.
48 Included in an advert for Jarrold's Ever-Welcome Toy Books is 'A brave tin soldier', *Hearth and Home* (29 November 1894), p. 141.
49 *Funny Folks* (21 August 1875), p. 52.
50 For examples see Mary Evans Picture Library: greetings card, late nineteenth century, Picture No. 10007805; New Year's Day card, with two children playing with a tiny boat on a water tub, 1890s, Picture No. 10994551. For girls playing with toy boats and soldiers, see Jane Hamlett, *Material Relations: Domestic Interiors and Middle-Class Families in England, 1850–1910* (Manchester and New York: Manchester University Press, 2010), p. 128.
51 Mary Evans Picture Library, Thomas Webster, *Contrary Winds*, Picture No. 10170466. Published in chromolithograph form thirty years later, in *Thorley's Illustrated Farmers' Almanack*.
52 'Good-natured Jack', *Our Young Folks* (7 February 1874), p. 84.
53 Joanne Begiato and Michael Brown, 'Visualising the aged veteran in nineteenth-century Britain: Memory, masculinity and nation', in Michael Brown, Anna Maria Barry, and Joanne Begiato (eds), *Martial Masculinities: Experiencing and Imagining the Military in the Long Nineteenth Century* (Manchester: Manchester University Press, 2019), pp. 102–36.
54 National Army Museum, Picture Number: 1997–10–89–1. Also published in *Christian Globe* (1890).
55 National Army Museum, Picture Number: 19777–06–81.
56 Cited in Brown, 'Modelling for war?', 238.
57 *Young Folks Paper* (17 September 1887), p. 189.
58 Brown, 'Modelling for war?', 238; Alix Bunyan, 'The children's progress: late-nineteenth-century children's culture, the Stephen juvenilia, and Virginia Woolf's argument with her past' (PhD dissertation, University of Oxford, 2001), p. 33. For a working-class example see Paris, *Warrior Nation*, p. 72.
59 *John Bull* (24 July 1848), p. 462.
60 For example, Mary Evans Picture Library, *Illustrated London Almanack*, 1882, Picture No. 10019925; Mary Evans Picture Library, Scrap 'Dog Saves Boy', Picture No. 10099008.
61 'Little Boy Blue', in *Lullaby-Land: Songs of Childhood* (Toronto, 1900), published in the *Woman's Signal* (26 November 1896), p. 342.
62 The following section is based on searches of online collections of ceramics from the Pottery Gallery, Sunderland Museum, Tyne & Wear Archives & Museums; National Maritime Museum; National Army Museum; and Fitzwilliam Museum. It is also informed by Myrna Schkolne, *Staffordshire Figures 1780–1840: Manufacturers, Pastimes, and Work*, vol. 1 (Atglen, PA: Schiffer Publishing Ltd: 2013); Reginald G. Haggar, *Staffordshire Chimney Ornaments* (London: Phoenix House Ltd, 1955); Thomas Balston, *Staffordshire Portrait Figures of the Victorian Age* (London: Faber & Faber, 1958); P. D. Gordon Pugh, *Staffordshire Portrait Figures and Allied Subjects of the Victorian Era* (London: Barrie & Jenkins, 1970).
63 For examples see, Madelena Antiques & Collectables, 'Staffordshire Pottery Figures – Discover' http://madelena.com/introduction-staffordshire-pottery-figures.php (accessed 12 September 2019). For the range of naval and military figurines see Balston, *Staffordshire Portrait Figures*, pp. 55–66; Pugh, *Staffordshire Portrait Figures*, pp. 3–4, pp. 323–71.
64 'Wounded Soldier', http://madelena.com/introduction-staffordshire-pottery-fig

ures.php (accessed 3 April 2018). Also see Fitzwilliam Museum, 'French Soldier and English Sailor' (c.1855), Object Number: C.1009–1928, http://data.fitzmuseum.cam.ac.uk/id/object/71130 (accessed 30 July 2019).
65 Tyne & Wear Archives & Museums, Edward Moore & Co.'s earthenware pot lid (1870), TWCMS: E710.
66 They were manufactured in Staffordshire, Yorkshire, and the north-east, mainly Newcastle and Sunderland. For an overview of their different forms see 'Mate sound the pump', www.matesoundthepump.com/ (accessed April 2018).
67 The portraits of notable men on ceramics included famous preachers such as John Wesley, literary heroes like Robert Burns, who adorned pottery that was produced in 1859 to mark the centenary of his birth, and cult liberal heroes, such as the radical MP Richard Cobden. See Pugh, *Staffordshire Portrait Figures*, passim.
68 Tyne & Wear Archives & Museums, pearlware jug, TWCMS: E2428.
69 Tyne & Wear Archives & Museums, creamware mug, TWCMS: P1549; also see same design on a barrel-shaped jug, which also has a view of the Iron Bridge in Sunderland, TWCMS: F6363.
70 National Maritime Museum, jug decorated with bands and splashes of pink lustre and hand-coloured, black transfer prints, Object No. AAA5163.
71 Simon Wendt, 'Introduction', in Simon Wendt (ed.), *Extraordinary Ordinariness: Everyday Heroism in the United States, Germany and Britain, 1800–2015* (Frankfurt and New York: Campus Verlag, 2016), p. 12.
72 Attributed to John Carr, North Shields, c.1830s–40s, www.matesoundthepump.com/ (accessed April 2018).
73 Tyne & Wear Archives & Museums, plain plate, c.1860, Ball's Pottery, TWCMS: 2004.2596.
74 See, for example, all Tyne & Wear Archives & Museums: jug, 1860, TWCMS: B1343; mug, 1855–60, TWCMS: D2290; bowl, 1860, TWCMS: D2249; creamware teapot, 1860–70, TWCMS: S1128.
75 Tyne & Wear Archives, earthenware bowl, TWCMS: D2037.
76 The transfer was used by Scott's and Moore's potteries in Sunderland, along with another known as Garrison. See the description of the transfers on the Sunderland ceramics in the Fitzwilliam Collection, Object Number: C.96–1997, http://data.fitzmuseum.cam.ac.uk/id/object/76460 (accessed 30 July 2019).
77 Tyne & Wear Archives & Museums, Dixon, Phillips & Co., c.1860, TWCMS: D2008; for figurines see Pugh, *Staffordshire Portrait Figures*, pp. 301–34.
78 For his popularity in Tyneside see Marcella Sutcliffe, 'Radical objects: radical and less radical effigies of Garibaldi', *History Workshop Journal* (2012), www.historyworkshop.org.uk/radical-and-less-radical-effigies-of-garibaldi/ (accessed 24 June 2019).
79 Tyne & Wear Archives & Museums, Moore's Pottery earthenware, TWCMS: D2037. Also see similar transfers on 'Sailor's Return Jug', Fitzwilliam Museum, Object Number: C.1090–1928, http://data.fitzmuseum.cam.ac.uk/id/object/71296 (accessed 30 July 2019).
80 'Miss Nightingale', c.1857, http://madelena.com/introduction-staffordshire-pottery-figures.php (accessed 3 April 2018).
81 National Army Museum Royal Patriotic Fund jug, Crimean War, 1855, https://collection.nam.ac.uk/detail.php?acc=1961-03-24-1 (accessed 12 September 2019). Also see the V&A collection, where it is described as a porcelain jug, CIRC.565–1963, http://collections.vam.ac.uk/item/O332874/jug-samuel-alcock-co/ (accessed 20 September 2019).
82 Thomas Dixon, *Weeping Britannia: Portrait of a Nation in Tears* (Oxford: Oxford University Press, 2015). Bernard Capp, '"Jesus wept" but did the Englishman? Masculinity and emotion in early modern England', *Past & Present* 224:1 (1 August

2014), 75–108. Also, Georgina Prineppi, 'Sailors in British broadside ballads, 1800–1850' (MA dissertation, University of Miami, 2015), pp. 34–5.
83 For example, see Tyne & Wear Archives & Museums, Dixon, Phillips & Co., c.1860, TWCMS: D2008.
84 This verse was very common. Another example is Tyne & Wear Archives & Museums, white earthenware quart mug, 1840, Scott's Pottery, TWCMS: D2258.
85 For the role of the wounded soldier in civilian attitudes to war, see Holly Furneaux, *Military Men of Feeling: Emotion, Touch, and Masculinity in the Crimean War* (Oxford: Oxford University Press, 2016) and Philip Shaw, 'Longing for home: Robert Hamilton, nostalgia and the emotional life of the eighteenth-century soldier', *Journal for Eighteenth-Century Studies* 39:1 (2016), 25–40.
86 Joanne Begiato, 'Tears and the manly sailor in England, c.1760–1860', *Journal for Maritime Research* 17:2 (2015), 117–33.
87 Annette Gero, *Wartime Quilts: Appliques and Geometric Masterpieces from Military Fabric from 300BC to WWII* (Roseville, NSW: Beagle Press, 2015).
88 For a detailed study of quilts made by soldiers, see Holly Furneaux and Sue Prichard, 'Contested objects: curating soldier art', *Museum & Society* 13:4 (2015), 447–61.
89 The V&A have precisely dated to it to a fairly short period of intense naval euphoria up to 1801. V&A, George III coverlet, Museum Number: T.9–1962, https://collections.vam.ac.uk/item/O165075/bed-cover-unknown/ (accessed 15 July 2019). Also see Jacqueline Riding, 'His constant Penelope: epic tales and domestic narratives', in Sue Prichard (ed.), *Quilts, 1700–2010: Hidden Histories, Untold Stories* (London: V&A Publishing, 2010), pp. 156–61. See also, Gero, *Wartime Quilts*, pp. 24–5.
90 This detail is based upon the description provided by the V&A, https://collections.vam.ac.uk/item/O165075/bed-cover-unknown (accessed 15 July 2019). Identified prints influencing the vignettes include Robert Dighton's *Descriptions of Battles by Land and Sea*, published in March 1801, and Copley's *Death of Major Peirson*, 1781, see www.tate.org.uk/art/artworks/copley-the-death-of-major-peirson-6-january-1781-n00733 (accessed 15 July 2019).
91 *British Workman* (November 1872), p. 138.
92 *Ibid.*
93 Those made by soldiers in India were distinguished by their more vibrant colour range since they used dress uniform as well as being influenced by mirrored and beaded fabrics in the country. Gero, *Wartime Quilts*, pp. 109, 138. Christopher Breward, 'Sewing soldiers', in Prichard (ed.), *Quilts, 1700–2010*, pp. 84–7. Examples of men sewing are cited in Nick Mansfield, *Soldiers as Workers: Class, Employment, Conflict and the Nineteenth-Century Military* (Liverpool: Liverpool University Press, 2016), p. 132. For a photograph of a uniformed soldier displaying such a quilt, dated around 1870, see Gero, *Wartime Quilts*, p. 113.
94 See V&A, Brayley quilt, probably made by Private Francis Brayley, India, 1867–77, T.58–2007, http://collections.vam.ac.uk/item/O144601/quilt-brayley-francis/ (accessed 15 July 2019).
95 The patchwork is from a private collection, Gero, *Wartime Quilts*, pp. 34–5. See also National Army Museum, patchwork and embroidered bed cover, 17th (The Leicestershire) Regiment of Foot, 1865 (c), NAM 1992-07-206-1, which has two regimental flags at its centre.
96 For crafts made as gifts for family also see Maya Wassell Smith, '"The fancy work what sailors make": material and emotional creative practice in masculine seafaring communities', *Nineteenth-Century Gender Studies* 14:2 (2018), www.ncgs-journal.com/issue142/PDF/smith.pdf (accessed 15 July 2019).
97 Gero, *Wartime Quilts*, p. 116.
98 *Ibid.*
99 Mansfield, *Soldiers as Workers*, p. 131; Gero, *Wartime Quilts*, pp. 9, 109, 116, 121.

100 It won a bronze medal. Gero, *Wartime Quilts*, pp. 70–3.
101 Gero has identified four British sailors' quilts and many more soldiers' quilts made during the long nineteenth century (not including those made in Europe and North America, or by military tailors). *Ibid.*, pp. 109–52.
102 *Ibid.*, p. 9.
103 'The Royal Military Exhibition', *Daily News* (6 May 1890).
104 This counters John Tosh's restatement of his thesis in 'Home and away: the flight from domesticity in late-nineteenth-century England re-visited', *Gender and History* 3 (2015), 570–1.
105 'The Royal Military Exhibition', *Daily News* (6 May 1890).
106 Furneaux and Prichard, 'Contested objects', 450.
107 *Band of Hope Review* (2 October 1871), cited in Gero, *Wartime Quilts*, pp. 124–5.
108 The illustration is reproduced in Gero, *Wartime Quilts*, p. 128, and discussed in Clare Rose, 'A patchwork panel "shown at the Great Exhibition"', *V&A Online Journal* 3 (2011), www.vam.ac.uk/content/journals/research-journal/issue-03/a-patchwork-panel-shown-at-the-great-exhibition/ (accessed 6 April 2018).
109 For examples of those made during convalescence, see Furneaux and Prichard, 'Contested objects', 451, 455–6; Furneaux, *Military Men of Feeling*, pp. 176–86.
110 Furneaux and Prichard, 'Contested objects', 453.
111 The portrait was reproduced as an engraving too. See *ibid.*, 455.
112 For a detailed account of Walker, see *ibid.*, 455–6.
113 *Ibid.*, 455–6.
114 *Ibid.*, 457.
115 For new work on the relationship between craft and masculinity, see Freya Gowrley and Katie Faulkner, 'Making masculinity: craft, gender and material production in the long nineteenth century', *Nineteenth-Century Gender Studies* 14:2 (2018), www.ncgsjournal.com/issue142/introduction.htm (accessed 15 July 2019). Wassell Smith, '"The fancy work what sailors make"'; Karen Harvey, 'Craftsmen in common: objects, skills and masculinity in the eighteenth and nineteenth centuries', in Hannah Grieg, Jane Hamlett, and Leonie Hannan (eds), *Gender and Material Culture in Britain since 1600* (London: Palgrave Macmillan, 2016), pp. 68–89.
116 For examples, see Pugh, *Staffordshire Portrait Figures*, pp. 298–9. For the feting of Havelock as a hero, see Paris, *Warrior Nation*, pp. 38–41.
117 National Trust Collection, Staffordshire equestrian figure of Henry Havelock, NT 341642, www.nationaltrustcollections.org.uk/object/341642.
118 National Trust Collection, General Charles George Gordon figure, NT 341721, www.nationaltrustcollections.org.uk/object/341721. Also see mounted Gordon, *c.*1870–1900, NT 341744, www.nationaltrustcollections.org.uk/object/341744. For the depiction of Gordon as a martyred hero, see Paris, *Warrior Nation*, p. 41.
119 V&A, wax and calico doll of Lord Frederick Roberts, MISC.12–1969, http://collections.vam.ac.uk/item/O1121620/doll/. See also National Portrait Gallery, Lord Kitchener, bisque-headed patriotic doll, *c.*1914–16, by unknown, www.portrait.gov.au/image/72882/72875/.
120 Kasia Boddy, 'Making history: life guardsman Shaw at Waterloo', *Critical Quarterly* 57:4 (2015), 2–3.
121 *Ibid.*, 3–7.
122 *Ibid.*, 12–14.
123 *Ibid.*, 1.
124 *Ibid.*, 14.
125 *Ibid.*, 17, 24.
126 *Ibid.*, 25–6.
127 *Ibid.*, 29.
128 *Chester Chronicle* (1 June 1849), p. 2.

129 Boddy, Making history', 34.
130 'Waterloo: the Cossall Monument', Thoroton Society Newsletter, Thoroton Society of Nottinghamshire, www.thorotonsociety.org.uk/publications/articles/cossall-monument.htm (accessed 4 May 2019).
131 According to one account, the medal was struck at the town's expense, with the City's Arms on one side. 'Gallant British tar', *Manchester Times* (12 April 1890). The medal is held in Tyne & Wear Archives & Museums, TWCMS: 2010.4463.
132 *Ibid*. The Earl of Camperdown returned it to Sunderland Town Council for display in the museum, *Newcastle Weekly Courant* (2 March 1888).
133 National Galleries Scotland, John Singleton Copley's painting, *The Surrender of the Dutch Admiral de Winter to Admiral Duncan at the Battle of Camperdown (The Victory of Lord Duncan)*, 1799, NG 2661.
134 For examples see National Portrait Gallery, *Jack Crawford* by Daniel Orme, line and stipple engraving, published 1804, NPG D23303 and *Jack Crawford* by Daniel Orme, line and stipple engraving, published 1797, NPG D23301; also Tyne & Wear Archives & Museums, TWCMS: 114936.
135 For examples see Tyne & Wear Archives & Museums: earthenware bowl, c.1897, TWCMS: C8085; earthenware jug, c.1890, TWCMS: D1882; Staffordshire porcelain teapot, c.1890. TWCMS: D1921; porcelain plate, c.1890, TWCMS: D1904.
136 Tyne & Wear Archives & Museums, *The Champion of England*, engraved by G. S. Shury, 1860 (colour lithograph), after Thomas Herbert Maguire (1821–1895) © Tyne & Wear Archives & Museums/Bridgeman Images.
137 *Huddersfield Chronicle and West Yorkshire Advertiser* (18 January 1890).
138 *Era* (7 October 1877); *Era* (6 October 1878).
139 *Lancaster Gazette and General Advertiser for Lancashire, Westmorland* (4 December 1841).
140 Reported in *Royal Cornwall Gazette Falmouth Packet, Cornish Weekly News, & General Advertiser* (29 April 1887), p. 6.
141 *Pall Mall Gazette* (5 July 1886); *Aberdeen Weekly Journal* (9 October 1895). When a new first-class battleship named the *Venerable* was launched, Crawford was still being feted as a manly exemplar: *Morning Post* (2 November 1899).
142 John Gorman, *Banner Bright: An Illustrated History of the Banners of the British Trade Union Movement* (London: Allen Lane, 1973), p. 113.
143 See *Dundee Courier and Argus* (17 July 1866); *Newcastle Weekly Courant* (20 July 1866); *Berrow's Worcester Journal* (21 July 1866), as well as papers in Birmingham, Glasgow, and Liverpool. The drinking fountain was reported under the title 'Memorial to "Harry Bluff"' in the *Morning Post* (10 September 1866), p. 3.
144 *North Eastern Daily Gazette* (7 August 1888).
145 For a detailed description of this 'happy' design of the Union Jack, see the *Dundee Courier & Argus* (10 August 1888).
146 *York Herald* (7 August 1888). In 2017, Sunderland launched a campaign to find the flap that Crawford nailed to the *Venerable*'s mast, to be displayed at the Tall Ships Race in 2018, www.sunderlandecho.com/our-region/sunderland/appeal-to-trace-the-flag-which-made-sunderland-hero-jack-crawford-famous-1-8832517.
147 *Newcastle Weekly Courant* (18 May 1889); *North Eastern Daily Gazette* (7 April 1890).
148 For an overview of boys' fiction, see Paris, *Warrior Nation*, ch. 2.
149 *Reynolds Newspaper* (13 April 1890); *Birmingham Daily Post* (8 April 1890); *Pall Mall Gazette* (8 April 1890). For the power of military parades and shows see Myerly, *British Military Spectacle*, pp. 140–2.
150 *Sunderland Daily Echo and Shipping Gazette* (12 May 1890), p. 4.
151 For battlefield souvenirs acquired by soldiers and sent home to family see Furneaux, *Military Men of Feeling*, pp. 163–75.
152 Boddy, Making history', 18–20. A plaster cast was made by Shaw's comrades, and

can be seen in the Household Cavalry Museum, www.nam.ac.uk/waterloo200/200-object/cast-of-skull-of-corporal-john-shaw/.
153 For the links between the sturdy oak of vessels and the courageous heart of sailors see Christiana Payne, *Where the Sea Meets the Land: Artists on the Coast in Nineteenth Century Britain* (Bristol: Sansom & Co. Ltd, 2007), pp. 29–31.
154 Cited in Chris McHugh, 'Towards a Sunderland Pottery for the twenty-first century: materializing multiple dialogues in museum display through creative ceramics', *Journal of Museum Ethnography* 26, Multiple Dialogues: Interpreting Ethnographic Collections in the Twenty-First Century: Papers from the Annual Conference of the Museum Ethnographers Group Held at the National Museum of Scotland, Edinburgh, 16–17 April 2012 (2013), p. 73.
155 *Sunderland Daily Echo and Shipping Gazette* (15 May 1890), p. 3.
156 John Kieschnick, 'Material culture', in John Corrigan (ed.), *The Oxford Handbook of Religion and Emotion* (Oxford: Oxford University Press, 2008), pp. 227–8.
157 Elina Gertsman, 'Matter matters', in Stephanie Downes, Sally Holloway, and Sarah Randles (eds), *Feeling Things: Objects and Emotions through History* (Oxford: Oxford University Press, 2018), p. 29.
158 Charles Sowerwine, 'Channelling grief, building the French Republic: the death and ritual afterlife of Léon Gambetta, 1883–1920', in Merridee L. Bailey and Katie Barclay (eds), *Emotion, Ritual Power in Europe, 1200–1920: Family, State and Church* (London: Palgrave Macmillan, 2017), pp. 157, 161.
159 For the concept of charisma, see Paul Binski, 'Charisma and material culture', in Brigitte Miriam Bedos-Redak and Martha Dana Rust (eds), *Faces of Charisma: Image, Text, Object in Byzantium and the Medieval West* (Leiden: Brill, 2018), pp. 128–55.
160 Cited in Boddy, 'Making history', 26.
161 For parades related to regimental colours see Myerly, *British Military Spectacle*, pp. 10–1.
162 *Girl's Own Paper* (6 May 1899), p. 510.
163 *Boy's Own Paper* (16 October 1886), p. 41.
164 *Ibid*.
165 Begiato and Brown, 'Visualising the aged veteran'.
166 *Englishwoman's Domestic Magazine* (10 October 1863), p. 266.
167 'At Messrs. Jevons & Mellor's, Corporation Street', *Birmingham Pictorial and Dart* (5 August 1989), p. 11.
168 'The man about town', *Country Gentleman: Sporting Gazette, Agricultural Journal* (27 May 1899), p. 645.
169 Captain Sidney Sheridan Bradford's wedding, 'Marriage and giving in marriage', *Hearth and Home* (1 April 1987), p. 838; also Major Arthur Jackson, 'People, places, and things', *Hearth and Home* (10 November 1892), p. 844.
170 For examples of this see the contributions to Downes, Holloway, and Randles (eds), *Feeling Things*.

4

Homeward bound: manliness and the home

Introduction

The chapters so far have used emotionalised bodies and objects to explore how manliness and unmanliness were constructed and reinforced. This chapter turns to the role of space in their formation, namely the place and concept of home. In 1871, the *British Workman* published the tale of a mariner, Darby, whose captain advised him to remember 'that "home" is a sacred word – 'tis a word that has a meaning in heaven. Yes, Darby, work for the "home". Save for it; spend by-and-by in it … God intended the thought of "home" to do much for a man.' He concluded, 'the man who has "home" in his heart, will, by God's blessing turn out well'.[1] In 1857 the same magazine contained a poem titled 'Come Back as Soon as You Can', illustrated by a top-hatted man bidding farewell to his daughter at the garden gate. The middle-class poet announces that his daughter always says goodbye to him by imploring, 'As soon as you can, come home.' He advises the businessman to 'get home', since that is where 'a man and a father be'.[2] As with working-class men throughout this book, they were instructed on how to be manly, but also served as exemplars onto which middle-class men projected their own concerns. Here was the ever-present tension for men: required to leave home to work, but told that home was central to their identity.[3] As this suggests, the imagined space of the home was the locus for concepts of manliness and unmanliness, but, paradoxically, most of its cultural power was situated in men's enforced absence from it.

This chapter examines how cultural accounts of men in the home inculcated feelings that produced, reinforced, and disseminated notions of gender. It shows that while manly men were often envisioned outside the home, they were nevertheless considered integral to its success, because they were fighting for it, defending it, or providing for it. Depictions of men's farewells and returns, often poised on their own doorstep, abound. Leave-takings had long had cultural significance, with ritualised markers in the seventeenth and early eighteenth centuries, but were naturalised and saturated with sentimental affect in the long nineteenth century.[4] Though men were shown to be absent, their minds, on the other hand, were understood to be directed towards home: all the time dreaming of cottage, wife, and family, and longing to be remembered. Together these were the motivating forces for their manly endeavours. When print and visual culture imagined men in the home, it was as catalysts for a 'happy' or 'unhappy' home, predominantly fashioned through their performance of key emotions. In some ways, therefore, the productive, heroic *absent* manly man resolved the conflict between the competing demands of home and work for masculine identity. The *present* unmanly man whose leisure and work disrupted the home was what must be avoided at all costs.

Farewell and separation

From the Revolutionary Wars of the later eighteenth century onwards, military men were the type most commonly imagined away from home for periods longer than a day in textual, visual, and material culture.[5] In prints and paintings, attractive sailors and soldiers bid farewell to parents, sweetheart or wife, and children.[6] They took their partings as Staffordshire figures and on all types of ceramic decorative vessels.[7] They were also sung about and recited in popular songs and poems, which were in turn widely published in the provincial press and almanacks.[8] There were some differences in these visual and textual cultures across the period. Sailors dominated visual depictions from the Revolutionary Wars to the mid-nineteenth century, with soldiers joining from the Crimean War period. Nonetheless, J. W. Hichberger's claim that common soldiers were only depicted from the mid-1850s in domestic scenes, once they were seen as heroic and were made-over by the dominant classes as respectable working-class husbands and fathers, is misleading.[9] Once poems and songs published before the 1850s are included, soldiers also bid farewell to home and loved ones to fight, and yearned for both while separated. Ironically, the idealised manliness so central and integral to a successful home was largely attained through these working men's absence.

The emotional motif of farewell moralised manliness by associating it with gendered values deemed essential to state and society.[10] When the idealised military man left his family to serve the nation, his sentimental manly form stirred patriotism through his self-sacrifice. The primary emotions elicited in the metonym of farewell and its tears were sorrow, pity, and pride, all evoked by his temporary, possibly permanent, absence from home.[11] Understandably, these depictions were particularly emotionally redolent during periods of war, emerging in the Revolutionary and

Napoleonic Wars, recycled and revivified in the Crimean period, and still common thereafter. As Carolyn Burdett remarks, this sentimental culture was a response to unsettling conditions of change in the long nineteenth century, offering a degree of consolation in transformative times.[12]

Though absent from their own homes, these men were conceptualised as the saviours of the nation's homes. As noted in Chapter 3, it was the danger and risk to mariners' lives that characterised the domestic and commemorative objects which linked sailors with departures from home and family. A bowl on a pedestal foot, probably from 1860–80, for example, describes: 'The Man Doom'd to sail/with the blast of the gale./ Through billows Atlantic to steer/bends o'er the wave,/which may soon be his grave.'[13] Such meditations were poignant commentaries on men's state-imposed distance from their home; the penalty of manliness dressed up as noble sacrifice. In 1840, the *Penny Satirist* reminded its readers that they owed their comfort and safety to sailors. The article used the emotionalised, damaged body of the Greenwich Pensioner to make this point:

> if it had not been for his [amputated] leg, the cannon-ball might have scattered us in our tea-parlour – the bullet which deprived him of his orb of vision, might have stricken *Our Village* from our hand, whilst ensconced in our study; the cutlass which cleaved his shoulder might have demolished our china vase, or our globe of golden fish.[14]

Tars formed, quite literally, 'walls of stout and honest flesh', enabling the prosperous middle classes, as indicated by the imagined domestic accoutrements, to live 'securely, participating in every peaceful and domestic comfort'. Consequently, these lucky folks had 'neither heard the roar of the cannon nor seen its smoke'. The tars' absence from their own homes thus saved the nation's domestic lives and kept intact other men's 'quietude'.[15]

The Crimean period's depictions of soldiers and sailors used the same tropes, reimagined in a highly sentimental form. George Baxter's 1855 print *The Soldier's Farewell* portrays a wintry scene outside a garden gate, where a guardsman wearing a busby and greatcoat takes leave of his aged parents. His mother despondently sits at his side, his father proffers a gift; the soldier's wife forlornly nestles in his arm and his little son looks up at his father.[16] Baxter pioneered mass-produced, cheaper colour prints that used such tropes and locations to sell them.[17] Pretty, colour images like these conveyed to a wider audience the moral underpinnings of the duties of manly men to their homes, families, and nations. For those to whom they appealed, these image could both demonstrate men's duty in serving the nation and offer a general portrayal of idealised manliness.[18] In George Elgar Hicks's *The Sailor's Farewell* (1867), for example, the mariner takes his leave of his wife within his cottage. Here is the emotionalised body discussed in Chapter 1: handsome, strong, and therefore manly. He is ideal also because he is affectionate, as the section 'Happy homes' explains, as displayed by his adoring wife and the couple gazing into each other's eyes. The home's material culture also displays his manliness by indicating his industriousness and, therefore, some disposable income. The couple and their children are dressed well. Though it is humble, the cottage has simple decorations and textiles, all clean and cared for (as the iron on the side indicates), and it contains possessions, such as mantelpiece ornaments, pictures, and pot plants on the windowsill. Of course, these are achieved because of the sailor's absence.

Henry Nelson O'Neil's *Eastward Ho!* (1858), which depicts soldiers on board ship leaving to quash the Indian Rebellion, is perhaps the most famous example of this genre.[19] The women left behind dominate the scene. The soldiers are cropped into disembodied arms and hands grasping their female loved ones, or reduced to faces full of emotion, some shining with excitement, others sad and anxious at leaving their wives. This painting and its pair, *Home Again*, reveal the feelings stirred by such sentimental depictions of farewells, since newspaper reports indicate that they were popular because they evoked powerful emotions. In 1863, the *Bury and Norwich Post* reported on the exhibition of *Eastward Ho!* and *Home Again* at Mr Spanton's Gallery, explaining that the paintings display the campaign's 'emotions, its painful anxieties, its terrible perils, and its triumphant issue'. For this reviewer, the 'prevailing expression of the "Eastward Ho!" is solemn, stern, and gloomy'.[20] Viewers were moved by what the *Liverpool Mail* called 'the separation of a troop of soldiers, bound for active service in a distant clime, from all their nearest earthly ties; the moment has arrived for the final parting – the last word – the last look – perhaps for ever'. The reviewer concluded that the paintings' 'truthfulness' and 'refined sentiments', 'excited the warmest expressions of genuine emotion from countless visitors'.[21]

Many such emotional scenes of men leaving home were also used to raise men's moral standards. The *British Workman* published *Eastward Ho!* as one of its full-page 'wall-papers' in 1859, framing it with biblical texts invoking manly self-control: 'Keep thy Father's Commandments', 'Swear Not at All', 'Forsake Not the Law of thy Mother', and 'To Do Good – Forget Not'.[22] Of course such improving words were meant to inspire men's manly behaviour within the home too.

Dreaming of home

Though men were imagined to be physically absent from home in the performance of their duties, they were considered to be psychologically and emotionally inseparable from it. Thus, the military man who longed for home was a very popular cultural motif. His meaning was deepened by the medical condition of nostalgia, in which the longing for home was pathologised and its physical and emotional symptoms manifested by soldiers who fought in European and American wars from the late 1680s to 1880s.[23] Nostalgia was linked to masculine identity in some of its diagnosis and discussion.[24] When medical practitioners wrote about soldiers suffering from nostalgia in the eighteenth century, they described 'ordinary soldiers exhibiting refined and "delicate" feelings such as melancholy and grief, feelings hitherto regarded as the privilege of the officer classes'.[25] American Civil War soldiers' longing for home helped them find 'a stable source of identity', one of the means by which they navigated the transformation in their lives wrought by war.[26] The soldier yearning for home was also linked to the message of patriotic manly self-sacrifice intrinsic to the military farewells discussed. In his analysis of French examples, Thomas Dodman remarks that their 'didactic message is arguably counterbalanced by the pathos of separation and the juxtaposition of (interior) domestic and (outside) public worlds'.[27] Yet, as this chapter reveals, feelings stirred by scenes of separation facilitated their didactic purpose.

This is evident in the evergreen poem 'The Soldier's Dream' by Thomas Campbell (1777–1844).[28] One of the most moving depictions of the absent military man, it was published as the nineteenth century dawned. It tells of a soldier sleeping in the aftermath of a dreadful battle where 'thousands had sunk on the ground overpower'd'. The soldier huddles on a straw pallet, guarded only by a small fire to scare off wolves. Three times he dreams a 'sweet Vision' of being transported to his idyllic rural home: 'the pleasant fields traversed so oft/ In life's morning march, when my bosom was young'. The sentimental motifs of homesickness dominate. The soldier notes that on greeting him in his dream state, 'My little ones kiss'd me a thousand times o'er,/And my wife sobb'd aloud in her fulness of heart'. The soldier is almost broken by his feelings for home, rather than consoled by them. In his dream he swears: 'From my home and my weeping friends never to part' and listens to his family begging:

> 'Stay – stay with us! – rest! – thou art weary and worn!' –
> And fain was their war-broken soldier to stay; –
> But sorrow return'd with the dawning of morn,
> And the voice in my dreaming ear melted away.

In the context of nostalgia as a deadly medical condition, kisses, tears, hearts, and sorrow prompted the reader to feel for the soldier and for his sacrifice. But admiration for his manly endurance was also expected and made stickier by these associated feelings.

It was a popular vision, immediately published in numerous provincial newspapers, such as the *Kentish Weekly Post* and *Staffordshire Advertiser*. This popularity was due to the intense feelings the soldier's dream displayed and stimulated. Like related cultural motifs, it was rejuvenated in the Crimean War period.[29] As a writer reviewing a musical concert based on the poem in the *Norfolk Chronicle* attested in 1820: 'The words are exquisitely tender.'[30] The *Worcester Journal* similarly recognised its emotive qualities in 1823, describing the ballad version as sung 'with a remarkable degree of feeling and affect'.[31] 'The Soldier's Dream' was regularly updated in new technologies. By the mid-century it had been rendered pictorially, set to music, performed in ballet, photographed as a daguerreotype, displayed at the Great Exhibition, and moulded in Staffordshire figurine form.[32] Seated, grasping a regimental flag in one hand, a canon at his feet, the rosy-cheeked, bearded soldier sleeps and, as the title suggests, dreams. New versions relocated the hero soldier to recent battles. In October 1855, the Royal Polytechnic launched its new entertainments for the winter, including a set of magic-lantern 'dissolving views' by Mr Hine. Representing scenes of the siege of Sebastopol, they used Campbell's poem as 'the plan of this work', offering a

> permanent picture of a wounded soldier slumbering on his lonely pallet in the hospital of Sentari; and the stern or triumphant memories of the trenches and of the combat ... were supposed to pass before his mind's eye, as they were depicted in the dissolving views, in the upper part of the curtain.[33]

In 1856, similar dissolving views of the dream were showcased in East Grinstead and the *Brighton Gazette* praised 'the vision of home, amidst the smoke of the expiring watch fire as it curls down the head of the sleeping Highlander'.[34] By the 1860s, the dream was the subject of slides for smaller more accessible mahogany dissolving-view lanterns.[35]

Victorian poets and artists reworked Campbell's popular poem to address soldiers' and the public's worries about army wives and families left without adequate provision in the Crimean War.[36] Tai-Chun Ho analyses two adapted versions, in which the dreaming soldier's fears that his children will be in want during his absence are met by a vision in which society and nation step in to aid them. These versions of 'The Soldier's Dream' sought to resolve the tension between the demands placed upon men to be provisioners while also expecting them to leave home to serve the state.[37] Nonetheless, it is important to note that Campbell's poem continued to circulate in its original form. Indeed, its original sentimental message that manly self-sacrifice and absence from home served the greater cause remained powerful, especially as home became ever more sanctified in the Victorian era. Its emotional significance is summed up in a 'Letter from the Camp', published in the *British Workman* in 1862:

> There is something in that little word 'home' which lifts the heart into the throat, and ever excites intense emotion in the British soldier on service. Let, for instance, but the bugle of a light regiment play 'Home sweet home', and you will perceive an uneasiness creep into every chatting circle; and then silence will ensue and many a head will be turned aside from the watch-fire to listen to that air, which perhaps more than any other, conjures up in the mind's eye of all of us the comforts of dear Old England.[38]

Here the soldier, cottage, and 'Old England' were combined in the concept of home and associated with apprehension, reverence, and loss to make appealing and 'sticky' the nobility of the man absent from home.[39]

By the 1860s, 'The Soldier's Dream' was used in the American Civil War, part of a popular literature that imagined tight links 'between home front and battlefront'. A lithograph published in the early 1860s, by Currier & Ives, portrays a sleeping Union soldier dreaming of being reunited with his wife and child (Figure 4.1). Underneath is a brief poem now shorn of Campbell's melancholy dread of war and instead declaring the soldier's simpler desire to return home to share his 'renown and honours' with his loved ones:

> Stretched on the ground the war-worn soldier sleeps,
> Beside the lurid watch fire's fitful glare;
> And dreams that on the field of fame he reaps
> Renown and honors which he hastes to share
> With those beloved ones who gathering come,
> To bid their hero husband father 'wellcome home'.
> Fond dreamer, may thy blissful vision be
> A true foreshadowing of the fates to thee.

As Alice Fahs argues, such soldiers were conventional sentimental antebellum types who embodied emotive themes of 'sacrifice, suffering, and redemption'.[40] Indeed, she found that many of the Civil War-era poems depicted unmarried soldiers yearning for mother and home, presenting the soldiers as boys. The military men discussed here, however, were often married, manly types whose emotional suffering, caused by their absence from home, communicated to the public the significance of manliness for individuals, families, and the nation.

Although the end-of-century militarism brought a far less sentimental tenor to depictions of soldiers, this vision of the military man suffering most acutely from his absence from home survived. Hardy, adventurous, imperial, and settler-colonial men in the period around 1870 to 1920 were themselves treated as sentimental objects of devotion, partly because they left the domestic sphere to endure the rigours of a hard frontier life.[41] An 1882 story in the American children's magazine *St Nicholas* follows a Civil War soldier's attempts to find his 'best and truest friend', Andy, following a battle at Hatcher's Run. When checking the ambulance trains, he locates a dying man who he thinks is his friend, rolling him over to reveal a 'manly, noble face'. It is not Andy, however. A week later, the soldier arrives in City Point, General Grant's headquarters, to search the hospital tents. To his joy, he discovers the recovering Andy. He also finds the man he had briefly mistaken for Andy in a nearby bed, suffering from a head wound, surviving despite all expectations that he would die, conscious but unable to speak or move. Andy explains that some of the wounded soldier's company visited him that day to return his valuables:

4.1 *The Soldier's Dream of Home* (New York: Currier & Ives, 1861–65).

among them was an ambrotype of his wife and child. Well, you just should have seen that poor fellow's face when they opened that ambrotype and held it before his eyes! He couldn't speak nor reach out his hand to take the picture; and there he lay, convulsed with feeling, while tears rolled down his cheeks.[42]

By this point, the memories of family were materialised to act as both a terrible reminder of the pity of war and to offer the absent man a virtual presence within his home. The motif also adds further weight to scholarship that rejects the vision of working-class family life and men as affectionless.[43] In all these cultural forms, after all, working-class men were imagined as loving deeply and suffering acutely when separated from their loved ones.

Forget me not: the absent presence

Men's 'presence' within their home and family during their physical absence was sustained and achieved through materialised memories.[44] The myth associated with the paired farewell and return images is that in sailors' families, the *Sailor's Farewell* was hung on the wall when the sailor left shore and would be swapped for the *Return* when he returned home safely.[45] Material culture alluded to this painful wait, such as the earthenware jug from 1870, which includes a verse that ends: 'Soon, soon before the light winds borne/Shall I be sever'd from your sight;/You left the lonely hours to mourn,/And weep thro' many a stormy night.'[46] This had high art antecedents in family portraits commissioned after the death of a deceased husband or father, which incorporated a portrait of him. Genre paintings of absent soldiers' families might also include their portraits. Ford Madox Brown's *An English Fireside in the Winter of 1854–5* (1855), for example, shows a young mother with a sleeping child on her lap, thinking of her husband away fighting in the Crimea, his portrait on the table beside her.[47] One of the features of this visual and material culture is that often sentimental entreaties to be remembered were included, a plea that men themselves also made through objects.[48] As with the dreaming soldier, such objects served to remind men of their obligations to domestic life, to reassure those they left behind that the men were devoted and not distracted by unmanly pursuits, and they symbolically preserved absent men's patriarchal dominance over their family and household.

One common verse on vessels variously dated from the 1830s through to the 1860s, was taken from Bernard Barton's (1784–1849) poem 'The Heart's Motto: "Forget Me Not"' (1820s). It selects four types of men who desire not to be forgotten: a painter and poet who hope to be remembered in posterity, and a soldier and sailor. The soldier, who dies for glory, 'Would own that fame a dream,/Did he not hope its better part/Would keep him unforgot'.[49] The stanza with the sailor was most repeated, however. Many earthenware vessels and lustreware plaques imagined:

> The sailor tost on stormy seas,
> Though far his bark may roam,
> Still hears a voice in every breeze,
> That wakens thoughts of home,
> He thinks upon his distant friends;
> His wife, his humble cot
> And from his inmost heart ascends,
> The prayer Forget me not.[50]

This was a reciprocal arrangement, since the man separated from home continued to love his sweetheart or wife in return for being remembered. In a 'Sailor's Farewell', published in the *Clonmel Herald* in 1839, for instance, the sailor rhetorically reminds his loved one: 'Though absent could I love thee less?' He declares that while he is 'doomed' to travel far from her, his 'heart dwells with my happy home'; as for his love, 'From absence it more strength derives'.[51] In return, absent men would be kept in their loved ones thoughts. A jug, circa 1860–80, with a 'Sailor's Farewell' and verse on one side declared: 'Far from home across the sea/To foreign climes I go,/While far away O think on me/And I'll remember you.'[52]

Men themselves crafted objects to serve as their absent presence in the home. Maya Wassell Smith shows that the handmade objects sailors made during deep-sea voyages, such as children's hammocks, cots, toys, and teething rings, as well as cooking utensils, knitting sheaths, stay busks, and needlework textiles, aimed 'to facilitate continued emotional contact and presence within a familial community'.[53] Bridget Millmore's study of love tokens made by the poor from repurposed coins, reveals the role of such tokens in expressing hopes, engendering duty towards family members, and aiding people to navigate life passages.[54] The 'sweetheart' pincushion is perhaps the best-known example of a material culture of absent 'presence'.[55] Soldiers and sailors made these large heart-shaped pincushions as decorative gifts, ornamented with beads, pins, embroidered regimental badges, and, in the First World War, cigarette silks, with verses asking the recipient to 'Think of me' and 'Forget me not'. Men made them as a way to fix their absent selves in their homes and female loved ones' minds.[56] There are written accounts of soldiers sewing them, as well as surviving examples.[57] A handworked velvet pincushion, dated around 1860, made by a convalescing solder to send home, combines the military and domestic, presumably to prompt remembrance. Its design is a Prince of Wales heraldic badge of three ostrich feathers made from seed beads – a typical element of regimental badges – and it spells out in glass-topped pins 'Ich Dien' ('I Serve', the motto of the Prince of Wales) and 'with love'.[58] Another from 1896 has pins spelling out 'remember me' on a red background.[59]

Sally Holloway shows that such handcrafted objects were material expressions of feelings, marking stages of life cycle such as birth and death. Similarly, she notes that the heart-shaped tokens that mothers left with their children at the London Foundling Hospital metaphorically placed the mother's heart in the child's possession.[60] The material culture associated with men's absence from home was equally invested with emotions that navigated the separation and kept the absent one's heart at home and in loved ones' hands. It spoke of the fear that absence also led to forgetting and, thus, these appeals for those at home to remember their absent men manifest the contradictory nature of masculinity and the home. While home was depicted as central to masculine identity, manliness also depended upon men's capacity and willingness to give it up with the knowledge that it could function without their presence.

Return and reunion

The counterpart of the farewell was the return, equally freighted with intense emotional power. The middle- and working-class appetite for depictions of various kinds of men returning home was voracious.[61] Following this chapter's earlier focus on military men's departures, sailors and soldiers returned home to swooning wives and delighted children.[62] In representations from the earlier part of the period, sailors returned with prize money and cosmopolitan clothing. In Julius Caesar Ibbetson's *A Married Sailor's Return* (1800), the sailor is surrounded by the accoutrements of his travels in the shape of objects to decorate and enrich the home.[63] Many verses have military men returning to sweethearts, vowing to settle down and marry. The conflicted national feeling about the Crimean War, driven by the public's greater awareness of its realities, thanks to the technology of faster reporting and photography, produced more ambiguous imagined homecomings.[64] Some were imagined as joyous, others as more complex. The *Bury and Norwich Post* described Henry O'Neil's *Home Again* as 'gay, joyous, and bright, with just a tinge of sadness here and there to render the scene more probable and natural'. It concludes that while one young man proudly waves his Victoria Cross, and others are overjoyed to return to their families, for the most part there is sadness. The review describes one 'wounded hero, whose appearance indicates that he has nobly fought', meeting his wife who, the *Post* says, views him with pride, compassion, and anxiety. Another 'invalid', however, has his pleasure 'blighted at the mournful news of his wife's death'.[65]

As this suggests, returning men were often imagined to return in a wounded, broken-down state, in need of support, to homes that were potentially not be the same as when they left.[66] These representations were popular reminders that some damaged male bodies could still be manly nonetheless, like the 'literary broken soldier' of late eighteenth-century visual and print culture, who brought the war home but diffused and contained its horrors through the tropes of service and sacrifice.[67] In James Collinson's *Home Again* (1856), a blind Coldstream guardsman returns to his cottage where numerous family members crowd around the large hearth. Patriotic themes dominate. A daughter sits with her sweetheart sailor, while two boys play-fight on top of a mangle, one holding the Royal Standard. Nearby is a washtub with two floating toy warships. On the wall behind them hangs a print of a battle scene, the mantelpiece boasts a model of the British Lion, and a stoneware vessel displays a royal crest. If the painting reflects the glory of military manliness, it is also intended to stir pity for a family whose head will no longer be able to work due to his injuries, and thereby troublingly reveals its precarious nature. Perhaps this is why the painting was not reviewed particularly enthusiastically.[68]

Depictions of returned soldiers that were well received often channelled grief over the effects of war through religious motifs and the notion of the home as sacred. Joseph Noel Paton's *Home* (1856) shows a Scots Fusilier Guards Corporal after his return to his cottage. His sacrifice is evident in his empty sleeve, his bandaged head, and his shattered weariness, as well as his loved ones' emotional response to him: his mother weeping and his wife's pale visage. This dimly lit cottage interior, with village church glimpsed through the window and open Bible on the table, was meant to prompt viewers to tears and Christian hope, as well as patriotism.[69] Indeed, men absent from home but yearning for it were a metaphor for human salvation. An example is Richard Wilton's poem 'Home at Last:

On Seeing Mr. Luard's Beautiful Painting', published in 1871, but inspired, as the title indicates, by John Dalbiac Luard's *Nearing Home* (1854–55), itself engraved on the following page.[70] *Nearing Home* depicts a scene on board ship of soldiers returning from the Indian Mutiny. In the centre is an exhausted wounded soldier lying on deck, his concerned wife in attendance, with a sailor boy offering consolation by gesturing to land coming into view. The other soldiers on board are turned outwards, drawn by the sight of England. In Wilton's verses the soldiers' 'brave hearts', gladdened and restored by beholding home, are allegories for humanity longing for its heavenly destination. Manly soldiers were once more an exemplar: Wilton concludes that all must 'show a soldier's bearing/In life's long and painful fight' to 'gain our HOME on high'.[71]

Home from work

The other popular imagery of the homecoming was of agricultural labourers returning home from a day's labour. This was a motif of pastoral poetry, which was revivified in Britain from the mid-eighteenth century and also featured in agricultural landscapes from the same period onwards. Gainsborough's cottage door scenes, for instance, track the weary labourer returning home to his family and some rest. Artists like Frances Wheatley, George Morland, and William Redmore Bigg sold pretty versions, shaped by sensibility and then sentiment, their works popularised in engravings.[72] Nineteenth-century rustic genre paintings took viewers beyond the cottage door into its interior, depicting happy families celebrating the recent arrival of the father. Historians of art and print have explored their numerous meanings. As Christiana Payne demonstrates, they appealed to their urban middle-class audiences' fear of social unrest and nostalgia for an imagined rural past, in which the lower classes were happy, deferential, pious, and unthreatening.[73] Brian Maidment considers the class dimensions of the returning artisan in popular prints between 1790 and 1870.[74] What still needs to be considered is that, like military homecomings, they too symbolised successful manliness. These sentimental scenes made manly provision central to their appeal, reinforcing its role as a marker of gender status.[75]

Many of the working men were envisaged at the cottage door rather than inside enjoying its supposed comfort. If the idealised women's place was in the home, her manly counterpart's was on the doorstep. George Elgar Hicks's *Sinews of Old England* (1856) is a particularly attractive version.[76] Its working man is handsome and well fed, possesses an attractive, cosy, well-tended cottage, glimpsed through the open door, as well as a doting wife and infant son. He is leaving for work, as indicated by his mattock on his shoulder and his purposeful face turned towards the world. The title indicates its patriotic intentions, since it is influenced by a line from Charles Swain's well-known poem 'The Peasantry of England' (c.1840), which was published in newspapers throughout the century.[77] This praised the 'English Peasantry' as the source of national strength and begged God to protect them and provide them with 'happy homes'. The second stanza begins: 'The Sinews of old England!/The bulwarks of the soil!/How much we owe each manly hand,/Thus fearless of its toil!' Nostalgic in the face of change, it also celebrated conventional gendered relationships.[78] The working man poised on his cottage doorstep underscored the supposed public–private divide of men facing the world and women bound by the domestic sphere. Nonetheless, it is more than a charming evocation of conventional gender roles and patriotic feelings. As a liminal space, the doorstep manifests the inherent tensions between manliness and home, where men were central to the latter but only by being absent from it due to paid work.[79]

Indeed, in 'The Homecoming of Darby Brill', published in the *British Workman*, 1871, securing and maintaining a home was both the protagonist's motivation to work and the marker of manliness. The story recounts Darby and Nancy's love story through their desire for a family home. As children they played with a toy house, which inspired Darby to spend his youth at sea saving for a real house in order to wed Nancy. Once acquired, Darby is shown working unceasingly to keep their home through adversity.[80] Eventually gaining his rightful inheritance of a ship and the prosperity that went with it, his rewards were described through home: 'Many a happy home-coming had our friend Darby' and 'there were few happier days spent anywhere or by any one than those of the home-comings of Darby Brill'.[81] The illustration of a mature bearded mariner, hoisting aloft his toddler, while his young wife gazes at both, evokes a long tradition of idealised images of labouring men returning home to dandle their small children on their knee.[82]

While working-class men were depicted away from home at work, however, they were still mentally and psychologically bound to it. Sometimes, they were described as ruminating upon it: an activity that kept them on the manly straight and narrow. In 'Dust Oh' (1871), the dustman, Mr Chouter, works hard and, because he abstains from drink, reflects on his lot. When walking from one house to another to empty bins, he ponders on God, considers the things he finds in the refuse, and dreams 'of how pleasant it would be to sit down to tea with Mrs. Chouter that evening, at seven o'clock, and see the little Chouters eat and drink and be merry on the proceeds of his labour'.[83] The illustration displays an archetypical emotionalised manly working body: a sturdy dustman, bewhiskered, cleanly dressed, and, significantly, cheerful.[84] This cultural motif prevailed throughout the century. A late version is seen in 'Two Ways of Life', 1898, in which the model working man is inspired to work by the prospect of returning home to his wife and baby, at which point 'every care vanishes and his cup of joy run over'.[85] As the next section, 'Happy homes', and Chapter 5 demonstrate, cheerfulness, contentedness, satisfaction, and happiness were an essential part of the urban middle-class vision of working-class manliness.

Happy homes

What happened when homeward-bound manly men got beyond the dwelling's threshold in sentimental art and tales? They created happy homes. Happy is a relentless motif in such popular fiction, symbolised visually through affectionate relationships and comfortable homes.[86] In this process, happiness was weaponised. It was something, so these stories and attractive images promised, to which the manly husband and father could 'easily' lay claim. All he needed to do was work hard, spend his money wisely, and not succumb to the temptations that drew him away from home. An early example are George Morland's *The Comforts of Industry* and the *Miseries of Idleness* (1780s). This pair of paintings showed the dire consequences of a man who failed to work and provide for his wife and children. His unmanliness is displayed in the worsening conditions of his cottage.[87] Several examples deliver a didactic lesson by showing that a man who did not drink could afford the materials and time to educate his children. This was part of the appeal of images of fathers reading the Bible, surrounded by their children, in a cosy rural cottage, such as David Wilke's *Cottar's Saturday Night* (1837).[88] In a story called 'Father, Please Come Home Early', published in 1856 in the *British Workman*, the author overhears a boy say these words to his father as the latter exits the door of his home in the morning to go to work. Remarkably similar to Hicks's *Sinews of Old England*, exhibited the following year, the accompanying illustration shows an emotionalised manly body: a handsome man wearing a cap, neat working clothes, a chinstrap beard, resting his working tool on his shoulder (Figure 4.2). At the cottage door, he takes his leave of his pretty and adoring wife, baby, and son. The boy is keen for him to return, because his father devotes his evenings to improving his children through entertaining lessons. The benefits accrued from such behaviour are children who 'learn to love HOME as the dearest spot on earth', content to spend their time there rather than roaming the streets. In turn, the children's love for their father means that he does not need urging to return home, 'for his heart turns to that home wherever he is, as the needle to the pole'.[89] In this way, happiness was a social pacifier too.

Emotionalised bodies and objects were, once again, central. Increasingly, hard-working, moral, temperate, working men were handsome and had beautiful homes to which to return. Thus, Morland's hard-working man looked fairly similar to his idle counterpart, the decline primarily identified through their demeanour and material culture. The contrasts were written into bodies as time went on, as Chapter 2 illustrates. 'The

4.2 *Please Father, Come Home Early*, British Workman 20 (1856), p. 76.

beneficial effects of temperance on a man and his family' c.1840 (Figure 4.3), for example, were displayed through bodies as well as objects. The young family takes tea outside the pretty, rose-arboured cottage. The ringleted wife and gorgeous children turn to the sprightly, handsome working man returning home. Their happiness, comfort, and plenty depend on him, signified by the decorative possessions and the incongruously large leg of meat on the table.⁹⁰ Bodily self-mastery was also emphasised. Manly acts of self-mastery were often manifested through savings, as in 'Twopence a-Day', where the father saves his daily beer money and hands it over as a lump sum to his son on his thirteenth birthday, so he can obtain the apprenticeship that suits his talents.⁹¹ In 'The House that John Built', John Banks turns to drink partly because he is forced to eat at the pub due to his young wife's inability to cook. However, once his first child is born he abjures from drink and saves his money. After some years he is able to build his own fine house and furnish it with 'excellent furniture', indicated materially in the illustration by a grandfather clock and ornaments and figurines on the mantelpiece. The family are joyous; as the narrator explains, this was 'Truly a happy home – a brilliant contrast to a drunkard's house.'⁹²

Men's affection and kindness were central to happy homes. An article in the *Bradford Daily Telegraph* in 1899 asked, 'What Makes the Home?' and answered: 'Loving words and kind acts.' ⁹³ Strikingly, the *British Workman* quickly moved to teaching working men how to create a happy home through affection and kindness, without explicitly discussing alcohol. In 'The Oiled Feather' in the *British Workman*, 1868, Samuel is contrasted with Joseph in behaviour. Both are honest and assiduous, but Sam is genial and civil while Joe is tart and brusque. Through the metaphor of Sam oiling the lock of his front door to keep it working smoothly, as well as numerous other objects, the reader learns that charm and kindness oils familial and social interaction. Sam's wife, son, and maid are happy because he calls them by pet names and treats them with kindness. Indeed, men were instructed that wives needed to be loved in order for them to perform their roles cheerfully and effectively. As Sam tells Joe, women will 'do anything for love – no use our riving them, our scolding, and ordering, and banging about; that only makes slaves of them; but give them a little love, and they'll do wonders'.⁹⁴ Sam is depicted inside his house at the open door, oiling a key, while his wife holds the bottle of oil, she and their son watching him contentedly.⁹⁵ Here, the manly man at his door instructs men to be agreeable, as well as industrious, to gain life's rewards. The same message informs 'The First Snowdrop' (1871), which shows Wedge, the village carpenter, learning by example how to achieve a happy home when carrying out work for Mr Cary, the squire. Present at the squire's return home at six o'clock, he is astonished to see him greet his wife with three kisses and a gift, while his children crowd round him with joy after only one day away at work. Wedge reflects that his own welcome home would be 'poor and cold, after that which he had just witnessed'.⁹⁶

Husbands who did not show affection when at home were inadequate, though not necessarily unmanly. They were not the unmanly brutes of the next section, 'Disruptive men and unhappy homes'. that loomed over the unhappy home. Indeed, the behaviour recommended was hardly demanding. Will Wedge, for instance, realised he was at fault because he never

4.3 *The Beneficial Effects of Temperance on a Man and his Family*, lithograph by W. Gunthrop (c.1840), after himself.

bestowed gifts on his wife, 'nor did he greet her with those kind words which would not have failed to draw the same from her'. Doing this, he discovered, 'so to speak, sawed Mary's heart right in two, and got the very inside, and planed down no end of knots and rough places, and French polished her off'. Indeed, her heart 'never closed up again'.[97] Similarly, the

Bradford Daily Telegraph criticised men for not talking to their wives when at home, for selecting the comfortable easy chair so that their wives were relegated to the straight-backed one, and refusing to stroll in the countryside with them. Those men who blamed their wives for being moody and obstinate were 'stupidly blind' and needed to 'realise that love and kindness go far in making the woman'.[98]

Such advice was partly aimed at helping the working classes to secure happy relationships. This had a political dimension, since the middle classes believed that affectionate family life improved status and condition. Indeed, Maidment argues that images of returning artisans had a powerful ideological purpose in their pre-1848 version, aiming to ally progressive, liberal middle classes with aspirational artisan classes.[99] Anna Clark shows that artisan men also used their family life and role as husbands and fathers to demand a political voice.[100] For the most part, however, the insistence that working-class men be judged by their manly domesticity was not a political opportunity for them. As Mary Poovey observes, although 'the politicization of middle-class men went hand-in-hand with the domestication of middle-class life', when the same notions of domesticity were imposed on working-class men, the intent was to deny them the opportunities 'to organise themselves into collective political or economic associations'.[101]

Happiness was, after all, a way to make people more satisfied with their lot, a middle-class means to the end of a quiescent, satisfied, and therefore peaceable and biddable workforce and working class. It was used to pacify men. As the *British Workman* declared in 1861: 'Workingmen! Strive to make "home" the happiest spot on earth! You will have a hundredfold reward.'[102] Happiness was held up as their reward for kind and orderly behaviour, since those who encountered it would be made happy in turn. As the author of 'The Oiled Feather' explains: 'a bright and happy home is a wonderful back-up to a man when he goes forth into a hard and cold world, to make his way through the day's business as best he can'. This formed a virtuous circle, for his family 'smiling him forth on his journey' and smiling him home again, were the benefit and the draw.[103] After all, Will Wedge's small gifts and kind words 'prompted Mary to do many loving deeds, the fruits of affection, which can make the humblest home a little paradise'.[104] Similarly, kindness and affection provided a 'Christ-like' acceptance of one's place. So in 'God's Gentlemen' (1898), the Reverend F. W. Farrar told his working readers that they were right to want to be gentlemen. However, he reminded them that this was not about fancy clothing, fortune, or recreation; it consisted of virtues which included 'affections gentle enough for the humblest services of earth, lofty enough for the aspirations of the skies'.[105] Such stories ignored structural inequity, persuading men once more that if they were manly, avoided temptation, and worked hard they would reap economic and emotional benefits.

Disruptive men and unhappy homes

Unmanly men were a disruptive force in the home, their actions resulting in 'unhappy' homes, a term used as shorthand for dysfunctional homes due to domestic violence or alcohol, or both.[106] These men populated sensation fiction, as well as newspaper reporting of murder trials.[107] Indeed, 'Unhappy Home' was a typical title for reports on marital violence, such as that on David Donaldson who was charged with violence against his wife in 1899.[108] In a sinister counterpart of the joyful manly homecomings, court or police intelligence reports frequently show the husband beating his wife on his return home in the evening.[109] Fairly typical was a report in an 1824 inquest that when William Gooderain 'returned home in a state of intoxication … high words ensued'. He beat his pregnant wife so that she died some days afterwards.[110] The wife abuser was considered especially unmanly, as the *Northern Whig* neatly demonstrated in 1899, in a report about a magistrate standing for election as mayor. An artisan asked him whether he would be severe on wife beaters, given that when previously performing his duties as magistrate, he had instructed an abuser 'that the next time he was tempted to indulge in such domestic amenities he should look in the glass, and if he saw a man there he would not strike a woman'.[111]

In fact, the textual and visual culture of wife beating reveals just how deeply problematic men's place within the home could be.[112] Pictures and cartoons from the mid-nineteenth century showed the violent husband as a large figure dominating the domestic environment, destroying its comfort, shattering ornaments, and turning over furniture.[113] Such men were brutish, ugly, often possessing simian faces intended to be physiognomically read as unmanly and racially inferior. Their emotionalised bodies spoke of class and race degeneration, filtered through melodrama's reassuring tropes of visible virtue, which suggested that a man became a disruptive force when his wife failed to make the home cheery, clean, ordered, and welcoming. This was explicitly stated in critiques of wife beating. Sir John William Kaye wrote an article in response to the Swansea MP Lewis Dillwyn's parliamentary bill of 1856, seeking to authorise flogging as a punishment for men who committed violent assaults on women and children. Kaye saw the roots of working-class men's anger in dirty, disorganised homes and middle-class men's abuse in a comfortable home spoiled by being poorly run.[114] Wives' household management needed to be hidden from men. 'Hints for the Wives of Working Men. By One Who Has Lived amongst Them' (1859), advised women to do the 'dirty work' during their husbands' absence, for example, 'so that the house may be clean and comfortable, and yourself *tidy* and ready to receive him'.[115] Men would then not be 'almost forced' to leave their home, as 'Family Secrets; Or, The Two Wives and the Two Homes' (1857) declared. It contrasted dirty and clean homes, observing that the secret of a 'lucky' husband's 'comfort and good temper lay in his wife's habits of early rising and prudent management'.[116] In these fantasy situations, the cosy cottage was not only the emblem of the happy home, it was a physical protection against unhappiness.

Even so, wives' ever-busy cleaning hands were insufficient to keep a man on the manly path; female patience and supplication were essential too. In the poem 'A Soft Answer Turneth Away Wrath, By a Birmingham Working Man', Thomas's wife waits for him to return home after the factory bell sounds. The cottage is 'tidy and straight', boasting a 'cheery fire' and 'bright-polished grate', food and tea are ready to serve. These are not enough, however. Thomas enters late, in a quarrelsome mood. Like a 'wise and good general', his wife keeps her temper, ignoring his annoyance and responding only with gentleness. Her patience restores his mood and the poem ends by finally acknowledging that men might make a similar effort: 'If men like their wives to be patient and kind,/They, too, should be patient with them.'[117] Understandably, feminists made political capital out of a rhetoric that envisaged unmanliness as the 'natural' default state of working-class men. Frances Power Cobbe, for instance, reminded her readers of 'the timid and meek-faced woman who tries too often unsuccessfully, the supposed magic of a soft answer to turn away the wrath of such a wild beast as he'.[118]

The most persistent threat in these accounts was a husband returning home when drunk, perhaps the most disruptive type of man imaginable. He entered the cottage embodying the abject unmanliness of the drunkard, depicted so terrifyingly in Cruikshank's *Bottle* series. In 'The Poor Man's House Repaired', 1858, a wife traces her husband's journey of redemption from drunkard wife beater to provisioning, caring father. The journey is a material one, told textually through the state of their home, but also visually in the header to the page (Figure 4.4). In a pictorially sequential narrative, it shows the broken-down external view of the cottage, then its smashed interior, followed by the 'poor man', Robert, outside his repaired home. For fifteen years, his wife testifies: 'Our house was the picture of wretchedness ... The windows were patched, the walls shattered, the furniture defaced and broken.' Robert is sent to the House of Correction after a dreadful night when he attacks his family and threatens to burn down the house. In the accompanying illustration, Robert raises his fist over his wife and small child who cower behind an overturned table from which the tableware has smashed onto the floor. Yet, for all his aggression, Robert is peculiarly passive throughout the narrative; it is his nameless wife's prayers and patience, rather than his own determination, which return him to the safe shores of manliness. Once he takes the pledge, the home is repaired, comfortable, and happy, demonstrated in the accompanying illustration with its cheerful fire, plentiful food, intact ornaments, and

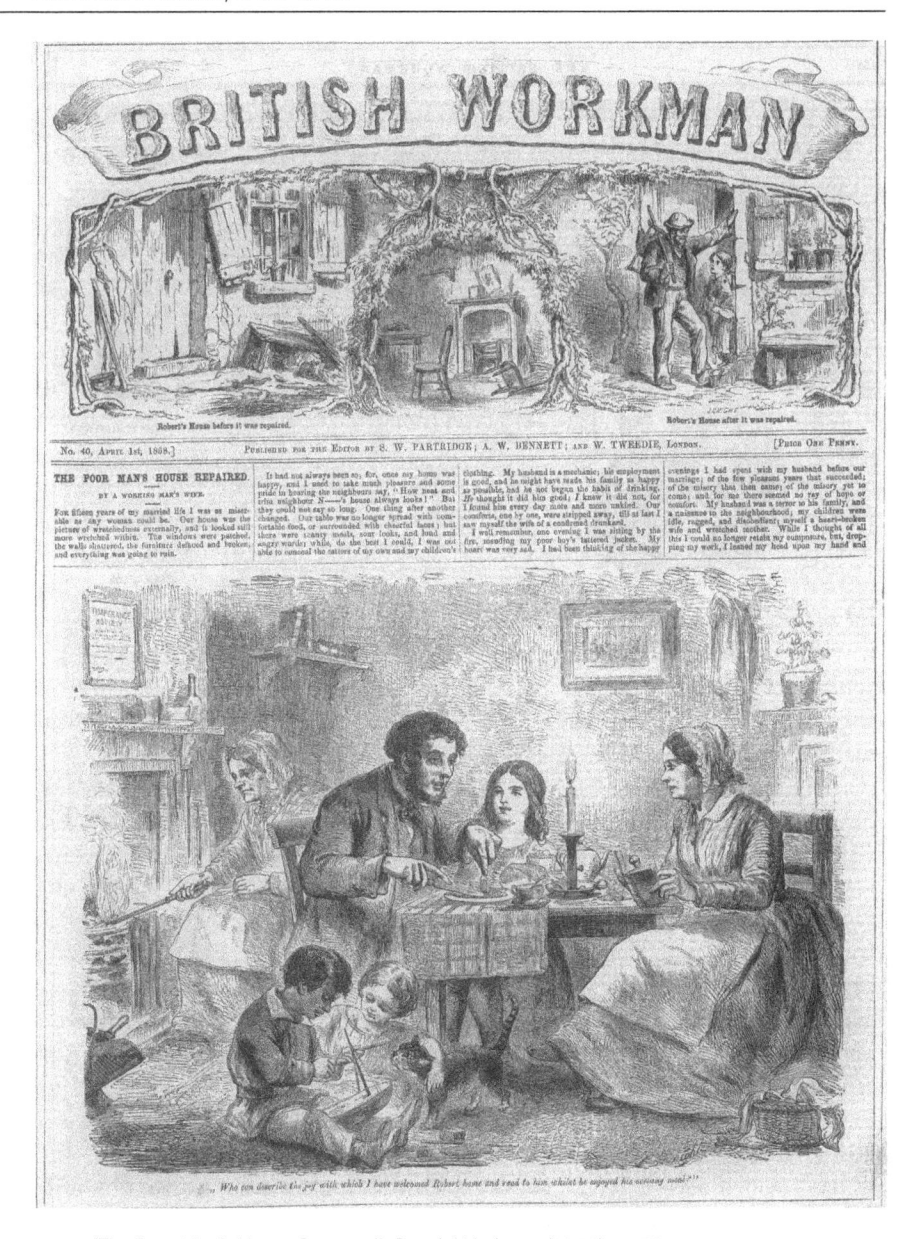

4.4 'The Poor Man's House Repaired', *British Workman* (1858), p. 37.

playful children and cat. The final 'frame' of the header makes his manly redemption very clear by showing Robert at his cottage door, working tools on shoulder, child welcoming him.[119] Space and material conditions were not only understood to determine the quality of marital and familial relationships, therefore, but the capacity of men to fulfil their potential to be manly through self-mastery.

Indeed, the issue of male self-control lay at the heart of these unhappy homes. As Chapter 2 showed, unmanliness originated in the failure to master one's appetites. One of the most emotive arenas in which this was played out was the home. Bridget Walsh argues that cultural representations of domestic murder reveal the vexed relationship between middle-class masculinity and the domestic, often centred on the demands for male self-mastery. In sensation novels of the second half of the nineteenth century, for example, some male characters' excessive sexual self-sacrifice was shown to have 'pathological' consequences, resulting in them committing violent acts.[120] Certainly, newspapers routinely reported wife murderers' self-defences that their wives had provoked them. In 1871, *The Times* published Reverend Watsons' claims that 'in a fit of fury I have killed my wife. Often and often have I endeavoured to restrain myself, but my rage overcame me, and I struck her down.'[121] In these cultural images, unmanliness was an ever-present menace.

Although the specific nature of men's work was rarely considered in the didactic tales, there lies at the heart of such tales an uneasiness about the relationship between men's employment and the home. The two were generally seen to be in tension. As Trev Lynn Broughton and Helen Rogers note, mid-Victorian cultural commentators were concerned that middle-class men were being marginalised within the domestic sphere, their role undermined by the demands that they work long hours outside the home.[122] Paid labour, while essential for economic success and masculine identity in allowing independence and the capacity to provide, drew men into the different, apparently antithetical, world of the workforce and its attendant temptations of leisure following the close of a day's work. Sarah Stickney Ellis deplored the demands of 'mammon' that denied middle-class men's 'longing to return [home]; yet every morning brings the same hurried and indifferent parting, every evening the same jaded, speechless, welcomeless return – until we almost fail to recognize the man, in the machine'.[123] Maidment sees the 'brutalising world of work' as haunting 'the conventional iconography of cottage contentment', with factory work seen as an opposing and alienating force.[124] This was perhaps most explicit in accounts of violent and disruptive men. Metaphors for wife beating often used the language of work, such as David Donaldson's wife's allegation in 1899 that he 'pounded her like a steam hammer'.[125]

In this kind of account, men's labour was not the source of comfort, it erupted into the home as a tool of violence, a signifier of the competition between home, work, and recreation that always underlay the discourse of happy and unhappy homes. Indeed, the class-specific rhetoric of wife beating that developed in the later nineteenth century drew on this tension for some of its visceral force, driven by various campaigners, including those supporting calls for harsher punishments and feminists drawing attention to the plight of women in the home. It focused on the apparel and instruments of men's work by alluding to the weapons some men used to beat their wives. This helped embellish and embed the stereotype of the working-class wife beater in public discourse and conscience.[126] Not only does it indicate the ways in which representations of unmanly working-class men were filtered through fears of racial and class degeneration, it exposes the uneasy relationship between home and work for narratives of manliness and happy homes.[127]

Unmanliness was materialised through workwear, a striking cultural metaphor which demonstrated that the home was not a haven from work when work intruded into it and its inhabitants' lives in the most grotesque fashion. The best example is the working boot, both clog and hobnail versions: industrial workers' footwear which became the most notorious object associated with wife beating. Wooden clogs were worn in metal- and textile-working industries to protect feet. Hobnail boots were similarly cheap, durable, and protective. Both were reinforced with metal toe caps and heels. As a result of some horrific cases where men murdered their wives by kicking them when wearing industrial footwear, the public mind identified them with working-class wife beating. Attempts to pass Lord Leigh's bill to introduce flogging to punish wife beaters in 1874, for example, presented evidence of cases of working-class husbands '"digging" the women with wooden clogs tipped and heeled with iron'.[128] In 1874, another article raised the spectre of an epidemic of violence in the north thanks to: 'The Rough who kicks an inoffensive passer-by to death, or who tramples, with his hob-nailed boots, on the body of his senseless wife, is often maddened with drink, but he is never, or hardly ever, quite irresponsible.'[129] A Letter to the Editor in the *Spectator*, December 1877, complained of a series of northern men who had killed their wives recently: 'Alfred Cummins, tailor, Moor Street [Blackburn], was charged with knocking his wife down and kicking her head and face so violently as to deprive her of sight in one eye.'[130]

Writers and artists conveyed their outrage and indignation over the unmanly working man through emotionalised bodies and objects. *Punch* published 'A Real Hard Case' (Figure 4.5) in 1875. Though seated, wearing the offending boots, this 'rough' still dominates the room; a sinister counterpart to happier associations of the father's chair and his comforting presence at home in the evening, underscoring only its links with male authority.[131] He comments on a report in the newspaper he holds: "'Ere's a go! – A man 'anged for kickin' his wife to death! I shall 'ave to take my boots off!' The potential danger of disruptive unmanliness is simply conveyed by the shadowy room, whose hearth manages not to exude the glowing warmth usually associated with the snug fireside, and by the vulnerable figure of the wife shielding her baby in the background. The men's clogs or hobnail boots were also emotional objects. Anyone who had seen, hefted, or worn a pair knew their weight and size, their roughness, and

A REAL HARD CASE.
(THE ROUGH'S LAST WRONG.)

Liverpool Ruffian. "'ERE'S A GO!—A MAN 'ANGED FOR KICKIN' HIS WIFE TO DEATH! I SHALL 'AVE TO TAKE MY BOOTS OFF!"

4.5 *A Real Hard Case. (The Rough's Last Wrong.)* by Charles Keene.

crudeness of form; those who heard the shoes on cobbles heard the nails ring. All knew these objects' potential threat as weapons and the way they turned one kick into a fatal blow. They also spoke of the anger of men who used them and prompted emotions in those who came to associate them with marital violence, of disgust, revulsion, and fear.

Although this material culture fixed wife beating as a working-class activity, in fact marital violence was not class-, occupation-, or place-specific. Studies of assault show it was scattered far more widely among different types of men.[132] Indeed, even though Frances Power Cobbe condemned 'Colliers, "puddlers", and weavers' in *Wife Torture* she actually named prosecuted men from a wider range of employments.[133] Nonetheless, there rapidly emerged a regional material culture of marital violence. Clogs and hobnail boots symbolised textile mills, mines, and iron-working; industrialised labour that centred on Lancashire, West Yorkshire, Liverpool, the north-east of England, and London. In 1876 Serjeant Pulling identified the 'kicking district' of Liverpool and, most famously of all, Frances Power Cobbe drew to the public's attention the 'kicking districts' of Lancashire in 1878.[134] Cobbe used the parliamentary reports on brutal assaults to estimate the proportion of wife beaters to population, concluding that London and Durham had the highest number. The other places she included were Liverpool, Lancashire, Stafford, and the West Riding of Yorkshire.[135] Cobbe identified the nature of working conditions as one of the causes: 'They are lives of hard, ugly, mechanical toil in dark pits and hideous factories.'[136]

The impact of this material representation of wife beating was profound. Elizabeth Foyster argues that by the mid-nineteenth century marital violence came to be seen as 'a symptom of social disorder that was in urgent need of attention ... a matter for social discipline and class control'.[137] The emotionalised material culture associated with unmanly working men helped constitute social and political life. As James Hammerton observes, it stimulated campaigns to educate the working classes and shaped social investigators' rationale and motivation for surveillance and intervention in poorer people's lives, since middle-class commentators believed that 'if environment created the conditions for domestic violence, its amelioration could offer the cure'.[138] The stereotyped unmanly working-class wife beater was also rhetorically deployed by English feminists to demand the vote and challenge arguments that men were suited to political citizenship simply because of their sex.[139] Finally, the unmanly entrenched class stereotypes offered a particularly offensive example of an 'other' against whom middle-class and 'respectable' working-class men could construct manly identities.

Conclusion

Men were considered vital to a successful home, which, in turn, was necessary for them to achieve manliness. Yet manliness was also predicated upon men securing the livelihood and success of families and homes by leaving them to serve economy, society, and state. This appears to correspond with Tosh's defence of the 'flight for domesticity', in which he observes that it was restricted to upper-middle-class men who sought out careers in the empire or, if they were married, pursued a 'qualified' flight through work and leisure. In contrast, he sees the lower middle classes as remaining connected to the ideals of the domestic, while the working classes became more wedded to them by the end of the century.[140] The class dimensions of these cultural accounts of men's absence from home offer a more complex picture. Although lower-middle- and working-class people consumed such accounts, they were created and enjoyed by the middle classes, who clearly still saw the value in keeping masculine identity fixed to the home even when such identity was fulfilled by absence from the latter.

Furthermore, all classes recognised the tensions between home and work for manliness, which was continually assessed within the domestic space and consistently found wanting.[141] When men were in their home, they were advised to perform some degree of emotional labour to sustain their place within it, typically by cultivating affection through kind words and deeds for family members, by rigorous self-control over their appetites, and by managing the often-competing demands of work and home. Their ability to do so was understood to break down or erupt into violence when men spent too much time away from home in non-domestic activities. The ambivalent relationship between masculinity, home, and work is perhaps most evident in the way that idealised men were so often depicted on the doorsteps of their homes. Metaphors for masculine liminality within the domestic, open doors also indicate the lack of working-class privacy. Working-class men's gender performance was under scrutiny when they stood at their doorsteps: their doors open to the intrusive judgemental middle-class eye. Chapter 5 explores how the concept of work and types of labour further shaped ideas of manliness for both middle- and working-class men.

Notes

1 *British Workman* (1871), pp. 74–5.
2 *British Workman* 33 (1857), p. 131.
3 Karen Downing has explored this from a more social perspective in *Restless Men: Masculinity and Robinson Crusoe 1788–1840* (Basingstoke: Palgrave Macmillan, 2014).
4 Lisa Toland, 'Late-adolescent English gentry siblings and leave-taking in the early eighteenth century', in Merridee L. Bailey and Katie Barclay (eds), *Emotion, Ritual and Power in Europe, 1200–1920: Family, State and Church* (London: Palgrave Macmillan, 2017), pp. 67–8.
5 For soldiers' narratives discussing separation, see Catriona Kennedy, *Narratives of the Revolutionary and Napoleonic Wars: Military and Civilian Experience in Britain and Ireland* (Basingstoke: Palgrave Macmillan, 2013), pp. 14–15. In France, scenes of conscripts leaving and returning home served similar purposes: David Hopkin, 'Sons and lovers: popular images of the conscript, 1798–1870', *Modern & Contemporary France* 9:1 (2001), 19–36.
6 For a coastal scene see National Maritime Museum, *The Sailors Farewell*

(caricature) PAH7359, http://collections.rmg.co.uk/collections/objects/147306.html#2IZ7EhCZoHhwpKHx.99 (accessed 1 April 2019).
7 For examples of 1855 Staffordshire figures, see http://madelena.com/introduction-staffordshire-pottery-figures.php; for the *Sailor's Return* on a jug celebrating Samuel Plimsoll, 1879, see National Maritime Museum, jug, 1879, ZBA4386, http://collections.rmg.co.uk/collections/objects/383670.html (accessed 1 April 2019) for the Soldier's Farewell. Also, it is just general category rather than a specific image. from the Crimean War era see Thomas Balston, *Staffordshire Portrait Figures of the Victorian Age* (London: Faber & Faber, 1958), plate 18 and p. 60; P. D. Gordon Pugh, *Staffordshire Portrait Figures and Allied Subjects of the Victorian Era* (London: Barrie & Jenkins, 1970), pp. 289–90.
8 For example of poem, see *Clonmel Herald* (6 April 1839).
9 J. W. Hichberger, *Images of the Army: The Military in British Art, 1815–1914* (Manchester: Manchester University Press, 1988), pp. 160–6.
10 French examples were statements that a youth become a mature man through the rite of passage of conscription and service. Hopkin, 'Sons and lovers', 34–5.
11 Joanne Begiato, 'Tears and the manly sailor in England, c.1760–1860', *Journal for Maritime Research* 17:2 (2015), 13.
12 Carolyn Burdett, 'New agenda sentimentalities: introduction', *Journal of Victorian Culture* 16:2 (2011), 187–94.
13 Tyne & Wear Archives and Museums, bowl, 1860–80, TWCMS: B3937.
14 Citing an article from the *Monthly and European Magazine*, the *Penny Satirist* (21 March 1840), p. 3.
15 *Penny Satirist* (21 March 1840), p. 3.
16 V&A, print by George Baxter, *The Soldier's Farewell*, or *The Parent's Gift*, Baxter-process print, untrimmed proof, England, 1855, E.2872-1932. Also Tyne & Wear Archives and Museums, TWAM NEWHG: BP.0538, http://collectionssearchtwmuseums.org.uk/#details=ecatalogue.324668 (accessed 13 September 2019).
17 Sonia Solicari, 'Selling sentiment: the commodification of emotion in Victorian visual culture', *19: Interdisciplinary Studies in the Long Nineteenth Century* 4 (2007).
18 Kendall Smaling Wood, 'George Elgar Hicks's woman's mission and the apotheosis of the domestic', *Tate Papers* 22 (2014), www.tate.org.uk/research/publications/tate-papers/22/george-elgar-hicks-womans-mission-and-the-apotheosis-of-the-domestic (accessed 30 April 2018).
19 Museum of London, 2004.152/1, On Display: Museum of London: Expanding City; also British Museum, mezzotint, 2010, 7081.6468, www.britishmuseum.org/research/collection_online/collection_object_details.aspx?objectId=3434349&partId=1&searchText=turner+wakefield&view=list&sortBy=objectTitleSort&page=1 (accessed 18 August 2019). For an assessment of *Eastward Ho!* and its companion piece *Home Again*, see Hichberger, *Images of the Army*, pp. 168–70.
20 *Bury and Norwich Post* (19 May 1863).
21 *Liverpool Mail* (19 January 1861).
22 *British Workman* 52 (1 May 1859), p. 212.
23 Thomas Dodman, *What Nostalgia Was: War, Empire, and the Time of a Deadly Emotion* (Chicago: Chicago University Press, 2017), pp. 3, 12, 63–92, 93–123.
24 Sarah Goldsmith, 'Nostalgia, homesickness and emotional formation on the eighteenth-century Grand Tour', *Cultural and Social History* 15:3 (2018), 333–60.
25 Philip Shaw, 'Longing for home: Robert Hamilton, nostalgia and the emotional life of the eighteenth-century soldier', *Journal for Eighteenth-Century Studies* 39:1 (2016), 25–40.
26 Susan Matt, *Homesickness: An American History* (New York: Oxford University Press, 2011), p. 99.
27 Dodman, *What Nostalgia Was*, pp. 106–7.
28 His other famous patriotic and military-themed poem was 'Ye Mariners of England'.

29 *Kentish Weekly Post or Canterbury Journal* (25 October 1803); *Staffordshire Advertiser* (29 October 1803). For an advertisement of the poem set to music, see the *Morning Chronicle* (17 July 1804).
30 *Norfolk Chronicle* (25 March 1820).
31 *Worcester Journal* (25 September 1823).
32 Pugh, *Staffordshire Portrait Figures*, pp. 289–90. The ballet was performed at the Adelphi Theatre, *Morning Post* (21 November 1826). For the Great Exhibition see *Morning Chronicle* (12 September 1851).
33 *London Daily News* (1 October 1855). The polytechnic later advertised these 'unceasing novelties', *Illustrated London News* (20 October 1855).
34 *Brighton Gazette* (3 January 1856). Another display was in the Teutonic Hall, Liverpool, 3d entry to the working classes. *Liverpool Mercury* (13 February 1856).
35 *Western Daily Press* (8 October 1861). For the leading role of the Royal Polytechnic as 'the vibrant centre of Victorian multi-media culture', see Joss Marsh, 'Dickensian "dissolving views": the magic lantern, visual story-telling and the Victorian technological imagination', *Comparative Critical Studies* 6:3 (2009), 333–46, esp. 344.
36 Tai-Chun Ho, 'The afterlife of Thomas Campbell and "the soldier's dream" in the Crimean War', *19: Interdisciplinary Studies in the Long Nineteenth Century* 8 (2015), 20, http://doi.org/10.16995/ntn.714 (accessed 9 June 2019).
37 Autobiographical accounts noted that men's role as provisioners meant they were often away from home working. Julie-Marie Strange, 'Fathers at home: life writing and late-Victorian and Edwardian plebeian domestic masculinities', *Gender & History* 27:3 (2015), 703–17, esp. 705.
38 American author John Howard Payne wrote lyrics to *Home Sweet Home*, which was from the opera *Clari*, which debuted in London in 1823. *British Workman* (1862), p. 292.
39 For the ubiquity of the cottage in mid-Victorian genre painting and a reading of Frederick Daniel Hardy's *The Volunteers*, 1860, see Trev Lynn Broughton and Helen Rogers, 'Introduction: the empire of the father' in Trev Lynn Broughton and Helen Rogers, *Gender and Fatherhood in the Nineteenth Century* (Basingstoke: Palgrave Macmillan, 2007), pp. 2–5.
40 Alice Fahs, *The Imagined Civil War: Popular Literature of the North and South, 1861–1865* (Chapel Hill: University of North Carolina Press, 2001), p. 95.
41 Melissa Bellanta, '"Poor Gordon": what the Australian cult of Adam Lindsay Gordon tells us about turn-of-the-twentieth-century masculine sentimentality', *Gender & History* 28:2 (2016), 401–21.
42 *St. Nicholas Scribner's Illustrated Magazine for Girls and Boys* (1 April 1882), p. 457.
43 For an overview of this position see Julie-Marie Strange, *Fatherhood and the British Working Class* (Cambridge: Cambridge University Press, 2015), pp. 1–7 and 15–17.
44 Maya Wassell Smith, '"The fancy work what sailors make": material and emotional creative practice in masculine seafaring communities', *Nineteenth-Century Gender Studies* 14:2 (2018).
45 Fitzwilliam Collection, *Sailor's Farewell*, Object Number: C.96–1997, http://data.fitzmuseum.cam.ac.uk/id/object/76460 (accessed 13 June 2019).
46 Tyne & Wear Archives and Museums, earthenware jug, 1870, TWCMS: B1339.
47 Walker Art Gallery, Liverpool, Ford Madox Brown, *Waiting: An English Fireside in the Winter of 1854–5*. Discussed in *Tate Gallery 1984–86, Illustrated Catalogue of Acquisitions including Supplement to Catalogue of Acquisitions 1982–84* (London: Tate Gallery, 1988), pp. 12–17.
48 For example, Maidstone Museum Love Token Collection, Kent, Unknown, 'Love token – So to my love the same I'll be', *When this you see remember me*, https://lovetokens.omeka.net/items/show/188 (accessed 30 April 2019). For love tokens see Bridget Millmore, 'Love tokens: engraved coins, emotions and the poor 1700–1856' (PhD thesis, University of Brighton, 2015).

49 Bernard Barton, *Poetic Vigils* (London, 1824), pp. 77–8.
50 The same verse is on a Moore's Pottery white earthenware jug, 1836, Tyne & Wear Archives and Museums, TWCMS: D2033, which was inscribed with the owner, Elizabeth Hoor's, name and the date 1836; also see Tyne & Wear Archives and Museums, Dixon, Phillips & Co., *c*.1860, TWCMS: D2008.
51 *Clonmel Herald* (6 April 1839).
52 Tyne & Wear Archives and Museums, jug, *c*.1860–80, TWCMS: F9539.
53 Wassell Smith, '"The fancy work what sailors make"', 1, 3, 22–8.
54 Millmore, 'Love tokens', pp. 268, 269.
55 There are sweetheart badges and brooches too, small metal badges intended for the soldier's loved one to wear, with regimental motifs, dating from around 1900. See the many examples in the King's Own Royal Regiment Museum, Lancaster, which are engraved with a lion and 'the King's Own', some adding more personalised messages, www.kingsownmuseum.com/sweetheart03.htm (accessed 13 June 2019).
56 Examples include: Imperial War Museum, pincushion, EPH 4231, www.iwm.org.uk/collections/item/object/30083766 (accessed 13 June 2019); Tyne & Wear Archives and Museums, TWCSMS: A258.
57 Nick Mansfield, *Soldiers as Workers: Class, Employment, Conflict and the Nineteenth-Century Military* (Liverpool: Liverpool University Press, 2016), p. 132.
58 Tyne & Wear Archives and Museums, pincushion, *c*.1860, TWCMS: J13107.
59 Ruth Kenny, Jeff McMillan, and Martin Myrone, *British Folk Art* (London: Tate Enterprises Ltd, 2014), pp. 38–9.
60 Sally Holloway, 'Materialising maternal emotions: birth, celebration and renunciation in England, c.1688–1830', in Stephanie Downes, Sally Holloway, and Sarah Randles (eds), *Feeling Things: Objects and Emotions through History* (Oxford: Oxford University Press, 2018), pp. 162–3, 168.
61 For Georgian examples see Joanne Bailey, *Parenting in England, 1760–1830: Emotion, Identity, and Generation* (Oxford: Oxford University Press, 2012); for mid-Victorian examples see Brian Maidment, 'Domestic ideology and its industrial enemies: the title page of the *Family Economist* 1848–1850', in C. Parker (ed.), *Gender Roles and Sexuality in Victorian Literature* (Aldershot: Scolar, 1995), pp. 25–56.
62 These were often in ceramic form. For example, see: Reginald G. Haggar, *Staffordshire Chimney Ornaments* (London: Phoenix House Ltd, 1955), p. 54.
63 Tate Gallery, Julius Caesar Ibbetson, *A Married Sailor's Return* (1800), N05793.
64 A survey of Royal Academy exhibitions shows that in 1855 seventeen painters and sculptors dealt with the war, in 1856 thirteen, and in 1857 seven. *Tate Gallery 1984–86*, pp. 12–17. For concerns over pensions and welfare for soldiers and their families see Hichberger, *Images of the Army*, p. 171.
65 *Bury and Norwich Post* (19 May 1863). Museum of London, Henry Nelson O'Neil, *Home Again*, 1858, Accession Number 2004.152/2.
66 An example is the Crimean War-era 'Wounded Soldier', Balston, *Staffordshire Portrait Figures*, plate 18 and p. 60.
67 Simon Parkes, 'Wooden legs and tales of sorrow done: the literary broken soldier of the late eighteenth century', *Journal for Eighteenth-Century Studies* 36:2 (2013), 191–207.
68 This is discussed in more detail in *Tate Gallery 1984–86*, pp. 12–17.
69 Royal Collection Trust, Sir Joseph Noël Paton (1821–1901), *Home (The Return from the Crimea)*, signed and dated 1859, RCIN 406954.
70 *British Workman* (December 1871), p. 95.
71 Ibid.
72 For the significance of such images for attitudes towards fatherhood and parenting, see Bailey, *Parenting in England*, pp. 114–18.

73 Christiana Payne, *Toil and Plenty: Images of the Agricultural Landscape in England 1780–1890* (New Haven, CT, and London: Yale University Press, 1993), pp. 1–4.
74 For this work and Maidment's stance see Brian Maidmont, *Reading Popular Prints, 1790–1870* (Manchester: Manchester University Press, 1996), pp. 102–4.
75 For men as provisioners see Joanne Bailey, 'A very sensible man: imagining fatherhood in England c.1750–1830', *History: The Journal of the Historical Association* 95:319 (2010), 267–92; Strange, 'Fathers at home', 705.
76 Yale Center for British Art, Friends of British Art Fund, George Elgar Hicks, *Sinews of Old England*, 1856, Accession Number B2003.14, http://collections.britishart.yale.edu/vufind/Record/3659731 (accessed 18 June 2019).
77 For example, *Berrow's Worcester Journal* (16 June 1853).
78 Karen Walker, 'Manly men and angelic women: gender and nostalgia in George Elgar Hicks's watercolour "The Sinews of Old England" (1857) and in an advertisement for Cadbury's Cocoa (1886)', http://open.conted.ox.ac.uk/resources/documents/manly-men-and-angelic-women-gender-and-nostalgia-george-elgar-hicks%E2%80%99s (accessed 18 July 2018).
79 The cottage doorway as transitional space is discussed by Maidment, *Reading Popular Prints*, p. 101.
80 *British Workman* (1871), pp. 73–5.
81 *Ibid*.
82 Bailey, *Parenting in England*, pp. 51–3.
83 *British Workman* 195 (March 1871), p. 58.
84 For the many and complex meanings of representations of the dustman, see Brian Maidment, *Dusty Bob: A Cultural History of Dustmen, 1780–1870* (Manchester: Manchester University Press, 2007).
85 *British Workman* (1898), p. 34.
86 Cottage interiors in rustic genre paintings were intended to demonstrate the virtues and good character of the poor, Christiana Payne, *Rustic Simplicity: Scenes of Cottage Life in Nineteenth-Century British Art* (Nottingham: Lund Humphries, 1998), pp. 5, 17–22.
87 National Galleries Scotland, George Morland, *The Comforts of Industry*, NG 1835; *The Miseries of Idleness*, NG 1836.
88 At Kelvingrove Art Gallery and Museum, Glasgow. Discussed by Payne, *Rustic Simplicity*, pp. 90–1.
89 *British Workman* 20 (1856), p. 76.
90 Wellcome Collection, W. Gunthorp, *The Beneficial Effects of Temperance on a Man and his Family*, lithograph, *c*.1840, after Gunthorp.
91 *British Workman* (1 February 1871), p. 58.
92 *British Workman* (1 August 1874), pp. 221–2.
93 *Bradford Daily Telegraph* (7 September 1899), p. 5.
94 *British Workman* 159 (March 1868), pp. 153–4.
95 *Ibid*.
96 *British Workman* 193 (2 January 1871), p. 50.
97 *Ibid*.
98 *Bradford Daily Telegraph* (7 September 1899), p. 5.
99 Maidment, *Reading Popular Prints*, p. 108.
100 Anna Clark, *The Struggle for the Breeches: Gender and the Making of the British Working Class* (Berkeley: University of California Press, 1995), ch. 8.
101 Mary Poovey, *Making a Social Body: British Cultural Formation, 1830–1864* (Chicago: University of Chicago Press, 1995), pp. 126–30.
102 *British Workman* 73 (1861), p. 293.
103 *British Workman* 159 (March 1868), pp. 153–4.
104 *British Workman* 193 (2 January 1871), p. 50.
105 *British Workman* (1898), p. 37.

106 For examples: *Greenock Telegraph and Clyde Shipping Gazette* (27 December 1899), p. 5.
107 Bridget Walsh, *Domestic Murder in Nineteenth-Century England: Literary and Cultural Representations* (Farnham: Ashgate Publishing, 2014), p. 94. Lisa Surridge also deals extensively with these issues, *Bleak Houses: Marital Violence in Victorian Fiction* (Athens, OH: Ohio University Press, c.2005).
108 *Dundee Courier* (17 October 1899), p. 6.
109 Maidment sees the shadow of the drunken threatening counterpart of the returning artisan in mid-nineteenth-century prints on this subject. Maidment, *Reading Popular Prints*, pp. 125–9.
110 *Bell's Life in London and Sporting Chronicle* (26 December 1824), p. 413.
111 *Northern Whig* (31 October 1899), p. 5. For the links between Victorian unmanliness and wife beating see Surridge, *Bleak Houses*, ch. 2.
112 Bridget Walsh makes this point in her study of reports and representations of domestic murder in sensation novels, *Domestic Murder*, ch. 4; Maidment, *Reading Popular Prints*, p. 127.
113 For the role of domestic space and objects in shaping marital violence and perceptions of it, see Joanne Begiato, 'Beyond the rule of thumb: the materiality of marital violence in England c.1700–1857', *Cultural and Social History* 15:1 (2018), 51–5 and passim.
114 John William Kaye, 'Outrages on women', *North British Review* 25 (1856), July 1857, 412. For the context to Kaye's text and its relationship with wider debates on wife beating see Surridge, *Bleak Houses*, pp. 4–6.
115 *British Workman* (1 June 1859), p. 119.
116 *British Workman* 34 (1 October 1857), p. 136.
117 *British Workman* 195 (March 1871), p. 59. *Gloucestershire Echo* (26 December 1899), p. 2.
118 Frances Power Cobbe, 'Wife-torture in England', *Contemporary Review* 32 (1878), 58–87; at 69. Feminists strategically used working-class marital violence to prove the inequities of an electoral system that gave the vote to wife beaters but refused to enfranchise middle-class, educated women. See Jo Aitken, '"The horrors of matrimony among the masses": feminist representations of wife beating in England and Australia, 1870–1914', *Journal of Women's History* 19:4 (2007), 112–17, esp. 114–17.
119 *British Workman* (1 April 1858), pp. 157–8.
120 She selects examples from Charles Dickens, Wilkie Collins, and Thomas Hardy. Walsh, *Domestic Murder*, pp. 106–10.
121 *The Times* (12 October 1871), p. 5. Cited in Walsh, *Domestic Murder*, p. 109.
122 Broughton and Rogers, 'Introduction: The empire of the father', p. 13.
123 Sarah Stickney Ellis, *The Women of England, their Social Duties, and Domestic Habits* (London: Fisher, Son & Co., 1839), cited in Broughton and Rogers, 'Introduction: the empire of the father', p. 13.
124 Maidment, *Reading Popular Prints*, pp. 126–7.
125 *Dundee Courier* (17 October 1899), p. 6.
126 Aitken, '"The horrors of matrimony"', 112–14; Elizabeth Foyster, *Marital Violence: An English Family History, 1660–1857* (Cambridge: Cambridge University Press, 2005).
127 For degeneration as one of the discourses around wife beating see Elizabeth Nelson, 'Victims of war: the First World War, returned soldiers, and understanding domestic violence in Australia', *Journal of Women's History* 19:4 (2007), 84; Aitken, '"The horrors of matrimony"', 107–31, esp. 115.
128 A. James Hammerton, *Cruelty and Companionship: Conflict in Nineteenth-Century Married Life* (New York: Routledge, 1992). For more on these debates see Susan Edwards, '"Kicked, beaten, jumped on until they are crushed", all under man's

wing and protection: the Victorian dilemma with domestic violence', in Judith Rowbotham and Kim Stevenson (eds), *Criminal Conversations: Victorian Crimes, Social Panic, and Moral Outrage* (Columbus: Ohio State University Press, 2005), pp. 247–66.
129 *Spectator* (5 December 1874), p. 9, http://archive.spectator.co.uk/article/5th-september-1874/9/aggravated-assaults (accessed 11 October 2019).
130 *Spectator* (22 December 1877), p. 13, http://archive.spectator.co.uk/article/22nd-december-1877/13/protection-for-english-christians-ct-the-enrrou-of (accessed 11 October 2019).
131 Megan Doolittle, 'Time, space, and memories: the father's chair and grandfather clocks in Victorian working-class domestic lives', *Home Cultures* 8:3 (2011), 245–64; Strange, 'Fathers at home', 705.
132 Joanne Bailey, *Unquiet Lives: Marriage and Marriage Breakdown in England 1660–1800* (Cambridge: Cambridge University Press, 2003), pp. 96–7.
133 Cobbe, 'Wife-torture in England', 59.
134 For more on Cobbe's campaign see Susan Hamilton, '"A whole series of frightful cases": domestic violence, the periodical press and Victorian feminist writing', *TOPIA* 13 (2005), 89–101.
135 Cobbe, 'Wife-torture in England', 55–87.
136 *Ibid.*, 59.
137 Foyster, *Marital Violence*, p. 72.
138 Hammerton, *Cruelty and Companionship*, p. 31.
139 Aitken, "The horrors of matrimony"', 108.
140 John Tosh, 'Home and away: the flight from domesticity in late-nineteenth-century England re-visited', *Gender and History* 3 (2015) 566–8, 572.
141 This is evident in lower-middle-class men's autobiographies, for example, A. James Hammerton, 'Pooterism or partnership? Marriage and masculine identity in the lower middle class, 1870–1920', *Journal of British Studies* 38:3 (1999), 291–321.

5

Brawn and bravery: glorifying the working body

Introduction

When the *British Workman* was first published in 1855, it boasted a handsome illustrated banner atop its front page. The graphic strips featured a range of workers arrayed to either side of a coat of arms representing the nation, with a scroll announcing, 'in all labour there is profit'. The workers busy themselves in front of structures that denote both the men's workplaces and economic significance, including a mill with smoking chimneys, a large building under construction, a transport bridge, and the Crystal Palace. The working men are navvies, agricultural labourers, carpenters, builders, and engineers. On the left and right are portrait vignettes, which at various times depicted dustmen, coal heavers, and sailors.[1] The periodical also published 'wall-paper' that revealed the types of working man most commonly linked with manliness: blacksmiths, navvies, railway workers, coal heavers and miners, mariners, lifeboat men, and firemen. For example, the 1871 volume's back page lists, among others, 'The Ambitious Blacksmith', 'The Life Boat', 'Musical Coal-Man', and 'The "Blue Jacket's" Sampler'.[2] These employments were no doubt intended to represent the magazine's readership, but they also offer valuable insights into the ways in which working men were imagined, consumed, and deployed in constructions of manliness.

Middle-class men wrote and illustrated the *British Workman*, so this chapter explores the role of such representations for their own social group. As such, it returns to where this book began, with desire for the male emotionalised body and the gender it embodied. Working men's erotic power lay in their aestheticised qualities and the association of their physicality with economic prosperity, akin to the associations of military bodies with national defence.[3] The first section explores the nobility assigned to the brawny, muscular body, cross-examined through the imagined blacksmith and navvy. The next section, 'Bravery and the heroic working man in the modern world', addresses the role of bravery, another alluring quality, primarily through miners, firemen, and lifeboat men. Such strong and appealing working men offered a very different vision of working-class masculinity to that in which they were politically and socially dangerous radicals, revolutionaries, malcontents, malingerers, or strikers, or physically and mentally warped by the degenerating forces of modernity. The chapter then scrutinises the images of working men that decorated friendly society and trade union emblems to show that the working classes created and disseminated their own highly emotional and material manifestation of working-class manliness. Comparing these constructions of working manliness, it argues that the glorified worker embodied idealised masculine qualities for middle- and working-class men, both of whom benefitted from the non-threatening persona that these representations cultivated. However, the emotions associated with them were subtly different and deployed in different ways. For all, he was an alluring inspirational figure. For middle-class men, however, he was reassuring and admirable; for working-class men he was a measure of their right to be included in the civic polity. As previous chapters propose, material culture was integral to all these connotations.

Brawn and the nobility of labour in an industrial society

One of the most commonly represented working men was the blacksmith, whose emotionalised body communicated a range of messages and whose cultural fascination had deep roots. In examples from the early eighteenth century, the body of the labourer was based on classical statuary. Joseph Wright of Derby's nocturnal paintings of blacksmiths, for example, include *The Blacksmith's Shop* 1771, in which three fine-figured men labour at the anvil.[4] Perhaps even more overtly indicative of the hearty beauty of male physical labour is the iron founder in Wright's *An Iron Forge*, 1772.[5] Overseeing the power-driven tilt hammer, he stands with his powerful arms crossed over his chest. Literally a glowing example of male strength, he is also surrounded by his family, indicating his virility and domesticity. As Matthew Craske observes, in these paintings Wright produced the opposite of the grand style of history painting, where the blacksmith stood as the lusty everyman essential to the village.[6] These works alluded to the natural health and beauty of the working man to remind those wealthy enough to consume such art that their appetites could result in an effete, enervated, and effeminate body.[7] The result was idealised virile workers who possessed an erotic charge for male as well as female consumption. For example, the *British Workman*'s illustration (Figure 5.1) of the blacksmith surely evokes his manhood, not only through his whiskered face and muscular arm, but by the phallic shadow his smith's tool casts across the

5.1 *Getting in the Thin Edge of the Wedge; Or, Strike while the Iron's Hot*, British Workman (1868), p. 182.

groin of his leather apron. Moreover, such manly bodies offered a benign virility: the opposite of the appetite-driven and brutal unmanly lower-class man.

While his size, attractiveness, and muscularity were consistent in these visual images, the imagined blacksmith's cultural function varied across the Victorian period. Although artists updated his pose and surroundings along with new technologies, he became a traditional figure in the transition from rural manufacturing to urban industry. Thus in 1855 the *British Workman* devoted a front page to 'Celebrated Blacksmiths'. Ostensibly portraying famous blacksmiths through time, many were actually famous men who were sons of blacksmiths. Blacksmiths were thus positioned as the perfect stock for fathering eminent men, because they were envisioned as physically powerful, decent, and honourable. Some of the blacksmiths singled out were autodidacts, another ideal quality for the self-help generation. They included Elihu Burritt, an American blacksmith and anti-slavery campaigner, whose illustration speaks to the new characteristics associated with this craft by middle-class admirers.[8] His sleeves are rolled up to gesture to muscular labour, but he was posed thoughtfully reading. Another was Aaron Arnold, pictured working at his smithy, 'at his lusty labour. He has on his great leathern apron, with a fringe to it. His shirt sleeves are tucked up nearly to his shoulders.' Crucially, Arnold was noted to be 'cheerful' and 'kindly' and contrasted with the wicked Squire Ringwood who oppressed the weak in his endeavour to increase profits.[9]

This combination of kindness and strength was a widespread trope. It was appealingly fictionalised in the form of Joe Gargery, Pip's brother-in-law (and father figure) in *Great Expectations* (1861). Pip recounted visiting the lawyer, Mr Jaggers, with Joe to hear of his 'great expectations'. Joe rejected the offer of financial compensation for Pip leaving his home to embark on his new life as a gentleman, on the grounds that Pip is his best friend. While Joe was gentle with his young brother-in-law, he used his bodily strength to attack Mr Jaggers' pejorative view of him. Pip recalled that Joe began 'suddenly working round him with every demonstration of a fell pugilistic purpose', warning Jaggers to stop 'bull-baiting and badgering me ... Which I meantersay as sech if you're a man, come on! Which I meantersay that what I say, I meantersay and stand or fall by!' Joe's kind-heartedness was conveyed by his body and feelings, as well as by his actions. Pip recalled that 'Joe laid his hand on my shoulder with the touch of a woman. I have often thought of him since, like the steam-hammer, that can crush a man or pat an egg-shell, in his combination of strength with gentleness.' Looking back as an older man, Pip remembered with shame his failure to appreciate Joe's worth, reflecting: 'I see you again, with your muscular black-smith's arm before your eyes, and your broad chest heaving, and your voice dying away.'[10] If at times dismissed by his wife, brother-in-law, and village as fair of face, but foolish, 'a sort of Hercules in strength, and also in weakness', Joe was nonetheless, Pip belatedly recognised, a man of true feeling and decency.[11]

In many ways, the idealised smithy became a generic emblem of a lost Merry England, the nostalgic 'visionary, mythical landscape' that writers and artists conjured in the nineteenth century as a means to manage the fears induced by a rapidly modernising society.[12] In this essentially conservative concept, the social and working conditions of modernity were contrasted with an Arcadian past in which the peasantry happily toiled and played, members bound together in a hierarchical society by a network of reciprocal obligations and duties.[13] Its adherents sought to recreate sanitised versions of pastimes and customs to generate a more reassuring present. William Howitt, for example, evoked the celebration of Whitsuntide in 'merry England' in his 1838 *The Rural Life of England*, through processions of friendly society members with their banners. At the head of the villagers wearing their best clothing and 'bearing the great banner, emblazoned with some fitting scene and motto', bedecked with posies of flowers, he placed 'old Harry Lomax the blacksmith, deputed to that office for the brawny strength of his arms'.[14] The smith was not the only worker used to perform similar cultural work. In 1871, the *British Workman* offered best wishes to Princess Louise on her wedding with a tableau of workers deemed representatives of 'our dear old Merry England'. Along with a blacksmith were a miner, shepherd, weaver, puddler, potter, seamstress, fisherman, and farmer. For the most part these workers were bodies in motion, whose 'stout hands' swung hammers, drove shuttles, rung axes, shaped stones, and plied needles.[15] They were also profoundly emotional bodies, their good wishes 'Rising up from hearts o'erflowing.' The blacksmith as feeling father was a common trope too. In a poem of 1871, 'A Dinner and a Kiss', a little girl brings dinner to her blacksmith father in an archaic smithy, his role simply to encourage the reader to ruminate on the importance of the working man being satisfied with his lot.[16]

Even when the smith was represented at the cutting edge of technology, his presence was a link to a comforting tradition. William Bell Scott's *Iron and Coal* (1856–60) musters every sign of modernity, from the engineering wonder of the High Level Bridge, to steam train and ship, to telegraph wires, with other flourishes including a photographer and fashionable ladies. Even the newspaper in the forefront is up to date, with its advert of a theatrical diorama of entertainment venues visited by Garibaldi, that other popular model of manliness. Yet, while the determined men forging the future are industrial smiths, they are familiar in leather aprons and blue shirts, rolled up to reveal muscular forearms.[17] In these accounts of labour, imagined manly workers were conjured to render progress safer and less threatening for the class who depended on them for labour, products, and success.

The manly workers offered reassurance in the face of political change too, particularly in the more liberal atmosphere of the 1850s and 1860s, when praising the moral qualities of ordinary people was part of political and intellectual discourse.[18] In the 1868 *British Workman* tale, 'Getting in the Thin Edge of the Wedge; Or, "Strike While the Iron's Hot"', two aptly named smiths, Tom Strokes and Ned Sledger, discuss the recent Second Reform Act of 1867, which extended the franchise to some working men. As the title 'Thin Edge of the Wedge' implied, this was seen as a step towards mass politics, which caused anxiety. Thus, Strokes and Sledger, by evoking the blacksmith of tradition, helpfully showed that enfranchised working men need not be a threat to society. Tom Strokes is described as 'about the strongest man in that part of the country', and in the accompanying illustration (Figure 5.1) the muscled arms and whiskered faces of both men, radiant in the furnace's flames, recall Wright's sumptuously lit and handsome smiths. Here muscularity, which could be threatening, was controlled and therefore made even more appealing. Linking these men with blacksmiths' cultural meaning as the stable heart of the village, the text also positions them as unthreatening 'independent' workers, whose only priority when enfranchised was to ensure that the Sabbath was protected by the MPs they had a hand in sending to Parliament.[19]

Unsurprisingly, therefore, the smith served as a vehicle for moral and Christian values. 'Jim Bowling's Twist' by the Rev. C. Courtenay (1898), takes Jim, the blacksmith's son, on a journey of redemption. He begins as a happy-go-lucky lad forced to abandon his nascent smithying due to drink. He becomes a sailor and encounters Miss Agnes Western's temperance movement and takes the pledge. With spiritual guidance he returns to the forge, now a pious smith.[20] The beating of the iron is a metaphor for his soul being hammered out into the right shape. It is illustrated by a conventionally idyllic image of a blacksmith hammering on an anvil in a village forge, a child peering in at the door; surely a deliberate contrast to the industrial unionised version of the blacksmith.[21] Other appealing manly workers were similarly deployed as exemplars for working-class men who did not threaten their social superiors. In the *British Workman*'s opening issue (1855), in the tale 'The Bag of Gold; or, The Noble-Hearted Navvie', the navvy turns charity on its head by giving his savings to a minister whose wife and all three children have died. Sir Morton Peto, the author, describes the navvy as an 'honourable example of an upright, conscientious Christian character, and of public usefulness'. As such, he seems to be as much a mirror for middle-class manliness as an example for working-class men.[22]

Indeed, there is evidence that such idealised workers inspired middle-class men. The 1860s and 1870s were decades when the governing elite had confidence in their countrymen and were prepared to see similarities between themselves and their social inferiors.[23] An excellent example is the socialist artist William Morris's 'emotional identification' with Dickens's fictional blacksmith, Joe Gargery.[24] Wendy Parkins shows that Morris regularly used Gargery's phrase 'Wot larks' in his correspondence with his daughters and his wife. Gargery provided 'a conduit for the expression of emotions associated with fatherhood', since he was depicted as a tender, loving, and playful paternal figure in *Great Expectations*. Nonetheless, it was not only Gargery's fatherly feeling which endeared him to Morris. As Parkins observes, Gargery was a simple, therefore pure, man, whose lack of social pretensions and charm endeared him to the radical socialist who envisioned manual work as a means to achieve a better society.[25]

Middle-class men thus also saw in these imagined working men a natural, untainted manliness. In some ways, the manly worker was positioned as a 'noble savage'.[26] In this myth, the original man of nature, innocent of vice and sin, and therefore of troubling passions and appetites, was noble in his uncorrupted state. It is possible to see such 'natural' qualities projected onto manly workers. In 1871, the *British Workman* approvingly described an archetypal Cornish miner thus. J. Scanlan's illustration shows him underground, sitting alone and at ease, strong-bodied, wearing working clothes with protective headgear (that evokes a helmet), large hammer held loosely by his side. He is not poised to work, but posed as confidently resting, looking off contemplatively into the middle distance. The author applauds his semi-independent status, wherein the miners would bid to work parts of the mine in groups, because this 'enlists him in mutual partnership with the mine owners and his fellow-workmen'. This, it is noted favourably, prevents strikes and lockouts. This aligned with anti-union rhetoric, which praised independence, showing men on their own or in domestic scenes, rather than working collectively or talking politics in alehouses. The Cornish miner's trustworthiness and skilfulness were such that he was 'the master of his work in all parts of the world' including Canada, California, Mexico, Peru, Chile, Brazil, and Australia. The narrator describes the Cornish miner as a man of simple tastes. On finishing work he washes and dresses 'tidy but gay', to enjoy an evening of simple pursuits. If a young man, he wrestles wholesomely with mates, if older he romps with his children; both age groups are churchgoers and educate themselves in their spare time. Although they speak in an 'unknown tongue', Cornish miners were trusty, intelligent, witty, pious: 'in their feelings, convictions and acts, they are genuine men, and not shams'.[27] Here was a skilled manual worker at once imperial in range, but simple and untainted by modern civilisation.

The concept of the inherent nobility of labour was woven into the fabric of several nineteenth-century political ideologies. Tim Barringer identifies two prevailing theories of work: 'instrumental', where labour was necessary for the economy, but disagreeable; and 'expressive', where work was integral to personal development and, even, salvation. Work was thus both redemptive and an act through which men realised their masculine potential.[28] Indeed, work was considered critical to English 'manliness' or 'self-reliance'. In the earlier nineteenth century, radicals emphasised the 'dignity of labour so that it appeared to be a noble alternative to (as well as qualification for) the exercise of political powers'.[29] Intellectuals metaphorically grappled with labour. The philosopher, historian, and polemicist Thomas Carlyle saw nobility as a product of being rather than birth, and work as one of the routes to improvement.[30] Indeed, he elevated work to a religion in his chapter on 'Labour', in *Past and Present* (1843), in which work made the man, and in so doing saved the individual as well as the national body and soul. This was partly because physical labour quelled the damaging emotions to which the modern man was subjected. He observed:

> Consider how, even in the meanest sorts of Labour, the whole soul of a man is composed into a kind of real harmony, the instant he sets himself to work! Doubt, Desire, Sorrow, Remorse, Indignation, Despair itself, all these like hell-dogs lie beleaguering the soul of the poor dayworker, as of every man: but he bends himself with free valour against his task, and all these are stilled, all these shrink murmuring far off into their caves. The man is now a man. The blessed glow of Labour in him, is it not as purifying fire wherein all poison is burnt up, and of sour smoke itself there is made bright blessed flame![31]

The elevation of the working man to noble status through his muscular emotionalised body in the act of labour was widespread in British art and literature in the second half of the nineteenth century. The archetypal mid-century example is Ford Madox Brown's masterpiece *Work* (1852–63), which centres on navvies laying water pipes in Hampstead. Navvies, 'navigators' who worked to build roads, tunnels, bridges, and railway tracks, were renowned for physical strength and virility. In some cases, this could be perceived to be threatening when navvies were seen as hard-drinking, violent, womanising, and lacking domestic roots.[32] They were, however, also represented in print and art as rough men with tender feelings and magnificent physiques.[33] Brown was a radical and socialist who was influenced by John Ruskin and Carlyle's views on work. Like them, he saw manual labour as the key to forging middle-class manliness. In the sonnet that he wrote to accompany the painting (February 1865), he eulogised work as beading the brow and tanning 'the flesh of lusty manhood', thereby 'casting out its devils!'[34] He also described the navvy as being in the 'pride of manly health and beauty'.[35] As Barringer explains, it is the central navvy's body, whose heroic pose Brown based on the Apollo Belvedere, that embodies true manliness, regardless of social status.[36] This sentiment was widely shared, as shown in critics' praise for *Work*, which used the language of manliness, celebrating it as manly, vigorous, and powerful.[37]

By the later nineteenth century, British socialists saw the fullest attainment of self through labour. For some, this was aestheticised as well as politicised. From the 1860s, William Morris developed a utopian version of the backwards-looking 'Little England' stance: a protest against the deleterious effects of industrialisation on the working classes. In this vision, a return to a more agrarian, artisan-based labour would eradicate inequalities.[38] Ruth Livesey explores this conjunction of work, aesthetics, pleasure, and politics in the 1880s and 1890s. She observes that socialists like William Morris and Edward Carpenter saw communal labour as the way 'in which the self achieved fullest expression, clearest realization – true manhood'. For both, in different ways, 'the masculine laboring body became an aesthetic site: the origin of the rebirth of the arts after the demise of capitalism'.[39] Manual labour was, therefore, a way for the professional classes to become their true selves. As Morris declared in *Signs of Change* (1888): 'I should not think much of the manhood of a stout and healthy man who did not feel a pleasure in doing rough work.'[40] It is not surprising, therefore, that these men revered the aestheticised male working body: it was the source of both political and personal identity.

For some socialists, the male working body was explicitly eroticised, even fetishised.[41] The combination of aestheticism, politics, and the erotic is most evident in the writings of Edward Carpenter, who conceptualised desire for the working-class male body as a means to throw off 'bourgeois bodily repression' and enable the rebirth of society. For Carpenter, the 'potent naked body of the laboring man writ large was the very emblem of Democracy'. This vision of 'priapic Labor', Livesey argues, differed from 'the aestheticised visions of the honest working man, visible from Ford Madox Brown's *Work* through to Soviet era statuary'.[42] For Carpenter, a future socialist utopia would be founded on desire and sexual contact with the labouring man. This would not only forge closer connections between social classes, it would improve higher-ranking men's masculinity.[43]

Bravery and the heroic working man in the modern world

The brawny, working, manly body – moral exemplar for working-class men, reassuring emblem of manliness for middle-class men, and metaphor for work as salvation and route to manly self-realisation – was not the only desirable representation of labour. The heroic working man was similarly popular. This was not the metaphorical heroic that artists like Brown captured in the classical form of a navvy, whose role was to update and radicalise the genre of history painting.[44] This was the ordinary hero – a worker who risked his life to save others during everyday employment or as part of his profession. Like their noble counterparts, these figures were simultaneously exemplars for the working class and reminders that middle-class manliness needed to raise its game. After all, heroism was a cultural language that middle-class men capitalised on to construct their own gender and professional identities. Michael Brown has shown, for example, that Victorian medical practitioners deployed discourses of heroism, in their case military self-sacrifice, to elevate their professional status and to draw attention to their contribution to the national good.[45] As such, middle-class men were sensitive to the gender and class connotations of heroic types. The brave working men that are discussed, then, possessed as much meaning for middle-class men as for their intended audience of working-class men.[46]

The seafaring man who rescued the drowning was one working man regularly lauded for heroism. Representations merged a strong, often handsome body, nobility of demeanour, and courage, and drew upon the rich symbolism and material culture of manliness embodied in the sailor.[47] In general, paintings of mariners extolled their manly virtues, such as James Clarke Hook's *The Fisherman's Goodnight* (1856) and *Hearts of Oak* (1875), which show attractive, sturdy, family men.[48] In 1860, the frontispiece of the *British Workman* depicted a 'Real Hero', Joseph Rodgers, a 'brave seamen' who had saved thirty-nine people from the wreck of the iron ship, the *Royal Charter*, in 1859, by swimming ashore through the stormy seas with a rope. This Maltese seaman was also captured by Henry Nelson O'Neil in the oil painting *A Volunteer* (1860), shown on the wreck, ready to swim in the turbulent sea, surrounded by desperate souls.[49] The *British Workman*, however, focuses far more on Rodgers himself. He stands at ease in the cover portrait, surrounded by a decorative frame made up of marine tools, one arm resting on his raised leg, looking off into the distance, hair swept by the wind, and face framed by a manly chin beard. The accompanying story approves the award of a National Lifeboat Institution gold medal and £5 to the 'heroic tar'.[50]

Lifeboatmen, in particular, were celebrated as 'modern heroes'. Christiana Payne observes that paintings of these men played a crucial role in fostering the ideals of the Royal National Lifeboat Institution after 1854.[51] Artists increasingly gave greater prominence to the rescuers rather than the wrecks as the century went on. Understood to be operating under enormous 'physical and nervous strain', in their portraits lifeboat men were represented, nonetheless, as steady and dependable.[52] The 1870 portrait of James Parsons, Deputy Superintendent of the Royal Humane Society (RHS), for instance, depicts him in brimmed hat, his jumper embroidered with an RHS emblem, both sleeves rolled up to show muscled forearms ready for action.[53] The capacity of such men to overcome nervous strain thus surely offered an example to middle-class men struggling with the stressful demands of their rather more sedentary jobs. The *British Workman* saw in such acts of life-saving a model for its readers, a cause for them to support, and a means to promote its temperance message. It set up a subscription in 1869 to fund a lifeboat, named *British Workman*, to present to the Royal National Lifeboat Institution. After all, as well as offering an opportunity to prevent 'fellow-creatures' dying at sea,[54] the lifeboat was a metaphor for Jesus saving souls.[55] It also conveyed the ideal of manly self-sacrifice in yet another material form.

Newspapers celebrated those working-class men who performed acts of heroism following industrial disasters, casting their actions in terms of wartime self-sacrifice and heroism.[56] The horrific Hartley Colliery disaster in January 1862, which killed 204 men, for example, was one such occasion. A beam supporting the steam engine that was used to pump seawater from the Northumberland pit broke, crashing into the mineshaft, killing those miners who were ascending at the end of a shift and trapping another 199 men underground. Despite the coordinated rescue operation with workers from neighbouring mines, it was six days before a passage was cleared, by which time poisonous fumes had killed the miners. The national coverage called on all the components of manly emotional bodies that have been seen in preceding chapters to describe the miners who made the rescue bid. The *Newcastle Chronicle* portrayed resting rescuers thus: 'While the ruddy glare of the fire was cast over their broad, manly features and well-moulded forms, they seemed to be the living embodiment of all those attributes of courage and strength which … [distinguish] the inhabitants of the British Isles.'[57] One of the heroic working men was illustrated by John Gilbert on the *British Workman*'s title page in April

1862: Thomas Watson, a miner in the broken cage. The author of the report notes that Thomas Watson was an 'honourable member' of 'the working class'. He is shown suspended on a cable above the shaft, a dramatic figure in motion, powerfully muscled and clearly in terrible danger.[58] He 'descended at the imminent peril of his life to pray with some of his dying comrades'. Here was a truly muscular Christian.

As with the accounts of self-sacrifice in Chapter 4, these miners' lives were described using the sentimental register so familiar in literary and visual cultures. Thus, a poem in the *British Workman* by John Harris, a Cornish miner, reflecting on the calamity, emotively described a miner's final day. At dawn, 'the miner/Arose, and kissed his boy'. He left for work: 'Thinking upon his baby,/And wife and home the while/He dashes off the tear-drop,/That steals into his eye;/And turns to see his dwelling,/Though scarcely conscious why.' The poet and readers know he will 'never see it more;/Or hear thy baby's footfall,/Upon the cottage door'. The poet accompanies him descending into the darkness with the men whose lives will soon end, recounts the crash of the riven engine-bob and its fall down the shaft, and, finally, the 'living tomb' where all men perished.[59] These heroic workers were also associated with the patriotic discourse of popular military heroism, outlined in Chapter 3. On 20 May 1862, Edward Glyn delivered a speech at the ceremony held in Newcastle in honour of the miners who had risked their lives to rescue their colleagues:

> We have heard of medals being presented for feats of war; we have heard of medals being presented by the excellent Humane Society for the rescue of lives from shipwreck; we have heard, in London at least, of the presentation of medals for saving life from fire, but this is the first time that we have heard of medals being presented for the rescue of lives in mining operations. The soldier who wore upon his breast the Victoria Cross or the Waterloo Medal might well be proud of it. But I say that these men here today who wear this Hartley Medal might be as proud of it as if they had gained it at Trafalgar, or Waterloo, or Delhi, or Sebastapol.[60]

Such military metaphors linked ordinary workers to the heroism and utility of military masculinity and material culture that helped disseminate these manly ideals of behaviour.

Outside of military heroes, one of the most popular 'professional' heroes throughout popular print culture from the mid-century was the fireman.[61] Like the blacksmith, the fireman was associated with the elemental. Yet he was a symbol of modernity, an urgent figure racing around the modern city to fight fire. His depiction in visual and textual culture took two forms. In some cases, it focused on notable firemen who had lost their lives in service, in other cases the subject was generic firemen. Both were presented as ideal manly working men in that they combined physical strength and gentleness.[62] The fireman added courage, selflessness, and kindness to the mix, typically embodied in a handsome form. These emotions stirred powerful cognate feelings of gratitude, admiration, and excitement, which made the fireman an especially potent symbol of manliness. Indeed, the stirring accounts of these men heightened the vicarious nature of fire rescues for the public. In 1874, a laudatory tale of firemen commented on the paradox underlying people's responses to witnessing a conflagration. Although they were concerned about those whose lives were endangered and whose property was being destroyed, they experienced 'with a thrill of something like exultation' the arrival of the engines drawing firemen to the action.[63] This excitement, even joy and pleasure, in seeing risk overcoming danger, was embodied in the fireman and made his intended manly exemplariness likely to be appealing.

Perhaps the most notable fireman of the era was James Braidwood, who died attending the Tooley Street fire at Cotton's Wharf near London Bridge station on 22 June 1861. The cover of the September issue of the *British Workman* was his head and shoulder portrait, flanked by a weeping Britannia and downcast Fame. The article offered a potted biography: born in Edinburgh in 1800, he was apprenticed as a builder; by twenty-three he was appointed Superintendent of Fire Engines in Edinburgh and became a noted hero by the age of twenty-six. In 1832, the newly formed London Fire-Engine Establishment invited him to organise a fire brigade in London. He was, the *British Workman* declared, superintendent of a 'band of devoted heroic men' who, it noted, followed him with obedience and love. Here, then, was an ideal working-class man, whose name was 'synonymous of all that is pure in life, noble in effort, and lofty in piety'.[64] Thus, his acts and personality were exemplary, and the *British Workman* instructed its readers that 'all of every rank, high and low, rich and poor, would do well to follow his example'. This call to men of all ranks is significant. The middle classes wanted more working men with Braidwood's qualities; after all, he was 'not only a very brave but a very peaceful man'. As the article reminded its target audience: 'We reverence the true hero, we love the good, simple-hearted man – the friend and peacemaker – the humble Christian.'[65] Here was a working man that the middle classes could trust with a vote. But he was also a model that could inspire middle-class men. When the article rhetorically asked about him: 'How beautiful is the union of gentleness and bravery – mildness and decision – coolness and energy', it is remarkable how much these beauteous qualities accorded with middle-class men's gender aspirations.

Art historians have discussed the emulative qualities of the fireman in conjunction with John Everett Millais's *The Rescue* (1855). He painted it having witnessed firemen fighting a fire that same year, because he wished to 'honour a set of men quietly doing a noble work'.[66] For Herbert Sussman, the fireman was an 'heroic exemplar ... from the warrior construction of masculinity', whose physicality was admired and envied by the middle-class man. As such, the depiction of the fireman rescuing children reinforced 'patriarchal order justified by male muscularity and courage'.[67] Indeed, the *Athenaeum* review of the painting claimed that the fireman was 'thoroughly English, cool, determined, and self-reliant ... resolute, manly, strong as iron, like one accustomed to pass through fire'.[68] Robyn Cooper argues, in contrast, that Millais's aim was only partially successful, since she identifies in the painting's reception evidence of middle-class men's unease about the depiction of a powerful working-class man penetrating a middle-class home to rescue its women and children.[69] Examining representations of fireman more generally, in fact, shows that their manliness was made safe and palatable for a middle-class audience.

In January 1874, for example, the *British Workman* published a full-page illustration titled *The Brave Fireman* (Figure 5.2). The fireman is depicted atop his ladder, in front of a thick jet of water aimed at the raging fire that surrounds him. He wears a brass helmet, his handsome, bearded face is resolute, his raised arm wields an axe. The inherent threat of his physically powerful body is countered in the accompanying tale, titled 'Our Brave Firemen', by his self-control and self-sacrifice. His domesticity is also remarked upon this story. It outlines a typical London fireman's day: 'On duty at all hours of the day and night, he is therefore liable to be taken at a moment's notice from family, household, or bed, and in three minutes prepare himself and be in his place on the engine.'[70] Thus, not only did he sacrifice the pleasures of home, the fireman had to cope with the likelihood of injury and even death.

Unsurprisingly, self-sacrifice dominated the military metaphors applied to firemen. The article introduced its cast: 'There exists in our midst an army whose duty compels each soldier to grapple with a foe as uncertain in its attacks as it is terrible in its effects'; the foe, of course, being fire rather than a human enemy.[71] This has strong parallels with the military metaphors that medical practitioners deployed. They stressed the humanitarian nature of their work, fighting disease and saving lives, thereby placing themselves on a superior moral plane to the army, while still garnering the reflected glory of heroic military masculinities.[72] Indeed, the *British Workman* author's commented that if each rescue of 'the screaming, terrified, and helpless victim' was recorded there would be a 'volume of courageous narrative by the side of which military triumphs would pale'. The non-hostile status of the firemen was further stressed in the author's comment, which noted that each member of this 'gallant regiment' remained 'quietly and actively at his work' in the face of chaos. Indeed, while the firemen's commander showed strategy and knowledge, he relied on 'the steady and enduring perseverance of the men', who are lauded for their hardiness. These 'heroic men' work on, wet and cold, after the fire is put out, 'long after the strength of ordinary *landsmen* would have been exhausted; for it may be here remarked that none but *seamen* are chosen for this employment'.[73] As we have seen earlier, to align an individual or group with the manly mariner was always likely to draw to mind powerful associations of appealing manliness.

In 1898, the *British Workman* devoted a full page to firemen, which further neutered the threat of a uniformed, powerful, axe-wielding working man by emphasising firemen's kindness. The full-page illustration of the fireman from 1874 (figure 5.2) was reproduced, now retitled *Desperate Work*. Unlike earlier examples in the magazine, the story takes the form of a narrative. The fire engine, with 'its load of bright-helmeted men' urging on the horses, is equipped with the latest appliances for 'battling with their enemy'. This is illustrated by a large image of a fire engine with three firemen standing on it, pulled by two galloping horses, all impelled towards their destination. As this suggests, military metaphors again abound: it is 'a battle royal, but the firemen are going to win'; they 'will remain until their enemy is cowed and beaten'. Again, they have emotional clout, the waiting crowd increasingly excited as the two firemen appear at a window, one bearing 'a child in his arms'; he runs 'down the escape with the little one – who even in her terror, keeps tight hold of her pet kitten'. The third image, titled *A Brave Rescue*, shows the fireman rescuing the child and her kitten. This, the author gushes, 'is the work of a moment'. Their self-sacrifice is applauded: they perform 'dangerous, desperate work; and the brave fellows who are engaged in it literally hold their lives in their hands'.[74]

The narrator continues with an account of the 'grand fellows'' qualities, which weave together the markers of manly labour: hard, rough bodies and gentle hearts:

> Judging by the grim doggedness with which they fight the flames, firemen may seem as rough as they are ready; but they stand revealed in another life when they are seen risking their lives to tenderly carry little children, or even dumb creatures, from danger to safety; or when it is known that their care for their horses is such that by an arrangement of pulleys the weight of the harness is lifted from the animals on duty in the stable.

The author chats with one of the men afterwards and remarks on the 'dangerous nature' of their work. The fireman responds, 'we never think of that', and takes the narrator to view their 'museum',

> where battered brass helmets, shreds of cloth, and other touching mementoes were displayed – all mutely eloquent of the brave deeds of real heroes.

'A man has to be strong, and active, and brave to be a fireman', he remarked as we turned away.

'And kind', I added, looking back at the pathetic evidences of noble self-sacrifice and devotion to duty.

'Yes,' he said, with a smile, 'and kind, too.'[75]

5.2 *The Brave Fireman, British Workman* (Jan 1874).

The association of kindness with idealised workers, conveyed through emotional objects, is critical to note. Kindness is a 'cluster concept', an act around which feelings and associations are formed. To date, it has been explored as an historical emotion in two ways. Studies of the meaning of kindness show that when performed by social and gender superiors it was a mediator of patriarchal authority or elicited reciprocal support within a patron–client relationship.[76] Recipients of kindness also used it to negotiate their situation, as well as, in some instances, sharing its values.[77] What happened when social superiors projected kindness onto an idealised gender and class subject? Linda Pollock's work on the origins of kindness and its meanings in early modern England offers insights. In scripture, kindness was conceived to consist of meekness and long-suffering: God commanded it from believers as well as demonstrating it to them. When merged with Greek understandings, kindness was understood to make individuals human, a quality which prompted them to aid each other and thereby build communities.[78] It was the former conceptualisation that shaped representations of the imagined manly worker, for it was the quality which made him less a spectre of revolution. The latter view can be discerned as underpinning working-class friendly societies' oaths, regulations, rituals, and banners.[79]

The use of kindness towards the elderly, women, children, and animals as a way to defang the working-class man is particularly evident in representations of railway workers.[80] In the *British Workman*, railway workers were portrayed as earnest and kind. In the December 1871 issue, the story of 'The Little Christmas Visitor in the Railway Guards Room' was illustrated by a very appealing depiction of railway guards gathered around a table, a robin perched on one man's shoulder. Uniformed and bearded, their earnestness is symbolised by their composure and the newspaper left open on the table. The Christmas story tells of a 'kind-hearted' guard caring for a starved robin by putting him in his breast pocket, which the author, Mr Point, reminds the reader, is 'near the heart'. The bird lives in the guards' room for nine of the twelve days of Christmas before flying off recovered. Mr Point explains to his working readers that such acts of kindness denote the men's hard work and thoughtfulness, which is beneficial to passengers and travellers. There follow short vignettes of a guard being kind to the elderly, women, and children. Civil and courteous, guards are portrayed as having 'good heart[s]' and unable to bear seeing others disappointed or vulnerable.

The author concludes with a remarkably voyeuristic paragraph: 'I like to look at cock-robin in this picture amongst these bearded men. And I like it all the better, because cock-robin was a real, and not a make-believe bird; and because all this is true – even the likenesses of the men will be recognized as exact.'[81] Clearly the author is aiming at emotional authenticity, subtly reminding readers of the veracity in this tale of kindness, but this description evokes Freud's concept of scopophilia, where people gain pleasure and identification from looking at other people's bodies as erotic objects.[82] Moreover, the timing of this tale is not perhaps coincidental. The Amalgamated Society of Railway Servants (ASRS), the first attempt to organise railway workers nationally, was established in 1871. By 1872, it had several thousand members.[83] The same year in July, the *British Workman*'s cover, entitled *All Right*, by RB, featured a L&NWR railway guard blowing his whistle.[84] This well-groomed, well-dressed, bearded guard was meant to be the epitome of steadiness, composure, and reliability, therefore unlikely to strike. He was a dependable figure one could 'recognise' and rely upon to serve in an increasingly anonymous urban world of strangers.

Working-class visions of working bodies

As we have seen throughout this book, working men's bodies were co-opted in a variety of ways. Middle-class men admired their imagined bodies because they stood for the success of national industry. The same men also idealised and consumed them as objects onto which they projected their manly ideals, an act which could be at once erotic and subordinating. These large working bodies had, after all, the potential to be threatening, speaking of 'natural' dynamism, of potential political threat, and, in a society that valorised strength, of sheer physical superiority over an increasingly sedentary social class. Thus, middle-class men's constructions of working-class bodies tamed them through notions of heroic sacrifice and benign emotions, especially kindness. This paradoxical vision of working men could be used by working-class men too, although the figure of the worker in their depictions differed from its middle-class counterpart. Sharing many conventions of the manly emotionalised body – handsome, muscular, posed and poised for action – the working-class version was less eroticised, less the subject of the consuming gaze in the same way. His form represented many similar qualities deemed manly, from self-control to hard work, domestic reliability, stoicism, and kindness. But these were shaped to serve working-class ends. He was, thus, perhaps less objectified, more a figure of dignity and assuredness than condescension, a model of manliness whose circulation through material culture and spectacle cultivated emotions that helped fix these ideals in those who encountered such constructions.

There is evidence from the turn of the eighteenth century that members of the working classes deployed politicised images of the handsome, working man resting at his cottage door, in songs, ballads, and images, to demonstrate that labouring men possessed the requisite independence and respectability for a political voice.[85] Working-class organisations, such as friendly societies and trade unions, increasingly harnessed the figure of the worker on their imagery, including ephemera such as certificates, trays, wooden emblems, and banners.[86] Variously, these were intended for personal ownership and display in the home, showcased in pubs or spaces where members met, and paraded as banners in villages and towns, a phenomenon which had increased enormously by the last quarter of the nineteenth century.[87] All were elaborately decorated with graphic depictions of working men as well as workplaces, work tools, allegorical figures, symbols, emblems, regalia, and mottos that drew on high art, classical and religious motifs, and natural and masonic imagery.[88] In the later 1820s and 1830s, when the organisations needed to be largely secret, designs were diverse and on a smaller scale. In the era of 'new model unionism' from the later 1840s, they took on a shared visual style and were larger scale, a change which survived until the 'new unionism' of the 1890s, when some shifts in pageantry and design occurred with a less busy but more defiant and militant iconography.[89] Most had cameos of the trade or labour represented and of sentimental family life to show their role in financial support for workers and their families following accidents and deaths at work.

This material culture was intended to foster a corporate identity among members, to visually represent this identity to communities, masters, employers, and government, and thereby demonstrate craft, union, or class legitimacy, whether conciliatory or defiant in message and intent.[90] Much of guilds, unions, and friendly societies members' 'pride, presence, identity, and cause' coalesced around the banner, which shared the imagery of other ephemera, frequently featuring the key component of certificate designs on their central panels.[91] This was a symbolism that, as Gwyn Williams explains, stemmed from workers' own 'rich subculture', with imagery drawn from 'old craft, Freemasonry, friendly society, temperance group, from the chapel and the Sunday school, from the bible and from Bunyan'.[92] It is the class and corporate identification stimulated and reinforced by such banners and events that has been most analysed; the latter's associated meanings for masculine identities have been relatively neglected.[93] All were, however, agents in constructing gender as much as class identities.

This material culture was replete with images of men, and it was paraded by working men in official public processions, first dignitaries, followed by those of lower social standing. In such civic ceremonies, the men carrying banners were flagged as 'sturdy, educated, orderly working men'.[94] They were emotionalised bodies and objects too. Newspaper reports of processions, for instance, which listed the processing trades and their banners used terms like 'handsome' and 'charming'.[95] Depictions of idealised working men on material culture deepened these associations, stirring excitement, pride, and identification in the images thereon. No wonder that, as Nick Mansfield notes, 'trade society banners have survived as half understood "holy relics" of a heroic past by modern trade unions'.[96] They were encountered in homes, meeting places, and streets – all spaces that served to disseminate and reinforce their associated notions of manliness. However, they were most potent when used in processions, generating positive emotions in those who paraded under a banner or those caught up in the excitement of viewing them.[97]

Moreover, it was working-class artists who produced and manufactured many of the designs for use on early ephemera, especially certificates.[98] Often educated in art schools, they had begun training by copying from antique sculpture and Old Masters. Lesser artists trained at night school would copy from art primers, pattern books, and engravings.[99] The industrial blacksmith James Sharples stated that he used Flaxman's *Anatomical Studies* to learn how 'accurately to delineate the muscles of the figures'. He also got his brother to stand for him as a model.[100] In this way, Barringer argues, Sharples 'appropriated the vocabulary of high art in order to fashion a corpus of visual self-representation'.[101] From 1837, George Tutill's company became the main manufacturer of banners, although some branch unions continued to make their own or use local suppliers.[102] Tutill was an accomplished artist who imbued the visual culture of workers' organisations with uniformity of style, and who amassed considerable wealth from his business; even so, he was from labouring origins and produced designs that workers selected and directed.[103] Other professional artists of emblems, such as engravers like James John Chant, John Saddler, and A. J. Waudby, were commissioned to produce designs that satisfied union and society members.[104] Furthermore, Sharples' certificate influenced middle-class artists' designs for the unions, and, it is suggested, the composition of Brown's *Work*.[105]

Working-class use of imagery varied over time. Annie Ravenhill-Johnson's analysis of the classical and Renaissance origins of working-class emblems and mottos shows that working-class people deployed the tropes of middle-class ideology and values that were transmitted to them. In the period before new unionism, they reflected them back to their employers to reassure them that they shared the same cultural and moral values and were not a danger to social stability. Yet, in 'appropriating high art', they laid claim to social and cultural capital, itself an empowering action.[106] As new unionism took hold, however, the sense of a shared visual culture withered. Middle-class commentators in the later nineteenth century sometimes disparaged the banners' decoration, describing them as crude, too colourful, in poor taste, even repugnant.[107] In 1887, a report in the *Leather Trades Circular and Review*, on the Northampton shoemakers' strike, for example, deployed racial slurs to belittle the 'flaunting of banners of more than Chinese gorgeousness and hideousness'.[108] No doubt, the viewer's response to such working-class material culture was shaped by his or her status and whether the banners were being displayed at civic celebrations or workers' strikes.

As such, these objects offer valuable insights into how working-class people saw themselves and wished to be seen.[109] Crucially, they chart working-class notions of idealised manliness, since working men were central features of this visual and material culture until the later nineteenth century, when machinery became more dominant in the iconography.[110]

5.3 Wooden hinged emblem, Stockport Branch of the Friendly United Mechanics (c.1830), People's History Museum, exhibition.

As Gwyn Williams evocatively states, 'banners had come to proclaim *homo faber*, Man the Maker'.[111] His form varied over time. Some early societies, in the 1830s, depicted men in fashionable dress rather than recognisably working attire. The wooden hinged emblem of the Friendly United Mechanics, for example, c.1830 (Figure 5.3), has two top-hatted men holding a coat of arms displaying mechanics, steamboat, and locomotives painted on its decorative panel, which was opened up for display during society meetings in pubs.[112] Similarly, the Berwickshire Shoemakers' banner, constructed in 1832 to celebrate the passage of the Reform Act, depicts a man on the left, smartly attired in white trousers and an elaborately buttoned jacket, alongside a woman in a simple, elegant white dress. Both are rosy-cheeked, presumably to show physical attractiveness and good health, attributes of idealised gender identities. Rather than being dressed as representative workers grasping tools of the trade, the man holds a boot and the woman a pump to signify shoemaking.[113] The well-dressed men on these early emblems indicate a concern to assume legitimacy through association with generic respectable or polite modes of civic and masculine identity, indicated by non-working poses.[114] As societies and unions moved into the open in the 1830s, the manly figures adorning such banners became more identifiable as workers through their dress and pose.

In the second half of the nineteenth century, working men stood at the heart of their bannerettes, banners, and certificates: their large, noble bodies elevated, signifying physical strength and health, their work tools indicating occupational identity.[115] Their execution became more sophisticated as design and manufacture was taken over by professionals and professional processes, and their representation varied according to the crafts and trades depicted and as clothing styles changed over time. Nevertheless, several generalisations can be made. Usually in pairs, the working men were intended to be both impressive exemplary workers and men. The main figures on certificates were typically posed standing on architectural structures, and thus raised higher in the design's hierarchical structure; they were at ease, rather than in motion, wearing clothing that indicated their craft, trade, or employment, and holding or surrounded by their typical working tools. Thus, the engineers on the Steam Engine Makers' Society certificate (1854) are pictured with hammer, measuring devices, plans, and a rule, respectively (Figure 5.4).[116] James Sharples' smith and engineer on the certificate of the Amalgamated Society of Engineers, Machinists, Millwrights, Smiths and Pattern Makers (1852) are youthful and handsome, hair fashionably styled, neatly dressed in their respective professional clothing.[117] Working men presented themselves as clean and well groomed to rebut the association of the labouring ranks with dirt and its associations of immorality and inferiority.[118] The smith politely declines Mars' offering of a sword for repair, a sign of the workers' pacific qualities, while the suited engineer accepts Clio's design. Both wear waistcoats and have their sleeves rolled up, though the smith has his waistcoat undone and protects his clothing with a long leather apron.[119] In later certificates, the workers are bearded, as fashion demanded, and therefore look more mature, their authority demonstrated through solid bodies and serious expressions.[120] An especially artistic example is the certificate of the Brass Founders, Turners, Fitters, Finishers, Coppersmiths Association circa 1890s (Figure 5.5).[121]

5.4 Steam Engine Makers' Society certificate (1854).

Dignified, serious, and authoritative figures, healthy and well built, these workers were examples of idealised working-class manliness for a working-class audience, as well as other social ranks who encountered this material culture. This was the workers' intention, evident from the

5.5 Brass Founders, Turners, Fitters, Finishers & Coppersmiths Association certificate (c.1890s).

second half of the nineteenth century in the trade union certificates whose elaborate designs were intended for close perusal rather than to be used in a procession. The 'Key to the General Union of House Carpenters and Joiners of Great Britain and Ireland emblem' (1866), sent out with the certificates, declared that the carpenter's face portrayed:

the Divine expression of 'Joseph' the Carpenter, reflecting the heavenly beam of mildness and benevolence, combined with manly determination to lead the way to truth, and act man's noblest part in honest labour. He is conversing with the modern and manly-looking Joiner opposite, who is leaning on the post with saw in one hand and compass in other.[122]

In the context of what this book has revealed about the significance of emotionalised bodies, these men were not simply intended to conform to ideals of manliness, they were meant to embody confidence and stir pride, love, and identification.[123]

Unsurprisingly, confidence and pride were often emphasised through symbols of national status. From the 1850s to 1880s, workers' associations stressed conciliation and positioned themselves as integral to metropolitan and national prosperity. Thus, the United Operative Plumbers' Association of Great Britain placed their representative workers in front of St Paul's dome, on either side of a figure of Justice, flanked by a lion and unicorn, with coats of arms quartered with lions, harp, and the tools of their trade. The patriotic workers are men at different stages of their lives, one younger and clean-shaven, the other full bearded; both smartly dressed in waistcoat, tie, and trousers, with jacket off and sleeves rolled up.[124] Unions were successful in constructing manly working identities. The *Eastern Evening News* published an 'outsider's' view of the recent gathering of delegates at the Trades Union Conference held in Norwich in 1894. Slightly critical of some features of the unionists' stance, the writer was still largely positive. He answered the question, 'What has trades unionism done', responding that it led to the formation of 'a kind of aristocracy of labour', commenting that the delegates who attended were typically fine speakers: 'Strong men always many of them, and a credit physically to England.'[125]

The general union emblems of 1890s often focused on industry, rather than individuals; nonetheless, some featured working men.[126] The certificate of the National Amalgamated Sailors' and Firemen's Union of Great Britain and Ireland is an excellent example (1891). Two workers flank a large central globe on which a ship was superimposed. Along with the flags from across the world arrayed along the top, this signified the reach and importance of the union. Both of the proudly posed workers were portraits: a fireman with a shovel, portrayed as Havelock Wilson (1859–1929), President of the Sailors' and Firemen's Union that he began in 1887; and a sailor in front of an anchor, with the face of the British MP Samuel Plimsoll (1824–1898), who campaigned for improved safety at sea. Such portraiture was increasingly common. Wilson, for example, who became a Liberal Party MP in the north-east, often featured on banners marched at galas and rallies.[127] The merging of workers' strong, capable bodies with notable men's faces raised the worker to a heroic level.

Perhaps one of the most common themes from the mid-1830s was the symbolic working-man's arm. Rich in cultural meaning, it was extensively deployed by a range of social classes. Muscular arms exposed by rolled-up sleeves ready for labour and grasping tools were the most potent symbol of 'heroic' men's labour. Initially, arms signified generic masculinity, not class-specific manhood, and connoted both the capacity to smite a national enemy and defend its subjects.[128] For the middle classes, sinewy muscular forearms also became the marker of Britain's industrial power.[129] They were central to the depictions of workers from Joseph Wright's iron-forge workers, to Hicks's agricultural worker, to Brown's Apollo-like navvy.[130] Working men adopted the visual iconography of muscular arms as part of their formulations of self and class identity. A single raised muscular arm bearing a hammer was originally the sign of the blacksmith and used in trade guilds' heraldry.[131] Alongside the handshake, a symbol of unity and concord, the arm became central to the iconography of working-class friendly societies, trade unions, and political movements like Chartism.[132] The emblem designed by William Hughes for the Order of Friendly Boilermakers in 1834, for example, was influenced by the design of the Friendly United Mechanics with the addition of what R. A. Leeson describes as the 'boilermaker's recognition sign' of a raised muscular arm wielding a hammer above the heraldic coat of arms. The two men flanking the coat of arms themselves are very early examples of working men with their sleeves rolled up.[133]

The iconography of men's tools on ceramic objects and in visual culture helped articulate a collective identity of craftsmen in the first part of the nineteenth century.[134] This was continued in the trade union visual culture in the later nineteenth century. In James Sharples' emblem of the Amalgamated Society of Engineers (1851), for example, both the dignified blacksmith and engineer have rolled-up sleeves.[135] A banner from the Cooperative Smiths of Newcastle, a small union of blacksmiths, survives from around 1870. Its major visual device is a raised arm with hammer painted on the plain-woven cotton. The banner claimed ancient dignity by adapting an archaic motto from the Worshipful Company of Blacksmiths 'by hammer and hand all art do stand'. As shown, this not only suggested lineage, it declared the workers' manly presence and power.[136] By the turn of the twentieth century, the muscular arm became a political symbol of an entire working class and thus a more threatening declaration of class militancy.[137]

Emblems and ephemera also incorporated vignettes of men working at crafts and trades, which depicted archetypical men in motion wielding tools. The membership certificate of the Amalgamated Society of Woodworkers, for example, features two smaller pictures of woodworking men. One is titled 'centring' and shows men constructing a wooden structure, the other is 'The Workshop' with men planing wood.[138] The Associated Blacksmiths Society has a vignette based on the central workers in Sharples' steel engraving, *The Forge*.[139] When a craft or trade's biblical origin was suggested, the men were partially dressed to reveal muscular forms. Working-class commissioners and creators also appropriated Greek and Roman culture to represent their union members.[140] Perhaps a particularly telling example is on the certificate of the Friendly Society of Iron Founders of England, Ireland and Wales, 1857, by the engraver John James Chant. It shows a typical architectural cutaway with working scenes at the bottom, and two ennobled working men at the top with rolled-up sleeves, holding their tools of trade. However, at the centre is an iron-ore miner hewing an enormous coal face. He is positively Herculean: bare-chested and heavily muscular.[141]

It is possible to see this imagery's strength in the moments when it was encountered by the public in processions. Some of the banners' emotional force during processions has been captured in published accounts. In 1862, the *Falkirk Herald*, for example, published a memory in verse of the Great Reform Meeting held in Falkirk on 7 May 1832. With around ten thousand attendees, the *Herald* notes, the procession 'was graced with seven bands of music, fifty banners and flags'.[142] The spectacle of proud tradesmen, including tanners, weavers, smiths, and sailors, along with the music, slogan banners, and various flags, clearly combined to stir feeling. As the verse notes, 'How mirth and melody did blend, Until the very air did rend'. Their combined impact on the 'host' was impressive: 'Confounded stood/The gazing crowd,/Baith mute and loud,/Warm was our *bluid*/When they did come in view, man'. The verse declares that the march, 'Wi' fifty banners borne above,/Wi' mottos firm and terse, man', was a sign of 'patriotism strong and keen'; and led the 'Antis there' to gape and stare.[143] It is clear that such events not only disseminated political ideologies, declared patriotic loyalty, displayed workers' unity, or stamped out class identity. When working men were portrayed, both on banners and in tableau form beneath, they also materialised ideal manliness.

This was often in celebratory rather than confrontational form. Thus, the opening of Bradford Town Hall in 1873 was the occasion of a procession of local trades through the park. The *Bradford Daily Telegraph* described the trades and their banners in considerable detail. Each trade had a 'directing board', or banner of silk, followed by tradesmen on horseback and walking. Strikingly, many enacted their trades on lorries pulled by horses. Dressed in their working clothes, wielding tools, alongside the machinery or products of their trade, they were living tableaux of what was on the banners lofted above them.[144] The Preston Guild Jubilee was one of the most spectacular examples of such occasions. A huge event, held every twenty years, it was covered in the national press. In 1862, the *Penny Illustrated Paper* described its origins and the week's events, which included a procession of the mayor and corporation, athletics and wresting displays, as well as one day of temperance and friendly societies' processions, with flags, banners, and brass bands playing, and another devoted to the 'long looked-for trades procession'. This was a 'gorgeous display', according to the newspaper, where the 'peculiarities of each trade were excellently and fully represented; and every detail was as correctly studied as if the promoters had been stage-managers of a first-class theatre'.[145]

The performative aspects were indeed noteworthy. The lorries conveyed individual performances of trades, which the press described in admiring detail. The smiths, for example, not only had a great banner and a band, but the process of each smithcraft was shown by men 'at work'. On the first lorry there 'were three smiths working at a forge; and through the joltings of the lorry, the stalwart striker missed his blow now and then, to the amusement of the spectators, some of whom called, "Now Jack, into it again, owd lad; and aim straight."' Their 'new white leather aprons' and other emblems are described, as was 'another mounted Vulcan, clad to the waist in iron armour'.[146] The power of such performances is captured by the illustrated engravings of the jubilee processions. The *London Illustrated News*, for instance, published engravings of the events in 1862 and 1882.[147] The 1862 trades procession illustration features the fire-service engine and a lorry arrayed with fishermen. The former conforms to the noble imagery described earlier. The fire engine is driven by a top-hatted driver, and transports six uniformed firemen carrying their fire axes, with two marching ahead of the horses, holding a large banner. Passing them is a rowing boat mounted on a wagon, which contains three fishermen, and others marching behind with lobster pots on their backs. The crowd throngs at each side, windows and roofs busy with others keen to view.[148] These men were living embodiments of manly workers, real emotionalised bodies at work as spectacle.

Class exploitation could lie behind such performances of labour. When Samuel Smiles added James Sharples to the celebrated lives in the second edition of *Self-Help*, in 1860, he requested his photograph to add to his collection of notable self-made men. Although there are several photographic portraits of Sharples in a plain respectable suit, the selected studio portrait posed him as blacksmith, sleeves rolled up, wearing a dirtied leather apron, holding his hammer.[149] Barringer points out that this photograph was thus a masquerade, designed to satisfy Smiles' construction of the artist/smith as 'the epitome of the worthy artisan'. The *London Illustrated News* supplement illustrating the 1882 Preston Guild Jubilee offers another example of the range of meanings emanating from such performances. It includes a medieval-style depiction of part of the trades' procession. Perhaps inspired by Walter Crane's Merrie England workers, the stylised tableaux show archaic artisans at work on the trailers of lorries pulled by pairs of horses. For all the styling, these are images of modernity, with new machinery on show, such as a sheeting loom and boiler.[150] The men are presented as happy workers rather than powerful men, toothless shadows of a socialist utopia. Nevertheless, these were 'masquerades' of labour that could be deployed by the labouring classes themselves. For example, in a context of industrial unrest that ended craft autonomy in the early 1850s, Barringer argues that Sharples' *The Forge* and unfinished Co-operative Society emblem contributed to new radical discourses of labour autonomy where 'the working man is the master of technology rather than its victim'. Similarly, working-class writers and audiences developed differing views of Sharples. The Blackburn journalist who wrote his short biography for a working-class audience following Sharples' death in 1893, constructed him as 'the essence of a local and regional type'.[151] Thus, if workers acting out their trade under bannered processions lost their muscular might in the later nineteenth-century press, the visceral force and passions they aroused were still experienced by the crowds who lined the streets and waited in parks in pouring rain to see them.

Friendly society and trade union ephemera were not only deployed to emotional effect at large public events, they were also domestic, deploying scenes of family life and displayed in the home. This further acted to stimulate emotions relating to manliness. Although all representations of heroic, noble, or dignified labour used manly muscular arms and bodies, the reality of excessive hours of toil and unsafe workplaces and practices was that workers' bodies frequently failed. As the Brushmakers' Society reminded members, 'Sickness might come at any moment, the rigorous health of youth might be shattered, the strong arm rendered weak or the skilfully trained hand lose its cunning.'[152] Since the societies and unions used contributions to provide welfare benefits to ill and injured workers, emblems and banners also depicted sick working men or their widows securing aid in their homes.[153] These 'picture parables' were especially elaborate in the 1890s and adhered to the moral and sentimental convention of before and after, good and bad comparisons.[154]

This was thrift and temperance from the workers' perspective, as Weinbren astutely observes, where 'thrift was more than a negative restriction, it was a heterogeneous set of practices, of working diligently, taking care of oneself and others, and being careful not to fritter money away'.[155] The material culture also deployed some of the motifs of the man absent from home. The Hull Seamen's and Marine Firemen's Amalgamated Association banner, a glorious scenic textile from 1887, for example, includes a cameo of the sailor's return home.[156] In the Hearts of Oak Society emblem, designed by A. J. Waudby (1869), the navy takes prominence in promoting this benefit society, whose primary function was insurance and savings. At its centre is a huge wooden 131-gun warship HMS *Hearts of Oak*, which represents security for its members. Under it is a large vignette of sailors aboard ship looking longingly towards land, 'Homeward Bound' spelled out on the deck plank. Here we see military masculinities being deployed within the domestic space, as discussed in Chapter 3, and absent manliness, explored in Chapter 4.

Certificates and emblems also made their way into homes. Trade unionist Sir Arthur Pugh (1870–1955), commenting on the British Steel Smelters' emblem (1893) in *Men of Steel*, observed: 'There were few active members of the union who did not adorn his home with an emblem certifying the date of his entry into the union, signed by the general secretary, mounted in a suitable frame.'[157] Some of the ephemera had particularly domestic connotations. The emblem of the Friendly Association of Cotton Spinners, a Glasgow society formed in 1806, for example, was printed on a japanned tin tray *c.*1825.[158] The image was a copy of the association's bannerette. In front of the power spinning machine stands a male worker extending his hand to a female child worker; neatly attired in a waistcoat, the former's sleeves are rolled up above his elbows.[159] The Carlisle branch of the Glasgow Association used the same image in its banner, probably around a similar date. The domestic nature of the banner, however, is particularly vivid, since the banner takes the form of a patchwork quilt, with the emblem reproduced in embroidery on an apron at its centre, surrounded by pieced cotton patches. The apron was apparently worn by a local cotton spinner when celebrating the passing of the 1832 Reform Act in a procession through Carlisle.[160] Here the public and domestic aspects of these emotional objects converged in one space.

Conclusion

The glorification of manly workers in the second half of the nineteenth century was a response to modernity and its repercussions for politics and society. For their middle-class creators and consumers, idealised, upright, trustworthy working men in print and visual culture smoothed the transition to political modernity and mass society. They were trustworthy figures that the middle classes could get behind and to whom they could concede political participation. After all, their strong (sometimes fighting) bodies were rendered less threatening by their gentleness, kindness, and temperate habits. In an age of technology, people needed to trust the moral and physical qualities of working men upon whose labour they depended in so many ways. They sought, therefore, a worker who was dependable: one who would not get drunk while working, or fall asleep, or be indifferent to the work in hand. They wanted to rely on the labour of happy men, not disgruntled or malign ones, nor those inclined to sabotage the products they manufactured. In short, the middle classes needed to construct a manly worker who took pride in his labour for its own sake and whose manliness depended upon his good work. Moreover, the middle classes were navigating the new conditions of urban modernity, and were reliant upon working-class strangers to provide services for them, to mediate and aid them in enjoying new technologies like the railways. In an era of urban and technological modernity, here were brave workers poised to rescue their social superiors from the threats of modernity, the fires, accidents, and shipwrecks that ensued from advancements in transport, working environments, and rapidly developing urbanisation. No wonder that representations of manly workers individualised them, separated them from the mass, and constructed them as attractive, earnest, kind, and helpful.

These cultural constructions were useful for working-class men too. They co-opted the imagery for their own organisational and political ends, reshaping it subtly so that it shed its condescension. The manly workers that they chose to represent them, and whom they performed in public for an audience, possessed remarkable confidence and assuredness. Perhaps, in some small way, this gendered identity could, over time, take on less conciliatory aspects to aid workers in asserting their rights.

Notes

1. For example, *British Workman* 11 (1855).
2. *British Workman* (1871), p. 97.
3. For the concept of the labourer as 'human machine' and its role in understandings of national regeneration and degeneration, see Anthea Callen, *Looking at Men: Anatomy, Masculinity and the Modern Male Body* (New Haven and London: Yale University Press, 2018), pp. 141–83.
4. Yale Center for British Art, Paul Mellon Collection, Joseph Wright, *The Blacksmith's Shop*, 1771, Accession Number B1981.25.712.
5. Tate Gallery, Joseph Wright, *An Iron Forge*, 1772, T06670, www.tate.org.uk/art/artworks/wright-an-iron-forge-t06670/text-summary (accessed 21 August 2018).
6. For the argument that the forge-man is portrayed as heroic, see Annie Ravenhill-Johnson, *The Art and Ideology of the Trade Union Emblem, 1850–1925*, ed. Paula James (London: Anthem Press, 2013), p. 35.
7. Matthew Craske, *Joseph Wright of Derby: Painter of Darkness* (New Haven, CT and London: Yale University Press, forthcoming). My sincere thanks to Matthew for sharing his book manuscript with me.
8. Samuel Smiles also included Burritt in *Self-Help, with Illustrations of Conduct and Perseverance* (London: IEA Health and Welfare Unit, 1996), 1866 edn, p. 80.
9. *British Workman* (1855), pp. 15, 57.
10. Charles Dickens, *Great Expectations* (New York: Collier, 1890), vol. 29, pp. 147–8.
11. Indeed, in the novel Joe is rewarded with a loving marriage and his own child that he names Pip. *Ibid.*, p. 503.
12. Roy Judge, 'May day and merrie England', *Folklore* 102:2 (1991), 131. For the conservative role this played in agricultural landscape art, see Christiana Payne, *Toil and Plenty: Images of the Agricultural Landscape in England 1780–1890* (New Haven, CT, and London: Yale University Press, 1993), pp. 4, 24.
13. This conservatism might extend to a socialist position. Oxford Reference: 'Merrie England', in Jacqueline Simpson and Steve Roud (eds), *A Dictionary of English Folklore* (Oxford: Oxford University Press, 2003), www.oxfordreference.com/view/10.1093/oi/authority.20110803100151694 (accessed 17 August 2018).
14. William Howitt, *The Rural Life of England*, 2 vols (London: Longman, Orme, Brown, Green, & Longmans, 1838), vol. 2, p. 187.
15. *British Workman* (1871), p. 63.
16. *Ibid.*, p. 91.
17. Robert Dare, 'History, progress and industry: William Bell Scott's *Iron and Coal*', *Word & Image* 12:3 (1996), passim. Michael Barringer interprets it as celebratory,

Men at Work: Art and Labour in Victorian Britain (New Haven, CT, and London: for the Paul Mellon Centre for Studies in British Art by Yale University Press, 2005), p. 159.
18. Peter Mandler, *The English National Character: the History of an Idea from Edmund Burke to Tony Blair* (New Haven, CT, and London: Yale University Press, 2006), pp. 69–70.
19. *British Workman* (1868), p. 182.
20. For this temperance campaign see Mary Conley, '"You don't make a torpedo gunner out of a drunkard": Agnes Weston, temperance, and the British Navy', *Northern Mariner* 9:1 (January 1999), 1–22.
21. *British Workman* (1898), p. 50.
22. *British Workman* (1855), p. 3.
23. Mandler, *English National Character*, p. 59.
24. Wendy Parkins, '"Wot larx!": William Morris, Charles Dickens, and fatherly feelings', *19: Interdisciplinary Studies in the Long Nineteenth Century* 14 (2012), 2, https://www.19.bbk.ac.uk/articles/10.16995/ntn.606/ (accessed 13 September 2019).
25. *Ibid.*, 5.
26. Barringer, *Men at Work*, p. 142.
27. *British Workman* (1871), p. 72–3.
28. Barringer, *Men at Work*, pp. 27–9.
29. Mandler, *English National Character*, p. 103.
30. For Carlyle's stance on character, see *ibid.*, p. 68. For John Ruskin's and Thomas Carlyle's views see Barringer, *Men at Work*, pp. 26–9.
31. Thomas Carlyle, 'Labour', *Past & Present* (1843), www.online-literature.com/thomas-carlyle/past-and-present/34/ (accessed 16 June 2015).
32. For literary perceptions of navvies see Ying S. Lee, *Masculinity and the English Working Class: Studies in Victorian Autobiography and Fiction* (New York and London: Routledge, *c.*2007), pp. 83–5.
33. *Ibid.*, pp. 88–9, 114–15.
34. Cited in Gerard Curtis, 'Ford Madox Brown's "Work": an iconographic analysis", *Art Bulletin* 74 (December 1992), 633. Barringer, *Men at Work*, pp. 34–5.
35. Curtis, 'Ford Madox Brown's "Work"', 631; Barringer, *Men at Work*, p. 37.
36. Barringer, *Men at Work*, pp. 37, 48–9.
37. *Ibid.*, p. 80.
38. Mandler, *English National Character*, p. 140.
39. Ruth Livesey, 'Morris, Carpenter, Wilde, and the political aesthetics of labor', *Victorian Literature and Culture* 32:2 (2004), 603. Not all elite men felt the same. Oscar Wilde derided the idea that manual labour was dignified in all its forms and critiqued this version of aestheticised socialism. See Livesey, 'Morris, Carpenter, Wilde', 608.
40. William Morris, *Signs of Change* (London, 1888), p. 26, cited in Livesey, 'Morris, Carpenter, Wilde', 607.
41. Barringer, *Men at Work*, p. 39. Callen, *Looking at Men*, pp. 160, 171–3.
42. Livesey, 'Morris, Carpenter, Wilde', 613.
43. *Ibid.*, 613–14.
44. Barringer, *Men at Work*, pp. 37–8.
45. Michael Brown, '"Like a devoted army": medicine, heroic masculinity, and the military paradigm in Victorian Britain', *Journal of British Studies* 49:3 (2010), 592–622.
46. *Ibid.*, 594.
47. Christiana Payne, *Where the Sea Meets the Land: Artists on the Coast in Nineteenth-Century Britain* (Bristol: Sansom & Co. Ltd, 2007), pp. 34, 157–63.
48. Discussed in *ibid.*, pp. 31, 185.

49 *Ibid.*, pp. 143–4.
50 *British Workman* (February 1860), p. 245.
51 Payne, *Where the Sea Meets the Land*, pp. 157–63.
52 'Heroes of the sea', about the lifeboat service at Ramsgate, *British Workman* (1898), p. 95. For RHS see Craig Peter Barclay, 'Heroes of peace: the Royal Humane Society and the award of medals in Britain, 1774–1914' (PhD dissertation, University of York, 2009).
53 *British Workman* (1 January 1870).
54 'Remember our sailors; Or, the "British Workman" life-boat', in which it is noted that 20,000 'brave seamen' have been shipwrecked in last ten years, *British Workman* (1 February 1869).
55 Richard Wilton, 'On the Launch of "The British Workman" Life-Boat', *British Workman* (1871), p. 51. This poem reifies the boat itself, rather than the men manning the boat and risking lives. For an earlier story which used a sea rescue to discuss God's rescue of sinners see 'He has drawn a breath', *British Workman* (1857), p. 131.
56 Jamie L. Bronstein, *Caught in the Machinery: Workplace Accidents and Injured Workers in Nineteenth-Century Britain* (Stanford, CA: Stanford University Press, 2008), pp. 73–7.
57 Cited in *ibid.*, p. 75.
58 The report notes the £70,000 raised by the country for the relief of the bereaved. *British Workman* (April 1862), p. 350.
59 *Ibid.*
60 Barclay, 'Heroes of peace', p. 104.
61 It has been suggested that the cult of the fireman did not fully reach its peak until the later nineteenth century. Robyn Cooper, 'Millais's *The Rescue*: a painting of a "dreadful interruption of domestic peace"', *Art History* 9:4 (1986), 474.
62 For the association of firefighters with heroism in America see Wolfgang Hochbruck, 'Volunteers and professionals: everyday heroism and the fire service in nineteenth-century America', in Simon Wendt (ed.), *Extraordinary Ordinariness: Everyday Heroism in the United States, Germany, and Britain, 1800–2015* (Frankfurt: Campus Verlag, 2016), pp. 109–38.
63 *British Workman* (January 1874), p. 5.
64 *British Workman* (September 1861), p. 322.
65 *Ibid.*
66 Cited in Cooper, 'Millais's *The Rescue*', 473.
67 Herbert Sussman, *Victorian Masculinities: Manhood and Masculine Poetics in Early Victorian Literature and Art* (Cambridge: Cambridge University Press, 1995), pp. 144, 146.
68 Cited in Cooper, 'Millais's *The Rescue*', 479.
69 *Ibid.*, 472–85.
70 *British Workman* (January 1874), p. 5.
71 This was common in visual and textual descriptions of firemen, Cooper, 'Millais's *The Rescue*', 474.
72 Brown, '"Like a devoted army"', 617.
73 *British Workman* (January 1874), p. 5.
74 *British Workman* 73 (1898), p. 5.
75 *Ibid.*
76 Linda A. Pollock, 'The practice of kindness in early modern elite society', *Past & Present* 211:1 (2011), 121–58.
77 Helen Rogers, 'Kindness and reciprocity: liberated prisoners and Christian charity in early nineteenth-century England', *Journal of Social History* 47:3 (2014), 721–45.
78 Pollock, 'The practice of kindness', 125, 136, 137.
79 Daniel Weinbren, 'Beneath the all-seeing eye: fraternal order and friendly societies'

banners in nineteenth- and twentieth-century Britain', *Cultural and Social History* 3:2 (2006), 170–1.
80 Also see story of a 'remarkable scene' on 26 October 1860 when one to two thousand workmen from Midland Railway Company's works at Derby came to the new large turning shop to listen to the Bishop of London. *British Workman* 74 (February 1861).
81 *British Workman* (1871), p. 94.
82 Oxford Reference, www.oxfordreference.com/view/10.1093/oi/authority.2011080 3100448183 (accessed 3 May 2019).
83 'Railway workers', Working Class Movement Library, www.wcml.org.uk/our-collections/working-lives/railway-unions/ (accessed 7 January 2019).
84 *British Workman* 211 (July 1872).
85 Matthew McCormack, 'Married men and the fathers of families: fatherhood and franchise reform in Britain', in Trev Lynn Broughton and Helen Rogers (eds), *Gender and Fatherhood in the Nineteenth Century* (New York: Palgrave Macmillan, 2007).
86 For friendly societies see Weinbren, 'Beneath the all-seeing eye', 167–91. Nick Mansfield's overview of the National Banner Survey and the banners held by the People's History Museum is a vital analysis of the material culture in its various forms: online Manchester University Working Paper. www.humanities.manchester.ac.uk/medialibrary/arts/history/workingpapers/wp_45.pdf (accessed 23 August 2018).
87 For estimates of the volume of emblems, ownership, and places of display see R. A. Leeson, *United We Stand: An Illustrated Account of Trade Union Emblems* (Bath: Adams & Dart, 1971), p. 6. The illustrations of emblems collected in Ravenhill-Johnson's study offers evidence spanning the century from the 1820s to 1920s, book plates 1–90.
88 For an introduction to the various types of imagery used see Hazel Bowden, 'Symbolism in trade union emblems from the collection of the Working Class Movement Library' (unpaginated pamphlet). Detailed analysis of the genre and its artistic origins is carried out by Ravenhill-Johnson, *Art and Ideology*, pp. 11–23. For similarities and shared roots of emblems in the iconography of the friendly societies and unions, see Leeson, *United We Stand*, p. 11.
89 Gwyn Williams, 'Introduction', in John Gorman, *Banner Bright: An Illustrated History of Trade Union Banners* (Buckhurst Hill: Scorpion Publishing Ltd, new edn, 1986), pp. 17, 21; Weinbren, 'Beneath the all-seeing eye', 187–8.
90 Williams, 'Introduction', p. 18; Weinbren, 'Beneath the all-seeing eye', 168.
91 Weinbren, 'Beneath the all-seeing eye', 168; Williams, 'Introduction', p. 19. For examples, see the Friendly Iron Moulders Society, *c.*1857, and the Chatham district banner of the Amalgamated Society of Woodworkers, *c.*1866, Gorman, *Banner Bright*, pp. 79, 81.
92 Williams, 'Introduction', p. 16.
93 Weinbren, 'Beneath the all-seeing eye', 169.
94 *Ibid.*, 174.
95 *Bradford Daily Telegraph* (10 September 1873).
96 Mansfield, 'Working paper', pp. 10, 20.
97 For the association of unrest with banners in the earlier nineteenth century see Weinbren, 'Beneath the all-seeing eye', 172.
98 Worker artists and the professional artists and companies who followed are discussed by Leeson, *United We Stand*, pp. 18–31. For changing forms of print reproduction of emblems and certificates see pp. 13–14, 16. For manufacture of silk banners, see Gorman, *Banner Bright*.
99 Ravenhill-Johnson, *Art and Ideology*, pp. 35, 38, 40.
100 Smiles, *Self-Help*, 1866 edn, p. 117.

101 Barringer, *Men at Work*, p. 139.
102 Over 75 per cent of all trade union banners after 1837 were made by Tutill's. Gorman, *Banner Bright*, pp. 17, 47–8. For other types of maker see Mansfield, 'Working paper', pp. 18–20.
103 For Tutill's impact see Mansfield, 'Working paper', p. 3.
104 Leeson, *United We Stand*, pp. 24–7.
105 Paula James, 'Introduction', in Ravenhill-Johnson, *Art and Ideology*, pp. 3, 4; see also Ravenhill-Johnson, *Art and Ideology*, p. 38.
106 Ravenhill-Johnson, *Art and Ideology*, pp. 32–3.
107 Weinbren, 'Beneath the all-seeing eye', 174.
108 Cited in Mansfield, 'Working paper', p. 30.
109 Leeson, *United We Stand*, p. 6; Mansfield, 'Working paper', pp. 31–2.
110 For the shift to depicting machinery, see Ravenhill-Johnson, *Art and Ideology*, pp. 45, 118.
111 Williams, 'Introduction', p. 20.
112 For coats of arms and their origins in guilds see Leeson, *United We Stand*, pp. 8–9. For an earlier example where the workers are dressed in plain craftsmen's attire, see the 1821 banner of the United Tin Plate Workers' Society, in Gorman, *Banner Bright*, p. 68.
113 Also depicts the shoemaker's half-moon knife on the crest that they support. People's History Museum, exhibition, c.1832, Duns, Berwickshire.
114 See Thomas Moorhouse's apprenticeship certificate, with the Brushmakers' Society, dated 1830. Working Class Movement Library, online reference Fr 347.
115 Ravenhill-Johnson, *Art and Ideology*, p. 107.
116 Working Class Movement Library, certificates from 'Framed/241 Box 3'.
117 Barringer, *Men at Work*, pp. 175–6.
118 Ravenhill-Johnson, *Art and Ideology*, p. 39.
119 Working Class Movement Library, certificates from 'Framed/241 Box 3'. Working Class Movement Library online reference FR242. For discussion see Ravenhill-Johnson, *Art and Ideology*, pp. 27–31.
120 For example, Amalgamated Society of Woodworkers, Working Class Movement Library, certificates from 'Framed/241 Box 3'.
121 Working Class Movement Library, certificates from 'Framed/241 Box 3'.
122 Cited in Ravenhill-Johnson, *Art and Ideology*, p. 65, p. 195n8.
123 Bowden makes the point that such confidence was radical, regardless of the conciliatory messages, 'Symbolism in trade union emblems'.
124 Working Class Movement Library, framed certificates on display, online reference Fr 291.
125 *Eastern Evening News* (8 September 1894).
126 For an industrial theme, see the Associated Iron Moulders of Scotland by Johnstones of Edinburgh, 1880s. Discussed in Leeson, *United We Stand*, pp. 42–3.
127 Leeson, *United We Stand*, pp. 45–6. For the use of portraits of public figures including statesmen, civic officials, and eventually national trade union leaders see Gorman, *Banner Bright*, pp. 41–2.
128 Joanne Begiato, 'Between poise and power: embodied manliness in eighteenth- and nineteenth-century British culture', *Transactions of the Royal Historical Society* 26:2 (2016), 141–3.
129 Ravenhill-Johnson, *Art and Ideology*, pp. 28, 38.
130 Barringer, *Men at Work*, p. 48.
131 Kim Munson, 'The evolution of an emblem: the art & hammer, 2010', unpublished paper, www.academia.edu/231841/Evolution_of_an_Emblem_The_Arm_and_Hammer (accessed 12 June 2015).
132 Ravenhill-Johnson, *Art and Ideology*, p. 31. Gorman, *Banner Bright*, p. 78. Munson, 'Evolution of an emblem', p. 9.

133 This emblem is reproduced in Leeson, *United We Stand*, p. 19. This book states that the emblems featured in it are preserved in the Library of the Trades Union Congress.
134 Karen Harvey, 'Craftsmen in common: objects, skills and masculinity in the eighteenth and nineteenth centuries', in Hannah Grieg, Jane Hamlett, and Leonie Hannan (eds), *Gender and Material Culture in Britain since 1600* (London: Palgrave Macmillan, 2016), pp. 69, 75–8.
135 Barringer, *Men at Work*, pp. 173–5; Ravenhill-Johnson, *Art and Ideology*, p. 28.
136 On display in the People's History Museum; also Williams, 'Introduction', p. 19.
137 Williams, 'Introduction', p. 20. Gorman, *Banner Bright*, p. 127.
138 Working Class Movement Library, certificates from 'Framed/241 Box 3'.
139 Framed certificates on display in Working Class Movement Library.
140 Ravenhill-Johnson, *Art and Ideology*, p. 2.
141 *Ibid.*, plate 21. For colour version of engraving, see www.unionhistory.info/Display.php?irn=7000001&QueryPage=AdvSearch.php (accessed 23 August 2018). Discussed by Leeson, *United We Stand*, pp. 24–5.
142 A large proportion of the banners located in the National Banner Survey were associated with the Reform Crisis of 1829–32. Mansfield, 'Working paper', p. 14.
143 *Falkirk Herald* (29 May 1862).
144 *Bradford Telegraph* (10 September 1873).
145 *Penny Illustrated Paper* (13 September 1862), p. 173.
146 *Ibid.*, p. 174.
147 *London Illustrated News* (13 September 1862) and (16 September 1882).
148 *London Illustrated News* (13 September 1862), 313.
149 For portraits of James Sharples see People's History Museum, NMLH. 1996.39.31; NMLH. 1996.39.32; NMLH. 1996.39.34. Barringer, *Men at Work*, pp. 149–53.
150 *London Illustrated News* (16 September 1882), p. 312.
151 Barringer, *Men at Work*, pp. 176–7, 182–3.
152 Cited in Gorman, *Banner Bright*, p. 42.
153 For such imagery on fraternal order and friendly societies see Weinbren, 'Beneath the all-seeing eye', 176–9.
154 Gorman, *Banner Bright*, pp. 40–1 and 91–101.
155 Weinbren, 'Beneath the all-seeing eye', 179.
156 Gorman, *Banner Bright*, p. 72.
157 Pugh was later Secretary of the Iron and Steel Trades Industry; cited in Leeson, *United We Stand*, p. 69. See also Leeson, *United We Stand*, pp. 30–1. 'The Hearts of Oak Benefit Society', certificate, *c.*1869, McCorquodale & Co, Science Museum/Science & Society Picture Library Image Ref. 10243045.
158 Glasgow Museum, accession no. A.1938.11.du, http://collections.glasgowmuseums.com/mwebcgi/mweb?request=record;id=139177;type=101 (accessed 13 September 2019). Also discussed in Gorman, *Banner Bright*, p. 70.
159 Gorman, *Banner Bright*, p. 70. Glasgow Friendly Association of Cotton Spinners, painted tin tray. Glasgow City Council, Glasgow Museums, Reference: 1420.78.502 / A.1938.11.du, www.theglasgowstory.com/image/?inum=TGSE00538 (accessed 23 August 2018).
160 Tullie House Museum & Art Gallery, Carlisle: cotton spinner's banner, www.tulliehouse.co.uk/thecollection/cotton-spinners-banner-victorian (accessed 23 August 2018).

The measure of a man: an epilogue

The phrase 'the measure of a man' features in motivational quotes, film and television series, song lyrics, book and memoir titles, and political speeches in the twenty-first century. Ranging from platitude to powerful demand for equal rights, the phrase is used to define the qualities that make a man: his humanity, his handling of his power and privilege, and his response to adversity. All measure men's strength and emotions, evidence that, long after the nineteenth century ended, men's emotionalised bodies and materiality make masculinity manifest. This epilogue, therefore, explores the continued resonances of emotionalised bodies and material culture for contemporary masculinities.

Studies of the traumatic events of the twentieth century acknowledge the centrality of men's bodies and emotions to the making and remaking of manliness through mechanised warfare and its aftermath.[1] Even so, the role of the specific nexus of men's bodies, emotions, and material culture in the formation of modern masculinity can bear further analysis. The power of emotionalised bodies and material culture to formulate, convey, and fix gender identities, after all, has become ever more potent with the growth of mass media and mass consumption in the twentieth century. In the twenty-first century, people regularly encounter images of male bodies on their hand-held devices via social media that drive engagement. Thus, the juxtaposition of image, text, and object is both powerful and personalised. As such, the measure of a man now encompasses appearance, bodies, and emotions, all aligned with masculine qualities and judged accordingly; the process has, perhaps, never been so intense or so intimate. Indeed, scholars, commentators, and men themselves, in blogs, print, television, and online videos, explore the impact of body image on men's sense of self and self-esteem.[2] Nonetheless, even as people are acutely aware of the personal distress caused by social and cultural pressures to conform to certain bodily ideals, and recognise that bodies and appearances convey gender and sex identities, the emotions associated with them and the roles they play are less often scrutinised.

This epilogue suggests some of these links by surveying the four themes that form the essence of this book. First, it considers men's 'spectacular bodies'; that is, the idealised emotionalised bodies encountered in entertainment and advertising, along with their more sinister political associations and uses. Secondly, the imaginative conjunction of emotions, bodies, and material culture in formulations of military masculinity are explored, whether deployed in recruitment drives, featured in the often romanticised and politicised tropes of servicemen's damaged bodies and minds, or in the creative projects that seek to materialise military men's experiences. Representations of the relationship of these men with home continues to be complex and charged with emotions. Thus, thirdly, this epilogue discusses how changed forms of male work, as well as unemployment, retirement, illness, and, more recently, paternal caring roles, are all configured through men's uneasy presence in the home: an arena in which manhood is still presumed to be undermined or compromised. Fourthly, throughout this book, the imagined body of the working-class man has been shown to impact greatly on the construction of manliness and unmanliness. In the post-industrial economy of British society, however, the manly emotionalised working-class body has changed as radically as notions of class itself. There are no noble images of working-class men at their labours. At best, middle-class 'hipsters' took on the nobility of physical labour through appearance: beards, workwear, and tattoos.[3] For the most part, the image of working-class men is derogatory, whether such men are perceived to be a dangerous political threat or a redundant and residual form of masculinity. No wonder, then, that the culture wars of late capitalism are fought over men's bodies and emotions.

The most visible idealised male bodies are those of actors and models; 'spectacular' in that they are both performative and muscular, the latter still typically conflated with masculinity.[4] Usually required to be large and well built, fashions have dictated men's form over time, varying from hefty and broad in the mid-twentieth century to the pumped bodybuilder physique of the 1980s to the lean, sculpted muscular bodies of the twenty-first century.[5] Other forms of masculine bodies have co-existed with them, lighter built and youthful, the Ephebe to the Herculean: graceful dancers in the 1930s, teenage rebels in the 1950s, floppy-haired pretty boys in the 1990s, nerds in the noughties, and the queer beauties of the twenty-first century.[6] Even so, their forms of masculinity are generally read as countercultural, challenging traditional manhood through their non-normativity.[7] Buff is simplistically equated with traditional masculine qualities of strength, courage, endurance, fortitude, restraint, aggression, heroism, and virility.[8] The film industry and business corporations use these bodies and the feelings they arouse, of desire, excitement, admiration, and love, to sell products.[9] In this process, emotionalised bodies remain bound up with the gender qualities with which they are associated.[10]

Yet spectacular bodies have their own complexities.[11] The white male action hero's body, for instance, is often 'repeatedly violated, penetrated in a variety of ways'; in Yvonne Tasker's words, martyred to demonstrate masculine self-sufficiency.[12] Here the tropes of self-sacrifice and suffering that we have seen so closely associated with manly bodies are reconfigured in new ways. Perhaps most problematically, as men exposed to the gaze of both males and females, these bodies cause anxiety for critics and audiences since their power is compromised by objectification.[13] One way to refute the feminisation of the erotic gaze and maintain masculine power is to stress hardness and muscular motion in the form of action and violence.[14] Notwithstanding, the muscular male ideal has shifted from 'predominantly instrumental to predominantly ornamental' in popular images.[15] It is perhaps the inherent anxieties concerning the eroticised male body that has led the film industry and critics to laud those male actors who can transform their bodies from slim to hefty, naturally built to ripped, emaciated to fat, and vice versa. Actors like Christian Bale, Jake Gyllenhaal, Michael Fassbender, Tom Hardy, and Matthew McConaughey are seen as reinvigorating careers or breaking free of conventional good looks through such acts of physical control.[16] Their roles are regarded as especially likely to elicit feelings. After all, these human chameleons also play with notions of good and bad when their bodies transmute from attractive to unattractive, from muscled, often meaning manly, if troubled, to thin or fat, which both equate with unmanliness, since emaciation can mean effeminacy or homosexuality, and corpulence corruption or weakness.[17] When these actors exert will, or wilfully adopt excess, to remodel their appearance, their acting abilities are awarded. Arguably, their mastery of their bodies is applauded because they shift the male body from ornamental to instrumental; their bodies are art rather than decoration.

One of the appealing features of these actors' depiction of masculinity, perhaps, is that they reveal that masculinity is fragile and contested. This may itself appeal to a female gaze, which enjoys the softening of the harder edges of spectacular bodies through signifiers of emotional tenderness or vulnerability. Perhaps the most successful symbol of masculine tenderness is fatherhood. Fathering children has long been considered proof of men's virility, but it is also seen as producing a more tender version of masculinity, most obviously through the visual pairing of an attractive man with a baby. An iconic early example is the Athena poster *L'Enfant* or *Man and Baby*. This 'artistic' black-and-white image of a muscular young man cradling a baby to his chest was shot in 1986 and became the company's most successful poster, selling millions of copies.[18] It was designed to stir feelings that evoked the sensitive 'New Man': a style of masculinity that combined a belief in the equality of the sexes, a preparedness to share familial and relationship duties, and consideration for women and their needs.[19] His twenty-first-century counterpart in popular print and social media is the 'sexy dad': a DILF counterpart to the MILF. Here the focus is explicitly upon male bodies, typically a celebrity cradling his young child.[20] The male body part that is objectified is the 'bulging bicep', a descendent of the workers' arm of the long nineteenth century, decoupled from class and labour. This sexualised and emotionalised body is a particularly female construct, catering to a female audience, and thus, arguably, a sign of women's pleasure and empowerment.[21] Still, it is advisable to recognise that cultural depictions of vulnerable emotionalised male bodies, along with fragile, damaged versions, which ostensibly offer a reconstructed masculinity, ultimately serve the interests of men rather than women.[22]

One type of masculinity that is regularly reconfigured and permitted to be troubled or damaged, as well as emotional and emotive, is that associated with the military. This is perhaps because, in the twenty-first century, military masculinities are still conveyed through the nexus of bodies, emotions, and materiality. The British Army, for example, has astutely drawn on emotions in its 2019 recruitment campaign. Its posters deploy the famous Lord Kitchener 'Wants You' format, with a series of conventional head and shoulder portraits of confident, attractive, uniformed soldiers. In contrast to the traditional style and typeface of the recruitment poster, however, they powerfully showcase racial and gender diversity, deploying emotions to attract young people. The text raises cliched stereotypes and turns them on their head: the army needs 'phone zombies', 'binge-gamers', 'class-clowns', 'selfie-addicts', 'me-me-me millennials', and 'snowflakes', for, respectively, their drive, focus, spirit, confidence, self-belief, and compassion. The broader campaign centres on a combination of action and emotional intelligence, updating military masculinities for a new generation of men and women.[23] More broadly, the resurgence of nationalism in Britain has resulted in servicemen being idealised in popular culture, especially the imagined Tommy of a nostalgic past. Indeed, a number of films in the second decade of this century, such as Christopher Nolan's *Dunkirk* (2017) and Peter Jackson's *They Shall Not Grow Old* (2018), deploy soldiers' emotionalised bodies as a key part of their narratives and, indeed, were assessed on their emotional detail and registers.[24]

Military masculinity is frequently represented as complex, combining trained bodies and fighting aggression with humane compassion and psychological trauma and physical damage.[25] As such, soldiers and veterans appear as the leads in television series and romantic literature in which their troubled emotions undercut their protective, heroic, masculine qualities. Their female lovers on the home front are shown saving them by helping them build emotional resilience: a neat trade-off of masculine vulnerability for female agency.[26] The damaged nature of martial masculinities is also materialised in art. Two particularly evocative examples can be seen in the works of Joyce Cairns and Chris McHugh. Cairns has produced a body of work responding to military themes in 'War Tourist', which uses artefacts related to conflict to create her 'memory paintings'. The most resonant in terms of embodied and materialised masculinity are her two pictures *Father's Memorabilia North West Europe* and *Father's Memorabilia Tunisia* (1995), which use her father's artefacts – photographs, postcards, medals, insignia, and uniform – from his service during the Second World War. Each lays out his uniform in the centre of the painting, surrounded by his military artefacts, touching evocations of the ramifications of war for men and their families. In these paintings, collectively exhibited in Aberdeen Art Gallery in 2006 and now on display in the National War Museum, Scotland, the martial material culture stands in for the man and invites viewers to fill the objects with feelings, of loss, absence, longing, nostalgia, and grief.[27] As in the long nineteenth century, the result is to associate military masculinity with these powerful emotions.

The ceramic artist and academic Christopher McHugh has also created a body of work that materialises soldiers' embodied experience of warfare, inspired by the Sunderland lustreware pottery discussed in Chapter 3. With eleven Wearside-born soldiers from 3 Rifles, who had served in Helmand Province, Afghanistan, 2009–10, he created ceramic objects intended to make the men's military experience 'empathetically "graspable"' through words, vision, and touch.[28] His 'tattooed pots', for example, are decorated with tattoos from the soldiers' bodies, along with images of their lucky charms. The tattoos and charms, themselves non-verbal expressions of emotions and identity, combine on these ceramic vessels to create embodied and emotionalised shrines to the soldiers' experiences.[29] Moreover, when viewed in exhibitions, such as 'Created in Conflict: British Soldier Art from the Crimean War to Today', Compton Verney Art Gallery (2018), these objects operate to convey martial masculinity in all its apparent contradictions of strength and weakness, power and vulnerability, aggression and compassion. McHugh is currently working with veterans from Forward Assist, to aid their well-being through their creation of ceramic artworks that embody their military experiences, often as gifts for loved ones. Rather than creating objects that operate as an absent presence in the home, their activities helped them in, as one veteran explained, 'getting out of the house'.[30]

As this suggests, there is still some ambivalence about men's presence in the home. Enforced presence through illness, unemployment, and retirement, for instance, are typically represented as presenting challenges for marital relationships, and for men's well-being and sense of masculine identity. At one end of the spectrum is the notion of men as domestic hindrances. Popular writer Gabrielle Mander has, for example, titled one of her books: *101 Things to Do with a Retired Man: ... to Get Him Out from*

Under Your Feet! (2012). At the other, as a number of opinion pieces and scholarship testifies, is the expectation that a man who stays in the home through retirement, unemployment, or being the primary child carer feels emasculated. A striking example is Kevin, the 'drippy stay-at-home dad' in the TV comedy *Motherland* (BBC, 2017), who is at turns ineffectual and despised.[31] This is partly because such men are not carrying out full-time paid employment, the key signifier of mature masculinity, but, also more surprisingly perhaps, because the home continues to be constructed as feminine and domestic, despite increases in those working from home.[32] What is worrying is that popular representations of such men elicit negative feelings of pity, contempt, and, perhaps for some, disgust.

The sense of home as a site in which men are emasculated is perhaps most acute where working-class men are concerned. Deindustrialisation challenged the generations experiencing it, and not simply because of economic difficulties working-class men encountered in unemployment or in securing alternative forms of work, typically precarious, in the 'feminised' service industries. It also undermined the especially embodied form of masculine identity that prevailed in the heavy industries of the twentieth century, predicated upon strong bodies, taking risks, and macho posturing.[33] This was not a masculine identity suited to domesticity. In fictional accounts, these men disrupted home. Mr Macdonnel, in *Dance of the Apprentices* (1948), for example, is described returning home after work, his 'tough, middle-sized physique' and his 'unnecessary, frenzied haste' literally shaking the house, his dirty clothes and body soiling its cleanliness.[34] Indeed, when forced to be at home, working-class men were depicted as casually and callously brutal. The cartoon character of Andy Capp, a work-shy, drunken Geordie, for instance, spent his early years from his creation in 1957 to the 1970s beating his wife Flo.[35] Globally popular, his depiction of an old-style masculinity entrenched class stereotypes located in an 'other' against whom the middle classes and 'respectable' working classes could construct their identities.[36]

The problematic vision of working-class masculinity in post-industrial Britain, where men were forced out of work by the closure of industry from the 1980s, is particularly evident in cinema.[37] Interestingly, in films like *Billy Elliot* (Stephen Daldry, 2000) and *The Full Monty* (Peter Cattaneo, 1997), clashes between old and new models of masculinity are worked out through emotionalised male bodies. Billy Elliot's dancing body not only questions gender and sex stereotypes about men, it is his outlet for the expression of emotions which help him realise his own subjectivity.[38] In *The Full Monty*, the men excluded from work, leisure, and commerce reclaim their masculinity, that is, their power, through the physical performance of their naked bodies. Though, of course, this is still a compromised, unstable form of masculinity since they strip for a female audience.[39] The deployment of bodies in constructing notions of problematic post-industrial working-class masculinity is also evident. The slew of attacks and contempt for 'chav culture' in the 2000s locates much of the contempt for men's supposed feckless behaviour and attitudes in their bodies and material culture. Working-class young men in post-industrial cities perform '"spectacular masculinities" of white male excess' through their bodies (dress, appearance, comportment, gait) and behaviours (dancing, drinking, swearing, sex, and violence), thereby accruing 'a body capital that has a currency and a local exchange value within the circuits they inhabit'.[40] Unfortunately, the popular representations of these practices often invoke negative emotions, which help make the pejorative views of working-class masculinities sticky.[41]

Grayson Perry has sought to create art around these conjunctions of class and masculinity, explored in his television series *Grayson Perry: All Man* (2016).[42] In 'Hard Man' he explored the hyper-masculinity of mixed martial arts cage fighters in the north-east alongside some of the victims of masculinity: those men who take their own lives. The art that materialised from this sensitive and sympathetic account of working-class masculinity is a ceramic vase 'Shadow Boxing' and a tapestry 'Death of a Working Hero'.[43] The latter movingly evokes the working-class ephemera described in Chapter 5 and was itself carried in procession in the Durham Miner's Gala. As with the trade union banners, the tapestry is dominated by two men: a miner on the left with 'provide' on his belt and a tattooed cage fighter on the right with a belt declaring 'protect'. Both are in fighting pose. The scroll above says 'A time to fight, a time to talk, a time to change' and underneath their feet: 'We work for the future and grieve for the past'. Underneath is a north-eastern landscape with Durham Cathedral, the Angel of the North, wind turbines, cranes, and, in the foreground, the coffin of the suicide victim surrounded by mourning women.[44] The rupture in representations of working-class masculinity and the power of emotionalised bodies and material culture are movingly encapsulated in a review of the episode which remarks on the poignancy that 'people march holding banners embroidered with sad emblems of manliness: miners, sailors and industrial buildings'.[45] Sad indeed, since Grayson's modern version evokes the tragedy of a form of masculinity that demands men restrain their emotions at the cost of their lives. His sensitivities materialise sympathy in the media and in art for the plight of a group of men who no longer understand their place in society and, in some cases, feel that their rightful place as men is thwarted, belittled, and dismissed by a service economy better suited to women.

As all this indicates, emotionalised male bodies are rarely innocent of political meaning. The third episode of Perry's *All Man* took him into London's financial sector. The artwork that resulted is a large glazed ceramic penis, *Object in Foreground* (2016). On it are the symbols of these men's status: banknotes, their faces, and the face of the then Chancellor of the Exchequer.⁴⁶ In its colour tones, the glazed cut-out images of men, its exclusively 'male' form and focus, and attempt to materialise an ultra-masculine world, it is reminiscent of Lord Byron's screen, which opened this book. Like Byron's screen, it graphically conveys the power of the male body as a locus for and disseminator of authority. Of course, this is most evident in the ways emotionalised male bodies are manipulated to suit political agendas. For twentieth-century authoritarian political regimes in the West, notably fascism, but also communism, and for twenty-first-century alt-right groups, white men's muscular bodies have been deployed in propaganda to symbolise masculinity as they claim it should be: masterful, dominant, superior to other types of male bodies of colour and all women.⁴⁷ These gendered bodies are inscribed as 'natural', though impossibly idealised and unattainable, and used to symbolise nationhood and racial superiority.⁴⁸ While they are intended to elicit feelings, they usually demand emotional as well as physical hardness from men. Similarly, in their campaigns, 'strongmen' populist leaders across the globe declare their own virility, potency, and physical size to win voters and persuade them of their ability to govern.⁴⁹ In modernity and late modernity, the hyper-masculinity that is displayed through emotionalised bodies and material culture is a backlash against more inclusive and progressive forms of gender and sexual identities.⁵⁰ Getting the measure of a man in this context has especially fraught and disturbing implications.

The second decade of the twenty-first century is undergoing a particularly vicious reaction against progressive politics and identity politics. Social media offers an outlet and rallying cry for white men who feel disempowered by a world whose 'future is female'. Their fights over the meaning of masculinity are often catalysed by the emotionalised bodies and objects they meet online. The response to the Gillette advert in early 2019 is a case in point. Linking itself with the #MeToo movement, the advert asserts: 'We Believe: the Best Men Can Be', reinventing the shaving product's slogan 'The Best a Man Can Get', to demand that men believe women's experiences and address them. Featuring men policing other men's behaviour by defending women from sexual harassment, guiding sons away from mindless violence, and encouraging men to express their emotions, the advert was cleverly positioned to provoke a powerful response, and it went viral, inciting online outrage and a Twitterstorm. Right-wing groups and controversialist commentators attacked it for 'virtue-signalling', assuming all men are 'horrible' and attacking the very foundations of real manhood; some even expressed anger that a woman, Kim Gehrig, directed it, rather than a man.⁵¹ 'Let boys be boys', they declared; while others decried corporate manipulation, implying that those men who took heed of the message were advertisers' pawns and, by association, emasculated.⁵²

Liberal feminist responses pointed out the dangers to all men's well-being of a toxic masculinity rooted in aggression and emotional restraint.⁵³

What is perhaps most disheartening is that the positive masculinity showcased in the Gillette advert is so conservative. After all, it simply plugs into long-standing 'traditional' notions of ideal manliness explored in this book: heroic, strong, tender men, who are clean-living and appropriately emotionally expressive. Nonetheless, there is something to be optimistic about. These brand role models are black as well as white and offer a more body-positive vision of masculinity. The men whose behaviour is criticised in the advert are conventionally muscular; those who behave 'best' are attractive but possess bodies that are not unattainable. As *Manliness in Britain* has shown, manly bodies are reified as symbols, progenitors, and defenders of gender, society, and nation, and thus are repeatedly manipulated and made-over to improve men and masculinity at an individual and collective level and across social classes. Masculinity matters, because we all live with its consequences.

Notes

1 This is a large area of scholarship. For an introduction to the First World War, see Sonja Levsen, 'Masculinities', in Ute Daniel et al. (eds), *International Encyclopedia of the First World War* (Berlin: Freie Universität Berlin, 2015), 1914–1918 Online, http://dx.doi.org/10.15463/ie1418.10531; Heike Liebau, 'Martial races, theory of', in Daniel et al. (eds), *International Encyclopedia of the First World War*, http://dx.doi.org/10.15463/ie1418.10702/1.1; and Jessica Meyer, 'Subjectivity and emotions (Great Britain and Ireland)', in Daniel et al. (eds), *International Encyclopedia of the First World War*, http://dx.doi.org/10.15463/ie1418.10412 (accessed 2 January 2019).

2 Viren Shinde, 'Men have body image issues, too: this is my naked truth', *Browngirl* (2018) www.browngirlmagazine.com/2018/05/men-have-body-image-issues-too-this-is-my-naked-truth/ (accessed 13 January 2019); Jessica Lovejoy, 'Body image issues are not just for women', *Huffington Post* (2014), www.huffingtonpost.com/jessica-lovejoy/body-image-issues-are-not-just-for-women_b_5034285.html (accessed 13 January 2019); *The Naked Truth*, BBC 3, series 1, episode 3: 'Male Body Image' (2018). For the impact of male muscularity in cinema on body image, see Todd G. Morrison and Marie Halton, 'Buff, tough, and rough: representations of muscularity in action motion pictures', *Journal of Men's Studies* 17:1 (2009), 58.

3 Jordan Detmers, 'Why hipsters dress like lumberjacks: the story of the "lumbersexual"' (November 2014), https://jordandetmers.com/2014/11/14/why-hipsters-dress-like-lumberjacks-the-story-of-the-lumbersexual/ (accessed 29 January 2019); Holly Baxter, 'Out of the woods, here he comes: the lumbersexual', *Guardian* (November 2014), www.theguardian.com/commentisfree/2014/nov/14/lumbersexual-beard-plaid-male-fashion (accessed 29 January 2019).

4 Yvonne Tasker, *Spectacular Bodies: Gender, Genre and the Action Cinema* (London and New York: Routledge Taylor & Francis Group, 1993); Morrison and Halton, 'Buff, tough, and rough', 68.

5 Vanessa Thorpe, 'What's their beef? Why today's leading men are driven to be buff', *Observer* (January 2019), www.theguardian.com/lifeandstyle/2019/jan/12/curse-of-perfection-male-actors-poldark (accessed 13 January 2019).

6 Ellie Hunt, 'Queer actor Ezra Miller is the hero we need right now: even Playboy gets it', *Guardian* (November 2018), www.theguardian.com/commentisfree/2018/nov/19/ezra-miller-hero-world-needs-now-playboy (accessed 13 January 2019); Jake Nevins, 'Boys on film: what we can learn about masculinity from Hollywood',

Guardian (November 2018), www.theguardian.com/film/2018/nov/26/boys-on-film-what-we-can-learn-about-masculinity-from-hollywood (accessed 13 January 2019).

7 For the prison movie as a site where competing discourses of masculinity are visible, see Dario Llinares, 'Punishing bodies: British prison film and the spectacle of masculinity', *Journal of British Cinema and Television* 12:2 (2015), 208.
8 Tasker, *Spectacular Bodies*, passim. Morrison and Halton, 'Buff, tough, and rough', 68.
9 For the commodification of the male body in film see Tasker, *Spectacular Bodies*, p. 2.
10 For their associations with national and racial identity, see *ibid*.
11 For the stereotypes in representations of black men's bodies in cinema see *ibid.*, pp. 37–9.
12 *Ibid.*, p. 39. Llinares, 'Punishing bodies', 209, 211.
13 Tasker, *Spectacular Bodies*, ch. 5.
14 *Ibid.*, pp. 77, 115–16. Llinares, 'Punishing bodies', 220.
15 Morrison and Halton, 'Buff, tough, and rough', 58–60.
16 For Hardy's physical transformation in *Bronson*, and Fassbender's in *Hunger* see Llinares, 'Punishing bodies', 218–19, 225.
17 For the association of personality traits with bodies in cinema, see Morrison and Halton, 'Buff, tough, and rough', 61, 69. The increasingly fragile, damaged image of masculinity in film is discussed in Phil Powrie, Ann Davies, and Bruce Babington (eds), *The Trouble with Men: Masculinities in European and Hollywood Cinema* (London and New York: Wallflower Press, 2004), passim.
18 Angela Smith, 'Building biceps and tender kisses: the sexualisation of fatherhood', *Social Semiotics* 28:3 (2018), 320. Cahal Milmo, 'The curse of "Man and Baby": Athena, and the birth of a legend', *Independent* (January 2007), www.independent.co.uk/news/uk/this-britain/the-curse-of-man-and-baby-athena-and-the-birth-of-a-legend-432331.html (accessed 16 January 2019).
19 Smith, 'Building biceps and tender kisses', 316–19.
20 *Ibid.*, 320–7.
21 *Ibid.*, 319–20, 327–8.
22 Phil Powrie, Ann Davies, and Bruce Babington, 'Turning the male inside out', in Powrie, Davies, and Babington, *The Trouble with Men*, pp. 13–14.
23 Claire Sadler, '"Your army needs you": army unveils latest recruitment campaign', *Forces Network* (January 2019), www.forces.net/news/your-army-needs-you-army-unveils-latest-recruitment-campaign (accessed 13 January 2019).
24 Stephanie Zacharek, 'Ambitious and harrowing, Christopher Nolan's *Dunkirk* is a masterpiece', *Time* (July 2017), http://time.com/4864051/dunkirk-review/ (accessed 17 January 2019); Ciara Wardlow, 'Christopher Nolan's emotional objects and the "Dunkirk" exception' (26 July 2017), https://filmschoolrejects.com/christopher-nolans-emotional-objects-dunkirk-exception/ (accessed 17 January 2019). Chris Knight, 'Peter Jackson's They Shall Not Grow Old sees the First World War made incredibly real again', *National Post*, https://nationalpost.com/entertainment/movies/peter-jacksons-they-shall-not-grow-old-sees-the-first-world-war-made-incredibly-real-again (accessed 17 January 2019); Adam Gopnik, 'A few thoughts on the authenticity of Peter Jackson's "They Shall Not Grow Old", *New Yorker* (January 2019), www.newyorker.com/news/daily-comment/a-few-thoughts-on-the-authenticity-of-peter-jacksons-they-shall-not-grow-old (accessed 17 January 2019).
25 For an overview of Western military masculinity from the later twentieth century onwards, see Veronica Kitchen, 'Veterans and military masculinity in popular romantic fiction', *Critical Military Studies* 4:1 (2016), 37.
26 *Ibid.*, 40 and passim.

27 Joyce Cairns, *Father's Memorabilia North West Europe* (1995) and *Father's Memorabilia Tunisia* (1995), National War Museum, Scotland, M.2006.3.2. Joyce Cairns website, 'My father's war', www.joycecairns.co.uk/my-fathers-war.html (accessed 29 January 2019); Janet MacKenzie, 'Joyce Cairns: interview', *Studio International* (2014), www.studiointernational.com/index.php/joyce-cairns-interview (accessed 29 January 2019); Georgina Coburn, 'Review Joyce Cairns: War Tourist, Aberdeen Art Gallery', *Northings* (March 2006), https://georginacoburnarts.co.uk/wp-content/uploads/2014/08/JOYCE-CAIRNS-WAR-TOURIST.pdf (accessed 17 January 2019).
28 Christopher McHugh, 'Clay and commemoration: materializing the somatic experience of warfare through ceramic practice', *Critical Military Studies* 3:1 (2017), 88.
29 *Ibid.*, 92–5.
30 *Ibid.*, 96.
31 Fiona Sturges, 'Motherland: a vision of child rearing that is panic-inducingly scary', *Guardian* (November 2017), www.theguardian.com/tv-and-radio/2017/nov/04/motherland-vision-child-rearing-panic-inducingly-scary (accessed 17 January 2019).
32 John Hart, 'Being a stay-at-home dad makes me feel manly', *Guardian* (December 2015), www.theguardian.com/lifeandstyle/2015/dec/26/being-a-stay-at-home-dad-makes-me-feel-manly (accessed 17 January 2019).
33 Ronnie Johnston and Arthur McIvor, 'Dangerous work, hard men and broken bodies: masculinity in the Clydeside heavy industries, c. 1930–1970s', *Labour History Review* 69:2 (2004), 135–51.
34 E. Gaitens, *Dance of the Apprentices* (Edinburgh, 1948), cited in Johnston and McIvor, 'Dangerous work', 142–3.
35 Rachel Wallace, '"She's punch drunk!!" Humor, domestic violence, and the British working class in Andy Capp cartoons, 1957–65', *Journal of Popular Culture* 51:1 (2018), 129–51. For a biography of Reg Smythe, the creator of the strip, and some examples, see the British Cartoon Archive, University of Kent, www.cartoons.ac.uk/cartoonist-biographies/c-d/RegSmythe_AndyCapp.html (accessed 20 July 2018).
36 Eric Hobsbawm saw the Capp cartoons as a gentle satire of traditional working-class culture in industrial regions, see 'Mass-producing traditions: Europe 1870–1914', in Eric Hobsbawm and Terence Ranger (eds), *The Invention of Tradition* (Cambridge: Cambridge University Press, 1983), p. 287.
37 John Hill, 'A working-class hero is something to be? Changing representations of class and masculinity in British cinema', in Powrie, Davies, and Babington, *The Trouble with Men*, 100–9; Claire Monk, 'Men in the 90s', in Robert Murphy (ed.), *British Cinema of the 90s* (London: British Film Institute, 2000), pp. 159–62.
38 Hill, 'A working-class hero is something to be?' pp. 104–8.
39 James Leggott, 'Like father? Failing parents and angelic children in contemporary British social realist cinema', in Powrie, Davies, and Babington, *The Trouble with Men*, pp. 163–7.
40 Anoop Nayak, 'Displaced masculinities: chavs, youth and class in the post-industrial city', *Sociology* 40:5 (2006), 813–31.
41 Carole Cadwalladr, 'Vajazzled! How chavs have replaced working class people on Britain's TV', *Guardian* (June 2011), www.theguardian.com/tv-and-radio/2011/jun/05/how-chavs-replaced-working-class (accessed 17 January 2019).
42 For class see Grayson Perry, *The Vanity of Small Differences* (London: Hayward Publishing, 2013).
43 For both, see Grayson Perry, *The Most Popular Art Exhibition Ever!* (London: Penguin, 2017).
44 Grayson Perry, *Death of a Working Hero*, tapestry (2016), http://paragonpress.

45 Filipa Jodelka, 'All Man: Grayson Perry on masculinity', *Guardian* (May 2016), www.theguardian.com/tv-and-radio/2016/may/05/grayson-perry-all-man-preview (accessed 17 January 2019).
46 Perry, *The Most Popular Art Exhibition Ever!*; Lorena Muñoz-Alonso, 'Grayson Perry crafts giant ceramic penis to represent London's bankers', *Artnet News* (20 May 2016), https://news.artnet.com/art-world/grayson-perry-giant-penis-sculpture-500663 (accessed 18 January 2019).
47 There are numerous examples in the Muslim and Hindu nations too. Pankaj Mishra, *Age of Anger: A History of the Present* (London: Penguin Books, 2017), pp. 243–4.
48 Pankaj Mishra, 'Jordan Peterson and fascist mysticism', *New York Review of Books Daily* (March 2018), www.nybooks.com/daily/2018/03/19/jordan-peterson-and-fascist-mysticism/ (accessed 18 January 2019).
49 Mishra, *Age of Anger*, pp. 328–9. Also, see Pankaj Mishra, 'The crisis in modern masculinity', *Guardian* (March 2018), www.theguardian.com/books/2018/mar/17/the-crisis-in-modern-masculinity (accessed 18 January 2019).
50 Mishra, *Age of Anger*, p. 326; Mishra, 'The crisis in modern masculinity'.
51 Alexandra Topping, Kate Lyons, and Matthew Weaver, 'Gillette #MeToo razors ad on "toxic masculinity" gets praise – and abuse', *Guardian* (15 January 2019), www.theguardian.com/world/2019/jan/15/gillette-metoo-ad-on-toxic-masculinity-cuts-deep-with-mens-rights-activists (accessed 18 January 2019).
52 Henry Williams, 'The Gillette advert has more to do with market control than #MeToo', *Spectator* (16 January 2019), https://blogs.spectator.co.uk/2019/01/the-gillette-advert-has-more-to-do-with-market-control-than-metoo/ (accessed 18 January 2019).
53 George Monbiot, 'The fear that lies behind aggressive masculinity', *Guardian* (16 January 2019), www.theguardian.com/commentisfree/2019/jan/16/men-masculinity-gillette-advertisement (accessed 18 January 2019).

co.uk/works/death-of-a-working-hero (accessed 20 December 2018); also detail in Perry, *The Most Popular Art Exhibition Ever!*, n.p.

Select bibliography

The following are key works for the ideas discussed in this book. For a more exhaustive bibliography, please contact me at jbegiato@brookes.ac.uk.

Ahmed, Sara, *The Cultural Politics of Emotion* (London: Routledge, 2004).
Barclay, Katie, *Men on Trial: Performing Emotion, Embodiment, and Identity in Ireland 1800–1845* (Manchester: Manchester University Press, 2018).
Barclay, Katie, 'Performing emotion and reading the male body in the Irish court, c. 1800–1845', *Journal of Social History* 51:2 (2017), 293–312.
Baron, Ava, 'Masculinity, the embodied male worker, and the historian's gaze', *International Labor and Working-Class History* 69 (2006), 143–60.
Barringer, Michael, *Men at Work: Art and Labour in Victorian Britain* (New Haven, CT, and London: Yale University Press, 2005).
Bedell, Rebecca, *Moved to Tears: Rethinking the Art of the Sentimental in the United States* (Princeton, NJ, and Oxford: Princeton University Press, 2018).
Begiato, Joanne, 'Between poise and power: embodied manliness in eighteenth- and nineteenth-century British culture', *Transactions of the Royal Historical Society* 26:2 (2016), 125–47.
Begiato, Joanne, 'Tears and the manly sailor in England, c.1760–1860', *Journal for Maritime Research* 17:2 (2015), 117–33.
Bellanta, Melissa, '"Poor Gordon": what the Australian cult of Adam Lindsay Gordon tells us about turn-of-the-twentieth-century masculine sentimentality', *Gender & History* 28:2 (2016), 401–21.
Boddy, Kasia, *Boxing: A Cultural History* (London: Reaktion Books, 2008).
Brown, Elspeth H., 'Racialising the virile body: Eadweard Muybridge's locomotion studies 1883–1887', *Gender & History* 17:3 (2005), 627–56.
Brown, Michael, 'Cold steel, weak flesh: mechanism, masculinity and the anxieties of late Victorian empire', *Cultural and Social History* 14:2 (2017), 155–81.
Brown, Michael, '"Like a devoted army": medicine, heroic masculinity, and the military paradigm in Victorian Britain', *Journal of British Studies* 49:3 (2010), 592–622.

Brown, Michael, and Lawrence, Chris, 'Quintessentially modern heroes: surgeons, explorers, and empire, *c.* 1840–1914', *Journal of Social History* 50:1 (2016), 148–78.

Brown, Nicola, 'Tender beauty: Victorian painting and the problem of sentimentality', *Journal of Victorian Culture* 16:2 (2011), 214–25.

Budd, Michael Anton, *The Sculpture Machine: Physical Culture and Body Politics in the Age of Empire* (Basingstoke and London: Palgrave Macmillan, 1997).

Callen, Anthea, *Looking at Men: Anatomy, Masculinity and the Modern Male Body* (New Haven and London: Yale University Press, 2018).

Capp, Bernard, '"Jesus wept" but did the Englishman? Masculinity and emotion in early modern England', *Past & Present* 224:1 (2014), 75–108.

Carter, Louise, 'Scarlet fever: female enthusiasm for men in uniform, 1780–1815', in Kevin Linch and Matthew McCormack (eds), *Britain's Soldiers: Rethinking War and Society, 1715–1815* (Liverpool: Liverpool University Press, 2014).

Carter, Philip, *Men and the Emergence of Polite Society, Britain 1660–1800* (London: Longman, 2001).

Clark, Anna, *Desire: A History of European Sexuality* (New York and Abingdon: Routledge, 2008).

Cocks, Harry, *Nameless Offences: Homosexual Desire in the 19th Century* (London: I.B. Tauris, 2003).

Cohen, Michele, *Fashioning Masculinities: National Identity and Language in the Eighteenth Century* (London and New York: Routledge, 1996).

Conley, Mary, *From Jack Tar to Union Jack: Representing Naval Manhood in the British Empire, 1870–1918* (Manchester: Manchester University Press, 2009).

Cook, Matt, *London and the Culture of Homosexuality, 1885–1914* (Cambridge: Cambridge University Press, 2003).

Dawson, Graham, *Soldier Heroes: British Adventure, Empire, and the Imagining of Masculinities* (London and New York: Routledge, 1994).

Deane, Bradley, *Masculinity and the New Imperialism: Rewriting Manhood in British Popular Literature, 1870–1914* (Cambridge: Cambridge University Press, 2014).

De Freitas Boe, Ana, and Coyendall, Abby (eds), *Heteronormativity in Eighteenth-Century Literature and Culture* (Farnham: Ashgate, 2014).

Deitcher, David, *Dear Friends: American Photographs of Men Together, 1840–1918* (New York: Harry N. Abrams, Inc., 2001).

Dixon, Thomas, *Weeping Britannia: Portrait of a Nation in Tears* (Oxford: Oxford University Press, 2015).

Downing, Karen, 'The gentleman boxer: boxing, manners, and masculinity in eighteenth-century England', *Men and Masculinities* 12:3 (2010), 328–52.

Downing, Karen, *Restless Men: Masculinity and Robinson Crusoe 1788–1840* (Basingstoke: Palgrave Macmillan, 2014).

Dyer, Gary, 'Thieves, boxers, sodomites, poets: being flash to Byron's Don Juan', *Proceedings of the Modern Language Association* 116:3 (2001), 562–78.

Forth, Christopher E., '"Manhood incorporated": diet and the embodiment of "civilised" masculinity', *Men and Masculinities* 11:5 (2009), 578–601.

Foyster, Elizabeth, 'Boys will be Boys? Manhood and Aggression, 1660–1800', in Tim Hitchcock and Michèle Cohen (eds), *English Masculinities, 1660–1800* (Harlow: Addison Wesley, 1999).

Furneaux, Holly, *Military Men of Feeling: Emotion, Touch, and Masculinity in the Crimean War* (Oxford: Oxford University Press, 2016).

Furneaux, Holly, and Prichard, Sue, 'Contested objects: curating soldier art', *Museum & Society* 13:4 (2015), 447–61.

Garton, Stephen, 'The scales of suffering: love, death and Victorian masculinity', *Social History* 27:1 (2002), 40–58.

Gero, Annette, *Wartime Quilts: Appliqués and Geometric Masterpieces from Military Fabric from 300BC to WWII* (Roseville, NSW: Beagle Press, 2015).

Gilbert, Pamela, 'Popular beliefs and the body: "a nation of good animals"', in Michael Sappol and Stephen P. Rice (eds), *A Cultural History of the Human Body in the Age of Empire* (Oxford: Berg, 2010).

Goodlad, Lauren M., *Victorian Literature and the Victorian State: Character and Governance in a Liberal Society* (Baltimore, MD: John Hopkins University Press, 2003).

Gorman, John, *Banner Bright: An Illustrated History of the Banners of the British Trade Union Movement* (London: Allen Lane, 1973).

Hannan, Leonie, and Longair, Sarah, *History through Material Culture* (Manchester: Manchester University Press, 2017).

Harari, Yuval Noah, *Ultimate Experience: Battlefield Revelations and the Making of Modern War Culture, 1450–2000* (New York: Palgrave, 2008).

Harvey, Karen, 'Craftsmen in common: objects, skills and masculinity in the eighteenth and nineteenth centuries', in Hannah Grieg, Jane Hamlett, and Leonie Hannan (eds), *Gender and Material Culture in Britain since 1600* (London: Palgrave Macmillan, 2016).

Harvey, Karen, *The Little Republic: Masculinity and Domestic Authority in Eighteenth-Century Britain* (Oxford: Oxford University Press, 2012).

Harvey, Karen, 'Men of parts: masculine embodiment and the male leg in eighteenth-century England', *Journal of British Studies* 54:4 (2015), 797–821.

Harvey, Karen (ed.), *History and Material Culture: A Student's Guide to Approaching Alternative Sources* (London: Routledge, 2009).

Harvey, Karen, and Shepard, Alex (eds), 'Special feature of masculinities', *Journal of British Studies* 44:2 (2005), 274–362.

Hau, Michael, 'The normal, the ideal, and the beautiful: perfect bodies during the age of empire', in Michael Sappol and Stephen P. Rice (eds), *A Cultural History of the Human Body in the Age of Empire* (Oxford: Berg, 2010).

Hichberger, J. W., *Images of the Army: The Military in British Art, 1815–1914* (Manchester: Manchester University Press, 1988).

Holloway, Sally, 'Materialising maternal emotions: birth, celebration and renunciation in England, c.1688–1830', in Stephanie Downes, Sally Holloway, and Sarah Randles (eds), *Feeling Things: Objects and Emotions through History* (Oxford: Oxford University Press, 2018).

Houlbrook, Matt, *Queer London: Perils and Pleasures in the Sexual Metropolis, 1918–1957* (Chicago: University of Chicago Press, 2005).

Houlbrook, Matt, 'Queer things: men and make-up between the wars', in Hannah Grieg, Jane Hamlett, and Leonie Hannan (eds), *Gender and Material Culture in Britain since 1600* (Basingstoke: Palgrave, 2016).

Janes, Dominic, *Oscar Wilde Prefigured: Queer Fashioning and British Caricature, 1750–1900* (Chicago and London: University of Chicago Press, 2016).

Kavanagh, Declan, *Effeminate Years: Literature, Politics, and Aesthetics in Mid-Eighteenth-Century Britain* (Lewisburg, PA: Bucknell University Press, 2017).

Kennedy, Catriona, *Narratives of the Revolutionary and Napoleonic Wars: Military* and Civilian Experience in Britain and Ireland (Basingstoke: Palgrave Macmillan, 2013).

Kenny, Ruth, McMillan, Jeff, and Myrone, Martin, *British Folk Art* (London: Tate Enterprises Ltd, 2014).

Kestner, Joseph A., *Masculinities in Victorian Painting* (Aldershot: Scolar, c.1995).

MacAloon, John J., 'Introduction: muscular Christianity after 150 years', *International Journal of the History of Sport* 23:5 (2006), 687–700.

McCormack, Matthew, *Embodying the Militia in Georgian England* (Oxford: Oxford University Press, 2015).

McHugh, Christopher, 'Clay and commemoration: materializing the somatic experience of warfare through ceramic practice', *Critical Military Studies* 3:1 (2017), 87–97.

McIvor, Arthur, and Johnston, R., 'Dangerous work, hard men and broken bodies: masculinity in the Clydeside heavy industries', *Labour History Review* 69 (2004), 135–52.

Maidment, Brian, 'Coming through the cottage door: work, leisure, family, and gender in artisan interiors', in Brian Maidment, *Reading Popular Prints 1790–1870* (Manchester: Manchester University Press, 2001).

Maidment, Brian, *Reading Popular Prints, 1790–1870* (Manchester: Manchester University Press, 1996).

Mangan, James, and Walvin, James (eds), *Manliness and Morality: Middle-Class Masculinity in Britain and America 1800–1940* (Manchester: Manchester University Press, 1987).

Mansfield, Nick, 'Online working paper: overview of the National Banner Survey and the banners held by the People's History Museum', https://www.humanities.manchester.ac.uk/medialibrary/arts/history/workingpapers/wp_45.pdf (accessed 23 August 2018).

Mishra, Pankaj, *Age of Anger: A History of the Present* (London: Penguin Books, 2017).

Moore, Louis, *I Fight for a Living: Boxing and the Battle for Black Manhood. 1880–1915* (Urbana and Chicago: University of Illinois, 2017).

Mosse, George L., *The Image of Man: The Creation of Modern Masculinity* (Oxford: Oxford University Press, 1996).

Mulvey, Laura, 'Visual pleasure and narrative cinema', *Screen* 16:3 (1975), 6–18.

Myerly, Scott Hughes, *British Military Spectacle: From the Napoleonic Wars through the Crimea* (Cambridge, MA, and London: Harvard University Press, 1996).

Myrone, Martin, *Body-Building: Reforming Masculinities in British Art, 1750–1810* (New Haven, CT: Yale University Press, 2006).

Newman, Simon, *Embodied History: The Lives of the Poor in Early Philadelphia* (Philadelphia: University of Pennsylvania Press, 2003).

O'Brien, Anne, 'Missionary masculinities, the homoerotic gaze and the politics of race: Gilbert White in northern Australia, 1885–1915', *Gender & History* 20:1 (2008), 68–85.

O'Connor, Erin, *Raw Material: Producing Pathology in Victorian Culture* (Durham, NC: Duke University Press, 2000).

Oldstone-Moore, Christopher, *Of Beards and Men: The Revealing History of Facial Hair* (Chicago: University of Chicago Press, 2016).

Olsen, Stephanie, *Juvenile Nation: Youth, Emotions and the Making of the Modern British Citizen, 1880–1914* (London: Bloomsbury, 2014).

Oppenheim, Janet, *Shattered Nerves: Doctors, Patients, and Depression in Victorian England* (New York: Oxford University Press, 1991).
Paris, Michael, *Warrior Nation: Images of War in British Popular Culture, 1850–2000* (London: Reaktion, 2000).
Park, Roberta, 'Biological thought, athletics and the formation of a "man of character": 1830–1900', *International Journal of the History of Sport* 24 (2007), 1543–69.
Park, Roberta, 'Muscles, symmetry and action: "Do you measure up". Defining masculinity in Britain and America from the 1860s to the early 1900s', *International Journal of the History of Sport* 22:3 (2007), 366–7.
Parkes, Simon, 'Wooden legs and tales of sorrow done: the literary broken soldier of the late eighteenth century', *Journal for Eighteenth-Century Studies* 36:2 (2013), 191–207.
Parsons, Joanne, and Heholt, Ruth (eds), *The Victorian Male Body* (Edinburgh: Edinburgh University Press, 2017).
Payne, Christiana, *Rustic Simplicity: Scenes of Cottage Life in Nineteenth-Century British Art* (Nottingham: Lund Humphries, 1998).
Payne, Christiana, *Toil and Plenty: Images of the Agricultural Landscape in England 1780–1890* (New Haven, CT, and London: Yale University Press, 1993).
Payne, Christiana, *Where the Sea Meets the Land: Artists on the Coast in Nineteenth Century Britain* (Bristol: Sansom & Co. Ltd, 2007).
Pearl, Sharrona, *About Faces: Physiognomy in Nineteenth-Century Britain* (Cambridge, MA: Harvard University Press, 2010).
Poovey, Mary, *Making a Social Body: British Cultural Formation, 1830–1864* (Chicago: University of Chicago Press, 1995).
Powrie, Phil, Davies, Ann, and Babington, Bruce (eds), *The Trouble with Men: Masculinities in European and Hollywood Cinema* (London and New York: Wallflower Press, 2004).
Prichard, Sue (ed.), *Quilts, 1700–2010: Hidden Histories, Untold Stories* (London: V&A Publishing, 2010).
Ramsay, Neil, '"A real English soldier": suffering, manliness and class in mid-nineteenth-century soldiers' tale', in Catriona Kennedy and Matthew McCormack (eds), *Soldiering in Britain and Ireland, 1750–1850: Men of Arms* (New York: Palgrave Macmillan, 2013).
Rice, Stephen P., 'Picturing bodies in the nineteenth century', in Michael Sappol and Stephen P. Rice (eds), *A Cultural History of the Human Body in the Age of Empire* (Oxford: Berg, 2010).
Rosenman, Ellen Bayuk, *Unauthorized Pleasures: Accounts of Victorian Erotic Experience* (Ithaca, NY: Cornell University Press, 2003).
Saha, Jonathan, 'Whiteness, masculinity and the ambivalent embodiment of "British justice" in colonial Burma', *Cultural and Social History* 14:4 (2017), 527–42.
Schkolne, Myrna, *Staffordshire Figures 1780–1840: Manufacturers, Pastimes, and Work* (Atglen, PA: Schiffer Publishing Ltd, 2013).
Shaw, Philip, 'Longing for home: Robert Hamilton, nostalgia and the emotional life of the eighteenth-century soldier', *Journal for Eighteenth-Century Studies* 39:1 (2016), 25–40.
Shaw, Philip, 'Wars of seeing: suffering and sentiments in Joseph Wright's "The Dead Soldier"', in Catriona Kennedy and Matthew McCormack (eds),

Soldiering in Britain and Ireland, 1750–1850: Men of Arms (New York: Palgrave Macmillan, 2013).

Shepard, Alexandra, *Meanings of Manhood in Early Modern England* (Oxford: Oxford University Press, 2003).

Sinha, Mrinalini, *Colonial Masculinity: The 'Manly Englishman' and the 'Effeminate Bengali' in the Late Nineteenth Century* (Manchester: Manchester University Press, 1995).

Smith, Angela, 'Building biceps and tender kisses: the sexualisation of fatherhood', *Social Semiotics* 28:3 (2018), 315–29.

Smith, Elise, '"Why do we measure mankind?" Marketing anthropometry in late-Victorian Britain', *History of Science* (2019), 1–24.

Smith, Helen, *Masculinity, Class and Same-Sex Desire in Industrial England, 1895–1957* (Basingstoke: Palgrave Macmillan, 2015).

Smith, Richard, *Jamaican Volunteers in the First World War: Race, Masculinity and the Development of National Consciousness* (Manchester: Manchester University Press, 2004).

Solicari, Sonia, 'Selling sentiment: the commodification of emotion in Victorian visual culture', *19: Interdisciplinary Studies in the Long Nineteenth Century* 4 (2007).

Strange, Julie-Marie, *Fatherhood and the British Working Class* (Cambridge: Cambridge University Press, 2015).

Streets-Salter, Heather, *Martial Races: The Military, Race and Masculinity in British Imperial Culture* (Manchester: Manchester University Press, 2004).

Surridge, Lisa, *Bleak Houses: Marital Violence in Victorian Fiction* (Athens, OH: Ohio University Press, 2005).

Sussman, Herbert, *Victorian Masculinities: Manhood and Masculine Poetics in Early Victorian Literature and Art* (Cambridge: Cambridge University Press, 1995).

Suzuki, A., 'Lunacy and laboring men: narratives of male vulnerability in mid-Victorian London', in R. Bivins and J. Pickstone (eds), *Medicine, Madness and Social History: Essays in Honour of Roy Porter* (Basingstoke: Palgrave Macmillan, 2007).

Tasker, Yvonne, *Spectacular Bodies: Gender, Genre and the Action Cinema* (London and New York: Routledge Taylor & Francis Group, 1993).

Tosh, John, 'Home and away: the flight from domesticity in late-nineteenth-century England re-visited', *Gender and History* 3 (2015), 561–75.

Tosh, John, *Manliness and Masculinities in Nineteenth-Century Britain: Essays on Gender, Family and Empire* (Harlow: Pearson Education, 2004).

Tosh, John, *A Man's Place: Masculinity and the Middle-Class Home in Victorian England* (New Haven, CT, and London: Yale University Press, 1999).

Toulalan, Sarah, *Imagining Sex: Pornography and Bodies in Seventeenth-Century England* (Oxford: Oxford University Press, 2007).

Turner, David M., *Disability in Eighteenth-Century England: Imagining Physical Impairment* (New York: Routledge, 2012).

Van Kleef, Gerben, 'How emotions regulate social life: the emotions as social information (EASI) model', *Current Directions in Psychological Science* 18:3 (2009), 184–8.

Wallis, Jennifer, *Investigating the Body in the Victorian Asylum: Doctors, Patients, and Practices* (London: Palgrave Macmillan, 2017).

Walsh, Bridget, *Domestic Murder in Nineteenth-Century England: Literary and Cultural Representations* (Farnham: Ashgate Publishing, 2014).

Wassell Smith, Maya, '"The fancy work what sailors make": material and emotional creative practice in masculine seafaring communities', *Nineteenth-Century Gender Studies* 14:2 (2018), http://www.ncgsjournal.com/issue142/PDF/smith.pdf (accessed 13 September 2019).

Wendt, Simon (ed.), *Extraordinary Ordinariness: Everyday Heroism in the United States, Germany and Britain, 1800–2015* (Frankfurt and New York: Campus Verlag, 2016).

Woods, Kathryn, '"Facing" identity in a "faceless" society: physiognomy, facial appearance and identity perception in eighteenth-century London', *Cultural and Social History* 14:2 (2017), 137–53.

Index

age *see* youth; old age
American Civil War 140, 142
anthropology 35, 49
anthropometry 6, 35, 38, 49
appetite 20, 68, 70, 73, 80, 83, 84, 86, 91, 119, 157, 161, 170, 173
   for alcohol 69, 79, 84, 94
   for food 69, 94
   and sin 69
   and vice 82, 84, 85
arms, muscular 41, 43, 44, 45, 50, 53, 102, 169, 171, 172, 192, 195
athleticism 3, 6, 7, 36, 37, 42

Baden-Powell, Robert 71, 73, 105
banners 14, 23, 74, 75, 184–96
   as emotional objects 185, 191
   depiction of men on 186–93
   friendly society 14, 171, 183, 184, 185, 192, 193, 195
   procession of 22, 74, 171, 185, 193–5
   trade union 124, 184–95
   visual art of 185–6, 192
battlefield objects 21, 104, 108, 125, 126
beard *see* facial hair
beauty, male 1, 2, 3, 35, 36, 43, 45, 122
   and health 5, 38, 54, 72–3, 80, 169, 175
   and male character 3–4, 16, 34, 38, 42, 45, 52–9, 68, 77, 80, 87, 89, 92, 147, 149, 150, 168, 173, 176, 178, 180, 188, 205, 211
   and male emotions 15, 19, 20, 47, 57–9, 89, 93, 138, 149, 176, 178, 184, 185, 197
blacksmiths 14, 22, 168, 169–73
bodies
   changes in form 19, 36–52, 204–5
   and emotions 1, 3, 5, 9, 10, 15–17, 18, 19–21, 22–3, 35–7, 59, 68–9, 71–5, 79, 83–4, 94, 101, 127, 136, 149, 154, 158, 170, 172, 177, 184, 185, 191, 194, 196, 206, 209–11
   historiography of 6–7, 13–14, 16–17, 71–2, 203–4
   idealised 4, 15, 22, 34–5, 40, 48, 50–1, 53, 188, 196, 204–5, 210–11
   motion, in 35–51, 57, 91, 172, 178, 188, 192, 205
   obese 9, 68, 72, 73, 80, 205
   'spectacular' 204–5
   working-class men's 3–4, 13–14, 22–3, 41, 42, 49, 77, 78, 83–4, 87, 154, 158, 170–96, 208–9
boxers 1–3, 37, 41, 42–6, 120
   as anatomical models 1, 43, 53
   and Fancy, the 3, 53
   and race 2, 45
   representations of 1–3, 43–4

boy scouts 71, 72, 105
bravery 7, 8, 11, 22, 45, 47, 50, 92, 103–4, 109, 112, 113, 119, 120–6, 127, 169, 176–83
　see also heroism
buttocks 20, 40
Byron, George Gordon, Lord 1–4, 56, 114, 210

carpenters 53, 151, 168, 190–1
ceramics 15, 17, 21, 45–6, 74, 75, 101, 108, 111–15, 120, 122, 137, 138, 141, 143, 144, 151, 192, 207, 209
　sailor's farewell and sailor's return 107, 113, 122, 138, 143, 144, 145, 195
cheerfulness 1–2, 19, 57, 59, 73, 105, 148–9, 171
cowardice 8, 87
Crawford, Jack 121–6
cricketers 46, 47–8, 49
Crimean war 11, 111, 113, 115, 119, 127, 137, 138, 140, 141, 146, 207
Cruikshank, George 20, 75–6, 107

degeneration 5, 13, 78, 79, 93, 154, 158
desire 70, 105, 107
　for gender attributes 3–4, 5, 20, 22, 35, 36, 45, 50, 52, 59, 105, 108, 114, 119, 127, 168, 205
　for the male body 3–4, 14, 19, 22, 34, 42, 48, 49, 52, 59, 168, 175–6, 205
disability 9, 20, 69, 87–8, 91, 94
disgust 4, 15, 17, 20, 68, 73, 74, 75, 79, 80, 84, 85, 91, 94, 159, 208
domesticity 6, 12, 21, 118, 153, 169, 180, 208
　see also home
drunkenness 74–9, 84–5, 87, 122, 155
　see also appetite, for alcohol

effeminacy 6, 40, 45, 69, 70, 73, 205
emasculation 7, 86, 119, 120
embodiment see bodies
emotional objects 15, 17–19, 102, 108, 111, 120, 126, 127, 159, 182, 196

emotions
　historiography of 5, 8, 9, 11, 15–19
empire 21, 41, 42, 71, 161
employment see work
Ephebe 36, 204
eroticism 3–4, 6, 14, 15, 22, 34–5, 41, 42, 47, 49, 50–2, 86, 168, 169, 175–6, 183, 184, 205

faces 6, 15, 19, 34, 38, 41, 52–9, 69, 77–8, 80, 83, 120, 139, 154, 169, 172, 190–1, 192
　open 37, 52, 53, 54, 57–8, 59, 90
　pale 79
　tanned 52, 54
　see also physiognomy; beauty, male
facial hair 36, 38, 41, 42, 47, 48, 52, 54, 56, 82, 92, 122, 141, 148, 149, 177, 180, 183, 184, 188, 191, 204
fathers 12–13, 22, 58, 136, 137, 142, 144, 147, 149–151, 155, 172, 173, 205–6
fear 8, 15, 20, 70, 74, 77, 79, 91, 94, 145, 147, 159
firemen 22, 168, 169, 178–83, 191, 194, 195
flight from domesticity 12–13, 22, 118, 127
fortitude 3, 11, 40, 45, 86, 92, 109, 121, 204

Garibaldi, Giuseppe 113, 172
gaze, the 15, 19, 22, 34–5, 42, 47, 48, 184, 205
gender see masculinities
Great Exhibition, The 118, 141
guilt 9

handsomeness see beauty, male
Hercules 36–7, 171, 193, 204
heroism 103–5, 120–5, 204
　democratisation of 10, 14, 112
　of the working man 176–83
home 12–13, 17, 21–2, 136–7, 160–1, 180, 204, 208
　absence from 137–9, 195, 207
　and cleanliness 154–5
　disruption of 75–6, 154–60, 208
　dreaming of 139–43

home (*cont.*)
   and happiness 149–54
   relationship with work 157–60, 184, 196, 208
   remembering 143–5
   return to 145–9, 195, 208
   and unhappiness 154–60
homoeroticism *see* eroticism
homosociality 3, 47, 85

imperialism 4, 6, 10, 41–2
intemperance 74, 77, 80–2, 85, 86, 90

Jack Tar *see* sailors
Jackson, John 3, 43, 120

kindness 21, 22, 58, 84, 110, 112, 151–3, 171, 178, 181–4, 196

legs 20, 38, 40, 43, 45, 49, 51, 52, 54, 72, 79, 88, 111
lifeboat men 168, 169, 176–7
love 3, 8, 15, 19, 21, 41, 58, 84, 104, 107, 112, 127, 144–5, 149, 151–3, 176, 179, 191, 205

mariners 22, 89, 138, 169, 176
   see also sailors
marital violence 15, 76, 154–60
   material culture of 156–60
masculinities
   as contested 205
   as fragile 205, 206–7
   and heteronormativity 4, 18
   historiography of 4–14
   hyper- 10, 209, 210
   queering the history of 4–5, 19, 34–5
   toxic 210
masturbation 69, 72, 79–80, 82, 86
material culture
   historiography of 7, 9, 10, 12, 14–19
medals 86, 102, 103, 104, 120, 122, 125, 146, 177, 178, 207
melodrama 15–16, 121
memorials 120, 121, 124, 125
Mendoza, Daniel 44–5, 46
men of feeling 5, 11
   see also soldiers, as 'military men of feeling'

mental-health disorders 10, 11, 14, 20, 49, 57, 69, 79, 80–3, 86–7, 90
Merry England 171–2, 194
militarism 4, 10, 41, 89, 108, 119, 124, 142
military spectacle 11, 103, 107, 124, 126
military uniform 21, 103, 105, 107, 108, 109, 115, 116, 119, 120, 121, 207
   allure of 105–7, 119
military weapons 89, 102, 103, 105, 106, 108, 110
miners 22, 168, 169, 174, 177–8, 209
modernity 6, 9, 19, 41, 42, 49, 55, 69, 70, 71, 169, 171, 172, 178, 194, 196–7, 210
Molineaux, Tom 2, 45
muscular Christianity 5, 7, 37, 178
muscularity 1, 3, 5, 20, 22, 35, 36, 37–41, 43–5, 47, 48, 53, 59, 73, 122, 125, 168, 169–71, 172, 175, 180, 184, 192–3, 195, 204–6, 210, 211

Napoleonic wars 19, 138
navvies 13, 168, 169, 173, 175, 176, 192
Nelson, Horatio, Lord 107, 112, 116, 120
neurasthenia 13, 49
nostalgia 11, 111, 139–40, 147, 207

old age 87, 88, 91–3

passions 8–9, 20, 69–83, 84, 85, 173
patriotism 4, 11, 15, 107, 110, 112, 113, 119, 120, 126, 137, 140, 146, 147, 148, 178, 191, 193
pincushions 145
physical culture 36, 48
physiognomy 6, 54–7, 68, 77, 154
pity 37, 84, 113–14, 137, 143, 146, 208
pleasure culture of war 10, 108–27, 137
politeness 5, 38, 188
pride 15, 37, 41, 45, 89, 107, 108, 112, 113, 120, 124, 126, 137, 146, 175, 185, 191, 196

prize-fighters *see* boxers
prosthetics 88
pugilists *see* boxers

quilts *see* textiles

race 2, 4, 6, 7, 8, 49, 68, 154, 186, 210
   construction of 6, 35
   and notions of the 'other' 8, 16, 35,
      42, 55, 68
   scientific racism 7, 10, 35–6, 42
railway workers 22, 168, 183–4
regimental colours 21, 101, 104, 116,
   120, 126–7, 141
relics 1, 21, 108, 111, 120, 125, 185
religion 8, 9, 71

sailors 9, 10, 11, 21, 22, 41, 59, 88, 92,
   101, 106–7, 111–14, 116–17, 118,
   124, 137–8, 143–4, 145–6, 168,
   173, 176, 191, 193, 195, 209
   appeal to women 9, 41, 50, 58,
      105
   see also veterans
Sandow, Eugen 36–7, 48–9, 50
Scott, Walter, Sir 56, 121, 125
self-help 8, 20, 35, 69–83, 91, 103, 109,
   170
self-sacrifice 11, 90, 104, 107, 113, 120,
   137, 140, 141, 157, 176–8, 180–2,
   205
sensibility 5, 6, 11, 15, 38, 147
sentiment 15, 147
shame 9, 10, 11, 20
Sharples, James 186, 188, 192,
   194–5
Shaw, John 120–1, 125–6
Smiles, Samuel 35, 45, 55, 70–1, 72,
   194
smoking 69, 73–4, 76, 77, 83, 85, 86,
   94
social Darwinism 13, 42
social purity movements 8
soldiers 21, 206
   appeal to women 9, 50–2, 59, 105,
      206–7
   as exemplars for men 10–11, 41–2,
      101, 103, 105–8

   as 'military men of feeling' 11, 116,
      142
   see also veterans
spermatorrhea 9, 20, 79–80, 86
stoicism 73, 110, 127, 184
strongmen 42, 48, 49, 210

tattoos 22, 41, 204, 207, 209
tears 8, 10, 11, 15, 58, 92, 103, 104,
   107, 113–14, 116, 137, 140, 143,
   146
temperance 14, 17, 72, 74–7, 80–2,
   83–6, 90, 91, 92, 118–19, 124, 150,
   173, 177, 185, 193, 195
textiles 15, 17, 21, 101, 114, 118, 127,
   139, 145
   wartime quilts 114–120, 127
torso 38, 43, 44, 48, 50, 122, 171, 205
toys 15, 21, 101, 108–11, 120, 144
   boats, toy 109–10
   soldiers, toy 108–9
trade union 14, 124, 169, 184–96, 209
   ephemera 14, 22, 184, 185, 186,
      192, 195–6
   iconography 186–93
   see also banners, trade union

ugliness 16, 20, 55, 68, 83, 93, 94, 154,
   160

veterans 88, 92, 103, 126, 206, 207
virility 9, 34, 41, 50–2, 72, 79, 85, 86–7,
   92, 94, 169–70, 175, 204–5, 210

Waterloo, battle of 10, 120–1, 125
Wellington, Duke of 19–20, 34, 40, 121,
   126
wife-beating *see* marital violence
work 13–14, 22, 35, 72, 91, 136, 137,
   147–9, 157–8
   as aesthetic site 175–6
   and attainment of self 70, 173–6
   nobility of 168, 173, 174–6, 180,
      204
   sedentary 7, 13, 42, 177, 184

youth 8, 9, 20, 35, 87, 88–92, 104–9,
   204

Ingram Content Group UK Ltd.
Milton Keynes UK
UKHW051510300323
419412UK00012B/182